Today's Teen

Seventh Edition

JOAN KELLY-PLATE, ED.D.   **EDDYE EUBANKS, PH.D.**

Glencoe

New York, New York   Columbus, Ohio   Chicago, Illinois   Peoria, Illinois   Woodland Hills, California

Contributors

Mark Bregman
New York, New York

Linda R. Glosson, Ph.D.
Plano, Texas

Christine Venzon
Eunice, Louisiana

Teacher Reviewers

Kathryn P. Crawford, Ed.S.
Family & Consumer Sciences
    Teacher, NBPTS certified
Huffman Middle School
Birmingham, Alabama

Carolyn Evans, M.S.
Family & Consumer Sciences
    Teacher
Armstrong Middle School
Starkville, Mississippi

Mary J. Haupt, M.A.
Life Management Skills Teacher
Louis E. Legg Middle School
Coldwater, Michigan

Anne Grab, M.S.
Home & Careers Teacher
South Colonie Schools
Albany, New York

Pat Luther
Family & Consumer Sciences
    Educator
Macks Creek R-V
Macks Creek, Missouri

Jenefer Rowley, CFCS
Child & Family Development
    Specialist
Granite School District
Salt Lake City, Utah

Gloria Taylor, M.Ed., CFCS
Family & Consumer Sciences
    Teacher
District of Columbia Public
    Schools
Washington, D.C.

Antoinette Turner-Jarrett
Family & Consumer Sciences
    Teacher
Henderson Magnet Middle School
Little Rock, Arkansas

Technical Reviewers

Deborah R. Craft, M.Ed., Ed.S.
Family & Consumer Sciences
    Teacher
Northwest Whitfield High School
Dalton, Georgia

Karen DeBord, Ph.D.
Extension Specialist, Child
    Development
North Carolina State University
Raleigh, North Carolina

Steven A. Hamon, Ph.D.
Licensed Clinical Psychologist
President, The Antioch Group
Peoria, Illinois

Sherri Hoyt, R.D., L.D.
Outpatient Dietitian/Nutrition
    Counselor
Missouri Baptist Medical Center
St. Louis, Missouri

Ray Sanchez, M.P.A.
Principal
Jefferson County Public Schools
Golden, Colorado

Printed in the United States of America

Send all inquiries to:
Glencoe/McGraw-Hill
3008 W. Willow Knolls Drive
Peoria, IL 61615-1083

ISBN 0-07-846369-6 Student Edition
ISBN 0-07-846374-2 Teacher Wraparound Edition

2 3 4 5 6 7 8 9 10   **027**   07 06 05 04 03

Contents in Brief

Contents

reduced

Special Features

HOW to...

Making a DIFFERENCE

TRY IT OUT

ACTIVITY

TAKE NOTE

Career Network

Highlighted Topics

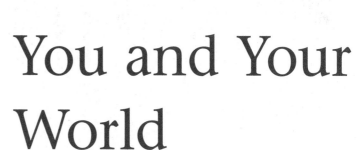

Unit 1

You and Your World

Reaching Your Potential

YOU WILL LEARN . . .

➤ How to identify strategies to reach your potential and make the most of your resources.
➤ Why goals are important.
➤ The relationship between short- and long-term goals.
➤ Guidelines to help you achieve goals.

TERMS TO LEARN . . .

➤ goal
➤ human resources
➤ long-term goals
➤ material resources
➤ potential
➤ resource
➤ resourceful
➤ self-confidence
➤ short-term goals

Imagine ...

. . . that you're a mountain climber going toward a summit. In your mind, you know exactly how it will look. Even though a mountain is a challenge to climb, you know it can be done. You start by choosing the mountain and then develop a climbing plan. Hand over hand and foot by foot your goal slowly becomes a reality.

Think About

• What are some of your dreams or goals?
• What progress have you made in achieving some of them?
• What obstacles must you overcome to reach your dreams?

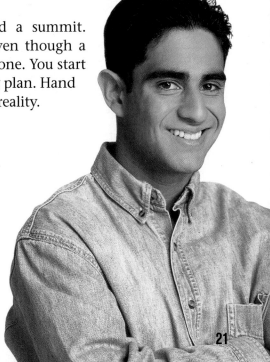

MAKING THE MOST OF YOURSELF

Each day is a step toward what you choose to build—whether learning a skill, staying drug-free, or making a new friend. Being successful at something you work for feels good. It helps make you feel more confident and willing to take on other challenges. Kate feels successful as a student council member. She's able to achieve goals that have an impact on other students' lives at school. You may feel successful in athletics or in certain classes. Pete's success at his part-time job helps him earn extra money and feel good about himself. It also makes him feel more confident in his classes.

Success and self-confidence go hand in hand. **Self-confidence** means people are *confident in their abilities*. They feel good about themselves and their accomplishments. When success comes, they feel there are other things they can achieve—if they work at them. They are usually ready and eager to try new things.

Think of tasks you weren't able to accomplish when you were younger. Maybe you hadn't learned to read yet, make a sandwich for yourself, or throw a basketball. How did you learn to do these tasks? In the process, did you tell yourself, "I'll never be able to do this?" or did you look at yourself more positively? Maybe you said to yourself, "I want to learn to do this. I know I can do it!"

➤ **Displaying a positive attitude and believing in yourself will lead to success.** Think of successful people that you know. What type of attitude do they display?

Move Toward Independence

When Pete first went to interview for a part-time job, he learned he was one of nine people applying for the position. He was confident he would be a good employee. He tried not to get discouraged by the competition he faced. The positive image he had of himself was affected by past experiences that had worked out well. Pete landed the job.

Think about experiences you've had since you were a young child. Hopefully, many of the experiences were positive as you learned to walk, talk, and understand more of your world. Even though no one is successful at everything, you've probably been successful at more things than you can recall. Even small successes can help you learn to believe in yourself and see yourself as a person of worth.

WHAT'S YOUR POTENTIAL?

Aleesha has won several awards in science and hopes to be a doctor someday. Rico loves to build things and wants to become an architect. Like everyone, Aleesha and Rico have **potential**, or *the possibility of becoming more than they are right now.* Reaching your potential means becoming all you can be.

➤ **Self-confidence is developed by believing in yourself.** What decisions have you made that will help you develop confidence?

What's your potential? How can you reach it? Try the suggestions below to get a head start identifying and reaching your potential:

- **Check out your interests and abilities.** Make a list of each one, asking others for additional input. Next, match your interests and abilities. For example, Su Ying loves the outdoors and enjoys growing plants. Because of her combined interest and ability, she plans to serve as a volunteer at the community park's gardens next summer. That will allow her to further develop her skills, explore her interest, and decide what steps she might take next.
- **Keep your efforts focused.** Many people don't reach their potential, because they let themselves get distracted many times along the way. Once you decide to accomplish a goal, stay focused. Keep in mind what's best for you and your future, and pursue that path.
- **Be health-smart.** You're far more likely to reach your potential if you're healthy and full of energy. Eat foods

➤ Your family members are human resources to help you reach your potential. What new things have you learned from a family member this year?

that promote good health. (Learn about healthy foods and eating habits in Unit 8.) Be sure you get enough sleep. Take time to exercise and stay fit. Stay away from substances that can harm your health, such as tobacco and drugs, including alcohol.

• **Use your potential in positive ways.** Curt probably has more computer skills than anyone at school. He hopes to find a way to use his skills to design software that detects diseases before they become serious.

Resources Impact Potential

Anything you use to help accomplish something is a **resource**. Resources can be either human or material. *Resources that have to do with people* are called **human resources**. All other resources are material resources. **Material resources** include *money, property, supplies, time, and tools*. They also include community resources such as libraries, schools, churches, hospitals, clinics, and parks.

Family members, teachers, and other school personnel are human resources that can help you achieve a goal. Friends, neighbors, employers, and people in the community offer other possibilities to help you reach your potential. Depending on what you hope to achieve, you might seek advice from a teacher, religious counselor, local artist, writer, or musician. Doctors, police officers, firefighters, and emergency service personnel are also valuable resources. Some resources may involve fees, but many are available at little or no cost to you.

Did you know that *you* are a storehouse of human resources? These include your health, interests, skills, knowledge, abilities, and attitudes.

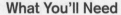

▼TRY OUT

Identifying Resources

ACTIVITY

What You'll Need
- 1 sheet of paper
- Pencil

What to Do

Divide your paper into two columns: Need/Want and Resources.

1. In the Need/Want column, identify something you need or want in the near future.
2. In the Resources column, make a list of the resources you could use for your need or want.
3. Join three classmates to form a group. Pass your papers to the right so that each of you receives someone else's paper.
4. Read your classmate's need or want and list of resources. List any additional resources you believe your classmate could use for the need or want.
5. Repeat the process until you each get your own paper back.

To Discuss
- What useful resources were suggested? Are these resources you could use? Why or why not?
- How can asking others to help you identify resources be useful?

Make the Most of Your Resources

After you identify your resources, put them to work for you. Whether they're plentiful or limited, you can make the most of the resources you have by ollowing these suggestions:

- **Expand your resources.** Get to know a variety of people. Individuals you meet may be able to help you learn a skill or find a job. Read newspapers, bulletin boards, and pamphlets available in your community to get a sense of opportunities you might pursue. Develop your own knowledge and abilities. When you train and sharpen your skills in a subject that really interests you, you start down a path that can lead to a successful adult career.

- **Conserve your resources.** Spending all your money on video games may be fun at the moment, but it's also a way to waste a valuable resource. Opening a savings account will reward you with more money in the long run. You can also save money, time, and energy by caring for your possessions. They'll last longer, and you won't have to replace them as often. What are other ways you can conserve resources?

- **Substitute resources.** Are you short on cash—with your best friend's birthday coming up? Substitute time and energy for money by making a birthday gift. If you enjoy books and tapes, save money by using the library instead of buying them. Rent a video and have friends over rather than going to the movies.

- **Share resources.** Work together in a study group for a difficult class assignment. Consider trading books, tapes, CDs, or sports equipment with friends. Sharing can be beneficial for everyone involved.

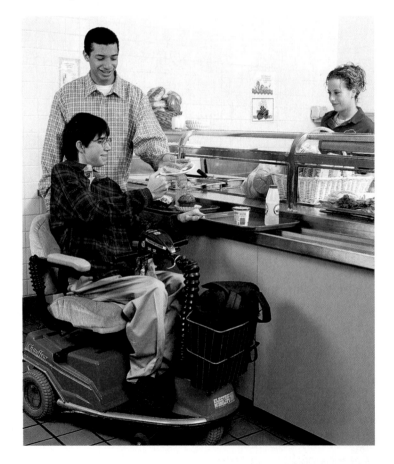

➤ Your time is a valuable resource. Sharing it with others can help them to reach their potential. You'll feel your time is well-spent.

Resources are everywhere. Look for them, and learn how to use them to help you accomplish your dreams. By doing so, you'll be **resourceful,** or *able to solve problems and succeed in life.*

THE IMPORTANCE OF GOALS

A **goal** is *something you plan to do, be, or have.* It's something you're willing to work for. Everyone has goals in life, but not everyone achieves them. That's why it's important to make sure your goal is:

• Stated in your own words.
• Positive.
• Realistic.
• Something you really desire.

Think for a moment about what you accomplished yesterday. Can you list specific achievements? What about the last month? Goals can help you see what you achieved—and did not achieve. When people look back in time, they often discover they didn't accomplish the very things they wanted most in life. Missed opportunities often cause deep regrets.

Goals force you to think about what you want and help you to take necessary steps to attain your objectives. Like road signs, goals give you direction, keeping you focused on just where you want to go. People who set goals and work to achieve them are much more likely to gain success and satisfaction in life. Without goals, it's easy to just drift along, letting circumstances control your future.

➤ **Set goals for yourself, then plan how to achieve them.** What are some of your goals? Identify which are short-term and which are long-term.

Personal Goals

Some goals, like finishing a homework assignment or applying for a part-time job, are **short-term goals**, or *goals that can be accomplished in the near future.* Graduating from college, starting your own business, and getting married are examples of long-term goals. **Long-term goals** are *more far-reaching and take longer to achieve.*

Making a DIFFERENCE

HIGH HOPES

"I know you have high hopes about going to college," Riley's dad said at dinner. "And you know we'll help out. But we don't have enough money to pay for all of your college expenses. You're going to have to help, too."

Riley planned to become a computer software designer. He'd thought a lot about his future and set some goals. "I know that, dad. I'm trying to keep my grades high. And I plan to talk to our school career counselor about colleges, scholarships, and financial aid."

"That sounds good," his dad said. "You know, Riley, I think you may just be on your way to seeing your dream come true."

Taking Action
1. What other steps would you suggest for Riley to reach his goal?
2. What steps can you take to reach a long-term goal of your own?

Both short- and long-term goals are important. Short-term goals, such as reading a book, cleaning your room, or writing a letter, are easier to complete than long-term goals. By setting and reaching short-term goals, you gain a sense of accomplishment. Short-term goals can also serve as stepping stones to long-term goals. As a Chinese proverb says, "The journey of a thousand miles begins with a single step."

Think about the long-term goal of playing a musical instrument in a band. Setting short-term goals would help make this longer-term objective seem less overwhelming. Short-term goals might include learning to play an instrument, practicing one hour each day, forming a band with friends, and eventually auditioning for a professional band.

In deciding what goals to set, you need to draw the line between dreams and reality. The chances of becoming a

➤ Groups learn to work together to meet goals. This band is practicing for statewide competition.

professional athlete are very limited, yet millions of teens share this dream. Lofty dreams are often the motivators for success. The risk of setting unrealistic goals is the possibility of deep disappointment. Examine your goals carefully. Are they realistic? What do you think?

Group Goals

Not all goals involve just yourself. People often share goals, with members of a group working together to achieve them. Families may have common goals, such as repainting a house, planning a holiday dinner, or planting a garden. As a group, the family maps out steps to take and works together to meet its goals. Working together to reach a goal can be as rewarding as the end result itself.

Sometimes working for group goals means that individual goals need to be put aside for a while. Can you think of examples when this might occur? What suggestions would you give someone whose personal goals had to be delayed?

Groups outside the family often share common goals. A community or religious youth group may decide to help less fortunate families. They meet their goal by holding a car wash, cookout, or sports event to raise money. When people pull together for common goals, they can accomplish what seem like miracles.

ACHIEVING YOUR GOALS

When setting goals, it's important to think about what matters most to you. That way, you can decide which goals to pursue. Even though parents, friends, and relatives may influence your goals, be sure the goals you set reflect what *you* want. To achieve any goal you must be committed, so

➤ Reaching goals takes effort. Keep your mind on your goals and be determined to reach them.

➤ **Suppose you want to work with the hearing impaired. Hard work and perseverance help you achieve your goals.**

that you're prepared to work hard for it. Use the following guidelines to achieve meaningful, realistic goals:

- **Keep your goals in mind.** Some goals, such as New Year's resolutions, are quickly forgotten. The same thing can happen with any goal you set if you're not careful. Create a mental picture of the goal. Also, write the goal down on paper and read it aloud often. That way, you're less likely to forget it.

- **Stay active with your goal.** Wanting to graduate from high school isn't enough. Go to each of your classes every day. Be on time. Study to meet your goal. *Action,* not wishful thinking, is the key to success.

- **Be determined.** Even if you have a strong will to succeed, at times stumbling blocks will likely interfere with your goal. Like roads, most goals have a few bumps, detours, or other obstacles that get in the way. Don't let them get you down. Confidence, determination, and enthusiasm can help overcome most obstacles. Remember, you benefit as much from working toward a goal as you do from eventually achieving it.

Review & Activities

Chapter Summary

- Self-confidence often leads to success. In turn, success builds self-confidence.
- You have the potential to become all you can be. There are certain steps you can take to help reach your potential.
- People sometimes fail to reach their potential because they get distracted.
- A variety of human and material resources can be used to accomplish your goals.
- Resources can be expanded, conserved, substituted, and shared.
- Both short- and long-term goals help you stay focused on what you want to achieve.
- Members of groups often work together to achieve common goals.
- When setting goals, you need to decide what is most important to you.

Family & Community

With Your Family

Think about some present goals you share with your family. Then talk to family members about goals you've achieved together in the past. Write down their comments to read in the future. How does your family's success in achieving goals influence your achievements?

In Your Community

Research local newspapers or interview local officials to determine some of your community's goals. Then, list activities you and your classmates could participate in to help improve your community. Select one activity, develop a plan, and carry it out.

- Having a mental picture of the outcome, actively working to achieve it, and being determined can help you achieve almost any meaningful, realistic goal.

Reviewing the Chapter

1. Briefly describe how success and self-confidence are related.
2. How can remembering small successes from your past help you?
3. What does reaching your potential mean?
4. What prevents many people from reaching their potential?
5. Give four tips for staying healthy so that you can reach your potential.
6. Explain how resources are used to achieve goals.
7. Give six examples of material resources that may be offered by a community.
8. List four ways that you might expand or substitute resources.
9. How can achieving short-term goals help you accomplish a long-term goal?
10. Give three guidelines to help you achieve your goals. Briefly describe each guideline.

Thinking Critically

1. **Make generalizations.** Which distractions do you think are the most challenging for teens to overcome before they can reach their potential? Explain your answer.
2. **Compare and contrast.** Compare the community resources available to you with those your parents or guardians had when they were your age. How are the resources different? How are they the same?

Making Connections

1. **Social Studies.** Interview someone who grew up in a different culture. How are this person's goals similar to yours? How are they different? Write a brief essay about what you've learned.
2. **Music.** Find examples of songs with references to goals that someone wishes to achieve, has achieved, or failed to achieve. Play the music or present the lyrics to your class. Discuss the impact music has on how well you and your classmates achieve goals.

Applying Your Learning

1. **Create a goals mobile.** Use cardboard or heavy paper to design a mobile that shows some of your goals. On the back of each goal, write one or more ideas to help you achieve it.
2. **Develop interview questions.** Imagine you're writing a profile of someone you admire for his or her past and present goals. Make a list of questions you might ask during an interview.
3. **Role-play.** Role-play a situation in which several teens encourage a friend who failed to achieve one of his or her goals. Afterwards, discuss how you'd feel if you were the friend with the failed goal.

What Would You Do?

Imagine a close friend set a goal to lose a certain amount of weight. Based on what you've learned in your classes, you think the goal is an unhealthy one. Your friend is upset because you and her other friends aren't supportive of her goal. She thinks all of you are undermining her intentions to improve her appearance. How would you handle the situation?

Growing and Changing

YOU WILL LEARN . . .

➤ The physical, social, emotional, intellectual, and moral changes that take place during adolescence.
➤ The difference between self-concept and self-esteem.
➤ How heredity and environment influence personality.
➤ How you can help others succeed.
➤ Signs of maturity.

TERMS TO LEARN . . .

➤ adolescence
➤ environment
➤ heredity
➤ hormones
➤ menstruation
➤ personality
➤ puberty
➤ self-concept
➤ self-esteem

Imagine ...

. . . that you could stop the clock and everything about you would never change. You'd stay the same age, height, and weight. You'd have the same friends and social life forever.

Think About

• Would you want to stay exactly as you are right now? Why or why not?
• What personal changes if any would you make before the clock stopped?
• What types of future experiences would you miss if your life remained frozen in time?

CHANGES IN YOUR LIFE

"I can't believe how time flies. Only yesterday we were kids playing in a sandbox," a childhood friend tells you. The years from birth to **adolescence**, the *stage of growth between childhood and adulthood*, is a period of amazing changes. During adolescence, you'll change faster than you ever will again.

➤ Teens experience adolescence at different ages. Physical changes in the human body vary. Some teens grow in spurts, while others grow steadily.

Physical Changes

Your body's rapid changes during adolescence impact the way you think and feel about yourself. They also deeply affect your relationships with others. Learning about adolescence helps you better understand and deal with so many changes.

Adolescence begins with **puberty**, *the time when teens start to develop the physical characteristics of men and women*. For girls, the start of **menstruation**—*a monthly discharge of blood from the uterus*—is an early sign that puberty has begun. For boys, the reproductive system begins producing sperm. Both girls and boys usually experience a growth spurt, or rapid increase in height. Girls may notice their body shape changes. Boys notice facial hair growth and their voices deepening. Both boys and girls feel strong surges of physical energy.

During puberty, your **hormones**, or *chemical substances in your body*, reach a very high level. Hormones help stimulate body changes and development of the male and female reproductive systems. Puberty lasts an average of three years, and starts at different ages for teens.

Many teens worry that they change too slowly or too quickly during puberty. Girls often undergo physical changes earlier than boys. Some look older than their peers—others look younger. Teens develop at different rates—*and this is perfectly normal*. Changes for both boys and girls usually start between the ages of 10 and 15. The

changes end between the ages of 16 and 20. Whether you start puberty early or late has no effect on the end product—the adult you.

➤ **You can relieve some of the tension of adolescence by participating in physical activities.**

Social and Emotional Changes

You may feel like you're on an emotional roller coaster during puberty. One moment you feel restless and irritable, the next, hopeful and full of life. Changing hormones in your body are often responsible for rapid swings of emotions. If you feel down about something, remember that your emotion will usually change after a short time.

Find positive ways to deal with your changing emotions and energy during adolescence. Play a sport, exercise, or volunteer in your community. You'll feel better and worry less about yourself. Take advantage of opportunities to make new friends. Learning how to get along well with others helps you develop lifelong winning social skills.

➤ These teens are part of their school newspaper staff. Decisions they make about its content requires making good judgment calls.

SAFETY First

Most people respond in a positive, healthy way to emotions such as love and hopefulness. However, learning to control emotions, such as anger, in a positive way is easier for some teens than others. Here are several ways to help control difficult feelings:

- Think about how you feel before you react. If you feel angry, count to ten, take deep breaths, or walk away from a stressful situation for a short time.
- Try not to let small irritations upset you. You'll see your attitude improve if you can let go of little things.
- Talk about the way you feel. Naming your emotions as you talk with someone can help you put a positive perspective on your feelings.

Intellectual Changes

During adolescence you also change intellectually. With increased experience and knowledge, you learn to solve more complex problems. You can think ahead to the consequences of how you act. The education you receive, along with your school and community activities, provide new insights and experiences.

Moral Development

During adolescence you start to make more decisions that deal with issues of right and wrong behavior. Although you want to do what's right, sometimes it's not clear how to act. Your choices may also be more difficult if you feel pressure from your friends. For example, Tamara is afraid of failing a class and asks Ally if she can copy her homework. In the past, Tamara has always come through for Ally. How should Ally handle the situation?

The challenge, as in Ally's case, is to base important decisions on a set of generally accepted guidelines for right and wrong behavior. From the time you were born to the present, your parents and other adults in your life set the standards for what's right and wrong. As you move through adolescence, it's up to you to apply these standards in the choices you make. For example, telling the truth and treating people fairly are commonly accepted standards of moral behavior. Lying and cheating are *not*. What other standards for moral behavior are part of your foundation? Having a strong sense of right and wrong can guide you through tough times. Parents, teachers, religious leaders, and counselors can help you deal with difficult situations.

TRANSFORMING SELF-CONCEPT

The mental picture you have of yourself, and the way you think others see you is your **self-concept**. Your self-concept is shaped by many experiences throughout life. The way family, friends, and others treat you helps mold the image you develop of yourself.

Who Am I?

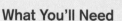
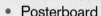

What You'll Need
- Posterboard
- Markers, colored pencils, crayons, scissors, and glue
- Magazines and newspapers

What to Do
1. Draw a vertical line to divide the posterboard in half. Label one side "Things I Like" and the other side "Who I Am." On each half create a collage of pictures, drawings, and sayings that represent you.
2. Explain your collage to your classmates. Display the posters in your classroom.

To Discuss
- Was it harder to think of things you like or characteristics about yourself? What did you discover about yourself as you made your choices for each part of the collage?
- What characteristics and likes did you share with your classmates? How do personal characteristics and likes make people unique? What would happen if everyone liked the same things or had the same characteristics?

Put these suggestions to work to boost your self-esteem.

- Be realistic. Some things can be changed—others can't. Spend your time and energy on realistic goals, not unrealistic dreams.

- Be willing to ask for help. Ideas and assistance from others can help you affirm your strengths and find new ways to deal with your weaknesses.

- Focus on your strengths. Everyone has strengths and weaknesses. Strengths, or the things you do well, help you work effectively toward your goals. If a weakness interferes with your goals, think about ways you can overcome or compensate for that weakness. You may discover some new strengths.

- Be proud of your accomplishments. Even small accomplishments are worthwhile. Often they're the stepping stones to bigger and better things.

- Get involved! Do volunteer work, join a club, play a sport. Just do it!

Having a clear view of yourself helps you focus on your good points and improve your weaknesses. Don't label yourself as "good" or "bad." Just try to see yourself realistically.

Building Confidence

The confidence and worth you have in yourself is called **self-esteem**. If you like who you are, you generally develop healthy self-esteem. If you don't feel good about yourself, you may develop low self-esteem.

Everyone has a bad day now and then. But if you can keep a positive attitude, you'll maintain healthy self-esteem. That makes you feel more self-confident. In turn, you can rely more on your own judgment, resist pressure from others, and stand up for what's important to you. Feeling good about yourself helps you feel and act successful. When you feel in control of your own life, you're able to achieve your goals.

➤ **The more knowledge you acquire, the more options you will have in your future. Believe it or not, learning can be fun.**

Appreciating Who You Are

Anna is an outgoing teen who enjoys people. She makes friends feel comfortable with her understanding and sense of humor. Life hasn't been easy for Anna since her father died and her mother took a full-time job. But Anna appreciates who she is, which shows in her behavior. Anna's self-concept and self-esteem are reflected in her friendly, outgoing personality.

Your **personality** is *the combination of feelings, traits, attitudes, and habits that you show to others.* This combination of characteristics makes you unique, or one of a kind.

The stage was first set for your personality before you were born. For example, genes you received from each of your parents determined physical traits like your height, eye color, and hair color. **Heredity** includes *traits and characteristics passed from parents to children.* Heredity also influences personality characteristics, such as your intelligence, abilities, and aptitudes.

Your personality may have begun with your heredity, but it's been shaped even further by your environment. Your

➤ Your self-esteem can come from doing your best—not just from winning. Positive attitudes can give you a good self-image.

environment is *everything around you, including people, places, things, and events.* Your family is usually your most important environmental influence. Children raised in an environment filled with love and emotional support are more likely to appreciate their worth. This, in turn, contributes to a healthy personality.

Unfortunately, it's not always easy to appreciate who you are. When Matt's parents divorced, his grades went down at first. He was upset about the divorce and felt powerless to deal with the situation. His self-confidence took a nose-

Signs of Maturity

One of the most common signs of maturity is age. Some laws require you to be a certain age before you can obtain a driver's license or vote. However, just because you are no longer a young child doesn't mean you're mature in all areas. Some signs of maturity include:

- **Independence.** Think about what you need to know before being on your own. You need to understand how to make good decisions, how to manage money, and how to take care of housing and health needs, for example.

- **Dealing with emotions.** Mature people learn to be in charge of their emotions, rather than letting their emotions overwhelm them.

- **Dependability.** You show you're mature by being dependable. That means you go to school or work every day, keep a promise, and show up on time for an appointment.

- **Willingness to work hard.** Very little is accomplished without hard work. Good grades come with effort. Winning teams develop with practice. Successful employees are rewarded for giving their all.

What signs of maturity do you think you need?

dive. He struggled to stay in school. Fortunately, Matt's school counselor helped him deal with his emotions about his parents' breakup. Gradually Matt recovered his healthy self-esteem.

Helping Others Succeed

Think about times when someone encouraged you to succeed. Did encouragement make you feel more capable and worthwhile? Do the same for people in your life. Positive comments such as, "I know you can do it," "I'm proud of you," and "I'm glad you're my friend" go a long way to motivate others to do their best.

It's easy to get caught up in your life and forget about others. But your life is closely intertwined with many people. The positive way you treat others returns to you. You truly can make a difference in the world by helping others succeed.

➤ Age does not measure maturity, your actions do. A positive attitude and dedication help you mature.

MOVING TOWARD MATURITY

How many times have you said, "I can't wait to grow up!" The desire to become an adult is normal and necessary. That's what gives you the incentive to learn about your own life and the world as you move toward adulthood.

Simply becoming an adult is not the real goal, however. Becoming mature is. There's a difference. Maturity means reaching full development, physically, emotionally, socially, intellectually, and morally. However, not everyone matures at the same rate. Also, some people mature rapidly in one area, but lag behind in others. For most people, personal development continues throughout life.

Review & Activities

Chapter Summary

- Adolescence is a time of many changes that affect the way you think and feel about yourself.
- Puberty marks the beginning of adolescence and the development of adult physical characteristics.
- During puberty, girls often undergo physical changes sooner than boys.
- Physical activities and volunteer service are some positive ways to deal with changing emotions and increased energy.
- Commonly accepted standards of moral behavior can help with decisions involving right and wrong.
- Experiences you have throughout life shape your self-concept. A realistic self-concept helps you focus on your good points and improve your weaknesses.

- If you have high self-esteem, you are more likely to feel self-confident and in control of your life.
- Your personality is shaped by your heredity and environment.
- Simply becoming an adult does not mean you are mature. For most people, personal development is a lifelong process.

Reviewing the Chapter

1. Name five physical changes that take place during adolescence.
2. Briefly describe some emotional changes that occur during adolescence. Name three positive ways to cope with changing emotions and increased energy.
3. Identify two moral standards that can help teens deal with difficult decisions.
4. Why is it important to have a realistic self-concept?
5. How can you benefit from healthy self-esteem?
6. Name four characteristics that make up a person's personality.
7. Briefly describe how environment can affect your personality.
8. Explain how you might help people succeed or do their best.
9. Explain how adulthood and maturity are not necessarily the same.

Family & Community

With Your Family

Talk with adult family members about changes they went through during adolescence and how they dealt with them. Which changes were the most difficult? Which were the easiest? Why? How are these changes similar or different from your own?

In Your Community

Think about people with disabilities who live in your community. What kinds of disabilities do they have, and what difficulties do they face? As a class, brainstorm some volunteer activities you could do to help them succeed in their daily lives.

Review & Activities

Thinking Critically

1. **Predict consequences.** Think of someone who needs encouragement to succeed at some goal or task. What might you do to help the person feel valued and important? What evidence would show that your efforts were helpful? What do you think might happen if you did nothing?
2. **Make generalizations.** Which of the physical changes during adolescence do you think is the most difficult for most teens to handle? Why?
3. **Recognize points of view.** Think about the set of moral standards held by someone you admire. In what ways are they similar to yours? In what ways are they different?

Making Connections

1. **Social Studies.** Use local newspapers and magazines to find examples of individuals in your community who have overcome obstacles such as disabilities, accidents, or serious illness to succeed in their lives. Share your findings with the class.
2. **Art.** Create one or more greeting cards that you could send yourself whenever you're feeling sad or discouraged. For each card, compose an original greeting—serious or humorous—that may be helpful.

Applying Your Learning

1. **Make a scrapbook.** Collect photographs of yourself taken over the years. Create a scrapbook documenting your physical growth and development.
2. **Make a list.** Imagine that you're your own best friend. Make a list of qualities about yourself that you appreciate, including actions you've taken that made you feel good about yourself.
3. **Write a letter.** Think about a family member or friend who could use some words of encouragement. Write the individual a short letter, offering your support and encouragement.

What Would You Do?

Imagine you're in line for lunch at school. A classmate says something that makes you angry. Your emotions are on edge, and you'd like to hit him or her. How would you handle the situation?

Building Character

YOU WILL LEARN . . .

➤ Why character is important.
➤ How to recognize character.
➤ What values are and how they are put into action.
➤ What it means to be a responsible citizen.

TERMS TO LEARN . . .

➤ character
➤ citizen
➤ citizenship
➤ ethical principles
➤ responsibility
➤ universal values
➤ values

Imagine ...

... that you are a role model for several younger children. They see you as someone they'd want to be like when they get older. They watch you closely and follow your example. They imitate your behavior, your language, and even the way you dress.

Think About

• Do you think the children's choice of you as a role model is a positive one? Why or why not?
• What aspects of your behavior, language, and dress are you most proud of? Which aspects are you least proud of?
• Who were your role models when you were younger? Who are your role models now? In what ways have you been influenced by their example?

WHAT IS CHARACTER?

Picture yourself as that role model for young children. Would your behavior show your true character? Calling someone a person of character may be the biggest compliment you can pay him or her. **Character** is *a combination of traits that show strong ethical principles and maturity.* **Ethical principles** are *standards for right and wrong behavior.* Your character shows in both your public and private behavior. You become a role model for people—both younger and older—to look up to. Character gives you the strength and courage to do the right thing every day. That, in turn, makes you feel confident and at peace with yourself.

Values to Guide You

➤ Role models can help you to become a more mature person. Choose role models with character and integrity. Who have you chosen as a role model?

The foundation of your character is based on a set of values. Your **values** are *the beliefs and ideas that help guide the way you live.* For example, taking time to visit and comfort a friend whose pet has died shows the value of *compassion.* You use your values to guide the choices you make every day.

Your values are reflected in your actions. For example, you show *honesty* when you don't shoplift. This value will guide your actions even when money is limited or peer pressure to steal is strong. Values also show in what you say—and how you say it. You display *courtesy* when you speak kindly and respectfully to others.

In addition, values can be seen in how you spend money. Buying a gift instead of a new CD for yourself displays *caring*. You postpone what you want to boost someone else's happiness. Finally, your values show in what you're willing to stand up for. A person who risks criticism from others to stand up for a principle sends a loud and clear message about *integrity*. Think carefully about what your values are and how they influence your behavior in a positive way.

➤ **You exhibit positive values when you care for others.** How do you display positive values in your day-to-day life?

Learned Values

You learn values at home from your family through what they teach you and the examples they set. For instance, Kevin's mom donates some time on weekends to a neighborhood clean-up project. She shows Kevin that *concern* for the community is an important value.

Throughout life you may also acquire values from other sources. Schools and places of worship teach values. So can friends, books, and TV. What values might a person learn from these sources? Which are most likely to be sources of values that keep the best interests of yourself and others in mind?

➤ Group values are reflected in what you and your friends do together. These teens are sharing their values by painting over graffiti on a wall in their community.

Shared Values

Look around and you'll see that people's values often vary. However, people of all cultures share some common values. *Values that are generally accepted and shared worldwide* are sometimes called **universal values.** They are the "glue" that makes positive and peaceful interaction among people possible. Universal values include:

- Courage.
- Fairness.
- Freedom.
- Honesty.
- Respect.
- Responsibility.
- Trustworthiness.

Although these values are held around the world, people place different levels of importance on them. Even among your own friends, you may share similar values but express them differently. For example, Barbara places high importance on *respect*. Her friends often confide in her because they know she'll listen and show respect without making judgments. Maria thinks *honesty* is most important—even when sharing her opinions leads to debates and disagreements with others. What are your most important values?

DEVELOPING CHARACTER

Personal character develops over time. It comes from thinking about and consciously putting your values into practice in a positive way. In time, putting your values into action becomes automatic—good habits are hard to break. Which of the following character traits have become habits in your life?

Making a DIFFERENCE

CLEAN-UP CREW

"Look at this place—it's a mess," Dave remarked to Jimmy about the community field where they played baseball. "There's so much litter you can't even see the bases. I don't like playing here anymore."

"So what are you going to do about it?" Jimmy asked. "Wait for somebody else to clean it up?"

"What am I supposed to do?" Dave replied.

"Well, why don't we clean it up?. And why don't we get some guys at school to help us keep it clean?"

"Why should *we* have to do it?" Dave said.

"Because if we don't, nobody else will," Jimmy shot back. "And if we do clean it up, it'll be a lot cleaner for everybody who wants to play here."

Jimmy and Dave formed a regular clean-up crew on Saturdays. They've played a lot of baseball there lately, and so have others.

Taking Action
1. What does Jimmy value? Why?
2. What could you do to make your community a better place to live?

- **Integrity** means you always act according to your values.
- **Honesty** means you're truthful and act real, not fake. Honest people don't cheat or take something that isn't theirs.
- **Trustworthiness** means being dependable. When people are trustworthy, you can take them at their word.
- **Patience** means that you keep the needs and wants of others in mind, and are willing to wait your turn. Patience is the opposite of hasty or impulsive behavior.
- **Self-discipline** means you have control over your behavior. You can control your temper, your actions, and your tendency to put off your homework.
- **Perseverance** means not giving up when things become difficult. When you "hang in there," you're persevering, or sticking with your goal. Perseverance also involves self-discipline.
- **Diligence** means you accomplish or achieve goals through hard work. Diligence involves how you use your time and energy at school, at home, in the workplace, and in the community.

➤ The value of compassion toward those who are hurting is a shared value around the world.

PERSONAL RESPONSIBILITY

Most teens look forward to being more independent and to having the freedom to make their own choices. Remember that along with this freedom comes responsibility. Personal **responsibility** is *character in action*. It involves choosing an action to take and accepting the consequences of your choice.

Taking Responsibility

It's easy to identify people who accept responsibility. It shows in their words and in their actions, such as when someone says, "Let me help," "I'll do it," or "I made a mistake and I'll correct it if I can." Responsible people don't need to be reminded or pressured to do a job. They simply work to accomplish things that need to be done. They keep their own and others' best interests in mind.

Think about ways those in your family show responsibility. Carol's mom drops Carol off at school on her way to work. Her little brother puts his toys away before going to bed. Sometimes Carol makes dinner and does the laundry. How do you show responsibility at home?

Every day you have dozens of ways to show whether you are responsible. Do you keep promises and avoid gossip? Do you refuse to be pressured into negative activities? Do you try to get the most out of school? Do you choose friends and activities that reflect your values? How well do you take care of your health?

➤ **When you volunteer to be the caregiver of the family pet, you are taking responsible action.** What do you regularly do to show you are a responsible person?

THE IMPORTANCE OF CITIZENSHIP

The newspaper headline reads, "Nominations accepted for Citizen of the Year." Would anyone you know qualify? A **citizen** is *a member of a community, such as a city or town, or country.* Unfortunately, just being a citizen doesn't automatically mean you are a good one. *The way that you handle your responsibilities as a citizen* is known as **citizenship.**

As community members, citizens are entitled to certain rights and privileges. For example, community members have the right to vote for city officials and the priviledge of fire protection. In return, citizens owe certain responsibilities to the community, such as abiding by its laws. This allows the community to run smoothly and serve the needs of its citizens. A thriving community requires responsible citizens.

HOW to...

Find Volunteer Opportunities

Many opportunities exist in most communities for volunteer service. One of the first things you should do is take a personal inventory of your skills and interests. Then look for opportunities within your community that match your skills and interests. Which opportunities motivate you most to serve?

- Tutor younger students.
- Organize games for children in your neighborhood.
- Get involved in student government. Help set rules and policies to make your school a better place.
- Become a hospital volunteer.
- Visit people who are confined to their home and run errands for them.
- Visit nursing home residents.
- Collect recyclable materials.
- Take part in food, clothing, or toy drives for people in need.
- Join a community clean-up group.
- Help with a community garden.
- Walk dogs at the local animal shelter.

Becoming a Responsible Citizen

You first learn and practice citizenship in your home and school. The two most important qualities of citizenship are caring and acting on your concerns. Danielle shows concern for her community by coaching a kids' baseball team. Beth is elected to a class office, because she treats classmates with honesty and respect. Drew volunteers at his community recycling center.

Your ability to contribute to your community is directly related to how much you know. Eventually, as a voter, you'll help choose public officials. The more information you know about your community, the more educated decisions you'll be able to make. By reading newspapers, and listening to radio and TV news, you can keep up with what's happening in your community and the world.

You'll have informed opinions that may enable you to influence others. When you know what's going on, you're more likely to make a positive difference—in your community and the world.

➤ **Good citizens make a good community. As a citizen, what can you do to improve your community?**

THE CHARACTER TEST

Learning to develop and display positive qualities of character and values takes time, but the rewards are great. People come to respect you for who you are. In turn, you learn to prize yourself. As you grow older and become more involved in your community, people may come to see you as a leader. Regardless of the role you choose to play as a valued citizen, everyone who knows you regards you highly for having passed the character test with flying colors!

3

Review & Activities

Chapter Summary

- Character, shown through behavior, gives people courage to do the right thing.
- Character is based on a set of values that guides the choices people make.
- You learn values from your family and from schools, places of worship, friends, books, and TV.
- People of all cultures share some common, or universal, values but place different levels of importance on them.
- Character comes from putting your values into practice in a positive way.
- Along with freedom to make your own choices comes personal responsibility.
- Citizens have certain rights and privileges, and owe certain responsibilities to the community.
- Home and school are the first places you learn and practice citizenship.

Reviewing the Chapter

1. In your own words, briefly describe what it means to be a person of character.
2. What are values? Give three examples of values.
3. How can a person show integrity?
4. Briefly describe how you learn values.
5. What are universal values and why are they important?
6. What is the difference between honesty and trustworthiness?
7. What personal qualities do responsible people have?
8. Give three examples of ways you can show that you are responsible.
9. What are the two most important qualities of citizenship?
10. What actions can you take to ensure that you are an informed citizen?

Family & Community

With Your Family

Talk with an older family or community member about an example of character he or she observed during his or her lifetime. If possible, record your conversation with this person. Which qualities of character were expressed in this person's example?

In Your Community

Children learn to be good citizens by example. As a class, brainstorm some volunteer activities you could do as a class to teach children to care for their school, neighborhood, or community.

Review & Activities

Thinking Critically

1. **Compare and contrast.** Compare your values with those reflected in the actions of your friends. How are they different and how are they alike?
2. **Make generalizations.** Describe someone whom you consider a person of character. How has the person's character influenced your values and actions?
3. **Cause and effect.** Think about a time when you or someone you know failed to act according to a positive set of values. Why was the action taken? What effect did it have on you or others?

Making Connections

1. **Language Arts.** Write a short story about a teen whose values are in conflict with those of his or her friends. Later, in a small group, share your finished work and discuss other instances in which values may conflict with one's friends. Give examples of how to deal with situations such as these.
2. **Social Studies.** Volunteer your time to work in a local shelter, or other area of need in your community. Write a brief report summarizing your experience.

Applying Your Learning

1. **Create a bulletin board display.** Feature a map of the world, and add newspaper and magazine photos of various people from different countries. Identify some of the values that the individuals may share, even though their cultures and countries are different.
2. **Write a letter.** Think about a citizen in your community who has worked to make it a better place for everyone. Write a letter, expressing thanks for the effort he or she has made, and send it to the individual.
3. **Design a help-wanted ad.** Create a classified advertisement seeking a responsible citizen for an unpaid position in the community. Include in the ad specific qualities that are needed for the position. Ask yourself if you or your friends would qualify.

What Would You Do?

Imagine that you are in a large department store. You see a woman accidentally drop a $50 bill and walk away. You're the only person who saw it. You feel torn. You lost your after-school job last week and are broke. Your family members would make you return the money if they found out you took it. How would you handle this situation?

Taking Responsible Action

YOU WILL LEARN . . .

- ➤ Different types of decisions.
- ➤ How various factors influence your decisions.
- ➤ Steps in the decision-making process.
- ➤ How your decisions can affect others.
- ➤ How to use the decision-making process to solve problems.
- ➤ Qualities of responsible leaders.

TERMS TO LEARN . . .

- ➤ alternatives
- ➤ decision making
- ➤ leader
- ➤ leadership
- ➤ needs
- ➤ wants

Imagine ...

. . . you need to make a choice that could change your future. Your school coach wants you to join the varsity basketball team. He thinks you have a shot at a college basketball scholarship. But your family thinks it's wiser to get an after-school job to save money for your college education. You can't do both, and you're torn.

Think About

- What would you do in this situation?
- What difficult decision have you had to make in your life?
- What do you think would happen if you didn't make any decisions at all about your future?

MAKING RESPONSIBLE DECISIONS

"Should I try out for a school team or seek an after-school job?" "Should I watch a TV special tonight that I've been waiting to see, or study for tomorrow's math test?" "Should I go to the mall with friends this weekend or help mom clean up around the house?" Decisions—large and small—play a continual part of your daily life.

Making responsible decisions—both major and minor ones—helps you achieve the goals you set for yourself. As you get older, you'll make a number of major decisions about school, health, work, and marriage. At times, your choice may be to do nothing about a situation, or let someone else decide for you. That's a decision, too.

> ➤ **Making decisions affects others, as well as yourself.** How will this teen's decision to quit his job affect others?

What Influences Your Decisions?

Think about a recent decision you made that turned out well. Did you make the decision yourself? Did you get help? A variety of influences shape your decisions. Some influences are external, like people and things around you. Others are internal, and come from your own attitudes and knowledge. Which influences below have played a major part in your decisions?

- **Family.** Even if they aren't giving you direct input, family members can strongly influence your decisions. Sometimes parents make a decision for you—especially if they feel you aren't ready or able to make the decision alone. They know that you learn by some mistakes, but it's their responsibility to protect and teach. They continue to offer advice because they don't want you to make mistakes that lead to serious trouble.

- **Friends.** As you grow older, you may turn to friends for help with decisions, which is natural. Keep in mind, though, that your friends often have no more experience or knowledge than you do. Some may want to influence you for their own reasons. Their influence can be positive or negative. You can always listen and learn from others, but in the end you must make your own decisions.
- **Values.** Many decisions you make are based on your values. As a result, your decisions express your values loud and clear. You're far more likely to make good decisions when you know exactly what your values are and follow them carefully.
- **Resources.** Your decisions are also affected by your resources, such as time, energy, knowledge, skills, available technology, and money. If you're low on money, do you go to the movies or stay home and read? If you just got paid from an after-school job, do you use your earnings to buy a new bike, or use your skills to repair the bike you already have?
- **Needs.** People's needs exert a strong influence on their decisions. Basic physical **needs** are *those things essential to your survival, such as food, clothing, and shelter.* Emotional needs include affection, security and safety, belonging, and achievement. An intellectual need is your desire to learn. Establishing positive relationships with other people is a social need.
- **Wants.** *Those things you desire, even though they aren't essential,* are **wants.** They also can have a powerful influence over your decisions. Sometimes it's easy to confuse wants with needs. Jamie says he needs a new pair of athletic sneakers, because he sees many of his friends buying them. Is this a want or a need?

➤ Many factors influence your decision making. Choosing to study for an exam while others goof off can affect your future. What do you allow to influence most of your decisions?

THE DECISION-MAKING PROCESS

Decision making is *the act of making a choice.* Many decisions you make each day are easy—you probably make them without a thought. You choose to brush your teeth, comb your hair, or pick out a jacket in your closet to wear

HOW to...

Take Steps in Decision Making

Whether you're thinking about getting a part-time job or choosing classes to take next semester, the steps in decision making can help you meet your goals.

Step 1: Identify the decision to be made. Clearly define the situation that requires a decision. Think about the goals or end results you desire to make an effective decision. For example, your goal might be to buy a new computer or get a part-time job.

Step 2. List your resources and options. What resources do you have or need to achieve your goal? Where can you get more information? Think about **alternatives**— *options or choices* you have. Make a list of your options. The more alternatives you think of, the more likely you are to find one that works.

Step 3. Analyze and study your options. Think through the possible results of each alternative. List the advantages and disadvantages of each. You may need to learn more about each alternative. Talk to a parent, school guidance counselor, or neighbor.

Step 4. Make your decision. Try to pick the best solution that fits your needs or wants. After researching new computer prices, you may decide to check out local papers for a used computer. After investigating after-school jobs to earn extra money, you may decide to babysit or mow neighbors' lawns instead.

Step 5. Act on your decision. Carry out your decision to the best of your ability. If you accept a part-time job, be a good worker. Have enough confidence in your decision to see it through and do your best.

Step 6. Evaluate your decision. Did you make the right decision? How has it affected you? Would you make the same decision again? If the outcome isn't what you expected or hoped for, you may have to make a new decision. Evaluate a decision and determine what could go better next time. You can avoid making the same error again.

Following these steps may seem awkward at first. With practice, however, the steps become automatic— making it easier to work on major decisions in your future.

to school. Other decisions are more complicated. Should you continue a friendship that seems troubled? Should you get involved in a school activity you know little about? Should you start to think about plans after high school? These decisions take time and consideration—they affect not only you but also your family, friends, and others. Some of your decisions will affect the society you live in and will have an impact on future generations. Fortunately there's a basic process that can help you make major decisions. This process is explained on the facing page.

➤ **You have 24 hours a day to make many minor and major decisions. Using the decision-making process can help you as you make those decisions.**

Learn from Your Decisions

Good decisions are choices you can be proud of. Think through your decisions carefully. Making choices you feel good about can result in:

- Improved self-concept and self-esteem.
- Increased respect from family and friends.
- More independence as you become responsible for yourself and your actions.

Every decision can't work out well. When you make a mistake, take responsibility for your action. Rather than blaming someone else, learn as much as you can from the experience. Sometimes you have to live with the consequences of a wrong decision and say, "I'll do better next time."

➤ **Suppose this happened to you without a witness around.** Would you take responsibility and help clean it up or would you just ignore your action?

Consider the Consequences of Your Choices

The consequences of some decisions you make—whether good or bad—affect only you. Some consequences may be minor, while some may be very serious. When Laurette decided she wanted to go to vocational college at the last minute, it was too late for her to apply.

Many decisions affect other people, too. That's why it's important to think about the impact of your decisions on family, friends, and your community. When you care about other people and want their respect, you'll make decisions carefully. Even seemingly small decisions, such as deciding not to use a safety belt when riding in a car, can have far-reaching consequences.

Remember that the decisions you make can alter the direction of your life. What do you think would happen, for example, if you decided to drop out of school? What effect would such a decision have on your own life? What effect would it have on your family and on your future? Choosing to stay in school and graduate is a responsible decision that will set you on a winning course in life.

➤ **The driver of this car decided to drink and drive.** If someone who had been drinking offered to drive you home, what would your decision be?

SOLVING PROBLEMS

"My father's health is failing, and we need to provide care for him." "My best friend is using drugs and I need to decide whether to continue the friendship." "My doctor says I should exercise regularly and I need to decide how to fit it into my schedule."

Making decisions is part of solving more complex problems. What are other situations that require in-depth decision making and serious thinking about future consequences?

It helps to break a complicated problem down into parts you can handle better. You're not as likely to be overwhelmed or make decisions you'll later regret. Consider your available resources and possible alternatives. What are the short- and long-term consequences of each alternative? What results do you want to achieve? Keep in mind that few solutions are perfect.

Problem-solving is a continuous process—and an opportunity to grow. Apply what you learn to new situations. In some cases, the process can prevent similar problems from happening over again.

Challenges of Group Decision Making

ACTIVITY

What You'll Need
- Clear jar filled with candies
- Paper and pen or pencil

What to Do

1. Try to guess the number of candies in a jar provided by your teacher. Write your answer on a piece of paper.

2. Work with a partner to agree on a guess. Next, join with another pair to form a group of four. Continue joining groups together until the whole class must make one guess. Each time write down the group's guess below your own.

3. When your teacher reveals the correct number of candies in the jar, circle the guess on your paper that was closest to the correct number.

To Discuss
- Are group decisions always good decisions for everyone in the group? Why? How can you be sure the group's decision is right for you?
- What should you do if you don't agree with the group's decision? What should you do if someone else disagrees with the group's decision?

RESPONSIBLE LEADERSHIP

Do you see yourself as a leader or a follower? A **leader** is *a person who has influence over and guides a group.* In many ways, a strong leader has mastered the art of decision making. As result, he or she can strongly influence and lead a group. The leader is willing to make decisions to solve often demanding problems. It takes a leader to motivate others to action, and it takes followers to get things done.

Leadership isn't just holding an office, such as student body president, it's *the ability to lead.* When Danielle organizes her friends to go bowling at a local charity event, she acts as a leader.

Qualities of Responsible Leaders

People have different ideas about what makes a good leader, but most agree on certain qualities and skills. Some skills can be learned and practiced—just like skating, playing piano, or making speeches. Which of the following qualities of successful leaders do you already have? Which ones might you work to develop?

- **Willingness to listen to the ideas, problems, concerns, and feelings of group members.** Good leaders listen to the feelings behind what is said as well as to words.

- **Ability to build a team from group members.** Good leaders are team-builders. One way is to recognize the worth of each member's ideas.

- **Ability to clearly identify group goals.** Leaders provide each member with information and direction about shared goals. Leaders aren't afraid to try new ways to achieve goals, to look for new solutions to old problems, or to risk failure.

- **Ability to solve conflicts within the group.** Leaders know how to handle conflicts or other personality clashes that could otherwise divide the group.

- **Willingness to participate with group members.** Good leaders don't consider themselves to be more important than the rest of the group. They pitch in and work hard, too. They also know that a group becomes strong when each member feels special and wanted.

- **Ability to manage time, money, and other group resources.** Leaders know what must be done to meet the group's goals. Good leaders are honest and are able to account for money and other resources that belong to the group.

What qualities do you have? Which do you want to develop?

➤ Everyone faces problems. Moving to a different town can be a problem for teens in school. How do you handle the problem of adjusting to new situations?

➤ **Some people have natural skills to become a leader. Leadership skills can also be learned.** What leadership skills do you have?

Leaders have two main functions: to get a job done, and to keep a group together. The "job" is whatever the group is organized to do. It might be a game, contest, or committee project. Graham takes charge of a group responsible for a class report.

Opportunities for leadership are all around you. In a group of friends, someone leads and directs the rest in deciding where to go and what to do. In school, some students spark class discussion and influence others by what they say.

In families, older brothers or sisters may set an example for positive behavior to younger family members. Just as you may look up to someone for guidance and behavior worth imitating, young people may do the same with you as their role model. A junior on the track team can show a freshman what it means to win or lose with a positive attitude. A long-time employee at a fast-food restaurant can show someone new on the job how to work well with others. Making the effort to practice leadership today can get you ready for even bigger opportunities in the future.

Review & Activities

Chapter Summary

- Making responsible decisions helps you achieve the goals you set for yourself.
- Decisions are influenced by a variety of internal and external factors.
- You are more likely to make good decisions when you keep your values in mind.
- Your decisions are affected by available resources and by your needs and wants.
- Following the steps in the decision-making process can help you make effective decisions.
- Decisions can have positive and negative consequences. Some consequences may be minor and may affect only you. Others are serious and may also affect other people.

- Complex problems often involve in-depth decision making, more than one decision, and serious consideration of future consequences.
- Leadership is the ability to lead and influence people.
- Leaders have certain qualities and skills that can be learned and practiced.

Reviewing the Chapter

1. Name five influences that affect people's decisions.
2. Why do you need to be cautious about turning to friends for help with decisions?
3. What is the difference between needs and wants? Give an example of each.
4. Briefly describe the six steps in the decision-making process.
5. Why is it a good idea to evaluate a decision?
6. What is the advantage of breaking complicated problems into parts you can handle better?
7. Why do leaders need to be good listeners?
8. What are the two main functions of leaders?
9. What are the benefits of practicing leadership in your school and home life?

Family & Community

With Your Family

Think about a decision you could make to improve the well-being of your family. Using the decision-making steps, write out the decision and how you intend to carry it out.

In Your Community

Many neighborhoods have one or more elderly residents who live alone, often without family members nearby. As a class, brainstorm some volunteer activities you could do as a class to provide assistance or companionship to one or more elderly individuals.

Thinking Critically

1. **Compare and contrast.** Think of two leaders in your community, state, or federal government. Compare and contrast the qualities of each. What are the similarities and differences of the two leaders? Which of the two do you think is more effective? Why?

2. **Make generalizations.** Which one of the steps in the decision-making process do you think is the most important? Which one of the steps do you think is the most difficult? Explain.

3. **Analyze the situation.** What advice would you give parents of a teen who failed to accept responsibility for his or her decision that negatively affected the family?

Making Connections

1. **History.** Select from history examples of decisions that affected large numbers of people, such as a national leader taking charge during a crisis. In small groups, choose one of the examples and discuss the consequences of the decision. Talk about the possible consequences that might have occurred if the decision had been reversed.

2. **Math.** Imagine you're going to make a purchase, such as an item of clothing, computer software program, or CD player. Follow the steps of the decision-making process and use your math skills to make your choice. Use newspapers and catalogs to contrast price differences among various products. Did price play a role in your final decision? Why or why not?

Applying Your Learning

1. **Write a letter.** Think about the positive influence of someone you respect on one of your decisions. Write a letter acknowledging his or her influence, and how it affected your decision.

2. **Role-play in class.** Enact a scene in which a teen's decision affected a friend or family member in a positive or negative way.

3. **Identify leaders.** Select photos from newspapers and magazines to create a collage of local, state, national, and international leaders. Select one of the leaders, and write a report on the leadership qualities that you think best describe the individual.

What Would You Do?

Imagine you're at the movies in a mall with several of your friends. Suddenly, one of your friends notices her purse is gone. Money she had saved was in her purse, along with her house keys. She wants you to go with her to look for her purse and to contact a security officer. You're in the middle of an action-packed movie. You want to help your friend, but would like to see the ending of the movie first. How would you deal with this situation?

Career Network

GRAPHIC DESIGNER

Large retail chain seeks creative graphic designer with demonstrated ability to develop effective marketing materials.
• Associate's or Bachelor's degree preferred.
• Computer proficiency required.

DIR. OF COMMUNICATIONS

Association needs organized director of communications to produce newsletters, brochures, press releases, and scripts for audiovisual materials.
• Excellent writing skills necessary.
• Four-year degree in English or journalism required.

ASSISTANT EDITOR

Professional organization seeks assistant editor for monthly publication.
• Review and edit articles related to health care issues.
• Excellent writing skills.
• Bachelor's degree required.

ANIMATOR

Progressive software company seeks imaginative animator for entry-level position.
• Bachelor's degree with art training necessary.
• Superior artistic ability, technical skills, and computer knowledge required.

MUSIC THERAPIST

Residential facility has opening for licensed music therapist to plan activities for individuals and groups.
• Must be comfortable working with emotionally disturbed patients.
• Master's degree required.

PHOTOGRAPHER

Portrait photographer needed to schedule and conduct school photography sessions.
• Must work well with youth ages 6-18.
• Associate degree or proven experience required.
• Extensive travel during school year.

More Career Options

Entry Level

• Model
• Florist
• Actor
• Visual Display Assistant

Technical Level

• Composer
• Interior Decorator
• Dance Instructor
• Set Designer
• Lighting Specialist

Professional Level

• Photo Editor
• Industrial Designer
• Commercial Artist
• Translator
• Publicist

PUBLIC RELATIONS SPECIALIST

Large metropolitan hospital has opening for public relations specialist to perform variety of PR functions, including promoting a positive image for the hospital.
- Must be comfortable dealing with media.
- Master's degree and excellent communication skills required.

SPORTS NEWSCASTER

Energetic newscaster needed for weekend on-air position.
- Must write and deliver sports news.
- Cover local and national sporting events during late evening broadcasts.
- Bachelor's degree required.

CAMERA OPERATOR

Cable television network has opening for camera operator to film local news events.
- Must work as part of news team at various locations.
- Excellent technical and problem-solving skills required.
- Post-secondary technical training required.

BROADCAST TECHNICIAN

Broadcast technician needed at small radio station to perform variety of duties.
- Need strong mechanical skills to install, operate, and maintain electronic equipment.
- Post-secondary technical training or two years experience required.

Linking School to Career

1. **Your Career Plan:** There are many paths that you can take to get from school to work. Did you notice that most of the want ads asked for specific levels of education? You can start thinking about your career path by looking at the classes you are taking now and how they relate to jobs. Write down the names of all of your classes. Beside each class, list three job titles that you think the class will help you prepare for.

2. **Researching Careers:** How long will it take to prepare for a career? Find out how long it takes to attain the following levels of education and discuss this information with the class: High School Diploma, On-the-Job Training, Apprenticeship Training Program, Associate Degree, Military Training Program, Bachelor's degree, Post-secondary Technical Training Program, Master's degree, and Doctorate degree.

3. **Social Studies:** Senior citizens often have valuable information to share regarding the history of events in your neighborhood or community. Interview someone 60 years of age or older about the events that have changed the area where you live in the past twenty years. How did any of the events impact the work opportunities for neighborhood residents?

Unit 2

Exploring Careers

Pathways to Careers

YOU WILL LEARN . . .

- ➤ Why people work.
- ➤ How school and work connect.
- ➤ Information you need to know to make career decisions.
- ➤ The best ways to explore careers.
- ➤ How people and resources can help you explore careers.

TERMS TO LEARN . . .

- ➤ aptitude
- ➤ career
- ➤ career cluster
- ➤ fringe benefits
- ➤ mentors
- ➤ occupations
- ➤ work

Imagine ...

... that you've won a 60-second shopping spree in your favorite store. Anything you can grab in one minute will be yours free. The catch is that the aisles in the store zigzag from department to department. The direction to take around the store is not easy to choose. Maybe you should just load your arms with everything that is within reach even if everything you get isn't quite right. This is a great opportunity. You want to make the most of it.

Think About

- How do you decide which items to take?
- What should you learn before your spree in order to get the most merchandise?
- How does having a plan help you make choices? In a similar way, how can having a career plan help you?

WHAT PATH WILL YOU TAKE?

Have you given thought to what your life will be like as an adult? Where will you live? How will you make money? What will your home be like? How will you spend your day? It's difficult to predict the answers to these questions, but it's important to start thinking about them now.

Work is *doing something productive with your time*. Everyone is expected to work. Work offers many benefits. The career paths you take and the work that you do will greatly influence your life. Some decisions you make as a student will help form your future.

Look around! The world is a very active place. People spend their days learning, making things, providing services, solving problems, and traveling from place to place. People perform a variety of jobs. No one person has the skills to make all the goods and services needed in life.

Most people work to make money that can be used to purchase these goods and services. Can you imagine what life would be like if you had to make your own clothes, shoes, TV, and sports equipment?

➤ **As a professional chef, this person helps meet the food needs of others.** What type of job might fit your needs now and in the future?

Paid work is a called a job. **Occupations** are *groups of similar jobs*. A **career** is *a series of occupations over a lifetime*. To choose your career, you need to understand your skills and interests, as well as the choices that are open to you. There are over 12,000 different occupational titles in the United States. That's a lot of jobs!

The jobs you hold and career choices you make will shape your entire adult life. Current research shows you could average six to seven career changes in a lifetime. You can use career information as a "road map" to choose your destinations, and sort out the best route to reaching your workplace goals.

What Is Work?

Work fulfills human needs in several ways. One way is directly from things that are made and services that are performed. Another way is from the income that you earn. Paid work provides money to buy the things you need and want, and gives you a sense of pride. When people work, they help themselves and their communities.

Money isn't the only reason people work. Many people enjoy what they do and wouldn't trade their work for another job, even if it paid more money. Work gives people a sense of doing something worthwhile and of belonging. Many people develop strong friendships at work.

How Do School and Work Connect?

School and paid work have some things in common. Learning in school can be hard work. It requires practice and commitment, even when you feel you'd rather be somewhere else. Most skills learned in school are necessary to succeed at work. Employers want to hire people who have above average grades and good attendance records.

There are also differences between school and paid work. In school, students are required to spread their efforts across a variety of subject areas. In the workplace, people try to pick jobs that allow them to work in areas they like and do well.

> ► Skills that you develop while in school can lead to success in your chosen career. **What are your best subjects in school? How might these skills fit into your future work?**

One difference between school and work is that employers often have less patience than teachers. Unlike teachers, employers pay wages and require people to work well in return for those wages. When a worker fails to show up at work, somebody else has to do his or her work. In the workplace, people who fail to meet expectations often lose their jobs. Those who have not performed well in past jobs, may not be considered for future jobs.

Many jobs now require lifelong learning. For example, Jim is a 30-year-old medical technician, Maria is a 40-year-old physician, and Chad is a 21-year-old maintenance supervisor. They all work at the same hospital. All three have earned licenses and degrees to qualify for their jobs. They're expected to continue their education in order to do better in their jobs. Each looks forward to vacation time to enjoy hobbies and interests. Yet all three see education, work, and leisure as important parts of daily living.

INVESTIGATING CAREERS

To understand your possibilities in the working world, start by looking at yourself. The more you know about your interests and skills, the easier it will be to pick your career path.

Your Interests and Skills

Interests are the things you like to do. Skills are the things that come easy to you. They're easy, because you have a natural talent or have practiced them enough. Over time, people tend to like most activities that they do well.

Remember, however, that skills and interests are two very different things. A person may be interested in an occupation, but not be willing to invest the time and effort to develop the skills needed to succeed at it. Another person may have natural talent, but not be interested in using these skills for paid work.

Looking at the "Big Picture"

What You'll Need
- Large sheets of paper and crayons or colored markers
- Large magazine picture cut in four pieces

What to Do
1. Divide into groups of four.
2. With puzzle pieces face down on the table, have each group member choose one puzzle piece. Without looking at other members' choices, take your puzzle piece, a large sheet of paper, and crayons or colored markers to an area of the classroom away from the rest of your group.
3. Glue your part of the picture to the center of the paper; then draw in what you think the rest of the picture might be.
4. Rejoin your group and share your pictures, then place the original pieces together to determine what the original picture was.

To Discuss
- How close were your drawings to the original picture? How would your task have been easier if you had seen the original picture first? How can you avoid making career decisions without considering the big picture?
- When making career plans, what information do you need? Where can you get this information?

Compare your answers to the following two questions:
- What activities do you enjoy the most?
- What activities do you think you would enjoy doing more than 2,000 hours each year?

If your answers to each question are different, don't be surprised. Some activities appear very interesting, but lose their attraction when you have to do them constantly.

Sara, for example, liked camping at her uncle's ranch. Yet she has no desire to work outside the whole year in snow, rain, or heat. She decided that camping was a hobby to enjoy as a change of pace from her office job as an accountant.

An **aptitude** is *a natural tendency that makes it easy for you to perform certain types of tasks.* Aptitudes are one type of skill. Students may possess different aptitude levels in school subjects, athletics, mechanical ability, public speaking, leadership, and the ability to understand the feelings of others. You can become aware of your aptitudes through school activities and career aptitude tests. Sara chose accounting as a career goal for several reasons. She had an aptitude for mathematics and an excellent memory for details.

➤ **This teen is developing her aptitude for art. She might consider a career in arts and communications.** What are your aptitudes?

Exploring Career Pathways

There are many ways to explore career paths. The best way to learn about jobs is to actually try them out. First-hand experiences such as field trips, internships, and employment are some ways to discover what you like. *Field trips* are visits to job locations that let students see a sample of what a certain job involves. *Internships* provide opportunities to actually do work, generally without pay.

You can also gain first-hand experience through paid employment. A student shows up to work on a regular basis, and an employer has specific expectations. Although an intern may have a broader range of experiences, student employees know they're doing real work because they're being paid.

Students can also benefit from developing special relationships with people who are experts in their jobs. **Mentors** are *successful workers who share their expert knowledge and demonstrate correct work behaviors*. You can learn a lot by working closely with a mentor.

Career Clusters

It's impossible to learn about all career opportunities through first-hand experiences. To save time and energy you may want to explore careers by looking at groups of occupations. A **career cluster** is *a large grouping of occupations that have certain things in common*. The clusters are usually formed around the types of services and products provided. Many states have identified career clusters to encourage career decision making and to help you choose appropriate study areas.

Job Shadow

Did you ever wonder how much you could learn by following a person around at work? Personal one-on-one field trips are called *job shadowing.* The person you're observing follows a regular workday, while you stay nearby and quiet—like a "shadow." The person being shadowed may take the time to answer questions and listen to your comments. Job shadowing provides a sample of the real work done on the job.

- Because job shadowing is an individual experience, you'll need permission of a parent as well as the person you're shadowing. You may also need permission from your school.

- Some schools permit students to do job shadowing as a school-related activity. If so, you can receive credit for shadowing and for reports you write about your experiences.

- Teachers and counselors can often help you find a person to shadow. Ask them about shadowing opportunities.

- Many businesses allow parents to bring their children to work on a special day each year so young people can explore careers. Ask your parents if you can participate.

USING CAREER CLUSTERS

Cluster Name	Product or Service	Sample Study Areas	Sample Occupation
Arts & Communications	Art, Music & Literature	Communications	Editor
Business & Management	Accounting & Management	Business Administration	Office Manager
Health & Medical Services	Medicine & Nutrition	Nursing	Nurse
Human Services	People & Education	Sociology	Social Worker
Engineering & Industrial Systems	Manufactured Goods	Manufacturing or Engineering	Engineer
Natural Resources	Food and Agriculture	Agricultural Services	Farmer

Name a career cluster in which your "dream job" might fall.

The common career clusters listed in the left-hand column of the chart on this page show six large groups of occupations. Can you name three occupations that you'd expect to find in each cluster? Clusters are useful in exploring career choices. Eventually, however, you'll need to narrow down your study areas to gain the necessary skills to succeed in specific occupations. The chart also shows sample study areas and specific occupations for each cluster.

Career clusters are also useful for identifying large groups of occupations that have no interest to you. For example, after observing an accountant all day, Andrew decided he wasn't interested in accounting.

Private companies, associations, and government agencies produce a wealth of information about career clusters and career opportunities. Your teachers, guidance counselors, and media specialists can help you gain access to these valuable resources.

Connecting with People

There's an old saying that people get jobs through the people they know. Many people credit someone else for helping them get a job. Some help by serving as personal references. Others help by encouraging people to explore career opportunities in a given area. They may be able to answer your questions or put you in contact with someone else who can. Do you know people who hold interesting jobs? Make a list and request interviews from them.

There are several reasons why personal connections are helpful. Word-of-mouth contacts are the best source of information about job openings in most communities. Employers want to know that others can verify a job applicant's skills, experience, and positive attitude before offering them a job.

➤ Many careers are available in each of the career clusters. Which career cluster is shown in this photo?

Researching Resources in Print

Most schools and public libraries have specific sections to help you explore careers and plan for the future. Career information includes information about jobs, workers, employers, and educational opportunities. There are several categories of information that job seekers need to know to make the best choice. The following types are most important:

- Educational requirements range from short-term, on-the-job training to as much as 10 years of college and a doctorate degree. Employers now require more post-high school education or training for job applicants.
- Earnings vary greatly among occupations and employers. Some jobs include regular pay increases based on the length of time a worker is employed. Wages may be earned on an hourly rate of pay or fixed salary.
- **Fringe benefits** include *vacation time, sick leave, health-care insurance, and retirement programs.* It's important to consider the fringe benefits offered with a job when comparing the income of two jobs. Sometimes it's better to select a lower-paying job that provides better fringe benefits than a higher-paying job.

- Nature of the work refers to the actual activities you do on a job. Nature of work includes the equipment used and supervision received. What work factors are important to you? Would you prefer to work alone or as part of a team?
- Working conditions refer to the environment where you work. Important conditions include work schedules, the chances of job-related injury, and perhaps travel requirements. Do you prefer to work inside or outside? Are you willing to work nights, weekends, or holidays?
- Job outlook refers to the future opportunities in an occupation. Job opportunities are often created because of new jobs, the replacement of existing workers, or a shortage of skilled applicants for job openings. Although new jobs become available when new businesses are created, two out of every three jobs become available when workers quit or retire.

Three of the best sources of national career information are available in most libraries:

- *The Occupational Outlook Handbook,* (OOH), provides information regarding the most common occupations in the United States.
- *The Occupational Outlook Quarterly,* (OOQ), provides updated information regarding changes in the work force and interesting articles about new occupations.
- *The Military Career Guide Online* is an important source of information regarding opportunities in the armed forces.

➤ **Many print resources are available to help you in your career search.**

Many sources of career information are also available on the state and local levels. Check with your school counselor about these options.

Using Computer Resources

The Internet is a rapidly expanding source of career information. Website addresses change on a regular basis, so you may have to conduct your own Internet search to find the latest ones. Conduct Internet searches using each of the following terms:

- Career information.
- Labor market information.
- Job bank.
- Industry employment.
- Occupational employment.

COLLEGE DEGREE LEVELS

Type of Degree	Years of College Required	Sample Degree
Associate Degree	At least two years	Associate of Arts
Bachelor's Degree	Four or more years	Bachelor of Education
Master's Degree	Bachelor's Degree + 1-2 years	Master of Business Administration
Doctorate Degree	Master's Degree + 2-3 years	Doctor of Philosophy

What degree would you need to attain in order to achieve your career goal?

CAREER OPPORTUNITIES UNLIMITED

Current resources do a good job of predicting the growth of existing jobs for the next five years. Some occupations will be eliminated because of changes in technology. Other jobs will be added as the result of new inventions and new ways of doing things. Medical technology, for example, is improving the quality of life and keeping patients alive longer. Consequently, the health care industry will offer thousands of new jobs.

The job market is constantly changing with increasing speed. What jobs and products can you think of that exist today that were nonexistent when your grandparents were young? You can expect to work in occupations that don't even exist today. Career opportunities will be unlimited for people who are willing to continue learning and adjust to change. The next two chapters describe the specific skills needed in the new work world and provide strategies to enter and advance in careers.

➤ The job market is rapidly changing. Just as technology has changed in recent years, so have many careers. What jobs do you think might exist in the future?

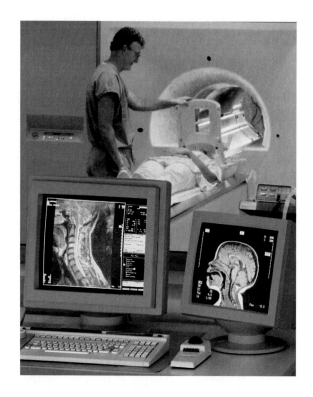

Review & Activities

Chapter Summary

- The career choices you make and the jobs you hold will impact your life.
- Work meets people's needs in many ways.
- School and paid work have some things in common as well as some big differences.
- People tend to make better career decisions when they understand the expectations of jobs, and their own interests and skills.
- There are several ways to learn about careers through firsthand experiences.
- Career clusters are a useful tool to examine occupations and make career decisions.
- Personal contacts help people explore careers, locate job openings, and receive job offers.
- Career information helps people make wise career decisions.

Family & Community

With Your Family

Talk to the older members in your family regarding their experiences making career decisions. Do they think you have more opportunities than they had? If so, why?

In Your Community

Identify at least five new businesses that have moved into your community in the last five years. Identify the kinds of job that they provide. Do people who work there live in the community?

Reviewing the Chapter

1. Explain the relationship between a job, an occupation, and a career.
2. Give two reasons, other than making money, that people work.
3. If a job requires lifelong learning, what must you expect to do?
4. Explain the difference between interests, skills, and aptitudes.
5. What are the differences between field trips and internships?
6. Describe the advantages of having a mentor.
7. What are career clusters? How do they help you choose a career?
8. List six important categories of information you need to explore when researching careers.

Thinking Critically

1. **Compare and contrast.** Compare and contrast school and paid employment by describing things they have in common and ways they're different. Which one do you think is harder?
2. **Draw conclusions.** If more and more jobs are requiring some type of post-high school education and only one-third of all jobs require a college degree, where will most people receive their additional education?
3. **Assess outcomes.** New jobs result from new inventions. List three jobs created as a result of new technology in the home or workplace. In what ways has technology affected jobs and careers in your community?

Making Connections

1. **Social Studies.** Name five current occupations that didn't exist in 1950. Name five current occupations that were already in existence when Columbus traveled to America in 1492.

2. **Science.** Identify three major inventions that have changed the world. For each invention, list five new occupations that came into existence as the result of that invention.

3. **Literature.** The ancient Greeks believed the goddess of wisdom disguised herself as a man named "Mentor" to help the busy hero, Ulysses, raise his son. While Ulysses served as the captain of a ship trying to find a way home, Mentor taught his son many things he'd need to know if he were to be king some day. What is the message of the story? Why do young people still need "mentors" today?

Applying Your Learning

1. **Make a career choice.** If you were forced to make a lifetime occupational choice today, what occupation would you choose? Why? Would your choice be different if you had to stay in the job only six months? Explain your answers.

2. **Write a letter.** Imagine you're nominating someone you know for "Outstanding Mentor of the Year." Write a letter explaining the reasons for your nomination and the traits that make the person a good mentor.

3. **Write a report.** Develop a brief report on an occupation of interest to you. Include the following in the report: educational requirements, earnings, fringe benefits, nature of work, working conditions, and job outlook.

What Would You Do?

Suppose your best friend asked your advice in choosing between two Saturday job opportunities. The first job is to operate the childcare room at a local health club. The job pays $6 an hour for five hours of work. The second job involves making sandwiches at the local fast-food restaurant. The restaurant pays $6.15 an hour for six hours of work. His long-term goal is to become a third-grade teacher. What advice would you give him? What's the difference in weekly pay between the two jobs? What factors should he consider besides the money?

Workplace Skills

YOU WILL LEARN . . .

- ➤ New requirements to enter and advance in the changing workplace.
- ➤ Basic skills that are needed.
- ➤ Thinking skills that are needed.
- ➤ Employability traits that are needed.
- ➤ The importance of workplace competencies.

TERMS TO LEARN . . .

- ➤ basic skills
- ➤ systems
- ➤ thinking skills

Imagine ...

... that you are a volunteer at the local animal shelter. Your job is matching animals that are available for adoption with families that want to adopt a pet.

Think About

- How do you learn what qualities the family wants in a pet, and whether a particular animal has these traits?
- How do you help a family decide between two promising pets?
- How do you determine whether you've been successful in helping the family?
- What skills would be the most important in your work at the shelter?

SUCCEEDING IN THE WORLD OF WORK

The skills you learn in school form the foundation of the skills necessary to succeed and advance in the workplace. Unlike many jobs in the past, jobs today require a combination of basic skills, thinking skills, and employability traits. This chapter outlines the new requirements to enter and advance in the changing workplace.

BUILDING YOUR WORKPLACE FOUNDATION

What skills do employers really want? The answer may vary from job to job, but this chapter discusses the skills most often requested by employers.

Basic Skills

Basic skills are *reading, writing, speaking, listening, and mathematics*. Basic skills are the tools for learning. They're building blocks that support all higher-level skills. Kathy and Justin, for example, complained to their math teacher

➤ **When deciding on a career for your future, consider your ideal way of living.** What type of work do you most enjoy? How important would mathematics be for this job?

about the large number of story problems they were assigned. Their teacher, Mrs. Cain, replied, "Problems in the real world are always story problems with many steps. You can't even bake a cake unless you can count money to buy ingredients, know how to measure them, set the oven temperature properly, and calculate time."

Reading skills include the abilities to read and interpret newspapers, magazines, manuals, directions, encyclopedias, dictionaries, and maps. Most jobs require a variety of reading skills. Higher-level jobs may also require the ability to read financial reports, technical journals, architectural plans, or legal documents. Workers need to be able to understand what they read, summarize the information, and apply it in real-world situations.

Writing skills for work include the abilities to communicate information, ideas, thoughts, and messages in written form. Writing skills are in high demand by employers. All occupations require the completion of job applications and other forms. Note taking is a skill you can expect in the workplace as well as in school. Higher-level jobs may also require the ability to write reports, speeches, or journal articles. The widespread use of computers has resulted in an increased need for writing skills in the workplace.

Speaking skills include the ability to organize ideas and communicate oral messages to individuals, small groups, and large groups. Much of oral communication in the workplace takes place in person, in group meetings, and over the phone. Oral communication is most effective when you present information in an organized way using effective communication skills.

➤ **Communication skills are vital to many careers, and demand courteous interaction.**

New requirements for teamwork in the workplace have increased the demand for speaking skills. Public speaking skills include the abilities to present reports before others and to participate in group meetings. Fear of speaking before an audience is often listed as one of the most common fears in America.

Have you ever been asked to make a presentation before a group? How did you feel? In any organization you'll need to talk to the people at your level and to those above you. If you're promoted, you may have people who work under your direction. Speaking skills are important in all three types of work relationships.

Listening skills include the abilities to hear another person's message, read body language, and understand the tone of voice of a speaker. Can you read the emotions of your family members just by looking at them? Listening skills are a companion to speaking skills. When listening to others, it's always important to show them that you hear what they're saying, whether you agree with them or not. When people are focused only on getting their ideas across, they often fail to hear what others are saying.

➤ **Learning something new every day will greatly broaden your knowledge level. When learning from an experienced worker, be sure to listen carefully.**

Basic math skills include the abilities to add, subtract, multiply, and divide all units of measurement. Math skills are very important in the changing job market. Managers and the workers who report to them increasingly use skills in algebra, geometry, and statistics.

Thinking Skills

Workers need to be able to think creatively, make decisions, solve problems, and know how to learn and reason. Do you like to come up with new ideas, design new products, and find new uses for old products? Are you able to see a product in your "mind's eye" before it's actually made? Can you imagine the taste of food just from looking at a recipe? Could you determine if you like a home just by looking at the plans?

The mental skills you use to learn and solve problems are commonly referred to as **thinking skills**. There are several levels of thinking skills. See the chart on this page for more information.

For example, Karen used six basic thinking levels while she learned to become an automotive technician:

- During the *knowledge* phase, she learned to name the various parts of an engine.
- In the *comprehension* phase, she learned to understand the purpose of each auto part.
- During the *application* phase, she learned to replace each part in the engine.
- In the *analysis* phase, she learned to take the engine apart.

➤ **These two teens were told to design a product that would sell, from this fabric piece. What products would you make if you were given this assignment?**

THINKING SKILLS

Knowledge	The lowest level of thinking includes *identifying facts and terms.*
Comprehension	The second level of thinking is *understanding the information.*
Application	The third level of thinking includes *the use of knowledge and understanding.*
Analysis	The fourth level of thinking involves *the ability to break a problem down into its component parts.*
Synthesis	The fifth level of thinking is *the ability to assemble parts into a whole.*
Evaluation	The highest level of thinking is *the ability to determine where problems exist and determine the best solutions.*

Try using these thinking skills as you solve everyday problems in school.

- In the *synthesis* phase she learned to put the parts back together into a working engine.
- Finally, in the *evaluation* phase she learned to diagnose engine problems by looking and listening to an engine before she took it apart.

A master mechanic who's reached the evaluation level is often capable of solving complicated problems on the first try.

Employability Traits

Employers complain that many employees lack necessary personal qualities to do a job well. They claim that many workers have poor relationships with their bosses, co-workers, and customers. As one employer says, "Most individuals I fire are let go not because they can't do the work, but because they don't get along with others."

Mike missed work three times in the first two weeks on the job. He provided no explanation for his absences. Each

> **Many employability traits are learned by showing responsibility at home.**

time he was given a task, Mike failed to complete it on time. His coworkers described Mike as careless about his work. He was finally dismissed from his job.

Employability traits necessary for success in the workplace include responsibility, self-esteem, sociability, self-control, and honesty. Responsible people are dependable and complete the tasks that they are asked to do.

The list of employability traits beginning on this page provides a wish list of qualities requested by employers. Do their views differ from your own? List the five employability traits you think are most important at work.

EMPLOYABILITY TRAITS

Trait	Description
1. Concentration	The ability to focus and pay attention.
2. Consistency	Tendency to act in the same way in repeated situations.
3. Creativity	Having the ability or power to make new, original, or imaginative solutions to problems.
4. Dedication	Sense of commitment to one's friends, family, or duties.
5. Dependability	Fulfilling obligations in a timely fashion. Reliability.
6. Drive	Energy, an organized effort to succeed.
7. Duty	The compulsion to meet all obligations.
8. Empathy	Understanding so strong that the feelings, thoughts, and motives of one person are readily understood by another.
9. Enthusiasm	Zeal, passion, and excitement about one's work.
10. Fairness	Treating others justly or equitably.
11. Flexibility	Willingness to respond positively to the need for change.
12. Honesty	Truthfulness, trustworthiness, willingness to admit mistakes.

(continued)

EMPLOYABILITY TRAITS (continued)

Trait	Description
13. Honor	Nobility of mind. Personal integrity without legal or other obligation.
14. Humility	Modesty, lack of boastful pride.
15. Initiative	Willingness to take the first step in an undertaking. Readiness to solve a problem without being told.
16. Integrity	Tendency to react the same way despite offers of additional rewards and punishments.
17. Optimism	A tendency to expect the best possible outcome.
18. Professionalism	Having the character, spirit, and skills of the best people in an occupation.
19. Respect	Willingness to show consideration, deference, or appreciation for others.
20. Self-control	Ability to limit and control your emotions and actions.
21. Self-discipline	Careful control and training of oneself.
22. Self-esteem	The confidence and worth you have in yourself.
23. Sense of humor	Ability to enjoy or express what is comical or funny.
24. Sociability	Ability to relate to the feelings of other people and develop positive relations with them.
25. Willingness to learn	Responsiveness to pick up new skills through education and training.
26. Wisdom	Common sense and good judgment. Understanding of what is true, right, or lasting.

Identify the employability skills you feel you meet and those you need to improve.

Making a DIFFERENCE

JOB TALK

"Thanks, Mr. Pollock, for letting me come talk to you about your job," Martha said, sitting across from the business manager in his office.

"I was really impressed by your thoughtful letter," Mr. Pollock replied. "Your thoughts were well-organized, and you expressed yourself well. We look for those qualities when we hire someone new."

"Can you tell me what your workday is like?" Martha asked.

Mr. Pollock smiled and spent a few minutes explaining his job. When he finished, he said, "You look like you have a number of questions."

"I do," said Martha, and fired away.

Mr. Pollock seemed impressed with her intelligent questions. When Martha got up to leave, he said, "I want you to stay in touch. If you have any questions about subjects to study in school that would prepare you for this kind of job, please call."

"I will," said Martha.

Taking Action

1. What traits does Martha demonstrate that would help anyone exploring future careers?
2. What could you do to contact someone in a job you'd like to explore?

BUILDING WORKPLACE COMPETENCIES

Once you have the foundation skills necessary for job success, the next step is to develop more specific workplace competencies. The five competencies listed below apply to most occupations found in America.

Allocating Resources

Work requires the investment of resources such as time, money, materials, space, and people. Because limited amounts of these resources exist, you have to make decisions regarding the best way to use them.

Using Information

Today, with so much information available, the challenge is to acquire information when you need it; to organize, evaluate, and interpret it; and to communicate it to others. What information would you need to pick out a new bicycle or running shoes? Where would you go to get information to compare different products?

Using Interpersonal Skills

"People skills" are central to success in the workplace. Workers are expected to work in teams, teach others, and serve customers. Successful workers are sensitive to people from different backgrounds and experiences. Employers especially want employees who can assume leadership roles

➤ Sharing your knowledge with others is an interpersonal skill. Practicing these skills will bring bigger opportunities in the future.

or follow the directions of others. Do you know people who seem to be natural leaders? Why do you think people are willing to follow their lead? Do you prefer to follow directions or lead others?

Understanding Systems

Systems are *orderly ways of doing things*. Systems include procedures and equipment used at work. Workers are expected to understand and correct problems using systems, such as network computers or complex machinery. Some workers improve and design systems. Systems have interconnected parts so that a change in one part can affect other parts of the system. People use systems in their personal lives, too. What system do you use to get ready in the morning? What changes in your system would get you ready more quickly? Your body and school are also examples of systems.

Using Technology

To be most productive, workers must be able to use and maintain technology in the workplace. Technology changes the size, cost, speed, and usefulness of tools that make our lives easier. With constant changes in technology, people must learn new ways to use tools and to include them in their lives. How do you use computers at school? How do you use computers at home?

REACHING FOR SUCCESS

Most jobs require more competencies than those described in this chapter. These additional competencies can be learned on the job or through education after high school. First, however, you must master the basic foundation skills, employability traits, and competencies covered in this chapter. Middle school courses, high school courses, internships, and paid employment provide many opportunities to practice and develop these basic requirements for success in your future.

MANNERS IN THE WORKPLACE

The following tips about manners will help you get along successfully in the workplace:

- Treat customers, co-workers, and employees with the same respect that you have for the person in charge.

- Always say thank you for any service received from others. Everyone wants to be appreciated.

- Apologize when you make a mistake. Everyone makes mistakes sometimes, but good employees accept responsibility and act to prevent mistakes.

- Listen intently when others speak to you. Speakers want you to listen to them. Make eye contact and lean towards the speaker.

- Don't cut off others when they speak. In an effective conversation people take turns speaking and listening.

Chapter Summary

- Jobs today require a combination of basic skills, thinking skills, and employability traits.
- Basic skills include reading, writing, speaking, listening, and mathematics.
- The six levels of thinking skills needed in the workplace are knowledge, comprehension, application, analysis, synthesis, and evaluation.
- Employability traits include responsibility, self-esteem, sociability, and honesty.
- Most occupations require workers to be competent in allocating resources, using information, using interpersonal skills, understanding systems, and using technology.

Reviewing the Chapter

1. Explain why basic skills are needed in the workplace.
2. Why has the demand for speaking skills in the workplace increased?
3. Why are thinking skills important in the workplace?
4. What is the difference between analysis and synthesis?
5. Why are interpersonal skills central to success in the workplace?
6. What are systems and why do workers need to use and understand them?
7. How must workers deal with constant changes in technology?

Family & Community

In Your Family
Discuss the employability traits list with others in your family. Do they have any traits that they would like to see added to or deleted from the list? Once you agree upon a list, ask them how they'd go about developing these traits in children and teens.

In Your Community
Some students in your community may lack the basic reading, writing, and math skills needed for success in the workplace. Many may be willing to be tutored to improve their skills. Ask your guidance counselor how you can help one of your fellow students to improve.

Review & Activities

Thinking Critically

1. **Draw conclusions.** In an age of rapidly expanding information, why do some people complain that they don't have enough information to make decisions?
2. **Make a generalization.** The rapidly changing workplace requires workers who can work effectively in teams. Do you think that schools do a better job of teaching competition or cooperation? Why?
3. **Make a self assessment.** From the list on pages 95 and 96, select ten employability traits that you believe are your strongest areas. Ask a close friend to identify ten traits that reflect your strongest areas. Compare the results and discuss differences.

Making Connections

1. **Social Studies.** Find two charts and two graphs in a newspaper or a magazine. Write a paragraph for each that explains what they show.
2. **Literature.** Shakespeare's character, Hamlet, said he could see his dead father in his "mind's eye." Thinking skills in today's workplace require people to visualize things in the "mind's eye." What do you think the term means?

Applying Your Learning

1. **Develop interpersonal skills.** Imagine that you are part of a school news team. With five or six of your classmates, prepare a newscast about recent events at school, including school issues, student council, sports, and even the weather. After a little practice, present your newscast to the class. How does teamwork help you develop interpersonal skills?
2. **Apply multiple math skills.** Assume you want to calculate how much it would cost to carpet your classroom. First, identify all numbers you need for your calculations. Then list the steps you need to take to determine the costs.
3. **Learn to interpret body language.** Watch a short video clip of one of your favorite TV shows with the volume completely off. Record your interpretations of the person's emotions. Watch the clip again, with sound, to see if your interpretations change.

What Would You Do?

Jessica suddenly stops getting the highest scores in her math and science classes. In fact, her scores are barely above average. She tells you she's doing it on purpose. She's afraid other students will make fun of her if she is "too smart." You think she's making a big mistake. What would you say to her?

Entering the World of Work

YOU WILL LEARN . . .

➤ How to apply for a job.
➤ How to write a résumé.
➤ How to prepare for a job interview.
➤ How to balance work and family.

TERMS TO LEARN . . .

➤ cover letter
➤ flextime
➤ résumé
➤ stress

Imagine ...

... that a job you want very much has become available. You've applied and been asked to interview for the position. A friend of yours helped you practice your interview skills. Now you're waiting in the interviewer's office, ready to make your case.

Think About

• How will practice benefit you during the interview?
• What will you do to control the impression you make on the interviewer?
• Is getting the job your ultimate goal? Explain.

HOW TO PRESENT YOURSELF

Getting a job can be a challenging process for anyone. Every job offer is a two-way agreement that benefits both the employer and the employee. The employer wants a good worker. You want a job that you can do well and that pays an acceptable wage. The way you present yourself when you apply for a job usually determines whether you get the job.

Applying for a Job

Few people are hired for jobs without going through a formal application process. Employers are required by law to use a fair and competitive process to hire new employees. The steps for a potential employee usually include:

- Completing a job application.
- Submitting a résumé and cover letter to a potential employer.
- Interviewing with an employer.

Résumés That Work

The first step in the job application process is a review of your own abilities and experiences. This self-review leads to developing a written summary of your job qualifications, or résumé. A **résumé** is *a typed document that provides a brief history of your work experience and education.* A résumé demonstrates your competence as a candidate for a particular job. A résumé also highlights your skills and includes some personal information.

Many employers ask for a résumé in addition to a completed job application. Employers will consult your résumé before they decide to interview you. See page 105 for more information on writing an effective résumé.

When employers receive large numbers of résumés for a position, they often narrow the field by selecting those candidates with the best prepared résumés. Poorly written résumés, or those with misspelled words, are usually eliminated regardless of an applicant's skills. If an employer seeks a specific skill, the reviewer will eliminate résumés that fail to identify the requested skill.

Using a Résumé

Work History Résumé

The work history résumé lists your most recent job first and moves backward to your first job. It identifies specific dates of employment, names of employers and job titles, as well as your educational experience. A work history résumé emphasizes a steady employment record and a pattern of promotions. The major headings for a typical work history résumé are as follows:

JAMES SMITH
123 Main Street, Springfield, IN 77007
(555) 555-555 (Telephone)
(555) 223-4568 (Fax)

● **Name, full address, phone number, and fax number.***

OBJECTIVE A paid position as a preschool teacher assistant.

● **Career objective.**

SUMMARY
- Three years of experience baby sitting for five families.
- Two years as an assistant coach for Little League baseball and helping care for my two younger brothers.
- Class president of Family, Career, and Community Leaders of America (FCCLA).
- Completed Red Cross CPR training course and D. A. R. E. program.
- Sophomore student at Hayes High School, currently on the Honor Roll for the first semester.

WORK EXPERIENCE AND ACCOMPLISHMENTS

● **Work history and accomplishments.**

2003 - Present	Child Care Worker	Mr. & Mrs. Greg Scott Family Sommersville, IN
2002 - Present	Child Care Worker	Ms. Martha Wilson Family Springfield, IN
2002 - 2003	Child Care Worker	Walt Green and Carol Born Family Sommersville, IN

EDUCATION AND TRAINING

● **Educational history and professional training.**

2002-2004	Hayes High School, 23 Oak Street, Springfield, IN 77007.
2002	Red Cross CPR Training Program Certificate of Completion.

SCHOOL ACTIVITIES
Current Activities
- Active Member FCCLA for two years, current class president.
- Manager, Junior Varsity Football Team.

Past Activities
- Boy Scouts of America member for three years.

COMMUNITY ACTIVITIES
Current Activities
- Assistant coach for Little League baseball, Springfield Recreation Department.

Past Activities
- D. A. R. E. program participant.

REFERENCES
References available upon request.

***You can include your e-mail address if you have one.**

Writing Cover Letters

A résumé should always be accompanied by a cover letter. A **cover letter** *informs the employer that you're applying for a position in the company.* A successful cover letter has four major parts:

- A salutation and a reference to the specific job for which you are applying.
- Information regarding your knowledge of the company.
- A positive statement about the contribution you can make to the company.
- Your desire for an interview, plus follow-up information.

Preparing for an Interview

➤ What you wear to an interview will give the interviewer his or her first impression of you. What impression do you want to give?

You *never* have a second chance to make a *first* impression. You can expect to be judged by the first impression you make during an interview. Interviewers tend to highly rate those candidates who appear genuine, enthusiastic, and share the same values as the company.

Dress properly for a job interview. You may not need to wear a suit for an interview as a teacher's aide, but denim jeans and a T-shirt aren't appropriate either. What do you think would be most appropriate in this situation?

During an interview, let the interviewer take the lead in the conversation. Focus on hearing questions and answering them directly. Sit up straight, smile, and lean toward the interviewer, so he or she knows you're interested in the job. Save questions regarding wages and benefits until you know that you're a finalist for the job. You should always end the interview with a positive statement of your interest in the job and an offer to participate in further interview activities.

HOW to...

Write a Cover Letter

Writing an effective cover letter is an important part of applying for a job. Use the following guidelines when putting together your letter.

Step 1

The beginning of your cover letter should include the date, the address heading of the potential employer, your salutation, and introductory paragraph. The opening paragraph of the letter should also indicate the specific job for which you are applying and how you learned about the position.

Step 2

The letter should show that you have taken some time to learn about the company. Positive comments about the location of the company, their good reputation, and the products and services that they produce show interest in the position.

January 23, 2004

Ms. Emily Jones
Safeway Airline Company
555 Cedar Highway
Anywhere, IA 55555

Dear Ms. Jones: (To Whom It May Concern)

Please consider my application for the position of flight attendant that was listed in the classified section of the Cedar Rapids Times on January 22nd.

I am very interested in the Safeway Airline Company and have been impressed by your outstanding safety record and commitment to customer service.

My family moved to Cedar Rapids ten years ago and I believe that it is great place to live and work.

I look forward to meeting with you to discuss my qualifications for this position. If I need to complete a job application or if you want additional information, please let me know at your earliest convenience. Thank you for your consideration.

Sincerely,

Andrea Smith

Andrea Smith

Step 3

You can also add some additional information in the letter that is not included in the résumé.

Step 4

Indicate your desire for a job interview and offer to submit additional follow-up information. Also include closing information and your signature.

Technology at Work

What You'll Need
- Classified section of local newspaper
- Paper and pen
- Glue

What to Do
1. Cut out 10 want ads for jobs that interest you and glue them to a sheet of paper.
2. Beneath each ad, list ways a person in this job would use technology.
3. Working with three other students, share your lists with your classmates.

To Discuss
- How is technology changing the workplace?
- What can you do to prepare for jobs that use technology?

Following Up

Follow-up activities are valuable parts of the interview process. Most employers appreciate a thank-you note from an applicant within one week of the interview.

BALANCING WORK AND FAMILY

Getting a job you want may give you a great feeling. But most jobs include a certain degree of stress. **Stress** is *the pressure people feel as the result of their ability or inability to meet the expectations of others and themselves.* You're expected to work hard, meet deadlines, and interact with coworkers and supervisors on a continual basis.

In addition, many people find it difficult to balance their commitments to their jobs, families, and friends. Some people find they have no time for their own interests and hobbies. Some feel frustrated that they don't have time to spend with others and accomplish their goals.

➤ A balanced work and family life recognizes the need for leisure activity and family togetherness.

Stress can be either positive or negative:

- Positive stress helps you meet challenges by giving you the extra push you need.
- Negative stress causes discomfort and decreases performance.

The cause and the intensity of stress determine whether stress is a positive or negative force in your life. Tragedies, such as the death of a loved one, a serious illness, or the loss of a job, foster feelings of negative stress. Uplifting events, such as a wedding, graduation, or job promotion, foster feelings of positive stress.

Positive stress is usually connected with feelings of success, and if kept at a low level, can improve your performance. But too much stress actually decreases performance levels. Did you ever perform poorly on a test because you were too worried about failing? Did you ever get so nervous in a game that you couldn't concentrate?

You can use several strategies to decrease the stress of balancing work and family commitments.

- Time management skills will help you set aside time for priorities.
- Strategies to work efficiently can help you complete necessary tasks.

➤ Stress on the job is similar to having too much homework or cramming for a test. This stress affects a person at work and at home.

See Chapter 24 for more information on stress.

• Eliminating unimportant tasks and activities can help you achieve success in your top priorities.

How can you improve your life by managing time wisely? In what areas do you want to become more efficient? What tasks do you want to eliminate?

Challenges for Families and Employers

Employers have the difficult task of supporting the needs of workers while treating them fairly and equitably. Company policies must be enforced equally for everyone, although workers may not show the same levels of commitment to their jobs.

Consider the example of two managers in a traditional company. Scott usually starts work 20 minutes early and continues to work at least 30 minutes after the end of the workday. Adam never starts early or stays late. If either has to leave early to take care of a sick family member, the boss charges both of them with a day of sick leave.

Benefits for Families and Employers

Events at work and at home have an effect on one other. People are happiest when their families can enjoy the benefits of their work. When people are worried about problems at home, it affects their performance at work. When workers lack success at work they often come home angry and frustrated. Most people are now aware of the deep connection between work and home life, and try to develop strategies to keep them in balance. When they do, workers and employers both benefit.

Some companies have adopted flexible work schedules (flextime) to meet the needs of their workers. **Flextime** *allows workers to adjust their start and stop times to meet the needs of their families* as long as workers put in the required number of hours on the job. As the result of flextime, parents can choose to take their children to school each morning or be at home when their children return. Additional benefits include healthcare, dental, and vision care plans for workers and their immediate families.

➤ More companies are providing flexible work hours, so employees can balance their work and family lives.

MANAGING RESPONSIBILITIES AT HOME AND WORK

Some people try to keep their work on the job completely separate from their work at home, but the two sets of responsibilities constantly impact each other. For a time, success in one of the two areas can balance a lack of success in the other. More often, however, problems in one area have a negative impact on the other. The happiest workers usually enjoy both their work and home lives.

Remember, paid work isn't a goal in itself. It's a way to earn money to buy the goods and services that improve the quality of life. People work to feel good about themselves and enjoy the fruits of their labor. When family members of employees benefit directly or indirectly from a person's job, he or she is likely to remain loyal and committed to an employer.

Chapter Summary

- When applying for a job, you usually provide a completed application form, a résumé, and a cover letter.
- A work history résumé emphasizes a steady employment record and pattern of promotions.
- A cover letter demonstrates your interest in the company.
- Dress properly for a job interview and focus on listening to the questions.
- Most people experience stress trying to balance commitments to jobs, families, and friends.
- Several strategies can be used to manage time and reduce stress.
- People are likely to be loyal to employers that provide benefits to their families.

Reviewing the Chapter

1. What is the purpose of a résumé?
2. What are the four parts of a successful cover letter?
3. What do employers look for in potential candidates during a job interview?
4. What kinds of clothes should you wear to a job interview?
5. Explain the difference between positive stress and negative stress.
6. Summarize three strategies you can use to decrease the stress of balancing work and family commitments.
7. How does flextime help workers reduce stress?

Family & Community

With Your Family

Most people feel they have some stress in their lives. Talk to others in your family to find out about their stress levels and the causes of their stress. Are there any ways you can make their lives less stressful? Offer your assistance.

In Your Community

Laughter, kindness, and humor help to reduce stress. Send a positive note or humorous card to someone you know. Include a drawing of how you feel when you are stressed out. You'll make their day.

Thinking Critically

1. **Make a generalization.** What does the phrase "You never have a second chance to make a first impression" mean? Does it apply to other areas of your life besides work? What opportunities will you have in the near future to make a positive first impression?

2. **Cause and effect.** In this chapter you learned that a little stress can improve performance, but too much stress can actually decrease performance. Why do the effects change? Can you give reasons for different responses to stress?

3. **Draw conclusions.** Some occupations are more likely to offer flextime than others. Determine which of the following occupations have a better chance of having flextime and defend your choices: farmer, writer, high school teacher, house painter, auto mechanic, long-distance truck driver, hairdresser.

Making Connections

1. **Social Studies.** Imagine you're a famous political leader in history, such as a U.S. president, and create a fictional résumé and cover letter for the job. You may also want to role-play the person's job interview.

2. **Science.** Imagine you're a famous scientist in history. Create a résumé and cover letter for your job. For example, Albert Einstein is applying for the job of a physicist or Madame Curie is applying for a job as a biologist. You may also want to role-play the person's job interview.

Applying Your Learning

1. **Write a résumé.** Create a personal résumé using information contained in this chapter. Imagine that you'll be applying for your dream job. How would you focus your résumé?

2. **Write a cover letter.** Create a cover letter following the guidelines in this chapter.

3. **Develop a plan to reduce stress.** Make a list of the things in your life that you find most stressful and identify three ideas to reduce your stress. If you're comfortable with the stress in your life, identify three actions you can take to help reduce the stress of others in your family.

What Would You Do?

Suppose you notice that one of your friends is very anxious about upcoming semester exams. He can't sleep and has been getting sick just before school. He just started a job as a grocery store bagger and has been criticized for being too slow. What advice would you give him? What changes could he make to improve his test scores?

Career Network

ACCOUNTANT

Large accounting firm seeks experienced Certified Public Accountant (CPA) to join auditing staff.
- Computer skills essential.
- Minimal travel required.
- Competitive salary and benefits package.

RETAIL MANAGER

Large retail store needs manager for sporting goods department. Will supervise employees and manage daily activities.
- Good customer service skills needed.
- Associate's degree required.
- Formal training provided.

MEETING PLANNER

Nonprofit association needs energetic certified meeting planner to coordinate annual meetings and conferences.
- Bachelor's degree required.
- Excellent organizational skills necessary.

MARKETING MANAGER

Rapidly growing small service business seeks marketing manager to develop and implement strategic plan for new products.
- Bachelor's degree or above desired.
- Successful sales experience required.

BANK TELLER

Bank teller needed to assist customers with banking transactions.
- High school diploma and good math skills required.
- Courses in banking and previous cash handling experience a plus.

ASSISTANT HOTEL MANAGER

New hotel is looking for assistant manager to oversee convention services. Primarily responsible for meetings, conventions, and special events.
- Hours include nights and weekends.
- Bachelor's degree required.
- Internship in hotel management a plus.

More Career Options

Entry Level
- Telemarketer
- Reservations Agent
- Stock Clerk
- Billing Clerk
- Retail Sales Clerk

Technical Level
- Brokerage Clerk
- Office Manager
- Cost Estimator
- Claims Adjuster
- Purchasing Agent

Professional Level
- Economist
- Bank Branch Manager
- Stockbroker
- Cost Accountant
- Product Manager

LEGAL ASSISTANT

Large law firm seeks a skilled legal assistant with superior communications skills and attention to detail.
• Post-secondary technical training required.
• Familiarity with legal software programs a plus.

FINANCIAL AID ASSISTANT

Private technical training institute has opening in student financial aid office to assist and advise students.
• Excellent interpersonal skills needed.
• Bachelor's degree with accounting background required.

MANAGEMENT CONSULTANT

Growing information systems consulting firm has opening for consultant with strong problem-solving ability. Will develop plans to expand operations in large companies.
• Master's degree plus experience required.
• Excellent communication skills necessary.

HUMAN RESOURCES DIR.

Expanding company seeks organized human resources director to oversee employee relations, benefits, and compensation programs.
• Degree in human resources desired.
• Previous supervisory experience required.

Linking School to Career

1. Your Career Plan: When thinking about the right career for you, you need to consider rewards, demands, and future trends. A career provides a number of rewards in addition to payment. It is also demanding in terms of the time and energy it requires. For various reasons, some careers have a more promising future than others. Think about a career that interests you. Write down the rewards you expect it to bring, the demands it will make, and what you expect from it in the future.

2. Researching Careers: What does it take to be a successful entrepreneur? List the traits that are common among entrepreneurs. Do you have what it takes to start and run your own business? What are the advantages of working for you? What are the disadvantages?

3. Math: Some jobs pay a monthly salary while others pay according to a specific hourly rate. Which of the following jobs pays more money?

A. $10.00 per hour for a 40-hour week.
B. $1600.00 per month for a 40-hour week.

Also, keep in mind that 25% of your income will go for taxes and benefits, such as health insurance. How much money would you bring home after deductions for both of the jobs listed above?

Unit 3

Building Relationship Skills

117

Respecting Others

YOU WILL LEARN . . .

- ➤ What it means to respect yourself and others.
- ➤ Why respect is important in daily life.
- ➤ What can happen when respect is lacking in your life.
- ➤ How to develop self-respect.
- ➤ Ways to show respect at home, at school, in your community, and for the environment.

TERMS TO LEARN . . .

- ➤ community
- ➤ empathy
- ➤ graffiti
- ➤ prejudice
- ➤ respect
- ➤ stereotype
- ➤ tact
- ➤ vandalize

Imagine ...

... that you live in the exact same world you do now, with one exception: You can do anything you want, whatever you like, and *no one* can punish you for it. This magical quality applies only to you.

Think About

- Would you obey your parents and teachers? Why or why not?
- How would you treat a possession someone loaned you and you wanted to keep?
- How would you deal with your parents or friends if you were angry at them?

RESPECT: WHAT DOES IT MEAN?

What does it mean to respect someone? **Respect** means *showing regard for the worth of someone or something.* It also involves showing regard for oneself. When Leo's high school coach asks him to organize sports equipment in the gym, Leo is glad to help out. Over the years, Mr. Jansen has earned Leo's respect by treating him and other school athletes with fairness and consideration.

➤ At your age, teachers have authority over you at school. Show respect for that authority by participating in class.

Coach Jansen has the authority to treat his sport teams fairly or roughly—but he chooses to treat players with regard for their worth. In turn, he earns his players' respect by his actions. Respect for authority comes from understanding that true authority figures take charge of the care of others. Without someone in charge, you can't run a family, a school, or a country.

You also gain respect by your actions. When you refuse to be pressured into going against your values, for instance, you send a message to others that you demand their respect.

Respect also means showing regard for all forms of property and the environment. Respect for other people's property means you understand that their property is an extension of themselves. Respect for the environment means you show regard for keeping your community safe and clean.

The Need for Respect

Respect is the key in all areas of life—from friendships to international cooperation. When people show respect and

> Have respect for people of all cultures. Prejudice limits your relationships and you miss a lot of fun.

common courtesy to each other, they help make life easier and more positive. Whether at home, in the classroom, at work, or on streets and highways, showing respect for others makes your world a better place.

Respecting Yourself

Self-respect means valuing yourself. You show self-respect when you treat your own life and body as deserving of worth. Caring enough about yourself to be your very best also shows self-respect. So does avoiding what could hurt you—physically, emotionally, and ethically. You show respect for yourself when you refuse to take part in self-destructive behavior such as drug or alcohol abuse.

People with self-respect have healthy self-esteem. Their self-respect shows in the way they take care of their health, develop their natural skills and abilities, and choose friends who have similar values to their own. In what ways have you tried to show that you respect yourself?

> Giving your body a nutritious jump-start at the beginning of the day is only one example of taking care of yourself. What other ways do you show self-respect?

When Respect Is Missing

Teens who lie, cheat, or steal show little respect for themselves. Combined with the fear of being caught for negative actions, their behavior may lead to guilt and regret, as well as many other serious consequences. Family members show love and concern for teens by setting limits and establishing guidelines and discipline that can help teens show respect for themselves and others.

It's easy to see when people fail to respect themselves or other people. Negative pressure from others, physical violence, and vandalism of property are just a few examples of lack of respect.

Stereotypes and Prejudice

When respect is missing, additional effects—stereotypes and prejudice—are often present. A **stereotype** is *a belief that an entire group of people fit a fixed common pattern*—that they're all alike in certain ways. Persons with disabilities, older men and women, and homeless people often are stereotyped. Some people fail to see these others as individuals. Instead, they see them as a group sharing the same characteristics.

Stereotypes often lead to prejudice. When people dislike or hurt others because of their differences, they show **prejudice**—*an unfair or biased opinion*. Often it's a judgment against a person or group made with lack of knowledge of the correct facts. For example, prejudice may be directed against people because of their race, religion, gender (male or female), or economic status. A person's age or disabilities are also sometimes used as a basis for prejudice.

Rather than smoothing the path to common ground and understanding, prejudice causes people to distrust and hate without just cause. People who are on the receiving end of prejudice often have feelings of anger, frustration, and sometimes despair. Some people act on these feelings. How do *you* want to be treated? No doubt, you want people to discover—and respect—who you are inside as a person.

OVERCOMING STEREOTYPES AND PREJUDICE

The best way to overcome stereotypes and prejudice is to learn more about the people you come in contact with in your community. Here are some actions that you can take:

• Learn about the cultures and backgrounds of people around you. Knowledge leads to understanding and can help get rid of stereotypes and prejudice.

• Try to identify the problems with stereotypes and prejudice in your school and neighborhood and what causes these problems. Then work on solutions with others.

• Identify language that is offensive to people or groups in your area. Avoiding offensive language smooths the way to acceptance and understanding and helps erase stereotypes and prejudice.

• Remove or help others remove offensive graffiti when you see it. Wiping out graffiti helps eliminate the "fuel" that often ignites stereotypes and prejudice.

➤ **Parents and guardians set curfew limits out of concern for teens. Teens who understand those concerns respect the limits.**

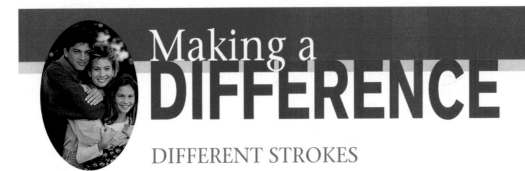

Making a DIFFERENCE

DIFFERENT STROKES

"Why are you nice to Maia?" Lauryn asked Kelly. "She's so weird. She wears uncool clothes, and has the strangest opinions on everything."

"That's just what I like about her—she's her own person," Kelly replied. "I don't agree with a lot of her opinions, but she's really smart. And she doesn't act fake by trying to fit in with everybody else. She has her own style. Why don't you give her a chance?"

"How would I give her a chance?" asked Lauryn.

"Talk to her," Kelly said. "Get to see who she really is as a person."

"I'll think about it," Lauryn answered.

Taking Action

1. How does Kelly show respect for Maia's differences?
2. What could you do to show respect to someone who seems very different from you?

RESPECTING YOUR COMMUNITY

A **community** consists of *a group of people with common interests who live in a certain area*. Look around your community. What evidence of respect and pride do you see in public spaces? Are sidewalks and streets, parks, playgrounds, libraries, and recreational centers clean and well-maintained? Are they in disrepair and littered with trash?

Respecting your community involves doing your part to take care of it. This includes disposing of trash in appropriate places. It means refusing to **vandalize**, or *destroy public or private property*. It means refusing to paint **graffiti**, *unwanted drawings and writing on walls and other property*. When you respect your community, you take care of public property—whether library books or playgrounds—as if it were your own.

➤ Litter is ugly. Do your part to keep the environment clean and beautiful.

At Home

Your home was the first community you ever lived in. Your home is where you learn to respect yourself and your family. As a teen, you show respect at home when you:

- Act with consideration for the feelings of family members, including differences of opinion and others' mistakes.
- Take initiative and help out willingly around the house.
- Clean up after yourself.
- Take responsibility for your actions and do not blame others for your mistakes.
- Follow rules, including curfews, and tell the truth about what you do and who you're with.
- Treat the possessions of others with care.

Showing respect at home helps make life easier for everyone, including yourself. What are other ways you can show respect to your parents, siblings, and other family members?

At School

Most of the ways you show respect at home also apply at school. Chris's actions express respect when he makes time for friends, listens considerately to teachers, completes assignments on time, and follows school rules.

Respect involves taking an interest in your classmates' interests and activities. You may not agree on issues, such as political or religious views, but you can show respect by listening. You also show respect when you're tactful with others. **Tact** is *communicating something difficult without attacking another's feelings.* To be tactful,

➤ **"Here's your jacket back, Dad. Thanks for letting me borrow it."** How do you show respect in your family?

➤ **Empathy is knowing just how others feel if they are happy or sad.** Have you ever felt truly happy when something good happened to a friend?

you need **empathy**, *the ability to understand what someone else is experiencing.* You empathize by putting yourself in another's place and trying to see things from his or her point of view. In most cases, the more respect you show, the more you'll gain in return—from teachers, other school staff, classmates, and friends.

In the Neighborhood

Neighbors show respect by watching out for each other's safety and well-being. They stay informed about community issues. Another way to show respect in your neighborhood is to properly dispose of trash and to recycle glass, newspaper, cans and plastic products. Courtney shows respect to her neighbors by keeping her stereo volume at a level that doesn't wake up her neighbor's baby.

Respect the Environment

When you respect the environment, you also show respect to yourself and your family. Everyone's health and well-being are directly related to the health and well-being of the environment—both at home and around the world.

INFOLINK

You can learn more about respect for the environment in Chapter 23.

➤ **All living creatures depend upon respect for the environment. Show that respect.**

Chapter Summary

- Respect involves showing regard for people, the environment, and yourself.
- When people show respect and common courtesy to each other, they help make life easier and more positive.
- Self-respect means caring enough about yourself to be your best.
- A lack of respect can lead to stereotypes and prejudice.
- You show respect for your community by doing your part to take care of it.
- To show respect at home: consider the feelings of others, help out, take responsibility for your actions, and follow family rules.
- Being tactful and empathizing with others are ways to show—and gain—respect.
- Neighbors show respect when they watch out for each other's safety and well-being.

Reviewing the Chapter

1. Briefly describe two ways to show respect to someone.
2. What are three signs that a person has self-respect?
3. How can you tell when people fail to respect themselves or other people?
4. What are three steps you can take to show respect for your community?
5. Name five ways that family members can show respect for one another. Why is showing respect at home important?
6. How does having empathy enable you to be tactful with others?
7. Give two examples of ways that neighbors can show respect for one another.
8. Explain how respecting the environment is directly related to respecting yourself and your family.

Family & Community

With Your Family

Think about ways to show more respect to someone in your family. What could you do to show that you care and value this person?

In Your Community

People in many communities are concerned about vandalism, graffiti, and other signs of disrespect in their neighborhood. Brainstorm some volunteer activities you could do as a class to clean up a local park or repair park benches, outdoor play equipment, or other pieces of public property.

Review & Activities

Thinking Critically

1. **Compare and contrast.** Compare ways you and your friends show respect for one another with how you show respect for family members. How are the ways different and how are they the same? What other actions show respect for friends and family members?

2. **Predict consequences.** Why are tact and empathy important in developing a respectful relationship with another person? What might be the consequences of a relationship in which one of the individuals does not show tact and empathy?

Making Connections

1. **Social Studies.** All communities depend on citizens to show respect for public spaces and property. In small groups, identify one or more areas of your school that reflect student pride and respect. Next, identify one or more areas that indicate a lack of concern. Talk about steps that students and faculty can take to increase school pride and respect. Share your suggestions with the entire class.

2. **Science.** Collect one or more newspaper articles showing how human activities have impacted an aspect of the environment, such as lakes, rivers, oceans, climate, or atmosphere. Share your findings with the class.

Applying Your Learning

1. **Write a newspaper article.** Write a profile for your school paper about someone in your community (home, school, or town) who is worthy of respect. Include a variety of reasons for your selection.

2. **Design a mural.** Use heavy paper, paint, and pens to create a mural showing various ways people can show respect for the community. Include a variety of local sites, such as schools, parks, libraries, and businesses.

3. **Teach children respect.** Write one or more lessons on respect that you might present to younger students. Focus the lessons on how children can show respect for the environment.

What Would You Do?

You see someone you know painting graffiti on a building. You know the person has been in trouble before for his actions. How would you handle the situation?

Chapter 9

Communication Skills

YOU WILL LEARN . . .

➤ The difference between verbal and nonverbal messages.
➤ How your body language sends messages to others.
➤ The importance of written messages in communication.
➤ How to recognize roadblocks to communication.
➤ Ways to be an active listener.
➤ Ideas for improving your communication skills.

TERMS TO LEARN . . .

➤ assertive
➤ body language
➤ communication
➤ e-mail
➤ nonverbal communication
➤ rapport
➤ verbal communication

Imagine ...

... you've been upset with a friend for weeks. You've heard your friend has gossiped about you to others, and you don't know how to express your anger without a fight. You care about your friend, but every time you're together now, you act cold.

Think About

• How does your manner express how you feel?
• How could you express your feelings without a fight?
• What would happen if you said nothing?

WHAT IS COMMUNICATION?

How do you express to others what you need and want, and what you feel and know? **Communication** is *the process of sending messages to—and receiving messages from—others*. Messages include facts, opinions, and feelings. You *send* messages in what you say and how you say it. You *receive* messages when you listen.

Verbal communication is *speaking to communicate. A message sent without words* is called **nonverbal communication**. Communication is usually a mixture of both verbal and nonverbal messages.

Verbal Messages

Although communication involves more than just talk, you need to use words effectively to communicate an accurate message. Whether you're speaking to a friend or in front of your entire school, you can improve your verbal messages if you:

- **Think before you speak.** Consider the points you want to make before they come out of your mouth. Don't embarrass yourself or hurt others by saying things you'll later regret.

➤ "Grandpa, how did you learn English so well in school? You always use perfect grammar." Ask questions to initiate a conversation.

> Show concern for others by being interested in what they say. In return, others will feel more involved and listen to you.

- **Express a positive attitude.** Try to express yourself positively, warmly, and enthusiastically whenever you can. No one likes to hear others complain or criticize all the time.

- **Consider the person receiving your message.** The way you talk to a close friend differs from the way you communicate during a class discussion, or how you express yourself to a young child. Consider the needs of the person or audience when you communicate.

- **Send specific messages.** Organize your thoughts before you talk. If you plan to speak in front of classmates, write down your main points, then list facts to support your points.

- **Speak clearly.** Pronounce words correctly and distinctly. Speak up so others can clearly hear you. Don't talk too slow or fast.

- **Make sure your listener understands you.** Check to see that another person or group understands what you're saying. Ask for feedback occasionally. If you feel you're not getting your points across effectively, try to express your ideas in a different way.

- **Be aware of give-and-take in conversation.** Find a balance between talking and listening. If you do all the talking, the other person may become bored and stop listening.

> Don't hog the conversation. Allow others to express themselves as well. How can people break themselves from talking too much?

HOW to...

Start a Conversation

Do you sometimes find it hard to start a conversation with someone you don't know—or don't know very well? The key to good conversation, especially among acquaintances, is to show interest in them. Here are tips to make good conversation:

- Ask open-ended questions that require a response in addition to yes or no answers, such as "What do you think of ... ?" That way, the other person is encouraged to keep a conversation going. Also, the conversation can more easily lead to other topics.

- Show you're interested in what the other person has to say. Pay attention to what is being said and respond to it.

- Look like someone you'd enjoy talking to. Smile, be enthusiastic, and positive in what you say.

➤ Body language is how you look when you are communicating. Your eyes, expressions, body positions, and gestures communicate how you are feeling about what you are saying.

Nonverbal Messages

You don't need to talk to communicate. You send many nonverbal messages without speaking a word. Your smile or frown instantly expresses delight or disapproval.

Body Language

Body language is *the way in which you use gestures and body movement to communicate*. Body language often says more than words. Facial expressions show enthusiasm, thoughtfulness, or sadness. All forms of body language, including your hand and arm gestures and posture, reflect your true inner feelings. Some body language, such as smiling and nodding, encourages communication. Other body language, such as frowning or crossing your arms, discourages it.

People send mixed messages when their words don't match their nonverbal messages. What they say is different from what they feel or think, and the difference shows in their actions and facial expressions. When Robby curls his mouth while giving a compliment, others don't know whether to believe him or take it as a put-down.

Written Messages

In the past, most written messages took the form of letters, notes, and cards. Today, many people also use computers to send written messages in the form of **e-mail,** or *electronic mail.* Perhaps you also use instant messaging to "chat" with your friends online.

All types of written messages require communication skills. Read your messages carefully before sending them to make sure your words are clear. Be sensitive to how your message will be received.

COMMUNICATION ROADBLOCKS

Roadblocks stop traffic at the site of a major accident. Vehicles are backed up for miles, and travel is impossible. Just like bad traffic, obstacles block open communication, too. They include:

- **Gossip, lies, insults, threats, and accusations.** Hurtful talk closes lines of communication, shows no concern for others, and destroys relationships.
- **Nagging and preaching.** Comments like "You better exercise more" or "I tell you every day, turn down your stereo!" turn listeners off.
- **A "know-it-all" attitude.** Not being open to other people's ideas or opinions also thwarts communication. There's almost always more than one way to look at a situation.
- **Sarcasm.** Sometimes people use a tone of voice called sarcasm that expresses the opposite of what they're saying. Someone may say, "You're so smart," but if his or her

➤ E-mail and Internet chat rooms have opened new channels of sending written messages to your friends. Use good judgment at all times.

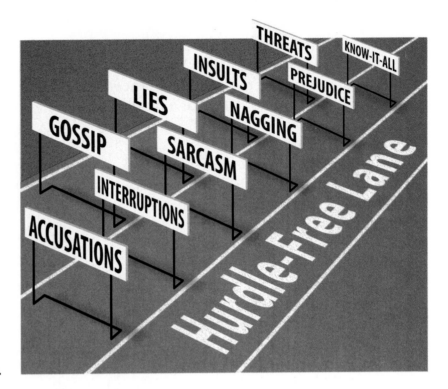

> Stay on track—Avoid the barriers to communication.

tone of voice is sarcastic, it communicates the opposite meaning. Sarcasm hurts others and prevents open communication.

- **Interruptions.** How should you respond to someone who interrupts before you finish speaking? Continue your message in a patient but determined way. You may need to say, "Pardon me. I didn't get to finish what I wanted to say."

DEVELOPING LISTENING SKILLS

Listening is as important to communication as speaking. Unfortunately, it's often the most overlooked communication skill. Have you ever tried to make a point when others weren't paying attention? If so, you know how important it is to listen when someone is speaking.

Be an Active Listener!

Active listening means listening and responding with full attention to what's being said. When you listen actively, you concentrate on what the speaker is saying, rather than on what you want to say.

Active listening involves giving both verbal and nonverbal feedback to the speaker. Verbal feedback might be a simple "Yes" or "Okay." It might be a question or statement. Nonverbal responses include maintaining eye contact, nodding your head to show you understand, or shaking your head when you don't understand.

DELIVERING YOUR MESSAGE

The way you speak is just as important as the words you use. For example, repeat the following sentence out loud four times: "I would be glad to do that for you." Each time emphasize a different word—*I*, *glad*, *that*, and *you*. Listen to how the meaning of the sentence changes each time.

Your tone of voice shows whether you're happy or sad, relieved or upset. The tone you use *should* always convey your intended message. Controlling your emotions makes it easier for people to clearly receive your message.

Choosing the right time to communicate is just as important for good communication. Pick a time when listeners are interested in communicating with you. When others are tired or preoccupied, they may not give you their full attention.

For good communication, establish rapport with your listener. **Rapport** (rah-POHR) is *harmony or understanding between people*. It's the feeling of being listened to and accepted.

One way to establish rapport is to put other people at ease. Show interest in them. Make them feel comfortable. Call them by name, and involve them in the conversation. Ask questions or ask for their opinions on a topic. Make sure you give them time to respond. If you act relaxed and comfortable, others will react in the same way, too.

➤ **Good listeners make good friends.** How would you rate yourself as a listener?

Be a Better Listener

You can become a better listener if you sharpen your skills in each of these four areas:

- **Hearing.** Tune in to what others are saying. Give the speaker your full attention.
- **Interpreting.** When you understand what a speaker actually says and means, you interpret the message. Be alert for nonverbal messages, too.
- **Evaluating.** Evaluate words, not the person speaking. Avoid letting preformed ideas or feelings get in the way of your evaluation.
- **Responding.** Your response shows the speaker whether you understand the message. You might nod your head, for example, to show understanding. If you don't understand the message, ask for an example. Try rephrasing in your own words what you think has been said.

Success at school or on the job often depends on understanding directions or instructions. Misunderstandings are less likely when you take the time to hear, interpret, evaluate, and respond.

How can you strengthen your listening skills?

Assertive Communication

Many people are afraid to express their feelings. They feel uncomfortable to say what they think or to ask for what they want. When people are passive, they don't stand up for themselves. They're afraid to say anything that might make others angry.

> ➤ **Use assertive communication in class by speaking up. Then listen to the opinion of others.** When is communication too assertive?

Some people are aggressive and want to be in control. They're often seen as pushy and rude, concerned mostly with their own needs and wants. They may try to get their way by bullying others.

People who communicate assertively are neither passive nor aggressive. **Assertive** persons *stand up for themselves and for their beliefs in firm, but positive, ways.* They don't bully others, but they don't cave in either. They state their opinions and also listen to others' opinions. When opinions differ, they try to reach an agreement that's acceptable to all involved.

Your opinions and your wishes are worthwhile. You have the right to express them, even though others may disagree at times. Everyone has to learn to accept give-and-take as part of open communication.

Review & Activities

Chapter Summary

- You communicate when sending messages to, and receiving messages from, others.
- Organize your thoughts and speak clearly.
- Feedback tells you if your messages are being understood.
- A balance between talking and listening is needed for effective communication.
- Many messages are sent nonverbally through body language.
- Mixed messages are sent when verbal and nonverbal messages don't match.
- Interruptions and hurtful talk are road-blocks to open communication.
- Active listeners fully concentrate on the speaker and give feedback.
- Assertive message delivery lets you communicate opinions firmly and positively.

Family & Community

With Your Family

Observe a conversation between two of your family members for one minute. Note the types of body language used. Along with one or more family members, discuss the types of body language each of you uses. Which types tend to send positive messages? Which project negative messages?

In Your Community

There are probably some older members of your community who have difficulty sending or reading written messages. Brainstorm things you could do as a class to help older citizens with their written messages.

Reviewing the Chapter

1. Briefly describe at least four ways people can improve their verbal messages.
2. When talking to someone, how can you make sure your listener understands what you are saying?
3. Identify three examples of body language used to communicate messages without words.
4. Describe a situation where a person is sending mixed verbal and nonverbal messages.
5. What is sarcasm? Give an example of sarcasm used in a hurtful way.
6. Briefly describe four ways to listen actively.
7. Why is it important to choose the right time to communicate some messages?
8. What are three ways to establish rapport with others?
9. Explain what it means to communicate assertively.

Thinking Critically

1. **Predict consequences.** What consequences occur when people send mixed verbal and nonverbal messages? What suggestions would you give a friend who sometimes sends mixed messages to others?
2. **Make generalizations.** What is the relationship between rapport and good communication? What actions do you think are most helpful in establishing rapport with a peer?

Review & Activities

3. **Clarify fact or fiction.** Some people feel that being aggressive helps communicate their messages in the most effective way. How do you respond when someone communicates aggressively with you? Give an example of an assertive response to aggressive communication.

Making Connections

1. **Language Arts.** Write a column for your school newspaper with one of the following titles: "Unmixing Your Mixed Messages," "Watching Out for Written Messages," or "Listening as Though Your Life Depended on It." Stress the importance of positive communication.

2. **Health.** Find examples in newspapers or magazines of how communication roadblocks affected one or more persons' health or safety. An example might be threats and accusations that led to a fight or a drive-by shooting. Then brainstorm ways that teens can deal positively and effectively with communication roadblocks.

Applying Your Learning

1. **Design a poster.** Use paper and other basic art supplies to design a poster that highlights one communication roadblock. Include suggestions for dealing positively with the obstacle. Share your finished project with the class.

2. **Present a one-minute speech.** Imagine you're the featured speaker before a class. Write a one-minute speech on a subject that interests you. List one main point and facts to support it. Practice your speech out loud in front of a long mirror. Also practice using effective nonverbal language. Present your speech to the class.

3. **Demonstrate assertiveness.** With a partner, write out three difficult situations teens might encounter in which assertive communication would be helpful. Develop a skit, based on these situations, contrasting passive, aggressive, and assertive responses. Present your skit to the class.

What Would You Do?

Suppose a friend has asked to borrow your favorite coat. You bought it with money you earned by working last summer. You'd rather not loan your coat, but don't want to risk your friendship. How would you handle this problem?

Conflict Resolution

YOU WILL LEARN . . .

➤ What causes conflict.
➤ How to recognize conflict.
➤ Strategies to resolve conflicts.
➤ Ways to control anger constructively.
➤ Steps to negotiate.
➤ How to use mediation to resolve conflicts.

TERMS TO LEARN . . .

➤ compromise
➤ conflict
➤ conflict resolution
➤ escalate
➤ mediation
➤ negotiation
➤ peer mediator
➤ tolerance

Imagine ...

... that you share a room with your younger brother or sister. Deep down, you love each other, but you often fight about personal space and privacy. Sometimes your sibling looks through your drawers when you're not around and borrows things. Once you caught him or her reading a personal note written to you. You don't want to continue sharing a room, but there isn't any extra space in the house.

Think About

• If you were a parent, what suggestions would you have for each of your children?
• If you were a younger sibling, how would you feel having to share a room with an older one?
• What types of conflicts have you experienced with siblings or other family members? Were the conflicts resolved? If so, how?

WHAT IS CONFLICT?

Conflict is *a disagreement, dispute, or fight between people with opposing points of view.* It can involve individuals or groups, such as friends, family members, community organizations, or even different nations.

Conflicts don't have to be contests in which one side wins and the other loses. The best solution is a fair one in which both sides win.

Types of Conflict

Conflicts are a part of everyday life. Many conflicts are settled easily, like a brief dispute with a friend. Others are continuous struggles. In some cases, conflicts impact the lives of many people over years. Whenever one person's wants, needs, or values clash with another's, conflict is almost always the result.

Conflicts may also be internal. For example, Emily strongly disapproves of a close friend's behavior, but doesn't know what to do about those feelings.

The outcomes of conflicts can be positive or negative. Sometimes, by expressing your thoughts and feelings about an internal conflict, you see how to resolve things in a positive way. Positive outcomes are also more likely if each person involved approaches the conflict with mutual respect, an honest effort to listen, and a commitment to finding a solution. Successful conflict resolution can actually bring people closer together. If anyone uses destructive tactics to try to solve a problem, the outcome is likely to be negative.

> ➤ **Some conflicts are like tug-of-war. You are pulled in opposite directions by your feelings.**

Causes of Conflict

Some conflicts seem so trivial, you may not even know how they began. Others have very specific causes. What creates conflict for one person may not matter to someone else. In general, several basic causes lead to conflict. These include:

- **Instant flare-ups.** Many kinds of situations can trigger sudden disputes or arguments. Anytime people interact—whether they live, work, or play together—conflicts can ignite. Sometimes just being in the wrong place at the wrong time can result in a heated conflict. Usually, the stronger the emotional ties and closeness between people, the stronger the conflict. Fortunately, such instant conflicts typically don't last long. People deal with a quarrel and go on with their relationships.

- **Personality differences.** Differences help make life exciting and fun, but they can also create conflict. Jonah likes being around large groups of people. His friend Liam feels uncomfortable in groups. As a result, conflict over what to do when they get together is an occasional part of their friendship.

- **Power issues.** Power struggles often take place when one or more persons wants to control a situation. Many arguments in families with teens concern power issues. For example, sometimes a teen's choice of friends leads to a power struggle with a parent. What options are available for parents and teens in a situation such as this? On what common ground could they meet?

➤ "Clean up this room!" Conflict can occur when two or more people's values differ. It takes working together to solve the situation fairly.

Other causes of conflict include prejudice, jealousy, and revenge. In addition, poor communication, stress, and drugs and alcohol frequently trigger conflict.

RESPONDING TO CONFLICT

When a conflict develops, you can either face it or ignore it. Before deciding which course of action to take, consider these points:

- Your personal well-being and safety should be your first concern.
- Walking away from a potentially dangerous situation is a positive choice—not a sign of cowardice.
- Weigh issues that lead to conflict. If the other person is a stranger or someone you'll never see again, it may be best to walk away. If the other person is someone you care about, try to communicate your feelings in a calm and reasonable way.

In some cases, people let conflicts **escalate**, or *grow into disagreements that are destructive or unsafe to everyone concerned*. Some teens think getting involved in a conflict may prove they're tough and fearless. Unfortunately, getting out of a difficult conflict isn't as easy as getting into one.

➤ **Keep rivalry on the field. School spirit should not create conflict between individuals.**

HOW TO RESOLVE CONFLICT

Whether you become engaged in a conflict that seems unavoidable, or one that tests your pride or values, you can learn to resolve conflicts in a peaceful way. **Conflict resolution**, the *process of settling a conflict by cooperating and problem solving*, is a proven approach.

Conflict resolution takes work. But anyone can learn problem-solving skills. Anyone can learn how to communicate effectively.

Steps in Conflict Resolution

Conflict resolution lets people involved in a dispute work out a solution to their problem. They try to brainstorm together to bring the conflict to an end by following these steps:

1. **Define the problem.** Each person takes a turn describing the problem from his or her point of view. Each person shows the other respect.

2. **Suggest a solution.** Each person suggests a solution to the problem.

3. **Evaluate a solution.** Each person identifies the parts of a solution that he or she agrees with or can't accept.

4. **Compromise.** If the parties are fairly close to agreement, they may compromise. This involves settling the conflict by each agreeing to give up something that he or she wanted.

5. **Brainstorm.** If individuals can't compromise, they brainstorm different ways to approach the problem and try again to reach a compromise.

6. **Mediate.** If no solution is reached, the persons ask a neutral third party to listen to their problem and make suggestions to resolve it.

How could you use these steps to deal with conflict with others?

➤ Treating people of all ages with respect helps avoid conflict. Tolerance for others is the basis for good relationships.

Respect and Tolerance

Many conflicts are avoided or resolved when one or both parties expresses respect for the other. When you show respect, you value another person as an individual. You also make it more likely the person will respect you. People who respect each other are more likely to listen with an open mind, consider the other person's views and feelings, and honor each other's basic values.

Tolerance is also vital to prevent and resolve conflict. **Tolerance** means *accepting and respecting other people's customs and beliefs.* People who are willing to accept persons as they are tend to have fewer conflicts than people who are unaccepting of others. Tolerance helps you understand that different people have a right to behave and express themselves in ways different from your own, as long as they don't hurt others in the process.

Tolerance also involves getting along with people of all ages and generations. Teens sometimes find it hard to get along with older adults because they have different ways of talking, dressing, and acting. You need to be willing to accept all people and learn to understand their points of view. You are deserving of respect. Be fair in respecting others, too, even older adults. (After all, you'll be an older adult someday, too!)

How to Control Your Anger

Everyone feels angry at times. When you're angry, your heart beats faster. Blood rushes to your face, and the palms of your hands may sweat as your body prepares to take action. If you learn to manage—or control—your anger, you can redirect these surges of energy to reach your goal.

When anger isn't controlled, conflict gets worse. Dwelling on how angry you are doesn't help defuse your anger. Instead, your anger can build up and lead to rage. At this stage, you may no longer be able to think clearly. The ancient martial art of jujitsu teaches those who practice the art to remain calm, to empty themselves of anger, and to gain the advantage in conflict by using their opponent's tendency to strike out in blind rage. Developing this type of self-control can help you deal with your anger and positively resolve conflict. Understanding your anger and how to deal with it can also help resolve conflict.

Anger has two aspects. The first can be called *pent-up anger*. It builds up over time. If not released in a healthy way, pent-up anger can explode when you least expect it. When you feel angry, here are positive ways to release pent-up feelings:

- Exercise: walk, jog, swim, or shoot some baskets.
- Talk out your feelings with a good friend.
- Listen to soothing music.
- Find a private place where you can feel emotional if you need to. Don't be afraid to cry. Crying releases anger and helps you acknowledge that you feel hurt.
- Sit quietly for a while.

➤ Feeling angry during a conflict is normal. Learn to control anger, not react to it. Physical activity can help you think of a solution.

The second aspect of anger can be called *hot anger*. It occurs very suddenly when conflict flares between you and another person. Here are some positive ways to control hot anger:

- Mentally tell yourself, "I choose to be focused; I choose to be relaxed."
- Rename your anger as energy. Mentally tell yourself, "I have the energy to get things done here and positively resolve this conflict."
- Breathe deeply. Pull air in through your nose and let it flow evenly and slowly out through your mouth.
- To calm down further, think of either a peaceful place in nature or of someone you love who loves you, too.

If you feel you need help in dealing with your anger, talk to adult family members, another adult, a teacher, or a counselor.

Learn to Negotiate

Negotiation is *a process of discussing problems face-to-face in order to reach a solution.* It involves talking, listening, considering the other person's point of view, and compromise. **Compromise** means *coming to an agreement in which each person gives up something in order to get what they both want.*

Keep these guidelines in mind to help negotiate a solution to a problem:

- **Select an appropriate time and place to work out your problem.** Choose a relatively quiet place and time that is agreeable to both of you. Avoid meeting if you feel rushed or impatient.
- **Keep an open mind.** Listen carefully to each other and consider both points of view.
- **Be flexible.** Be willing to bend and meet the other person halfway.
- **Accept responsibility for your role in the conflict.** Be willing to apologize if you see you've unfairly hurt the other person. Accepting the fact that you may be wrong is a sign of courage and maturity.
- **Work together to find a positive solution.** Brainstorming possible solutions together can be very productive.

SAFETY
First

To help prevent the spread of violence:

- Choose friends who value peaceful behavior. Don't become a member of a gang.
- Learn and practice the skills of communication and conflict resolution.
- Walk away from physical conflict and other acts of violent behavior.
- Work at building your self-esteem. When you feel good about yourself, you're more likely to deal with difficult situations in positive, nonviolent ways.

➤ Suppose you need or want to negotiate an increased allowance. Give your reasons, then listen to your parents' or guardians' reasons. The result may require each of you to compromise.

- **Don't give up.** If negotiating isn't going well, it's okay to work at it another time. Suggest a future time and place where you can continue the process.
- **Seek help.** Consider asking another person to help you both reach a solution.

Be a Peacemaker

Sometimes people can't resolve a conflict, even when they use the problem-solving process. Deadlocks, in which no one will budge, occur when two or more people can't agree on a solution to a conflict. To solve a deadlock, they may need mediation. During **mediation**, *a neutral third party is used to help reach a solution that's agreeable to both sides.* With a mediator, people can often agree on a solution.

Many schools offer peer mediation programs. A **peer mediator** is *a young person in the middle between two students who are locked in conflict.* Mediators are trained to withhold judgment and to be careful listeners. They ask questions of both parties and respond fairly and evenly. Mediators try to resolve conflicts by using problem solving. They don't solve problems. Instead, they help both parties seek a solution, usually through compromise.

Schools with peer mediation programs tend to have more cooperation, fewer fights, and less overall violence. Many families and communities now use mediation to resolve disagreements and prevent violence. When people resolve differences peacefully, each side benefits.

Making a DIFFERENCE

MAKE UP

When Cal found out that Tess had put him down to his best friend, he became furious. Cal lost his temper and yelled at her in front of a group of friends at school. He called her names.

Stunned, Tess didn't know how to react. But she thought fast and said very calmly, "You're right, and I apologize. But this isn't the time or place to talk about it. Why don't you call me tonight, and I'll tell you what I said and why I said it."

Cal was so taken aback he couldn't say anything. But Tess's manner had calmed him down. "I'm sorry I yelled at you, and we'll talk about it tonight," he finally replied.

Their group of friends cheered and high-fived them.

Taking Action

1. Do you think Cal handled the conflict in the right way? Why or why not?
2. Do you think Tess handled the conflict in the right way? How would you have handled the situation if you were Tess?

WORK THROUGH CONFLICTS

Some conflicts are never resolved, but both sides learn to accept and respect each other's differences. Zoe and her parents may never agree on types of music, but they can agree to respect each other's choices.

Fortunately, most conflicts can be resolved when people are willing to cooperate and work toward positive solutions. By learning as much as you can about conflict resolution, you can do your part to bring about and keep peace at home, at school, and in your community.

➤ A peer mediator may be assigned by your school to resolve conflicts between students. They help the students to come to a peaceful solution.

Review & Activities

Chapter Summary

- Conflict is a struggle or disagreement between people with different or opposing wants, needs, values, or points of view.
- Conflicts are a part of everyday life. Some conflicts are settled easily; others may last indefinitely.
- Personal interactions, personality differences, and power issues often cause conflict. Other causes include prejudice, jealousy, revenge, poor communication, stress, and drugs and alcohol.
- It's not a sign of cowardice to walk away from a potentially dangerous situation.
- Conflict resolution is a proven method for successfully resolving conflicts.

With Your Family

Think about times when you were younger and became angry with members of your family. How did you express your anger? How did family members respond to your angry feelings and actions? How do you tend to express your anger now that you're older? Make a list of positive actions you can take to deal with angry feelings now and in the future.

In Your Community

Many people are worried about violence in their community. Brainstorm some volunteer activities you could do as a class to reduce violent conflict and promote peace.

- Tolerance helps prevent and resolve conflict. Tolerance involves respect and acceptance of people of all ages.
- There are positive ways to control anger and release pent-up feelings. If anger is not controlled, it may build up and lead to rage or violence.
- The process of negotiation helps people compromise and reach mutually agreed-upon solutions to problems.
- Peer mediators are used in schools to help students resolve conflicts, usually through compromise.
- Most conflicts can be resolved if people cooperate and work for positive solutions.

Reviewing the Chapter

1. Identify three basic causes of conflict.
2. What options do you have when a conflict develops?
3. Under what circumstances might it be best to walk away from a conflict?
4. Why is it dangerous to allow some conflicts to escalate?
5. Why is respect important in preventing and resolving conflict?
6. What is tolerance? How does it help prevent and resolve conflict?
7. Name three ways a person's body responds to angry feelings. List at least five positive ways to release pent-up anger.
8. Identify two ways to control hot anger in yourself.
9. What is mediation? Name three positive results of peer mediation programs.

Thinking Critically

1. **Draw conclusions.** How could conflict strengthen a relationship? How could it weaken or destroy a friendship?
2. **Compare and contrast.** Compare ways you dealt with conflict two or three years ago with how you deal with conflict situations now. How are they different and how are they the same? How would you rate your current conflict resolution skills? Explain the reasons for your rating.
3. **Draw conclusions.** Imagine that you are in charge of selecting a peer mediator for your school. What qualities would you look for in a person for that position? What qualities would you not consider suitable for a peer mediator? Explain your answers.

Making Connections

1. **Social Studies.** Conflicts take place between individuals and groups all over the world. In small groups, examine current newspapers and magazines to identify one or more conflicts in this country and other countries. Discuss causes of the conflicts and their consequences.
2. **Drama.** Act out a situation in which two teens use negotiation skills to work through a conflict. Present your situation to the class. Brainstorm a list of other conflicts experienced by teens that might be resolved through negotiation.

Applying Your Learning

1. **Create a poster.** Create a poster that shows how teens can learn to control their anger. Share the poster with your class.
2. **Teach a lesson.** Work with a partner to plan a 10 to 15-minute skit for elementary school children on the importance of respect and tolerance. If possible, present your lesson to an elementary school class in your community.
3. **Write a letter.** Write an anonymous letter about an unresolved conflict you've experienced. Describe the emotions you feel about it, without naming any individuals involved. Have your teacher gather samples, and pick a few to read aloud. Brainstorm with classmates how to resolve each conflict.

What Would You Do?

Suppose a friend invited you to a party. At the last minute, your dad bought tickets to a major sports event and invited you to go. The event was held at the same time as the party. You chose to go with your dad, and your friend is angry. You want to keep the friendship. How would you handle this problem?

Dealing with Peer Pressure

YOU WILL LEARN . . .

➤ The difference between positive and negative peer pressure.
➤ How to avoid manipulative behavior.
➤ How to respond effectively to negative peer pressure.
➤ The difference between passive, aggressive, and assertive responses to peer pressure.
➤ How to use refusal skills.

TERMS TO LEARN . . .

➤ manipulation
➤ peer pressure
➤ peers
➤ refusal skills

Imagine ...

... that you're shopping with your best friend. You both have your eye on the same jacket, but it's too expensive for you. Your friend turns to you and whispers, "Come on, no one's looking. Let's just take it." You know that stealing the jacket is wrong, but you don't want your friend to think you're afraid.

Think About

• How would you respond to your friend's pressure? Why?
• Why do you think friends sometimes pressure others to do things that are illegal or harmful?

WHAT IS PEER PRESSURE?

It's normal for **peers,** or *people the same age,* to try to influence each other. *The pressure you feel to do what others your age are doing* is called **peer pressure**. Because most teens are very sensitive to their peers' opinions, peer pressure can be very hard to resist.

Positive Peer Pressure

Positive peer pressure is what you feel when people your age encourage you to do something worthwhile. Tina's influence on her friend to study hard for a big test is very positive. So is Andrew's pressure on his friend to get in shape for a team sport.

Positive peer pressure supports your values and beliefs. It almost always results in positive consequences for everyone involved.

➤ Having friends your age enriches your life. This teen is using positive peer pressure by influencing his friend to study for a test.

Role Models

Good role models—peers or others that young people look up to—exert positive influence. They may inspire you to work harder, to think about your future, and to choose right behaviors. You may be a positive role model to someone who looks up to you and is influenced by your actions.

Role models can also serve as good examples of what *not* to do. A teen whose role models *don't* use tobacco, alcohol, or other drugs may be positively influenced to follow their example. Unfortunately, not all role models are positive ones. Some people who influence you may encourage you to act against your own values and beliefs.

➤ **Everyone can be a role model.** When have you inspired someone to work harder and choose positive behavior?

TAKE NOTE

A Look at Gangs

What do you really know about gangs? Consider the following facts:

- A gang is a group of people who associate with one another because they have something in common.
- Not all gangs are bad, but many are involved in criminal activities.
- Most of their crimes involve some type of violence or intimidation.
- There are many alternatives to joining a gang. If you're lonely or bored, search out a youth group, sports team, volunteer opportunities, or other activities in your neighborhood or community.
- If peers are negatively pressuring you, think about starting a group that works for positive change, such as tutoring or cleaning a vacant lot.
- If you're harassed by gang members and are scared, get help. A family member, community group, school counselor, or police officer can help protect you and give you support.

How could you use the above facts to resist negative gang pressure?

Negative Peer Pressure

Negative peer pressure is what you feel when your peers try to persuade you to do something you don't want to do. Going along with the crowd can be fun if what the crowd does supports your values and beliefs. But what if the crowd's actions betray what you believe is right? What if the actions have negative consequences?

Peers may try to persuade you to do something unhealthy, dangerous, or illegal, such as use tobacco, alcohol, or other drugs—or to do something that hurts other people. They may urge you to try something you feel you aren't ready for, or that goes against your better judgment.

Manipulation

People sometimes pressure others through **manipulation**—*a dishonest way to control or influence someone.* People who manipulate others aim to get what they want regardless of the consequences. How do you feel when friends manipulate you to do things their way? Three common types of manipulation work in ways that:

- **Appeal to your courage.** A person may use put-downs, such as "What are you, chicken?" to shame you.
- **Appeal to your desire to belong.** Statements like, "We only asked people we thought were cool to join us" or "Only nerds say no" and the familiar "Come on, everybody's doing it."

If you're pressured by others to act against your beliefs or take part in behavior that has negative consequences, stop and think carefully. Ask yourself these questions:

- Will this hurt anyone or their property?
- Will it be harmful to me?
- Are there risks involved?
- Would my actions negatively affect the way my family, teachers, other friends, and people in the community view me?

If any of the answers are "yes," then respond with a firm "no." If you think you need to, give a simple reason for not going along with what your peers want you to do. Then change the subject or walk away. You don't need friends who don't care about your well-being. Look around to find friends who do.

➤ Peer pressure occurs when your peers pressure you to do what they are doing. Apply your own values when responding to their pressure.

- **Appeal to your guilt.** "Man, I thought I could count on you!" is an example of manipulation with guilt.

A true friend won't push you to do something you don't want to do. In the same way, your peers should be able to count on you to respect their values and beliefs.

INFOLINK

See Chapter 12 for more information on the qualities of a true friend.

RESPONDING TO NEGATIVE PEER PRESSURE

Learning to stand up to negative peer pressure is one of the most important skills you can learn. It's never easy to say "no" to friends when you want to be part of a group. You may be afraid of hurting someone's feelings or losing a friendship. You may fear being laughed at or excluded.

How you respond to negative peer pressure is up to you. You can give up your self-control and let others direct your life. Or you can decide to be the one who is in charge of your life.

Passive Responses

Passive responses to peer pressure include giving in or backing down from standing up for your needs and wants. Celia is passive and thinks she wins friends by going along with her peers. Instead, her peers view Celia as a pushover and not worthy of respect.

Aggressive Responses

Aggressive responses are hostile and violate the rights of others. Even though aggressive people think they'll get their way and may be seen as powerful and popular, their approach often backfires. People either tend to avoid those who are aggressive or jump in and fight back.

➤ Throughout your life, you will develop new interests and friendships. Your true friends will respect your personal choices and like you for being yourself.

Assertive Responses

When you respond assertively to peer pressure, you stand up for your rights in firm, but positive ways. You don't bully or back off. Instead, you directly and honestly state your thoughts and feelings. You show that you mean what you say. Most people respect others who show the personal courage to be true to themselves.

DEVELOPING REFUSAL SKILLS

What if a friend tries to convince you to do something you don't want to do? Maybe it's something that goes against your values. If you say yes to something that doesn't feel right, you'll end up feeling disappointed in yourself. Saying "yes" to something too risky can harm you physically and emotionally. It can also hurt the people you care about most.

Refusal skills can help. **Refusal skills** are *communication skills you can use to say no effectively*. Use these skills to say no without feeling guilty or uncomfortable. Other people will respect you for your honesty and firmness.

Taking a Stand

When you choose to take a stand against negative peer pressure, use the following guidelines for refusal skills:
- **Say "no" and mean it.** When you're pressured to do something you don't believe is right, say "no" and mean it. Practice saying "no" out loud until you sound like you really mean it. If you seem to waver, the other person may try to change your mind. Use eye contact to show you mean what you say. If the other person won't take "no" for an answer, try repeating your refusal and your reason for it.
- **Offer alternatives.** If a friend presses you to do something that makes you uncomfortable, suggest another activity that's acceptable to you.
- **Take action.** Back up your words with actions. If you're pressured to act against your better judgment, make it clear that you won't do it. If that doesn't work, just leave an uncomfortable situation. It's perfectly okay to say, "I'm going home."

SAFETY First

Watch out for manipulative behavior by friends and acquaintances who:
- Make threats to use violence or other negative actions to get their way.
- Make you feel guilty to get what they want.
- Flatter or praise you insincerely to influence you.
- Promise you money or favors if you do what they ask.
- Tease you in mean or destructive ways.

A MORE CONFIDENT YOU

You're capable of standing up for what you want and believe in. It's up to you to take charge of your life. Rather than letting others pressure you into behavior you may regret, start now to follow your own values and dreams. You really can make a positive difference in your life—and in the lives of others.

Making a DIFFERENCE

PAINT JOB

"Hey, what are you doing?" Jesse asked Alan one night when they were horsing around.

Alan had taken a can of spray paint from his satchel and started to scrawl his initials on an apartment wall in their neighborhood. "What does it look like I'm doing?" he retorted. "Come on, spray your name, too."

"Stop it!" Jesse ordered him. He stood firm and looked Alan in the eye. "How'd you like somebody to do that to your building?"

"Somebody already has," Alan replied. "Come on. Let's both do it."

"Does that mean you have to act like a child and do the same thing to other people's property?" Jesse asked. "If you want to do something, why not paint over the graffiti on your building?"

"Why do you care?" Alan asked.

"Because I live in this neighborhood, too," Jesse answered with conviction, "and I'd like to show some respect for it, not make it worse."

Alan stopped and turned. "I never thought of it that way."

Taking Action

1. Why were Jesse's words and actions appropriate?
2. What do Jesse's words and body language say about the way he handles peer pressure?
3. In what ways can you make a difference like Jesse did?

Review & Activities

Chapter Summary

- You experience peer pressure when others your age urge you to join in their activities and accept their beliefs.
- Peer pressure may be positive or negative. It's positive when it supports your values and beliefs and causes no harm to others.
- Good role models encourage you to be your best.
- Negative peer pressure encourages you to betray your values and beliefs.
- People who use manipulation aim to influence others in order to get what they want regardless of the consequences.
- Learning to handle negative peer pressure is an important skill. When you respond assertively to peer pressure, you stand up for your rights firmly and positively.
- Refusal skills help you say "no" without feeling guilty or uncomfortable.

Family & Community

With Your Family

Think about someone in your family who has served as a role model for you. Make a list describing this person's qualities.

In Your Community

Some consequences of negative peer pressure, such as gangs and vandalism, may create a problem in your community. Brainstorm some volunteer activities you could do as a class to work with children, teaching them how to respond effectively to negative peer pressure.

- Having positive alternatives in mind can be helpful when you are pressured to do things you don't wish to do.
- When pressured to go against your good judgment, back up your words with actions. In some cases, you may need to leave an uncomfortable situation, end a friendship, or make other friends.
- Dealing effectively with peer pressure allows you to take charge of your life without being pressured into behavior you may regret.

Reviewing the Chapter

1. Give two examples of positive peer pressure.
2. What is a role model? Explain how a role model can serve as a good example of what not to do.
3. How do three common types of manipulation work?
4. What are some reasons why it's hard to stand up to negative peer pressure?
5. Give two examples of passive responses to peer pressure. Why might individuals who respond passively not be viewed with respect by others?
6. Briefly describe an assertive response to peer pressure.
7. What are refusal skills? How can they help you deal with peer pressure?
8. Briefly describe three guidelines to follow when taking a stand against negative peer pressure.

Review & Activities

Thinking Critically

1. **Compare and contrast.** Compare several responses to peer pressure that you have observed in friends and acquaintances. How were the responses different and how were they similar? Which responses were the most effective? Which were the least effective?
2. **Fact or fiction.** "Peer pressure isn't much of a problem after people finish high school." Does peer pressure apply only to teens? Are adults immune to pressure from others? Explain.
3. **Analyze behavior.** What is the relationship between negative peer pressure and manipulation? What advice would you give a friend to identify and deal with manipulative behavior?

Making Connections

1. **Music.** Find examples of songs with lyrics that show examples of positive and negative peer pressure. Discuss the potential influence of the lyrics on listeners.
2. **Language Arts.** Find examples of peer pressure in short stories or novels. Discuss in class.

Applying Your Learning

1. **Role-play.** In a small group, role-play situations in which a teen experiences positive pressure from his or her friends. For example, show a student who coaches another to do better in class or on a team. Perform the role-play in class. Then discuss other ways that friends influence each other positively.
2. **Write a short story.** Put yourself in the place of a teen who experiences negative peer pressure. Write a short story, with two different endings, that shows how the teen responds to peer pressure. In the first ending, describe the consequences of giving in to negative peer pressure. In the second ending, describe what happens when the teen successfully resists the pressure.

What Would You Do?

Suppose that three of your friends decide to buy the same jacket to show they're part of a group. You don't want to do it—you like expressing your own individuality. You care about your friends and don't want to lose them. How would you handle the situation?

Career Network

HUMAN SERVICES

FIREFIGHTER

Applications now being accepted for new firefighting training class.
- High school diploma required.
- Must be least 18 years of age, and pass written and physical exams.
- Self-discipline, mechanical aptitude, and strong sense of public service a must.

CHILD CARE WORKER

Mature, dependable, creative people needed to join our teaching team! Must enjoy working with children from 6 mo. to 6 yrs. of age.
- Self–directed people with excellent communication skills should apply.
- High school diploma required.
- Course work in child development preferred.

LIBRARY TECHNICIAN

Local library seeks dependable, detail-oriented technician. Will assist patrons in locating information and provide instruction on navigating the Internet.
- Associate's degree preferred.
- Evening and weekend hours required.

SOCIAL WORKER

Licensed social worker needed to assist with patient recovery and rehabilitation plans. Must maintain accurate case records and help clients locate necessary services.
- Four-year degree required, Master's degree preferred.
- Must be available to work evenings and weekends.

FOSTER PARENT

Foster parents needed to provide secure homes and meet basic needs of temporarily displaced children.
- Responsibilities vary with age of child.
- Monthly stipend provided.
- Must pass home inspection.

TEACHERS

Growing school district has immediate openings for experienced full-time teachers in Middle School Mathematics and High School Family & Consumer Sciences.
- Bachelor's degree and current state teaching license required.
- 10-month positions with excellent benefits.

More Career Options

Entry Level
- Correctional Officer
- Home Health Aide
- Security Guard
- Nanny

Technical Level
- Community Outreach Worker
- Case Management Aide
- State Highway Patrol Officer
- Recreation Worker

Professional Level
- Recreation Therapist
- Lawyer
- Psychologist
- Director of Student Services
- Geriatric Social Worker

POLICE OFFICER

City Police Dept. has several openings. Duties include enforcing laws, investigating complaints, and community service.

- Must deal effectively with people in both normal and stressful situations.
- Associate's degree preferred. Police officer training provided.
- Applicants must pass civil service exam.

REHABILITATION SPECIALIST

Full, part-time, flexible hours, and live-in opportunities available. Will work with developmentally disabled adults.

- Requires direct care and assisting with daily living skills in home environments.
- Must be at least 18 years old, have valid drivers license, and high school diploma.

DIR. OF YOUTH PROGRAMS

Community center needs organized director to plan and manage recreation programs.

- Will supervise staff and direct athletic programs and community events.
- Excellent leadership and people skills necessary.
- Degree in recreational programming with knowledge of first aid preferred.

CAMP COUNSELOR

Outgoing individuals needed to supervise and instruct early teens in variety of recreation programs. Seasonal work.

- Live-in staff positions require nights and weekends.
- Some post-secondary course work and talent in recreational activities preferred.

Linking School to Career

1. Your Career Plan: Family members have many roles and responsibilities that require a variety of skills. What skills do your family members use at home that are also used in the workplace by the people who perform in one of the jobs listed in the want ads? Of the skills that you listed, which ones can be learned in school?

2. Researching Careers: Human services occupations are considered "people-oriented" because they involve persuading, instructing, or providing services for others. Human services jobs also bring special rewards associated with helping others. Choose three of the human services jobs advertised on these pages, do research to find out more about them, and list the rewards you think they would bring.

3. Reading: Look up the definitions of the following terms that are found in the want ad listings:
- Licensed
- Rehabilitation
- Dependable
- Developmentally disabled

Unit 4

Your Friends and Family

Quality Friendships

YOU WILL LEARN . . .

- ➤ The importance of friendship.
- ➤ To identify the qualities of a true friend.
- ➤ Ways to make and keep friends.
- ➤ Reasons why friendships end.
- ➤ Ways to end a friendship when necessary.

TERMS TO LEARN . . .

- ➤ acquaintances
- ➤ cliques
- ➤ dependable

Imagine ...

... you could find an ideal person who had all the qualities you want in a good friend. Whatever you value in a friend, that person would have it. You'd spend time together, have fun, and be there for each other in times of need.

Think About

- What qualities would you seek in an ideal friendship?
- In reality, does any one person you know have all those qualities?

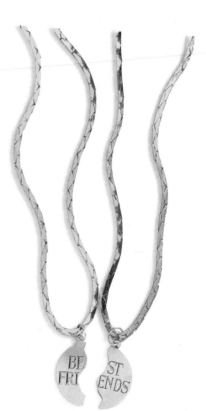

THE IMPORTANCE OF FRIENDSHIP

Angela's best friend, Margie, recently moved to another city. Angela misses her friend, and sometimes feels lonely. She and Margie have known each other for years and spent most of their free time together. Regardless of the distance that separates them, Angela and Margie hope to remain friends the rest of their lives.

Some people form childhood friendships that last a lifetime. Others make new friends as they move to high school and beyond. Good friends enjoy spending time together. They go to each other for advice or just an accepting ear. They listen to one another and offer moral support.

Friendship is important to nearly everyone. Friends broaden each other's life.

Qualities of a True Friend

> ➤ Relationships are an important part of your life. Think about friends from your past. What special things have you learned from them?

Qualities you may want in a friend vary depending on the degree of friendship. *People you may know—but who are not personal friends*—are called **acquaintances**. For example, a neighbor down the street or someone you say hello to at school may be an acquaintance. In time, the person may become a friend, someone you know well and like to spend time with. A friendship generally goes through stages on the way to becoming a close relationship.

You may have known some of your friends for as long as you can remember. Others may have recently grown from acquaintances to friends. Regardless of how you met, or how long you've known each other, four qualities are generally true of all good friends:

- **Caring.** Friends care for and about each other. They accept each other's weaknesses as well as strengths. Also, caring friends value each other's feelings as much as they do their own.

Quality Friendships

What You'll Need

- 20 4 x 6-inch note cards, scissors, markers, masking tape, ruler
- Paper and pen or pencil for keeping score
- 1 bean bag per group

What to Do

1. Working in a small group, brainstorm 10 positive and 10 negative qualities a friend might possess. Write each on a note card.
2. Assign points as follows: highly desirable (10), desirable (5), undesirable (-5), and highly undesirable (-10). Write points beneath each quality.
3. With the cards placed face down, mix well; then number 1 to 20. On a blank wall, tape cards in order, four across, five down, numbered side up.
4. Standing ten feet from the wall, have each person throw a beanbag at the cards, rotating until everyone hits five cards. Write down the card numbers of the cards each person hits. To find each person's score, turn each card over and record the assigned points. Finally, total the score.
5. Repeat with the cards taped to the wall with the quality side out.

To Discuss

- Compare the scores from the two rounds. Was it easier to hit the positive qualities that are important in a friend when you knew where they were? How can getting to know someone first help in choosing friends?
- What is the difference between a close friend and a casual friend? Why is it important to choose your close friends carefully?
- How do your friends influence what you think? How you behave? What might happen to someone who hangs out with the wrong crowd?

- **Dependability.** Friends are **dependable,** or *able to be counted on.* Dependable friends do their best to keep promises. For example, you can rely on them to be on time when expected.

> Caring for others is an important relationship skill. What can you do to show others that you care about them?

- **Loyalty.** Real friends stick by you. They like you for who you are—not for what you have or what you can do for them. Loyal friends are there when you need them. They respect your values and never ask you to go against what you value as important.
- **Empathy.** Good friends understand how you are feeling. They have empathy, or the ability to understand what you and others are experiencing. They put themselves in your place and try to see things from your point of view.

Each of these qualities is important in a true friendship. Which of the qualities do you offer as a friend? Which ones do you receive from a friend?

Making Friends

Angela's parents encourage her to make new friends. Ever since her friend Margie moved away, Angela has spent much of her free time alone, wishing her friend would move back. By reaching out to others, Angela can develop new friendships. New friends won't replace Margie, but they can enrich Angela's life and help her deal with the sadness she feels.

Getting Started

It usually takes time for a friendship to develop. Some people remain acquaintances, never growing beyond a passing "Hi. What's going on?" Others move on to become good friends.

Most people enjoy being—and having—friends. Because they find pleasure in friendship, they often look for ways to begin new ones. Here are some ideas to get started:

➤ Participating in group organizations or clubs often leads to new friendships. This is a great way to meet others who have interests or hobbies similar to your own.

Have you ever moved to a new community—a place where you didn't know anyone? Here are some ideas for forming new friendships now and in the future.

- **Make yourself interesting.** Read, watch the news and other TV programs of interest, and get involved in community activities.

- **Be a good listener.** Many potential friends love to talk—and love a good audience.

- **Remember names.** When you meet new people, make a point to remember their names and interesting things you discover about them.

- **Be yourself.** Don't try to be something you're not. Be sincere and real instead.

- **Walk your pet.** Pets often attract other pet lovers who are open to making new friends.

- **Don't give up.** Keep a positive attitude. Other people out there are also looking for friends. Look for individuals that share your values and beliefs.

- **Smile.** A friendly face is the first signal that you're willing to begin a friendship. Check out your expressions in the mirror to see if they seem friendly to you.

- **Start a conversation.** When you're around someone you might like as a friend, ask a question that doesn't require a simple "yes" or "no" answer. Then listen and respond to the answer. Mention any common interests you might have. Good friendships often begin with a simple conversation.

- **Go where there are people.** Get involved in clubs, sports events, and other programs sponsored by schools and your community. Be open to activities that bring people together.

- **Invite someone to join you in an activity.** Instead of waiting to be asked, take the first step. You may be surprised to learn that the other person was hoping you'd reach out. If someone turns you down, don't worry about it. This happens to everyone. Just try later with another person.

- **Don't rush a friendship.** It takes time and effort for a friendship to develop. The more time you spend together, the easier it is to make a friendship happen.

Maintaining Friendships

Being a friend takes some effort. If you want a friendship to last, you must give as well as take. This involves spending time with your friends, listening to what they have to say, and offering to help when needed.

Look at the following situations and ask yourself how a friendship would be affected in each one:

- Kyle, Chad's friend, is worried about next week's math exam. Chad is good in math and volunteered to help Kyle study for the test.
- Gale feels jealous when her friend Juanita talks to other girls at school. She wishes Juanita didn't have any other friends but her.

➤ You can use your personal values and advice from those you trust to make good decisions.

FRIENDS OF ALL AGES

Think about the friends you have. Are any of them a different age than you? Perhaps you've become a friend to an older neighbor. Although many of your friends will be your age, not all friends have to be. Having a variety of friends makes life interesting. Friends come in different ages, shapes, sizes, and colors.

Peer Friendships

Your peers are likely the people you associate with the most. They're friends who are your own age. During teen years, peer friendships are often the most common kind. You may have one close friend and a few others who aren't so close. You may see others who appear to have many friends and always seem included in everything. However, popular people may not always be as happy as you think. Some teens struggle to be popular—even to the point of doing things they know they shouldn't. Some miss out on having special close friends.

Making a DIFFERENCE

FRIENDLY OFFER

"Hi," Curt said to Lee, a new teen in his class. "It seemed like you were having a hard time with the math lesson. If you need help, just ask."

Lee nodded gratefully. "I appreciate it. I just moved here last week, and this class seems tough."

"Well don't be shy," said Curt. "If you want help, holler."

"Thanks a lot. I don't really know anyone at this school yet, so it's nice to have a friendly offer."

Two months later, Curt and Lee were tight friends.

Taking Action

1. Have you ever gone out of your way to make someone new at your school feel comfortable? What happened?
2. How did you meet a good friend in the past?

Cliques

In any setting where people gather, they tend to move into groups in which they feel comfortable. There is nothing wrong with that. Many teens, as well as adults, form groups to have a sense of belonging.

Unfortunately, some groups—or **cliques**—*exclude people from their circle of friendship.* In one way or another, the members of a clique reject those who they think don't fit the group's ideals. Only by the group's approval can someone join in. The basis for acceptance is often superficial, based on external qualities such as appearance, clothing, income, or status. When this kind of rejection occurs, it hurts people.

Perhaps you've been in a clique and have seen someone rejected by the group. Or maybe you've been the one who was excluded. There are a number of ways that you can

> **Often teens participate in friendship groups.** What types of activities do you participate in with your friends?

fulfill a need for belonging without rejecting others. They include:

- Avoid groups that treat others unfairly.
- Form your own circle of friends who don't exclude or judge people.
- If the "clique mentality" comes up in your group, challenge it. Do your best to include, rather than reject, others.

Younger Friends

Latasha enjoys spending time with her friends at the community center. Besides being a friend, she serves as a role model, a person who helps others see what's expected of them and shows them how to act in certain situations. The younger girls look up to Latasha and value her friendship.

Although most of your friends are probably other teens, children make good friends, too. Because you're older, your attention is very special to them. You may feel more relaxed and appreciated with younger people than you do with others.

> Teens make good mentors for younger children. **What skills do you have that you can share with a child?**

In today's world, children can use your friendship. Like Latasha's young friends, many children need good role models. The quality of their lives could improve greatly if you give them some time. You might teach them a skill you have, or just sit down and talk. What you learn about children can be carried over to your own future, perhaps as a parent or teacher someday.

Having younger friends can broaden your understanding of people in general. Also, friendships with younger people may help you gain insight into your own thoughts, feelings, and actions. Sometimes, listening to others' questions and concerns can help you better understand yourself.

Older Friends

Sometimes it's hard thinking of adults as friends. One of the reasons is because many adults have authority over teens. This means the adults are in charge. They set the rules to be followed. When teens are learning and aiming for independence, this isn't always easy to handle.

Being the adult in charge isn't always easy, either. Mr. Garza, a math teacher, cares about his students. He's especially concerned about Wayne, one of his students, who seems headed for trouble. Wayne constantly clowns around and causes disturbances in class. He doesn't care if he learns anything. Mr. Garza knows that it's his responsibility to keep order in the classroom. If his students don't learn the math, they'll have a harder time in future math classes—and in life. Also, if they don't pass the district proficiency exams, his teaching will be questioned.

For adults such as Mr. Garza, setting and enforcing rules is part of their responsibility to young people. Enforcing rules isn't fun, nor is it always easy to do. Rules are made to provide guidance for appropriate behavior—a necessary part of functioning in an orderly world.

Most adults, even when they have authority over you, want to be your friend. They also have personal problems and concerns. Try to put yourself in their place. Show respect, and offer your friendship. Like you, adults can make mistakes sometimes. When you fail to understand why an adult acts in a certain way or sets a rule you don't agree with, you may want to talk about it with that person. Be respectful and considerate. After all, you'll be an adult someday, too.

➤ You can share friendship with adults and benefit from their experience. What positive relationships have you had with an adult friend?

ENDING FRIENDSHIPS

Even young children learn that not all friendships last forever. When you were little, perhaps you—or your best friend—moved to another town. Because of the distance, maybe you never saw each other again. Even in later years,

Appreciating Your Heritage

If you were to write a biography about your family, what would you write? Perhaps your great-grandparents were born in the town where you live. Maybe they moved to your town from another country. No matter where your family may have originated, learning about—and appreciating—your heritage can be interesting and fun.

Families pass on their heritage from one generation to the next in many ways. Older relatives may share stories, photographs, or recipes with younger family members. They may also keep videotapes or journals of family events that can be treasured for generations.

What can you and your family do to celebrate your heritage? Each of the following ideas can be both fun and informative:

• Set out family albums and play "who's who." Document as many photos as possible with names, dates, and places.

• Map your family. Use a state map, U.S. map, or world map—whichever is appropriate. Place a marker over places where family members may live or where ancestors came from.

• Share a favorite story from your childhood. Tell the story or read the book that you loved best when you were small. Consider writing a letter to future generations about your life now.

• Create a family "time capsule." In a shoebox or other similar container, have all members of your family contribute items that show who they are today. Suggestions include a school paper, a finger painting, an office memo, a photograph, etc. Put your time capsule in a safe place, and bring it out one year from now to see, together, how the family has changed and grown.

Activity: Choose one of the activities listed above to work on with your family. Or, choose another heritage-related activity you may like better.

separation poses a threat to many friendships. When considerable distances separate friends, it's hard to stay emotionally close. Communication may suffer, and there may be fewer opportunities to keep in touch and share experiences. Only strong friendships that are deeply valued by both individuals usually survive long periods of separation.

Some friendships end because of conflict or misunderstandings. Feelings of jealousy and possessiveness can end—or threaten—a friendship. In other cases, people mature, change, and no longer want exactly the same things from their friendship. Changing interests, goals, and experiences can end friendships that aren't strong enough to deal with the changes.

In some cases, a friendship no longer works or may simply fade, because you don't give enough time to each other. In other situations, a friendship may be unhealthy or destructive, and you need to get out. If someone causes problems or is unpleasant to be around, a friendship can be harmful.

➤ When a friendship ends you may feel sad or hurt. Focus your energy on activities that keep you busy. In time, these sad feelings will lessen.

If you must deliberately end a friendship, do it with sensitivity. One way to do so is by easing out of the relationship. Find other activities that gradually take more and more of your time. Getting a part-time job, volunteering in the community, and making other friends can be effective.

In the case of a friendship that's not healthy or constructive, you may need to be direct, but kind, in your actions. Explain why you need to end the friendship. Focus on how you feel, not on the other person; and be honest about the reasons. For example, "I don't like being around people who smoke" or "I feel bad when we put down other people. I know some of them, and they're okay." Giving reasons rather than blaming the other person takes courage. However, doing so can help you end a friendship in as positive a way as possible.

If a friendship ends against your wishes, understand that this just happens sometimes. For awhile, you may feel sad or angry. You may even blame yourself. After a period, these feelings will go away, and you'll remember good times you had. As you move on to other friendships, you can take what you've learned with you.

Experience will help you recognize which friendships are worth keeping. Special friendships shouldn't be taken for granted. Doing your part to show respect and caring for the other person—and the other person's possessions—can help you make and keep friends.

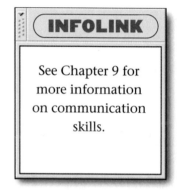

INFOLINK

See Chapter 9 for more information on communication skills.

➤ Respecting the opinions of your friends can lead to long-term friendships.

Chapter Summary

- Friendships broaden your life and give you people to spend time with.
- Good friends are caring, dependable, loyal, and empathetic.
- To make new friends, take the first step and smile, start a conversation, or invite someone to join you in an activity.
- Peer friendships are the most common kind of friendships during the teen years.
- Cliques are groups that exclude others from their friendship circle.
- Making friends with younger and older people can be very rewarding.
- Not all friendships last forever, When moving on to other friendships, remember the good times and take what you have learned with you.

Reviewing the Chapter

1. What is the difference between an acquaintance and a friend?
2. Briefly describe the four qualities that are generally true of all good friends.
3. List five things you can do to help start a friendship.
4. What do you need to do if you want to maintain a friendship?
5. What are four qualities that often form the basis for membership in a clique?
6. Give two advantages of having younger friends. Older friends?
7. Describe two ways to end a friendship with sensitivity for the feelings of the other person.

Family & Community

With Your Family

Ask your family members to identify qualities they value in a true friend. Then ask them to share some of their favorite memories involving family friends. Plan a picnic or potluck meal for one or more special friends of the family.

In Your Community

Some communities have young children who lack positive role models. As a class, brainstorm some volunteer activities you could do to make friends with younger children and share time with them. Follow through on some of your ideas.

Thinking Critically

1. **Draw conclusions.** How might your experiences as a friend differ from the experiences your parents had as teens? How might these differences influence their attitudes and actions as parents?
2. **Analyze behavior.** How would you rate yourself as a friend? Is it true that friendships always change as you grow and develop? Explain your answers.
3. **Make generalizations.** Think about friends you've had in your lifetime. Which of these friendships are still ongoing? What factors have made your friendships last?

Making Connections

1. **Language Arts.** Imagine that you've been asked to write a guest editorial for the school newspaper. Choose one of the following topics for your editorial: The Importance of Friendship; The Effects of Cliques; or When Friendships Must End.
2. **Social Studies.** Members of some gangs are pressured to prove their loyalty to the gang by getting involved in unhealthy or illegal behavior. In small groups, identify differences between true friendships and gang membership. Is there a difference between a clique and a gang? If so, how do they differ?

Applying Your Learning

1. **Write a note.** Write a note of appreciation to your best friend. Be sure to explain what you appreciate about him or her.
2. **Develop questions.** With a partner, develop a list of questions you might ask others when starting a friendship. Then take turns asking each other questions and answering them.
3. **Draw a word picture.** Complete the following statement: "I believe a true friend is . . ." Draw a "word picture" about the completed statement.

What Would You Do?

Suppose that you have been best friends with someone since third grade. Lately, however, your friend seems to enjoy being around other people—not just you. When you call him, the line is often busy. Later, he says he was "just talking to someone." You feel insecure, knowing the friendship isn't as strong as it used to be. You've never had to bother with making other friends and don't know where to start. How would you handle this problem?

Going Out with Friends

YOU WILL LEARN . . .

- ➤ Interest in the other gender is part of adolescence.
- ➤ Responsibilities you have when going out with others.
- ➤ Ways to deal with infatuation and rejection.

TERMS TO LEARN . . .

- ➤ crush
- ➤ infatuation

Imagine ...

... that there's someone of the opposite sex in class whom you'd like to meet. You're not quite sure if the person is interested in meeting you, or if the person might want to go to a movie with you sometime.

Think About

- How would you start a conversation with the person?
- Can you imagine having someone of the opposite sex as a good friend? Why or why not?

TO DATE, OR NOT TO DATE

Tamra enjoys going to the mall on Saturday afternoons with a group of friends. The group includes both males and females. They share a pizza and play video games or go to the movies. Although she hasn't started dating, Tamra enjoys being around friends of the opposite sex.

➤ Teens mature at various ages, so the age for dating varies.

Adolescence is the time when most people develop an interest in the other gender. Teens mature at different rates, especially during the early teen years. Because of this, not all teens develop an interest in the opposite sex at the same time. For example, Jeremy likes girls as friends, but he's not interested in going out with them yet. For him, spending time with the guys is first priority. If he's anything like his older brother, he might not even start dating until after high school.

Brad, one of Jeremy's classmates, is just the opposite. He began dating at an early age and rarely spends time with his old group of friends.

Holly thinks she'd like to date, but she hasn't met anyone special. In the meantime, school and a part-time job keep her plenty busy. Plus, she enjoys spending time out with a group of guys and girls who do things together, such as play games or go to the movies.

You probably know teens who aren't in a hurry to date. Some have interests that are more important to them than dating. Others may be shy and don't feel at ease with a person of the other sex. This is entirely normal and shouldn't be cause for concern.

GOING OUT WITH FRIENDS

One of the first steps that many teens take toward dating is going out in mixed gender groups. Getting together with such a group—without having an actual date—helps build understanding of each other the easy way. It gives you a variety of opportunities to examine and compare the feelings, thoughts, and actions of both guys and girls. Also, by being in a group, people tend to have fewer pressures than in a one-to-one dating situation.

At this stage of your life, it's a good idea to wait until you feel comfortable about dating. Don't let anyone pressure you into doing what you're not ready to do. Going out with a group of friends of both sexes can be a lot of fun. You can get to know everyone better at your own pace—without being rushed into pairing off with someone. Until then, there's plenty of time for dating as you go through adolescence and enter young adulthood.

Where to Go? What to Do?

When Alicia goes out with her friends, their favorite place is a nearby mall. The group enjoys snacking on food from various shops while talking and watching people go by. At other times, they like to go to the community center and skate or practice some new dance steps.

CHOOSING FRIENDS OF THE OPPOSITE SEX

Now that you're a little older, you have greater opportunities for meeting and choosing male and female friends. To form meaningful friendships with people of the opposite sex, be selective and choose friends who:

- Share values and beliefs similar to yours.
- Support and encourage your best qualities.
- Make you feel valued as a friend.
- Share equally in the friendship without being possessive.
- Are trustworthy and respectful of your personal limits.
- Don't pressure you to behave inappropriately.

➤ Friendship groups are a fun way to socialize with others. These teens each brought an ingredient to make homemade pizza together.

Whenever you go out with a group of friends:

- Let your parents or guardians know where you're going and what time you'll return home (within the limits set by your family).
- Tell your parents or guardians who you're going out with.
- Always carry change for the telephone.
- Keep in mind the responsibilities you have to yourself, to others, and to the community – and follow them.
- If the activities of an individual or group get out of hand, or fail to be in line with your values or standards of behavior, leave! Call your parents, other relatives, a taxi, or the police to ask for a ride home.

Some communities offer a wide variety of fun places to go and things to do. Other communities have fewer choices. In such cases, some creative thinking can help provide ideas. If Alicia lived in your community, what group activities might you suggest for her and her friends? Which of these are your favorites?

Cost and transportation can restrict what many teens are able to do. If this is true for you and your friends, look for inexpensive and simple ways to spend time together. An afternoon or evening spent watching a video at a friend's house, listening to music, playing games, or making popcorn or pizza, can be fun.

Your Responsibilities

When you spend time with others in a group, don't forget that you have some important responsibilities. Malls and most other places where teens go are used by other people as well. People who own property want to preserve its value. When you and your friends gather in community places, think about how your actions affect others. For example, what might happen to a restaurant if a large group of people routinely take up booth space while ordering only soft drinks? Without a chance to make enough money to pay its expenses, the restaurant would go out of business. If you were the owner of a restaurant or store frequented by your teen friends, how would their actions affect your business?

Going out with people of the opposite sex involves additional responsibilities. First of all, you must make decisions about your conduct. It's important to set your standards of behavior ahead of time. Having them clearly in mind can help you if any difficult situations come up.

You also have a responsibility to people you go out with. Show respect by treating them the same way you want to be treated. Think about how you'd handle each of the following situations when you go out with your friends:
- Choosing a time to leave and to return.
- Deciding what to do.
- Handling expenses.
- Showing consideration and appreciation.
- Ending the activity.

➤ Show respect for your family and friends by being on time. Learning promptness now will bring you great rewards in the future.

Responsibilities to Your Family

Another important responsibility is to your family. Talk over family rules with responsible members when you're thinking about going out. Some families have a particular age in mind for you to begin going out with mixed-gender groups. Other families look for signs of readiness in a teen. Family rules may involve curfews, transportation, and where teens may and may not go. Cindy disagreed with some rules her family had about going out. Her older sister suggested she discuss them with her parents and show a willingness to listen. Cindy took her sister's advice and learned a valuable lesson: Instead of arguing, being willing to listen can lead to cooperation and perhaps compromise on both sides of an issue.

Once rules are set, you'll find that it helps to be mature and follow them. Parents make rules because they're responsible for your safety and well-being. Breaking rules causes family members to worry and lose trust. Think about how you'd feel if you were a parent. What rules would you set for young teens in your family? How might you feel if they failed to follow the rules?

➤ You may have a crush on a celebrity, a teacher, a coach, or someone your own age. It's normal, and maturity usually brings more realistic feelings.

Tori Amos

LOVE AND INFATUATION

Trey is having trouble doing his homework. Thoughts about Janie keep getting in the way. She's a new member of his group of friends, and he's attracted to her. He'd like to spend time with her alone rather than with the group.

Trey is experiencing **infatuation** or a **crush,** *a type of love experience based on an intense attraction to another person that is generally one-sided.* You may have had similar feelings about a movie star, one of your teachers, or a classmate.

When people are infatuated, they're in love with what they imagine the other person is like. Infatuation can be pleasant or painful, depending on the attitude and actions of the other person involved.

Crushes are common feelings, especially for teens. The emotions are very real and powerful, but aren't true love. Crushes seldom last long. Once over, you may even wonder why you felt the way you did. Trey's feelings of infatuation are already fading, since Janie is showing interest in someone else.

HOW to...

Handle Rejection

Because rejection is something that almost everyone experiences, you need to learn to handle it as positively as possible. First, remember that rejection is only as hurtful as you allow it to be. If feelings of rejection are difficult to deal with, here are some other ideas to consider:

- Share your feelings with a friend or family member. He or she can offer support and helpful suggestions.

- Be kind to yourself. Just because someone rejected your friendship doesn't mean you're a bad person. Perhaps your friendship simply outgrew itself, and your friend responded first.

- On bad days, make a list of your good points and refer to your list when needed.

- Examine why you were rejected. If there's something you truly need to change about yourself, take steps toward improvement.

- Don't say negative things about the person who rejected you. Getting stuck in the mud of negative words and feelings will get you nowhere.

- Move on. Put the experience aside and get involved with daily life. In time, the painful feelings will weaken, and later, go away.

Most teens simply let such feelings run their course. If the feelings are hard to handle, talking to family and friends can help.

Handling Rejection

Rejection can happen in any kind of a friendship, including one with a person of the opposite sex. Sometimes two people simply don't hit it off. As in Trey's case, one person may not share the same attraction or feelings as the other person. Sometimes an individual knows this immediately and turns down the first invitation. At other times, it takes time before the discovery is made. Whatever the case, one party may experience rejection.

➤ You may face rejection when you ask for a date. This can teach you to cope with adversity in other situations.

Review & Activities

Chapter Summary

- Not all teens are ready to start dating. Some have other important interests.
- It's normal for some teens to feel shy and ill at ease with persons of the opposite sex.
- Going out in a group of males and females can be a healthy first step toward dating.
- When spending time with others in a group, you have important responsibilities to yourself, to the people you go out with, and to your family.
- Show respect by treating others the same way you want to be treated.
- Willingness to follow the family rules may lead to cooperation and compromise.
- Many teens experience crushes or feelings of infatuation.
- Rejection can happen in all kinds of friendships.

Family & Community

With Your Family

Think about some of your family rules and how they impact your safety and well-being. Talk with your family members about rules their families had when they were young. What were the consequences if they failed to follow the rules?

In Your Community

Many communities are concerned about teens who aren't responsible for themselves, to each other, and to the community whenever they are out in mixed groups. As a class, brainstorm some volunteer activities you could do to encourage teens to be more responsible when out together.

Reviewing the Chapter

1. Name three advantages of going out with a group of males and females rather than just one other person.
2. Suggest four activities friends might enjoy when cost and transportation are limited.
3. Explain how the actions of teens may impact others when they and their friends gather in a community place.
4. Why is it important to set personal standards of behavior before going out with people of the opposite sex?
5. What are five factors to consider when showing responsibility to people you go out with?
6. Identify two ways that breaking the rules impacts the family.
7. Give an example showing how a teen might handle infatuation in a positive way.
8. Give four examples of ways to handle rejection.

Thinking Critically

1. **Compare and contrast.** Think about friendships you have with people of the opposite sex. In what ways are these friendships similar to same-sex friendships? How are they different? Explain.
2. **Draw conclusions.** Imagine you're out with a group of male and female friends. Draw some conclusions about what you can do if you are being pressured to pair off with someone.
3. **Recognize alternatives.** What advice would you give a younger sibling or friends about saying "no" to someone who asks him or her to behave in an inappropriate way?

Making Connections

1. **Social Studies.** Teens of different cultures sometimes have different customs when relating to members of the opposite sex. Use library and Internet resources (or personal interviews with people from other cultures, if possible) to learn how teens in other countries and cultures meet and make friends with members of the opposite sex. Write a summary of your findings.
2. **Speech.** Write a two-minute speech supporting the parental viewpoint about the importance of family rules for teen safety and well-being. Present your speech to the class. Discuss some consequences you think would be fair for teens that fail to follow family rules.

Applying Your Learning

1. **Interview.** Interview older family members and friends to discover the similarities and differences in dating practices over the years. Share your findings with the class.
2. **Create an announcement.** In small groups, create a public service announcement about teen responsibilities in the community. Encourage teens to consider how their actions impact local businesses and shopping centers.
3. **Develop a quiz.** With a partner, write a quiz to help teens distinguish between feelings of infatuation and real love. Give the test to some of your friends and discuss the results.

What Would You Do?

Suppose a friend told you that he is "in love" with a young woman who works at a local store. He thinks that she also "loves" him because of the way she smiles at him. Your friend's grades are suffering because he daydreams about her. You've observed the young woman out with someone else. You also know that she smiles at everyone who comes into the store. You know your friends feelings are one-sided. How would you handle this situation?

Building Strong Families

YOU WILL LEARN . . .

- ➤ The functions families fill in your life.
- ➤ The roles and responsibilities family members.
- ➤ How families change.
- ➤ What strong families are like.
- ➤ How you can get along better with your family.
- ➤ Ideas for strengthening family ties.

TERMS TO LEARN . . .

- ➤ age span
- ➤ family life cycle
- ➤ sibling rivalry
- ➤ siblings
- ➤ traditions

Imagine ...

… that your family is like a quilt. Each square in the quilt represents a person in the family. There's an overall pattern to the quilt, but no two squares are exactly alike. Maybe your quilt consists of just the people living at home right now. Maybe it's big enough to include your grandparents, aunts, uncles, and cousins. Thousands of stitches keep the quilt together. The border of the quilt holds the squares together, much like family traditions and values hold a family together.

Think About

- What colors would you use in your quilt—bright or soft?
- How do all the "squares" in your family's quilt fit together?
- What binds your family together like the border of the quilt?

YOU ARE PART OF THE WHOLE

One quilt square can't keep anything very warm. That's much like a family. You laugh and learn together. When everyone comes together as a whole, each person is happier and more effective. The others help you through tough times and you help them.

Make a habit of thinking of yourself as part of "us" instead of just "me." That will help you remember that whatever you do affects other members of your family. If you wipe up a spill, then no one else will slip and fall. If you call your grandfather, his day will be brighter—and yours too! It's easier to make good choices when you remember to keep others in mind. Your family "quilt" stays together only when every member works at unity.

Why Families Are Important

Without families there wouldn't be neighborhoods, or cities, or countries. That's because families are the building blocks of society. You will find this is true in every culture. Children are born into families. In families they grow and learn to become independent adults who'll form their own families.

➤ Strong families develop with hard work and positive attitudes. They overcome difficulties together.

Who's in the FAMILY?

- **Nuclear family.** This consists of a mother, father, and one or more children born to them.
- **Single-parent family.** One parent raising one or more children.
- **Blended family.** Formed when two people marry and at least one already has children
- **Extended family.** Another relative, such as a grandparent or aunt, lives with the family.
- **Adoptive family.** Parents legally adopt a child not born to them.
- **Foster family.** Includes a child not related to the family but cared for by them as a family member.

Families differ in who the family members are and how they are related.

Think of situations when one family fits more than one category.

This process doesn't just magically happen. What family functions encourage the growth of strong, caring adults?

- **Families meet basic needs.** They provide food, shelter, clothing, and education.
- **Families give emotional support.** They help family members believe in themselves and help each other through difficult times.
- **Families teach values.** Parents teach right from wrong and what things are most important in life.
- **Families pass on culture and tradition.** In the family, children learn how to get along with other people. They also learn about their family's heritage.

Each Family Is Unique

No one else is just like you, and no two families are exactly alike. You may know a family that is very similar to your own. Even so, if you spent a day with that family, you would be able to make a list of dozens of differences.

Families vary depending on their cultural background, too. Some cultures emphasize large families while others prefer smaller families. Some cultures place emphasis on having a close-knit family that takes part in many activities together. Several generations of the family may live together in one home. Other cultures emphasize independence, encouraging their children to move out into the world and develop their own interests and activities.

Families who value their cultural history usually make a point of carrying on its traditions and beliefs. They want their children to learn traditional songs and stories, and stay in touch with their cultural heritage. At the same time, they teach their children to respect and appreciate other cultures.

Think again about the stitches in the quilt that represents a family. All the stitches that hold the front, the middle, and the back together come from everyday family experiences. Some are your family routines and traditions. Others are the rules your family follows and the problems you have shared.

Family Roles and Responsibilities

To better understand families, it's helpful to think about what each member contributes. Be aware of each person's roles and responsibilities in your family. Who is carrying the heaviest load? Are there ways to even things out?

Playing Your Part

The people who make up a family each have certain roles within that family. Some roles—like mother, father, child, or older sister—come with the person's position in the family structure. Others—such as income earner, at-home parent, and student—refer to the major way the person spends his or her time.

Each person has more than one role. You might be a son, a younger brother, and a grandson all in one! At the same time, you might be a friend, soccer team member, and paper carrier outside the family.

➤ **Responsible teens can have many roles and still do their chores.** Name some of the roles you have at your present age.

TRY IT OUT

Family Portraits

What You'll Need
- Index card
- Pencil

What to Do
1. Divide your index card into three columns: Parents/Guardians, Siblings, Other Family Members. Don't write your name on the card.
2. Under each column, indicate how many in that category live with you.
3. At the board, tally the numbers on all the cards for each category. Divide each total by the number of class members. This gives you an "average" for each category.

To Discuss
- Were the class averages higher or lower than you expected? Identify some possible reasons.
- Do you think your class averages are typical of families in your school? Your city? Explain.

Showing Responsibility

Certain responsibilities go along with each of your roles. Within the family, Erin is expected to clean her room, clear the table after meals, take out the trash on Tuesdays, and keep the grass mowed. Your own list might be quite different. It depends upon how many people are in your family and what must be accomplished.

It's easy to slip into the complaint, "I have to do *everything* around here!" Is that really true? Take another look at your family. What are each person's roles inside and outside the home? What responsibilities go with each of those roles? In your family, who pays the bills, keeps the car running, fixes meals, and does laundry? Every person can and should do some things to help. In fact, growing up means taking on more and more responsibility.

➤ **Working together saves time and can be fun.** What are some household tasks you can do with a sibling or a parent?

Families Change

Just as life changes, families change, too. Think about what has happened in the last year in your family… in the last five years. How is your family different from families in the early 1900s?

The Family Life Cycle

Couples expecting their first child know that their life is about to change dramatically. They'll have less freedom and much more responsibility. As children grow up, the school years bring more changes. Finally, the children set off on their own and the parents are alone again as a couple. As they grow older, their needs, wants, and responsibilities continue to change. Social scientists who study families call this the **family life cycle.** These are *the stages that many families go through during their lifetime together.* The diagram on the next page shows the family life cycle. Knowing about it will help you better understand families.

Families Mirror Society

Over the centuries, family life has changed along with daily life. In the 1800s, many people lived on farms. Having large families meant more help in the fields.

In the early 1900s, many of today's conveniences hadn't yet been invented. To arrange a visit with cousins in the next town, you might send them a letter saying when you would come. No telephones!

➤ **Because of today's busy lifestyles, cellular phones make it easier for families to communicate.** What are other types of improved communication?

Today, life is changing faster than ever. In most families, there's no parent at home full-time. Families keep in touch with cellular phones and computers. Fewer families eat dinner together. What other changes can you identify?

The Family Life CYCLE

At what stage is your family in the life cycle?

Beginning Stage
A young couple without children.

Parenting Stage
Families expand. Children are born and develop. Parents care for children and provide for all their needs.

Launching Stage
Teens become independent and leave the family home.

Retirement Stage
A time when children have left home. Parents adjust to being a couple again and enjoy the activities of the retirement years.

➤ Open communication improves family relationships. This family has regular family meetings to resolve problems and plan family activities.

BUILDING FAMILY STRENGTHS

Just what does it take to have a strong family? Researchers have identified some characteristics of strong, successful, loving families. They:
- Have a positive attitude about life and family.
- Enjoy spending time together.
- Show appreciation and love for each other.
- Share beliefs, values, and goals.
- Are committed to each other and to the family.
- Show consideration and respect for each other.
- Are tolerant and forgiving.
- Take time for laughter and play.

It takes a few of these traits to make a family strong. Which fit your family? Strong families don't just happen. It takes time and effort from everyone to make and keep a family strong. You can positively impact your family relationships through the actions you take.

GETTING ALONG IN YOUR FAMILY

Getting along is a challenge every family faces. Think about all the ways family members are different—age, gender, personality, and life experiences. Add differing interests, abilities, and obligations and you have quite a mix of people living under one roof!

What can you do to improve family relationships? More than you may realize. First, you can control your own attitudes and actions. It's easy to just react to what happens, saying or doing things without thinking. Often that hurts others and pulls you apart. If you think about the situation first, you will make better choices. Talk through problems without an "I win, you lose" attitude.

➤ Ask your parents to share what their teen years were like. You might be surprised that they felt what you feel now.

You and Your Parents

As you move toward more independence, your relationships with your parents change. You need to find ways to get along and stay close. Here are some suggestions from teens who have done that successfully.

Increase Your Understanding

How well do you know your parents? What have their lives been like? What responsibilities and problems do they have? Understanding means learning about the reasons behind your parents' beliefs and actions. Maybe they are trying to protect you from problems that they had at your age.

Understanding also depends on how well your parents know you. Unless you share your thoughts and feelings with them, they can't understand you. Find times when you can be alone together. Thomas and his mom talk as they walk the dog together every night. Shelly's become closer to her dad and stepmother because they ride into town together every Saturday. Think of times that might work for you.

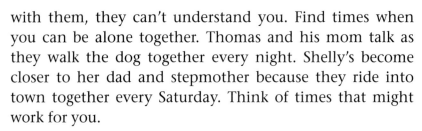

INFOLINK

See Chapter 8 for more information on respect.

Show Respect

When you understand why people act as they do, it's easier to show them respect. It's easy for disrespect to creep into a family. Everyone's happiness suffers. Try taking mental movies of how you interact with others. What message did your words give? Your tone of voice? Your body language? How can you be more respectful?

Be Responsible and Dependable

Teens who are willing to be responsible and dependable are often given more privileges. Here are some examples of responsibility:

- Be honest with your parents. Admit mistakes when you make them.
- Complete your jobs at home without constant reminders.
  - Tell your parents where you are when you're away from home.
    - Do your best in school.
      - Watch out for younger brothers or sisters—whether it's your job or just because you see that you are needed.

When you do your best to be responsible, you help strengthen your family. Where do you rank on the responsibility scale?

➤ **Strong families show love and appreciation for other family members.** What can you do to strengthen your family relationships?

Show Appreciation

How often do you give a friend a compliment or say "thank you?" Appreciation is just as important in families, but it's often overlooked. A hug, an offer of help, or even a request for advice all can show that you realize how much your family helps you. Start a trend in your family!

➤ Supporting your siblings will help you give them respect. This creates positive feelings for everyone.

You and Your Siblings

These same skills will also work with your **siblings**, or *brothers and sisters.* Understanding, respect, responsibility, and appreciation are key skills in any relationship.

How easily you get along with your siblings depends on many factors. If you have common interests, it's much easier.

The **age span,** or *number of years between siblings,* also plays a part. Some older siblings are very protective of the younger ones. Others feel frustrated when a younger brother or sister hangs around and asks questions all of the time. Try figuring out what your sibling really thinks and feels. Then you can find better ways to get along.

Are You Rivals?

Sibling rivalry, or *competition for the love and attention of parents,* is common between siblings. Have you ever felt that fairness was a problem in your family? Do you keep track of gifts, awards, privileges, and compliments that each of you receives? Try not to fall into this trap.

Every situation is different. As a parent, how would you keep track of everything said to, bought for, or rawarded to each child? It's impossible!

Cool Sibling Rivalry

Do you ever feel you are competing with your siblings? Do you find yourself keeping score on parental attention? Here are some ideas for cooling the rivalry with your siblings and improving your relationships.

- Try to look at the situation from the other person's point of view when you're feeling things aren't fair. How might the situation look different?

- Find similar interests that you can talk about or activities to do together.
- Teach each other new skills.
- Work together on household jobs. They'll be easier and more fun.
- Do something nice for each other.
- Ask before borrowing anything and return things in good condition.
- Talk to each other often to share your feelings and viewpoints.

➤ Sibling rivalry is a common occurrence.

When you feel competitive, remember that you have your own special qualities and abilities. They may not be the same as those of your siblings, but that doesn't matter. Discover what you do well, and develop those skills. See "How to Cool Sibling Rivalry" on this page for tips on improving relationships.

MAKING TIME FOR EACH OTHER

The time you spend with your family is much more important than what you do together. For some families, having fun together might involve washing the dog, baking cookies, having dinner together, or taking a biking trip. Sharing time together can strengthen family ties and create memories to treasure the rest of your life.

Building Family Traditions

Think about your favorite family times. Often these include family **traditions**—*customs that are followed again and again.* Traditions are often passed from one generation to another.

Traditions can help make families strong. Chandra's relatives all come for Thanksgiving. After they eat, they tell family stories. Pete's family watches a movie together on Friday nights and snacks on popcorn. In Andrea's family, each person has a silly nickname. Traditions involve creating memories, sharing love, and building strong family bonds. What are some favorite traditions in your family?

➤ Looking at old family pictures is a fun way to spend time with your family. These photos bring floods of memories of the past.

PULLING TOGETHER

When you think about all of the things that combine to make families strong, there's one last point to remember. People need the support, love, and friendship of their family. Friends can drift apart, but parents and siblings share a bond like no other. If you want your family to be there when you need them someday, then it's well worth your effort to work toward building strong family ties now.

Chapter Summary

- You are part of a family; whatever you do affects others in your family.
- There are different types of families, but all have the same functions.
- Every member fulfills several roles in a family and has many responsibilities.
- Families go through a cycle of change. Families also change with the times.
- Strong families have common characteristics that bind them together.
- Controlling your attitudes, actions, and reactions can improve family relationships.
- Showing understanding, respect, responsibility, and appreciation helps improve relationships with your parents.
- You can improve your sibling relationships and lessen sibling rivalry.
- Family traditions help make families strong.

Reviewing the Chapter

1. Briefly describe at least four types of families.
2. Name four functions that families are responsible for.
3. How do roles affect responsibility within the family?
4. Identify at least four characteristics of strong families.
5. How can you show respect for parents?
6. How does responsible behavior lead to greater independence for teens?
7. What is helpful to remember when someone feels that fairness is a problem in the family?
8. List at least five tips for getting along with siblings.
9. Why is it important for family members to spend time together?

Family & Community

With Your Family

Think about some of your favorite experiences with your family. Then talk to others in your family about their favorites. Gather pictures and write about these experiences to make a memory scrapbook.

In Your Community

Many people are concerned about families in their community who go hungry. Brainstorm some volunteer activities you could do as a class to combat hunger.

Thinking Critically

1. **Draw conclusions.** How might your experiences as a teen differ from the experiences your parents had as teens? How might this influence their attitudes and actions as parents?

2. **Compare and contrast.** Compare the roles you currently fill in the family with those of your other family members. How are they different and how are they the same? Which roles do you think are most important?

3. **Make generalizations.** Which stage of the family life cycle do you think would be the most difficult for parents to go through? Why?

Making Connections

1. **Social Studies.** A variety of cultures and family customs exist in every community. In small groups, identify the cultural background of group members. Then share some customs that are unique to that culture.

2. **Literature.** In the book *Anna Karenina*, author Leo Tolstoy wrote, "Happy families are all alike; every unhappy family is unhappy in its own way." Discuss the meaning of this quote. Do you agree or disagree? Why?

Applying Your Learning

1. **Design a quilt square.** Using paper or fabric, design a quilt square that shows how colors and patterns combine to display the unique characteristics of your family.

2. **Write a letter.** Imagine that you are the parent of a teen your age. Write a letter explaining your reasons for making a decision or taking an action that the teen thinks is unfair.

3. **Describe a good relationship.** Draw a "word picture" describing your response to the following statement: "My idea of a good family relationship is . . . ."

What Would You Do?

Suppose that you are shopping at the mall with your friends. Everyone in your group decides to go for pizza at a popular place a few miles down the road. Your mom is picking you up at the mall in 45 minutes. She's out running errands and can't be reached by telephone. You feel torn. You really want to go for pizza with your friends, but don't want to break your mom's trust by leaving the mall and going someplace else. How would you handle this problem?

Chapter

15

Family Changes and Challenges

YOU WILL LEARN . . .

- ➤ Examples of changes and challenges that families face.
- ➤ Ways that families can deal with changes and challenges.
- ➤ Resources available to families who need help.

TERMS TO LEARN . . .

- ➤ addiction
- ➤ alcoholics
- ➤ alcoholism
- ➤ creditors
- ➤ credit rating
- ➤ crisis
- ➤ financial
- ➤ spouse

Imagine ...

... that you and your family have driven through country you've never seen before on a weekend getaway. As you turn back and start to head home, you notice the route seems unfamiliar. After several miles and a few uncertain turns, you realize your family is undeniably lost.

Think About

- What are some likely reactions of family members to the situation?
- What resources can you use to find your way home?
- How can each family member contribute to a solution?

CHANGES AND CHALLENGES IN THE FAMILY

➤ This family is packing study supplies to send the older brother off to college. Families experience a variety of changes as they go through life.

Getting lost on a weekend drive with your family can be an unexpected challenge. But it's one challenge that usually doesn't take too much effort to solve. If your mom or dad knows how to read a road map, or can find someone to provide directions, your family will soon be on the right road again.

Change and challenge are part of the normal ups and downs of life. Some changes are exciting: Your dad gets a job promotion and you move to a new home. Your mom has a baby, and suddenly you have a new sibling. Other challenges can be far more difficult.

When families experience major problems that deeply impact each member, you need to know how to cope. With time and effort, anyone can learn the best strategies to handle difficult problems. The big question is *how*.

New Family Members

Many families experience change because of a new addition. Maybe you have a new brother or sister. Or maybe a cousin has moved in to attend a local college. Anytime a family stretches to include another person, everyone needs to make adjustments. A new brother or sister can shake up daily routines. You may need to share your space and possessions. It's only natural to find yourself feeling a certain amount of insecurity and resentment. But that's the negative, or down, side—*if* you choose to see it that way.

You have the option to view the change as a way to learn more about yourself and your family. Loving and entertaining a new baby can be more fun than you ever imagined. Thinking of as many reasons as possible to value a new addition to your family makes it easier to make change work for you.

➤ **Families can gain additional support from family members who move into the home.** What families do you know who have grandparents living with them?

Moving

Have you ever moved to a new community? If so, you know it can be both exciting and challenging. You have to adjust to a new school, unfamiliar surroundings, and neighbors you've never met. Feeling strange about a new community is perfectly normal, but usually the feeling disappears after awhile. Soon it can feel as if you've lived there your entire life.

You can fit in faster at a new school by signing up for an activity or sport you enjoy. That can make it easier to meet other students with similar interests. Be friendly and show your interest in others. Discovering classmates who share your interests is a first step to cementing new friendships.

Unemployment

Sometimes you have to deal with a parent who loses a job. Temporary unemployment is a fact of life for many families, and can be stressful for each member. It's common in such situations for family members to experience feelings of low self-esteem, anger, and frustration. But feelings are usually temporary.

MAKE NEW FRIENDS IN SIX EASY STEPS

1. Look friendly and show an interest in others. Don't be afraid to smile and have something pleasant to say.

2. Offer to help someone. Reach out and let other people know you want to be friends.

3. Telephone or e-mail someone you talked with in class or during lunch. Keep the conversation balanced so both of you can participate.

4. Make sure you have something to talk about. Develop or continue activities that interest you—and that make you interesting.

5. Try out for a sports team or join a club or other group.

6. Take part in volunteer activities. Working together forms bonds of friendships among people.

Financial Problems

➤ Learn to understand your family finances. Financial problems can be stressful. Be part of the solution, not the problem.

Financial, or *money-related,* problems are often triggered by the loss of a job, natural disaster, serious illness, or even death. Some families routinely struggle with financial problems because their income simply doesn't stretch far enough. Here are some facts to keep in mind:

- When bills are overdue, most **creditors**—*people or companies you owe money to*—are willing to schedule new arrangements for payment. This can protect your **credit rating**—*a record that shows your ability and willingness to pay your debts.*

- Consumer credit counseling services are available in many communities to help individuals and families with financial problems. They offer plans to help people control their spending and get out of debt. In some situations, they work with creditors to arrange realistic payment plans. These services are listed in the yellow pages of the phone book under "Credit."

- Understanding goes a long way when finances are tight. Money for clothes and entertainment may be scarce. Learning ways to alter, or re-style, your clothes can help. So can taking advantage of free and low-cost sources of entertainment.

- A teen's ability to handle financial difficulties in positive ways eases some of the financial pressure for parents. Although it may be stressful at the time, learning to carefully manage financial resources makes people far better money managers throughout their adult lives.

Homelessness

Homelessness is a problem all over the world. Some families have no permanent place to live. This problem has become more common in recent years. When people lose their homes, financial troubles or job loss is often the reason. A downturn in the economy can make jobs scarce. Sometimes people lose their home through natural disasters such as floods, fires, hurricanes, and tornadoes. Even temporary homelessness puts a major strain on a family.

Most communities are able to provide a safety net for those who find themselves with nowhere to go. The Red Cross and other groups and agencies are usually able to place people in shelters until they can get back on their feet.

ILLNESS AND LOSS

When a parent, child, or close relative becomes seriously ill or disabled, families experience stress. But those families who know how to pull together fare best. Learning about a parent's illness or disability can help you better understand his or her daily needs.

Doctors, clinics, libraries, and Web sites offer extremely valuable information. Others who've gone through similar difficulties can provide encouraging advice and support. Family members who show an attitude of understanding and compassion can help maintain a loving and strong family even in tough times.

➤ Homelessness sometimes occurs after a natural disaster.

Making a
DIFFERENCE

DEALING WITH ADJUSTMENTS

"We need to talk," said Jason's mom.

Jason could tell by her tone of voice that it would be a serious discussion. They sat down in the living room.

"You know Grandpa's not well," she started. "And I know it would be hard for us if he moved in for a while, but I think it would really help him get better. And it would mean a lot to me." Before Jason could reply, she explained her reasons.

"So what does it mean for me?" he asked. But he knew the answer. "I know. It means I'll have to share a room with Larry." Larry was Jason's younger brother.

Jason and his mom talked out the situation, weighing the pros and cons of the decision. After sharing their feelings, Jason thought about it. He'd always enjoyed spending time with his grandfather, but he wasn't too excited about sharing space with Larry. "Okay" he said finally. "Let's try it out."

Mom gave him a big smile.

Taking Action

1. How could Jason's decision make his family stronger?
2. What would you do in a similar situation?

Death

Leila's father was killed in a work-related accident. A loss like this creates a **crisis,** or *an extreme change* in a family. Some losses are temporary, while others are permanent.

When death strikes the family, everyone experiences grief. The closer you were to the person, the greater your loss. The person's age and circumstances of the death can also impact how you feel. People go through grief in different ways.

Some people need to express intense emotions. Others need to talk quietly to a trusted relative or friend. So family members need to respect each other's grief and allow each other to mourn in his or her own way. Participating in an event such as a funeral or memorial service can help people better accept the reality of death.

A family needs to deal with many details following a death. Conflict among family members is common due to increased emotions during this period. But families can grow closer and stronger as a result of loss. Sharing emotions and memories with each other—and with good friends—can be valuable and lessen the pain of coping with loss.

Separation and Divorce

When parents separate or divorce, one parent moves out of the family home. Some couples separate for a period of time, but after resolving their differences, get back together again. In other cases, they decide to divorce, and the original family undergoes major changes.

The children of parents who separate or divorce often go through a difficult period of emotional adjustment. They may blame themselves for the breakup, thinking that if they had behaved differently their parents would have stayed together. For this reason, they need to receive loving support from both parents and reassurance that this is not the case.

> Divorce in families may bring on increased responsibilities to teens. They may have to make adjustments and accept a new way of life.

Teens whose parents divorce often feel isolated and lonely. They may feel that they are the only people on earth who have experienced the effects of divorce. At such times it's important to realize that many marriages end in divorce, so there are many teens who experience similar feelings.

Parents often make mistakes when a separation or divorce process involves bitter feelings. They may make negative comments about each other to their children, and want children to take sides. One parent may even try to take the children illegally.

It's easy to feel torn between two parents going through a separation or divorce. For this reason, you need to spend time with both parents and share feelings. You have the right to express how your parents' actions make you feel. If you are unsure about how to tell your parent(s) how you really feel, you might try dealing with angry or sad feelings by writing a letter that you don't intend to send. Such a letter would express your feelings in your own way, and would be for your own use.

Coping after a divorce takes a lot of thought and special effort. Teens may have increased responsibilities in the home and spend less time with both parents—not just the absent one. Although many effects of divorce are unpleasant, most people learn how to make adjustments and grow to accept their new way of life. Talking out conflicting feelings with parents can help you come to terms with your parents' decision. Another trusted adult—maybe a teacher, school counselor, or religious leader—can help, too.

➤ Alcoholism is a form of drug addiction. If a friend or family member needs help to overcome an addiction, you may need to assist them in seeking help.

SUBSTANCE ABUSE AND ADDICTION

Substance abuse can prove a fast track to the breakdown of a family. In some cases, substance abuse occurs when medications for illness are misused. It also occurs when drugs such as alcohol, inhalants (substances that are breathed in), and illegal drugs are used. Often people develop an **addiction** to a drug, or *a physical or psychological dependence on the substance.* They'll do almost anything to get the drug they crave. Serious health problems, and even death, result from substance abuse.

Alcohol is the most commonly reported example of drug abuse. The result is often **alcoholism,** *the physical and mental dependence on alcohol. People who are addicted to*

Help Someone Who Abuses Alcohol

If you're concerned about someone close to you who is abusing alcohol, the following guidelines can help:

- Let the person know you're concerned and willing to help.

- Discuss the problem calmly. Call the problem by its name, alcoholism, and tell the person how you feel about it.

- Don't assume responsibility for the drinker. This just enables the person to continue drinking.

- Never argue with someone who's been drinking. The person isn't able to think clearly and may react violently.

- Let the person know help is available. Give the person information about community resources and their locations. Realize, however, that the alcoholic must be ready to seek assistance.

- Even when the alcoholic is unwilling to find help, friends and family members can learn how to deal with an alcoholic. They can seek help in order to promote possible recovery and keep the family together. Alateen and Al-Anon are two organizations that offer suggestions and support. With help, many alcoholics and their families have succeeded in traveling the road to recovery.

alcohol, in the form of beer, wine, or other liquor, are called **alcoholics.** They're considered to have a disease.

The Effects on the Family and Society

Whether young or old, people with a substance abuse problem can make life very trying for their families. Their behavior often causes other family members to live in constant tension and fear, never knowing how the addicted person will act. Out of touch with themselves and reality, abusers may even deny they have a problem. They may neglect their responsibilities and behave irrationally. Their actions may be violent, endangering themselves and others. Financial problems can occur due to the cost of a drug or loss of a job as a result of abuse. Addicts may even turn to crime to pay for a drug habit.

INFOLINK

See Chapter 26 for more information on health risks.

When teens use alcohol and other drugs, they face serious consequences that can affect them for life. Long-lasting physical, psychological, and emotional problems can interfere with how well teens perform in school or at work. They may frequently fight with parents and show off a "don't care" attitude. Since their use of alcohol and other drugs is against the law, they may face serious legal troubles.

Drug abuse problems in a family can cause anger, frustration, and pain. The result is often damaged or broken families. But the family isn't the only unit to suffer. Drug abuse impacts society, too. A society plagued by drug abuse becomes equally damaged. Obviously, the way to halt the cycle is to stop substance abuse in its tracks—with the individual.

➤ Family support is essential to overcoming a chemical dependency. Family counseling or drug treatment may be necessary to solve the problems.

Considering Solutions

Prevention is the best solution to the problem of drug abuse. If you don't start using alcohol or any other drug you won't have a problem. That means resisting any pressure from peers to try drugs, and avoiding places where drugs will be available. Saying "no" to drugs might be difficult at times, but doing so could prevent a lifetime of problems.

VIOLENCE IN THE HOME

Another kind of abuse occurs when one person harms or threatens another's physical or mental health. Abuse can harm any member of a family—a **spouse** (*one's husband or wife*), child, disabled person, or older adult.

Abuse may take various forms:

- Leila grew up feeling that she was worthless. Constant put-downs from her mother fueled this *emotional abuse.*
- Mr. Turner *physically abused* his wife by hitting her when he was angry.
- *Neglect* was cited when two small children were found in an apartment without food or adult supervision.
- *Sexual abuse* occurred when a young girl was forced into sexual activity by an adult.

There is no excuse for any kind of abuse or neglect. Every type of abuse is wrong and severely damaging to the victim. Anyone who is abused needs help. An abused person must find someone who will listen and provide shelter if needed. Some teens run away from abusive situations. Sadly, running away can turn out to be just as dangerous—or even worse—than staying in the home. Strangers may take advantage of runaways and abuse them as well.

Many communities provide safe shelter for victims of abuse. You can locate them by calling 911 (or the emergency number in your area). You can also ask for a referral at a hospital emergency room or from various community organizations.

Cycles of Abuse

Any kind of abuse is destructive to families. Physical abuse usually has little, if anything, to do with the victim's actions. Instead, the abuser explodes and strikes out. After hurting an individual, the abuser often feels guilty and may be very loving and caring. However, in many cases, abuse is almost certain to repeat itself. A cycle continues within the family until help is sought.

A person who is abusive in any way needs to learn self-control. This may not happen unless victims seek help first. Unfortunately, when abused children grow into adulthood, they often repeat the same pattern in their own families. They grow up believing that striking out is the only way to vent frustration or settle disputes.

Breaking the Silence of Abuse

When someone is being neglected or abused, outside help is needed right away. Whether abuse or neglect is physical or emotional, it's harmful. Effects are long-lasting. No one has the right to neglect or abuse others, and no one should have to accept neglect or abuse.

In situations such as this, you may feel helpless or scared. You may even be confused and reluctant to take action. Even so, someone must be told so that victims can be kept safe from further harm.

First, tell your parents, guardians, or another trusted adult. Keep in mind that reports of abuse and neglect can be made *anonymously*—without giving your name. If you think the victims are in immediate danger, call the police. They'll come to the home or inform an appropriate community agency. All cases of suspected child abuse and neglect must be reported to police or government social service agencies. Under many states' laws, if a report indicates that a child is in immediate danger, a social worker must be assigned to the case and must respond immediately.

Telephone crisis hot lines may also be available in your community. The numbers are listed in the yellow pages of the phone book under "crisis hot lines" or "crisis intervention." Information given is kept confidential, and callers don't have to give their names.

What sources of help are available in your community for those experiencing abuse?

In most communities, law enforcement officials respond actively to reports of abuse. In some cases, they prosecute a suspected abuser even if the victim doesn't file charges. Offenders are usually required to seek treatment and are sometimes sent to prison.

Crime

Have you, or someone you know, been a victim of crime? It can happen to anyone. Children, teens, and people who live alone, or are elderly or disabled, feel especially at risk. Following safety rules is the best defense.

Victims of crime can become emotionally scarred. Family and friends need to rally around the victim to give support. Report any crime immediately to your local police.

When a family member commits a crime, the rest of the family suffers. The best approach is to get legal help and try to get the person's life back on track.

GETTING HELP

Most families have to deal with unexpected changes and challenges. Through love, care, and support for one another, members are better able to face stress and crisis. At times, however, seeking help outside the family is necessary to cope with problems:

- Relatives, neighbors, and friends often can provide aid in times of need.
- Many communities offer a variety of services for families. Libraries and various Web sites are useful sources of information. Police and fire departments provide assistance in emergencies. Medical services and support groups are available in most communities.
- Support groups are made up of people who have personal experience with similar problems. Religious and community organizations often provide families with services, such as crisis centers and hot lines. Professionals, including social workers, religious leaders, school counselors and trusted teachers, also can help. Remember, when you or your family can't handle a problem alone, asking for outside help is a sign of courage and maturity.

➤ **Violence in a family may lead to temporary escape from the home. Shelters offer safety, while the abuser gets professional help.**

15

Review & Activities

Chapter Summary

- Every family faces changes and challenges.
- There are positive strategies you can use to handle changes and challenges.
- Adding new family members, moving to a new community, unemployment, and financial problems can cause stress.
- Homelessness is a problem for families around the world. Various agencies provide assistance to families in need of housing.
- It helps to learn about a family member's illness or disability.
- By sharing emotions and memories, families are better able to cope with the death of a loved one.
- It's common for children to blame themselves for their parents' separation or divorce.

- Substance abuse can cause the breakdown of a family and has serious consequences for the abuser.
- Emotional, physical, and sexual abuse are severely damaging. In many cases, abuse repeats itself until help is sought.
- While most families can deal with changes and challenges, outside help is sometimes necessary.

Reviewing the Chapter

1. When is a change in a family likely to be positive or exciting? Name three major difficult challenges for families.
2. Briefly describe some of the feelings a teen may experience with the arrival of a new sibling.
3. What are three steps you can take to adjust to a new school more easily?
4. Why is it important to contact creditors when bills are overdue?
5. Why is it helpful to learn about a family member's illness or disability? List four sources of information about an illness or disability.
6. How might a funeral or memorial service help families cope with the loss of a family member?
7. How can parents help their children deal with the effects of divorce?
8. In what ways are families and society affected by substance abuse problems?
9. Why is running away from an abusive situation often an unwise decision?
10. Name six sources of help for families in times of need.

Family & Community

With Your Family

Think about some of the ways you might help if your family experiences a change or a challenge. Then talk to your parents or guardians about some of the changes and challenges their parents faced. Ask how their family members dealt with difficult problems. If faced with similar problems today, would they do the same? Why or why not?

In Your Community

There may be new residents in your community who would like to make friends and get involved in various activities. Think of volunteer activities you could do as a class to welcome new residents and make them feel part of the community.

Review & Activities

Thinking Critically

1. **Fact or fiction.** Some people think homelessness is always caused by substance abuse, people's unwillingness to work, or other faults of their own. How would you respond to this position?

2. **Make generalizations.** Which two changes and challenges do you think would be the most difficult for families to go through? Why?

3. **Predict consequences.** Describe possible consequences of neglect in a family with young children or disabled or elderly family members. What suggestions would you give those people who witness the neglect?

Making Connections

1. **Health.** By conservative estimates, several million Americans are addicted to prescription medicines. Use classroom resources to identify some of these medicines and reasons why they are prescribed initially.

2. **Language Arts.** Alcoholism is considered a disease by the American Medical Association. If not treated, alcoholism may result in the individual's death. Locate and read newspaper or magazine articles or books about individuals who died because of their alcoholism. Discuss how the abuse may have affected the individuals, their families, and society.

Applying Your Learning

1. **Write a poem.** Think about someone important in your life who died. The person may have been a relative, friend, or neighbor. Write a poem expressing what the person meant to you.

2. **Write a note of thanks.** Think of an individual who helped you or someone you know deal positively with a change or a challenge. Write a note to thank him or her for the support and assistance.

3. **Make a mobile.** Design a mobile showing various sources of help for families in your community. Display the mobile. With the class, identify and discuss some of the sources of help.

What Would You Do?

Suppose that you noticed bruises on the arms of your best friend. You ask what caused the bruises, and your friend admitted they were from an older sibling who got angry and hit her several times. Everybody in the family seems scared of him, especially when he's doing drugs. You don't want to be a snitch, but you're worried about your friend and her younger brothers and sisters. How would you handle this problem?

Career Network

LIBRARIAN

Large metropolitan library has immediate opening for librarian with supervisory experience.
• Responsibilities include public relations, fund raising, purchasing materials, and supervising employees.
• Master's degree in library science required.

SPEECH PATHOLOGIST

Speech pathologist needed to join a growing practice in evaluating and treating communication/speech disorders for regional school districts.
• Effective skills in working with preschoolers and elementary children.
• Master's degree, clinical experience, and state license required.

EMPLOYMENT COUNSELOR

Search firm specializing in placement of computer analysts/programmers needs employment counselor to interview potential candidates.
• Bachelor's degree and good communication skills needed.
• Salary plus commission.

SOCIAL WORKER

Licensed social worker needed to assist with patient recovery and rehabilitation plans. Must maintain accurate case records and help clients locate necessary services.
• Four-year degree required, Master's degree preferred.
• Must be available to work evenings and weekends.

HOME HEALTH AIDE

Caring individuals needed to work with patients in their homes providing personal care.
• Must be able to check vital signs; assist patients in bathing, exercising, and dressing.
• High school diploma, valid driver's license, and reliable transportation required.
• Training provided.

HOMEMAKERS

Dependable individuals needed to take care of homes and raise families throughout the nation.
• Responsibilities vary with age of family members.
• Ability to juggle multiple tasks is required.
• Good consumer, management, and leadership skills needed.
• Willing to work evenings, weekends, and holidays.

More Career Options

Entry Level
• Teacher Aide
• Preschool Worker
• Social Work Assistant

Technical Level
• Physical Therapy Assistant
• Dental Hygienist
• Technical Support Worker

Professional Level
• Guidance Counselor
• Pediatrician
• Family Therapist
• School Principal
• Volunteer Coordinator

CHILD PSYCHOLOGIST

School district seeks psychologist to observe, interact with, and help children who have behavior and learning problems.
• Good observation skills.
• Ability to communicate with children, teachers, and parents.
• Doctoral degree required.

CHILD CARE WORKER

Mature, dependable, creative people needed to join our teaching team! Must enjoy working with children from 6 mo. to 6 yrs. of age.
• Self–directed people with excellent communication skills should apply.
• High school diploma required.
• Course work in child development preferred.

DIR. OF YOUTH PROGRAMS

Community center needs organized director to plan and manage recreation programs.
• Will supervise staff and direct athletic programs and community events.
• Excellent leadership and people skills necessary.
• Degree in recreational programming with knowledge of first aid preferred.

PRESCHOOL TEACHER

High quality early learning center has opening for enthusiastic teacher for afternoon class of three-year olds.
• Positive work environment.
• Associate's degree and certification required.

Linking School to Career

1. **Your Career Plan:** A "want ad" is a description of a job opening. It tells what is needed for a person to get the job— the job requirements. What are job requirements? Read the want ads and write down five job requirements that you find. What would you have to do to meet the requirements that you have listed?

2. **Researching Careers:** One of the best ways to learn about a career is to talk to someone who already works in the field. Interview family members or friends about the jobs they hold. Find out about the rewards and demands of the job. Ask how the job has changed over time, and how it is expected to change in the future. Write a short report based on one of your interviews.

3. **Reading:** Look up the definitions of the following terms that are found in the want ad listings:
• Evaluate
• Public relations
• Fund raising
• Leadership

Unit 5

Relating to Children

How Children Grow

YOU WILL LEARN . . .

- ➤ The stages of child growth and development.
- ➤ How children develop physically, intellectually, emotionally, socially, and morally.
- ➤ How heredity and environment influence development.

TERMS TO LEARN . . .

- ➤ conscience
- ➤ developmental tasks
- ➤ fetus
- ➤ initiative
- ➤ toddlers

Imagine ...

... you could watch a continuous videotape of yourself from birth to adolescence. You'd see yourself as an infant laughing and crying. You'd watch yourself develop as you learn to speak, dress yourself, and tie your shoes. The videotape could teach you amazing things about yourself that you don't remember at all.

Think About

- How old do you think you were when you learned to control emotions such as laughing and crying?
- What were the first words you ever said?
- What has a parent told you about the way you grew and developed as a child?

STAGES OF DEVELOPMENT

You may remember little about your own development, but all children go through stages of development—each at his or her own rate. In each stage, *children master a number of expected skills* called **developmental tasks**. The stages of development and some key tasks include:

- **Prenatal stage**. This stage usually lasts about nine months as the **fetus**, or *unborn child*, develops inside the mother's womb. During this period, a single cell develops into a baby capable of surviving in the outside world.

- **Infancy**. This stage begins at birth and lasts about one year. Physical development occurs more quickly during infancy than at any other stage of life. One task for an infant is learning to crawl.

- **Early childhood**. Infants become **toddlers**—*from age one when they begin walking through age two*. Toddlers learn many new physical skills making them more independent.

- **Preschool**. Children ages three to five gain increasing control over their bodies. They experience a growing sense of independence and begin to learn **initiative**, *the ability to start activities on their own*.

- **Late childhood**. This stage starts around age five or six and lasts until the beginning of adolescence—usually around eleven or twelve years of age. Children learn to complete and manage tasks at school and at home and learn to interact with others.

➤ Just think! You were once like this newborn infant. You have experienced many physical and emotional changes to reach your age. Remember the past, then think about how you will continue to change.

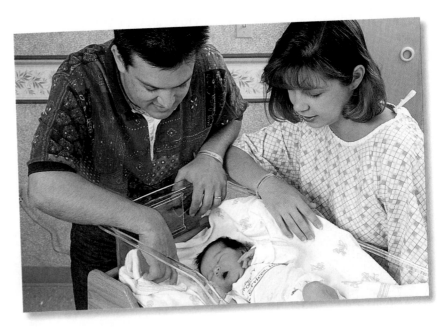

How Do They Grow?

What You'll Need
- Parenting magazines
- Paper, scissors, glue, and pen or pencil

What to Do
1. Work in a group of four. From parenting magazines, cut out 20 pictures of children from birth to age five that tell the age of the child. Glue each picture on a separate sheet of paper. Number each picture. Group the photos into infants, toddlers, preschoolers, and school-age children. Identify the type or types of development shown in each picture. On a separate sheet of paper, create a key giving the picture numbers and age of each child.
2. Exchange pictures with another group. Without looking at the ages written on the backs of the pictures, create a timeline of childhood from birth to five years of age.
3. Obtain the key from the other group and check your answers.

To Discuss
- How difficult was it to create the timeline? Would it have been easier if all the pictures had been of the same child?
- What characteristics did you observe in children at each age?

HOW CHILDREN GROW AND DEVELOP

Children grow and develop in several different ways and the types of development often take place at the same time. But the rate of growth differs for each child. The key types of children's development include:
- **Physical development.** They grow in size, muscle strength, and coordination.
- **Intellectual development.** They grow in their ability to learn, think, and judge.
- **Emotional development.** They learn to control emotions and express them in appropriate ways.
- **Social development.** They learn to interact with people.
- **Moral development.** They learn right from wrong.

Physical Development

During early childhood, physical development takes place at a rapid pace. Physical development includes the body's growth and developing abilities. See page **237** for more details about how children develop.

Intellectual Development

The first years of life are crucial to intellectual development. During this period, the brain is developing rapidly. A child who is talked to and given many different experiences develops more brain connections, which improve the speed and ease of learning. As children grow intellectually, they gradually understand more words and concepts. They're able to pay attention longer as they grow older.

Infants learn with their eyes, ears, mouths, and hands. Colorful toys, simple books, and songs provide learning experiences. So does talking to the baby.

One of the main intellectual skills young children learn is language. Most children begin to speak words and phrases around the middle of their second year. By the third year, most speak full sentences. They can connect two thoughts, such as, "The oven is hot and can burn me!"

By the fourth year, most children seem to ask questions continually. Children need to hear words in order to learn to speak, think, and understand language. They must also have someone they trust to communicate with.

➤ Children have curiosity about life. They respond emotionally to almost everything.

Emotional Development

At first, infants show emotions only by body movements and facial expressions. They show they're unhappy or un-

Physical Growth & Development

Infancy

During the first year, healthy infants:

- Triple their birth weight and increase their height.

- Develop the ability to see, hear, and use their other senses.

- Begin to develop motor skills—skills that allow them to use and control their muscles. Movements begin at the head and gradually work toward other parts of the body.

- Begin to move around and explore their world. With increased strength and muscle control, infants can get up on their knees and crawl.

- Develop hand-eye coordination, the ability to move their hands precisely in relation to what is seen. They learn to pick up items, including food.

Toddlers

During early childhood, toddlers become more independent and capable of doing things for themselves. Signs of physical growth and development during this stage include:

- Increased weight and height.

- The appearance of teeth.

- Further development of motor skills. Most toddlers can hold and drink from a cup, turn on a faucet, and button large buttons. They also can walk, run, climb, and jump.

- Changes in sleeping habits, usually requiring less sleep than before.

- Development of muscles that control elimination. Toilet training usually begins between the ages of eighteen months and three years.

Preschool

The preschool stage involves vigorous activity and practice and refining of physical skills. Signs of increased physical development are:

- Increased weight and height, with legs lengthening rapidly.

- Continued development of basic motor skills.

- Ability to get dressed and undressed.

- Greater coordination of finger, arm, and hand movements.

- Stay calm and speak softly to the child.

- Distract the child. Get out a favorite book, puzzle, or toy, or look out the window together. Try to entice the child to sit down with you to talk and play.

- Try holding the child. Holding a child firmly and affectionately during a tantrum helps some younger children regain control. The hold may turn into a hug as composure is regained.

➤ **A child experiences all forms of development at the same time. This child is learning social development skills.** What do you remember as your first feeling of learning independence?

comfortable by crying, kicking, and squirming. They respond with pleasure when being fed, rocked, or when someone speaks soothingly to them. It is very important to respond to a baby's needs positively.

As children grow older, their emotions become more specific. Toddlers' emotions change rapidly. They may cry one moment and laugh the next. Gradually, children learn to express joy, anger, fear, curiosity, jealousy, and affection. As they grow older, children learn to control their emotions more effectively.

Social Development

Social development involves learning to interact with people in socially acceptable ways. Here are some social tasks that children learn during early childhood:

- **Trusting others.** Children learn to trust when their caregivers feed them, answer their cries, and show them love and affection.
- **Learning independence.** Parents help their children become independent. By making their surroundings safe, parents allow children to learn by exploring. By choosing clothing that's easy for children to put on, parents make it easier for children to learn to dress themselves. This helps give children confidence to learn other skills.

- **Learning acceptable behavior.** A two-year-old may scream, "No, No!" when told to share a toy with another child. At age three, he may clutch a toy tightly and refuse to share it. By age five, through consistent interactions with his parents and other children, he usually learns to share his toys.

Moral Development

Moral development grows as children start to learn right from wrong. Children gain a foundation in moral development mainly in the home, at school, or in places of worship.

At first, young children don't understand the difference between right and wrong. They only know that some behavior makes adults upset and that other behavior makes them happy. Gradually, with help from parents and caregivers, they develop a **conscience**, *an inner sense of right or wrong.* This helps children monitor their own behavior.

WHAT INFLUENCES DEVELOPMENT?

Have you ever wondered what makes people unique or special? Two factors work together to shape you into a one-of-a-kind individual. These are heredity and environment.

> ➤ Learning not to take things without permission, helps children develop an inner sense of right and wrong.

Heredity and Environment

Heredity refers to all the traits you inherit from your parents. These traits include your body type and the color of your hair, skin, and eyes. You also inherit certain abilities, such as being musical or artistic.

Environment is what surrounds you and affects your development and behavior. The way a family treats a child and the opportunities a child has to grow and develop are environmental influences.

Both heredity and environment are responsible for how children grow and develop. Children need both the ability and the opportunity to learn. Without positive interactions and a good educational environment at home and at school, children may not develop the full range of their abilities.

Family

Even though many aspects in a child's environment are important, none quite compares to the importance of family. Praise, encouragement, and support from family members are crucial to developing healthy self-esteem. Children who feel good about themselves are better able to work hard to complete challenging tasks. Children who aren't encouraged often feel insecure about themselves and become afraid to try new things.

Families help children develop their learning ability by working together on projects at home, such as gardening or building models, taking family trips to museums, and reading to each other.

➤ Heredity affects how you look and your ability to grow and develop. What evidence of heredity can you see in these two children?

Special Needs

Some children have special needs that require special help from parents and caregivers. The children may have a physical disability that inhibits normal movement or a mental disability that inhibits intellectual development. Some children experience emotional disability that affects behavior patterns. Others experience learning disabilities, while still others are highly intelligent, gifted, children.

All of these children require some assistance to help them cope with their special needs and achieve their potential. Other than that, they want to be treated just like other children and they have the same basic needs for praise, support, and encouragement as anyone else. Many schools today have a policy of inclusion: children with special needs are placed in regular classes with others their age.

School

At school, children gain knowledge and skills that prepare them for life. Schools also teach important ideas about social behavior and ethics. In school, children learn to relate to people outside the family. At school, children further develop their personality and self-concept. While studying different subjects and meeting new people, children learn more about their own likes and dislikes, as well as their strengths and weaknesses. The world opens up to them through education.

Knowing how children develop and what influences shape development help you better understand yourself and others. If you babysit for children, take care of them, or decide to become a parent, learning about child development gives you important childcare skills to use all your life.

➤ **Providing an environment of learning greatly affects a child's development.** How can you help a child learn?

Chapter Summary

- All children go through specific stages of development, each at his or her own rate.
- Children master certain developmental tasks during each stage of development.
- Physical development is the most rapid during the first year of life.
- Stages of development include physical, intellectual, emotional, social, and moral development.
- Emotional development involves learning to express feelings in appropriate ways. Social development involves learning to interact with others.
- Moral development includes the development of an or inner sense of right or wrong.
- Both heredity and environment influence children's growth and development.

With Your Family

Make a list of some favorite experiences you had with your family when you were younger. Write a brief report explaining how these experiences influenced your growth and development—physically, mentally, emotionally, socially, or morally.

In Your Community

Families in many communities can use assistance in helping their young children grow and develop to their fullest capacity. As a class, brainstorm ways to help families in your community. List some volunteer activities you could do to help out.

- Children inherit physical traits from their parents. They also inherit certain abilities.
- Children with special needs require assistance to help them meet their potential, but otherwise have the same basic needs as other children.
- Praise, encouragement, and support from family members help children develop healthy self-esteem.

Reviewing the Chapter

1. Briefly describe the five stages of a child's development.
2. Name and describe five types of development.
3. What is the main intellectual skill learned by young children?
4. How do young infants show they are unhappy or uncomfortable?
5. Name three ways that caregivers help children learn to trust others.
6. Give an example of how parents can help a child learn independence.
7. What is moral development? Name three places where children may gain a foundation in moral development.
8. What is the difference between heredity and environment? Give an example of each one.
9. Why is the development of healthy self-esteem important in a child's life?
10. What role does school play in children's growth and development?

Review & Activities

Thinking Critically

1. **Predict consequences.** Describe what might happen to a child in the following situations: a child imitates an older sibling who has an explosive temper; a caregiver frequently makes fun of a young child's efforts at independence; a child's parents seldom spend time reading or speaking to her.

2. **Draw conclusions.** How might parents encourage a preschooler's moral development? What influences do you think played a part in your moral development? Why?

3. **Fact or fiction.** Some people think that heredity is the most important influence on a child. Others feel that a child's environment is the most important. How would you respond to these two positions? Why?

Making Connections

1. **Art.** Design an advertisement for a toy suitable for children in certain stages of development. Share your advertisement with the class, and discuss why the toy is appropriate for the particular age range.

2. **Reading.** As part of a childcare kit, start a card reference file of library books that young children might enjoy. Include the author, title, appropriate ages, and a brief description of the book. Include space to write notes about children's responses to the book.

Applying Your Learning

1. **Design children's car games.** Think of educational games that could make special use of the time families spend in the car. Write down your ideas, and share them in class.

2. **Create puppets.** In a small group, create a puppet show to teach young children a basic skill, such as counting or making a snack. Present your show to preschool children you know.

3. **Identify developmental toys.** Look through toy catalogs or advertisements for toys that encourage a toddler's physical development. Next, identify toys that may assist intellectual development. Select two of the most appropriate toys in each category and discuss the reasons for your choices with the class.

What Would You Do?

Suppose you're at a friend's house while he cares for his two-year-old sister. The toddler is very active and wants her brother's full attention. Your friend has little patience with the toddler and yells at her to sit down and be quiet. He gets angry when the child starts to cry. You don't want to get in the middle of the situation, but you feel sorry for the little girl. How would you handle this problem?

17

Caring for Children

YOU WILL LEARN . . .

➤ How to care for children of various ages.
➤ How to prepare meals and snacks for children.
➤ How to keep children safe.
➤ What to do in an emergency.

TERMS TO LEARN . . .

➤ first aid classes
➤ poison control center

Imagine ...

... you're asked to take care of your cousin's one-year-old baby. There's no one else who can care for the child. You have taken care of older children before, but have never been responsible for a baby.

Think About

- What would you do if the baby starts to cry?
- What would you feed the baby if it's hungry?
- What would you do if the baby started to get sick or choke?
- What would you do before accepting the responsibility?

CHILD CARE: AN IMPORTANT RESPONSIBILITY

CHILD CARE BASICS

Follow these tips for taking safe care of children:

- Learn about a child care job before you go: time and date, names and ages of children, how long parents will be gone, and transportation details. Also, agree on your fee.

- Write down the name, address, and phone number of the family. Give this information to your family.

- Arrive about 15 minutes early for the job. This gives children time to get used to you before parents leave.

- Get emergency phone numbers—doctor, poison control center, fire, and police. Also, write down the phone number where parents can be reached.

- Ask parents for special instructions about medication, meals or snacks, and bathing and bedtime routines.

- Have parents show you the children's rooms, bathroom, and first aid supplies.

- Stay with the children at all times. When they go to sleep, check on them frequently.

Rosa's first job was as a baby-sitter. She quickly learned that *baby-sitter* isn't a very accurate term. In fact, most of her jobs since have been caring for young children, not babies. She also usually doesn't have much time for sitting—except when children are asleep.

There may be times when you are asked to care for the children of family, friends, or neighbors. Caring for children is a very important responsibility. When you know what to expect, you can do a better job. Remember, the children's safety and welfare are your responsibility.

➤ **Babies feel secure when they are held by a caring parent or caregiver.** What are some ways to hold a baby safely and comfortably?

Caring for Infants

Children of different ages have different needs. For example, infants need a lot of physical care and protection. You need to know how to hold them firmly while supporting their head and neck. Never leave babies on a bed, sofa, or other surface where they can wiggle and fall off. Also, keep harmful objects out of their reach.

When babies cry, find out what's troubling them. Are they cold or too warm? Maybe they're hungry, sick, or have a wet diaper. Changing diapers is a frequent and necessary part of child care. Make sure all necessary supplies are nearby before you begin.

Caring for Toddlers and Preschoolers

The needs of toddlers and preschoolers are different from those of infants. For example, toddlers tend to be into everything, so safety is a real concern. They need to be watched every moment.

Preschoolers also need your attention, but they can do more for themselves. They like being read to, played with, and talked to.

Caring for School-Age Children

Caring for older children can be a challenge. Some children may feel they're too old to need your care. Others may be jealous of attention given to younger children. Some may try to get away with behavior their parents don't allow.

Try to make friends right away with older children. Show a sincere interest in their ideas and activities. If a child deliberately misbehaves, remain calm. Be fair, but firm. Often the most effective discipline has a clear connection to the misbehavior. For example, if a child bumps into others with a tricycle after being told not to, you might take away the tricycle for a while. Often children who misbehave are really looking for attention. Try playing a game or reading a book together.

BATHING A BABY

Follow these tips for safety and comfort when giving a small infant a bath:

- Check water temperature before putting a baby into a tub. Make sure the water isn't too hot or too cool.

- Put a towel or rubber mat in the tub to make the baby comfortable and prevent slipping. Keep the baby seated in the tub.

- Place the baby in the tub with a secure grip. Hold the baby under the arm with your wrist supporting the back and head. Start by washing the baby's face with clear water, and pat it dry. Continue to wash and rinse the rest of the baby's body.

- Don't let the baby drink bath water or suck on a washcloth. Instead, offer the baby a drink of fresh water or a teething toy to suck on.

- Lift the baby from the water with a secure grip. Place the infant on a clean towel, and immediately wrap the towel around the baby to prevent chilling, Then gently pat the baby dry.

Making a

DIFFERENCE

HELPING OUT

Rafael's older sister phoned to ask, "Could you take care of Maria while I go to the dentist this afternoon?" Maria was her two-year-old daughter.

"I can't," Rafael replied. "I've a got a baseball game after school."

"I don't know who else to ask," she said. "I can't find a sitter on such short notice."

"Besides," Rafael said, "I'm not sure I'd know what to do if she gets hungry."

"I thought you told me you studied child care in one of your classes," his sister said. "If you come early, I'll show you exactly what to do."

Rafael knew his sister wouldn't ask the favor if she didn't really need him. It might be fun, since he loved playing with his niece. "Okay," he agreed. "What time?"

Taking Action

1. If you wanted to learn more about caring for a child, what resources might be available to you other than in class?
2. What could Rafael do to make his time with his niece fun for both of them?

INFOLINK

See Chapters 28 and 29 for more nutrition information.

MEALS AND SNACKS

Sometimes caregivers are responsible for feeding children while their parents are away. Find out from the parents what food should be served and when. Are other foods off limits? Remember that young children eat smaller servings than you do. Here are tips for feeding children:

- **Infants.** When caring for an infant, you may need to feed him or her a bottle of formula left by the parent with instructions. Before feeding, put a bib on the infant to protect clothing. You can feed an infant formula at room temperature, or warm it by placing the bottle in warm water for several minutes. Check the formula's temperature by shaking a drop out on the inside of your wrist. It should feel warm, not hot. (Never warm a bottle in a microwave oven. The liquid might get dangerously hot.) You will need to burp the baby during and after eating.

Older infants may be eating baby cereal or baby food. Be prepared for messiness. Protect the baby's clothes and your own. The child is likely to play with the food, as well as eat it. That's normal. Be sure to make mealtimes fun and enjoyable.

- **Toddlers.** Toddlers can eat some regular food. They like simple finger foods—small, bite-sized pieces they can pick up with their fingers. Use a bib to protect a child's clothes. If you need to use a high chair, keep it in a safe, easy-to-clean place. Never give young children hard candy, nuts, or any other food that might cause choking.
- **Preschoolers.** Simple foods, such as milk, cheese, crackers, peanut butter, fresh and dried fruit, and vegetable sticks are popular and healthful foods for preschoolers. Preschoolers may lack good manners, but they're somewhat skilled at eating. Avoid foods that are high in fat and sugar. Check with parents about any food allergies, special diets, or other restrictions.

➤ Eating is a new skill for babies. Be prepared for a messy situation when you care for infants.

BEDTIME

When caring for young children, bedtime is often a challenge. Toddlers and preschoolers may not want to go to bed because they like to play. Ask parents what their routine is, and follow it. Putting on pajamas, brushing their teeth, and a quiet story can help prepare children physically and

> Bedtime for a child should be a consistent routine. A quiet activity helps prepare a child for bedtime.

emotionally for bed. If children are awakened by a bad dream, cuddle and comfort them until they go back to sleep.

KEEPING CHILDREN SAFE

Caring for children requires your full attention—to them and to their surroundings. Make sure those under your care are safe, both inside and outside the home.

> Those who care for children must always think of safe ways of providing that care.

Indoors

When caring for small children, think about how *they* see things. Check for anything on the floor that could hurt a crawling baby. Look for any small items young children might swallow. Remove items from tables that infants or toddlers might pull off.

To keep children safe, stay with them all the time. Don't leave young children in the bathroom alone. They may lock themselves inside or get into medicine cabinets. When you bathe a child, *never* leave him or her alone in a bathtub.

Play with Children

Children need to play in order to grow and learn. In fact, play is sometimes called children's work.

- **Infants.** Turn routine activities into games for infants. Sing, talk, make eye contact, or imitate the baby's sounds. Choose safe toys and objects to catch the baby's attention.

- **Toddlers.** Toddlers enjoy simple toys that can be taken apart and put together again. Safe household items, such as measuring cups and spoons, are also ideal. So are simple puzzles, storybooks, large crayons, and paper. Walking and running are fun, too.

- **Preschoolers.** Make-believe play lets children try out different roles. Old clothes, hats, jewelry, shoes, puppets, and other toys let children create fantasy situations.

Infants and younger toddlers can easily fall down stairs. Keep them away from stairs and fasten any gates at stairways. Older toddlers and preschoolers need to be taught to hold onto a handrail to prevent falls.

Doors and Windows

Make sure that all windows and outside doors are locked when small children are around. Safety is especially important in high-rise apartments where windows may be high above the ground.

During an emergency:

- **Stay as calm as possible.** This helps reassure a child and helps you think more clearly.
- **Evaluate the situation.** What seems to be wrong? Is the child burned, bleeding, or unconscious?
- **Make the child comfortable.** Use a blanket, jacket, or large towel if a child is cold.
- **Call for help if needed.** If you aren't certain what the problem is or how to care for the injury, contact the child's parents, a neighbor, a doctor, or 911.
- **Give the minimum necessary first aid treatment.** Knowing what you should "not" do in an emergency is as important as knowing what you should do. Some injuries, such as broken bones, can be made worse by moving an injured person. If you don't know what to do, get help from someone better trained.

Poisons, Matches, and Lighters

Ordinary household products can be very dangerous for children. Some are poisonous if swallowed. Others cause damage if inhaled into the lungs or if they come into contact with skin or eyes. Common poisons include insecticides, cleaning supplies, and drugs such as aspirin and vitamin pills. Here are some typical symptoms of poisoning:

- Choking, coughing, stomach pain, or dizziness.
- Unconsciousness or difficulty breathing.
- Vomiting.
- Skin rashes or burns.

If you think a child has been poisoned, immediately call 911 or a poison control center, hospital emergency room, or doctor right away. **Poison control centers** are *special hospital units that advise and treat poison victims*. Staff members will tell you exactly what to do.

Other dangers include matches and lighters, which can be deadly. Keep them out of reach of all children. Also, keep children away from ranges, heaters, hot-water faucets, and hot drinks.

Toys

Some toys can be dangerous to small children. Be sure each toy you give a baby is clean, unbreakable, too large to swallow, free of sharp edges, and has no small parts that could be swallowed.

Some loud-sounding toys can scare small children and even damage hearing. Toys with long strings or cords may cause choking. Never hang toys with long strings, cords, loops, or ribbons in cribs or playpens where children might get tangled in them.

Remember toy safety for older children, too. Check to see that toys are in good working condition. Don't let children play with broken toys. They should wear safety equipment for activities such as biking and rollerblading.

Outdoors

Caregivers must supervise young children at all times wherever they go. This includes:

- **Playgrounds.** Playgrounds should have a soft surface, such as shredded tires, beneath equipment.
- **Streets and roads.** Never let children play in streets or roads. Make sure older children know how to cross streets safely and do so. Bicycle safety rules may need to be reviewed.
- **Wading and swimming pools.** Watch children closely when they're in a wading or swimming pool.

HANDLING EMERGENCIES

Would you know what to do if a child fell from a swing or into a swimming pool? You may have to take emergency action that affects a child's safety. **First aid classes**, offered in schools and through the American Red Cross and other community agencies, *provide instruction in basic emergency care.* Contact your school nurse or the nearest office of the American Red Cross about first aid classes.

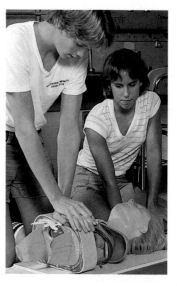

➤ Emergencies occur more often than you think. Take first aid courses in basic emergency care. Courses are available in schools and through community agencies.

▼TRY IT OUT

Storybook Puppet Show

ACTIVITY

What You'll Need
- Children's storybooks appropriate for children ages three to five
- Paper lunch bags
- Crayons or markers, glue, construction paper

What to Do
1. Choose a storybook. As you read the story, make a list of the characters and their descriptions.
2. Using paper lunch bags, crayons, glue, and construction paper, create puppets to represent each character in the story.

To Discuss
- To what age child would this story appeal? How would you use the puppets?
- How could you use this idea if you were baby-sitting both school-age children and preschoolers?

Review & Activities

Chapter Summary

- Child care is an important responsibility. If you know what to expect, you can do a better job.
- Infants require a lot of physical care and protection.
- School-age children may feel they are too old to need your care. Try to make friends with them and take an interest in their activities.
- Most caregivers are responsible for preparing and serving children healthy meals and snacks.
- Following regular routines can help when preparing children for bedtime.
- Young children need supervision both indoors and outdoors at all times.
- Keep dangerous household products out of reach of all children. If you suspect a child has been poisoned, summon help immediately.
- First aid classes can help you learn what to do in case of a child care emergency.

Reviewing the Chapter

1. Why is *baby-sitter* an inaccurate term?
2. Briefly explain how caring for infants is different from caring for toddlers and preschoolers.
3. Give four suggestions for caring for older children.
4. Why is it important not to warm a baby's bottle in a microwave oven?
5. List six simple and nutritious foods that are popular with preschoolers.
6. What is the most important step a caregiver can take to keep children safe?
7. Name four symptoms of poisoning.
8. Why is it important to keep toys with long strings or cords away from infants and young children?
9. Where can people go for classes to learn to handle emergencies involving children's safety?

Family & Community

With Your Family

Think about your favorite playtimes as a young child. Did the playtimes involve certain family members? Favorite toys or family pets? Write about one of these experiences and share your written memories with family members.

In Your Community

As a class, research what's needed in your community to meet recreational needs of children. Brainstorm creative and low-cost activities you could do as a class to help children.

Review & Activities

Thinking Critically

1. **Make generalizations.** How would you rank your own child care qualifications? Why? What actions can you take to develop or enhance your qualifications?

2. **Fact or fiction.** "If you have younger siblings, you know how to take care of children." Think about the responsibilities of child care. Does having younger siblings qualify someone as a good caregiver? Explain.

3. **Predict consequences.** What consequences might occur if a teen takes a job caring for toddlers and has no knowledge or experience in child care.

Making Connections

1. **Health.** Conduct a study of community resources dealing with child safety, such as a local poison control center, children's hospital, Red Cross chapter, etc. Make a list of each resource and a description of the help available.

2. **Drama.** With a partner, write a scene in which a teen calls from someone's home with a child care emergency. On the other end of the phone is someone at a hospital giving advice about the situation. Present the scene, then discuss how well each person handled the emergency.

Applying Your Learning

1. **Write an emergency list.** Develop a list of emergency numbers, names and ages of relatives, addresses, etc. that you can refer to when caring for children.

2. **Create a toy exhibit.** Collect a variety of toys appropriate for children of various ages. Arrange the toys according to their appropriateness for infants, toddlers, and preschoolers. What can a child learn from each toy?

3. **Interview a peer.** Interview one or more teens who frequently have jobs caring for children. Make a list of questions, including what suggestions they have for feeding children, keeping them safe, handling bedtimes, and playing with children.

What Would You Do?

Suppose one of your friends frequently takes care of an infant and a three-year-old until 11:00 each night. Your friend has confided in you that the job is tiring and that she often falls asleep after putting the children to bed. Last night she failed to hear the toddler get out of bed and didn't wake up until the child asked her for a drink. She needs the job to help with her family's finances, but the children need someone who is alert and awake. How would you handle this situation?

Understanding Parenting

YOU WILL LEARN . . .

- ➤ Factors to consider when deciding whether to be a parent.
- ➤ The special problems teen parents face.
- ➤ The responsibilities of parenthood.
- ➤ Guidelines for handling discipline.
- ➤ Resources available to parents.

TERMS TO LEARN . . .

- ➤ discipline
- ➤ immunization
- ➤ nurturing
- ➤ parenting

Imagine ...

... you had to take a test before you could become a parent. You'd be tested on how much you honestly wanted to raise a child. You'd have to answer questions on how much you knew about caring for children. And you'd have to explain how you planned to financially support a child.

Think About

- Have you thought about raising a child in the future? What are your thoughts?
- How much money do you think it would take to raise a child? How would you earn the money?
- How would you do on the test?

THE PARENTING QUESTION

What if everyone had to pass a test before they could become parents? Even though becoming a parent is a very important job, no test, license, or training is required. Instead, for many people, parenthood happens with little preparation. Some people give little thought about whether having a child is the right decision for them.

Deciding to Be a Parent

People have children for various reasons. Not all reasons are good ones. Some people may feel pressure from family or friends to have children. However, any potential parent needs to seriously consider whether the decision to have children is the right one.

Before deciding, couples need to ask themselves, "Do we want to have children?" For many people, having children because they want them is the right decision. Having children because of pressure from others isn't a good reason. Choosing not to have children may be the right decision for some people.

Couples who are committed to loving and caring for children may face a second question: when to have children. At this point, they need to ask themselves:

- "Have we finished our education?"
- "Do we have enough money to support ourselves and the baby on our own?"
- "What do we know about babies and the responsibilities of parenthood?"
- "Are we willing—and able—to make personal sacrifices needed to care for another person?"

Answers to these questions and others like them can help a couple decide if and when to have children. Waiting to have children can give some couples a better start in life. It also makes it easier to raise children later, when parents are ready.

➤ There are important decisions to make when planning to have a child. The first is to "plan" to have a child.

Teen Parents

Becoming parents too soon disrupts the lives of teens and is also very hard on children. Many children are raised by teen parents who are not ready to be good parents. They don't have the resources, knowledge, and skills to raise children.

Having a child greatly limits teens' choices for the future. The time, energy, and money needed to raise a child are far greater than most teens can imagine. Often the responsibility to raise a child falls onto the mother. Although some teen fathers take an active role in parenting, many don't live up to their responsibilities. If either parent drops out of school, the lack of a high school diploma is a lifelong barrier to a good job, and completing school becomes difficult.

Think about your plans for yourself and your future. Where do you want to be in 5 years, 10 years, 15 years? Would having a child fit into your plans? The happiest and healthiest children are those who are born to parents who honestly want and are ready for them. The decision to become a parent is a permanent one. A child's birth changes the lives of the parents—and their families—forever.

➤ **Parenthood requires a great deal of responsibility. Teen parents must make many personal sacrifices to care for a child.**

THE RESPONSIBILITIES OF PARENTING

"Isn't that baby cute? I'd love to have one of my own to play with," Melissa said. Like Melissa, many teens only see the cute side of babies and have little or no understanding of what parenting really involves. **Parenting**, *the process of caring for children and guiding their growth and development*, is demanding work.

Parenting requires knowledge of child growth and development. It also requires teaching, counseling, and even nursing skills. Large amounts of patience, understanding, and a sense of humor are needed, too. Unfortunately, many parents learn these difficult skills by trial and error. Taking time to learn them ahead of time can help.

To balance work and family life:

- Consider your values. Which is more important to you: a spotless house and little time for family, or a picked-up house and time to be with your family?

- Share child care and household tasks with your spouse.

- Consider dividing tasks, with one parent caring for children while the other works to support a child.

- Consider working from home part-time. This may allow one or both parents to arrange working hours to suit the family schedule.

➤ **Children can cause physical and emotional fatigue for parents. You can give parents a break by offering to care for the children.**

Parenting skills aren't just for parents. Many people help raise children. Relatives, friends, and professional child care workers need parenting skills just as much as parents do.

Meeting Children's Physical Needs

Food, clothing, and shelter are only some of the physical needs of children. Children also need plenty of rest and exercise. Medical care and *protection against common childhood diseases*—with **immunizations**—must also be provided. A mature parent is better able to take care of children's many needs.

➤ **Immunization is important to protect against common childhood diseases. This is only one responsibility for the physical care of a child.** Name some of the physical needs of infants.

- **Teaching children.** Children begin learning as soon as they're born. Parents must provide the tools and opportunities for intellectual development of their children. What can you as a parent do to help children learn? Talk, read, and listen to children from the time they're born. Provide opportunities for children to play and learn. Most communities offer various resources, such as library story hours, that help meet children's intellectual needs.

- **Nurturing children.** Children need a lot of **nurturing**—*the giving of love, affection, attention, and encouragement.* Nurturing makes children feel secure and accepted. It gives them a sense of worth and confidence. It also helps them relate well to others. Children who learn to be comfortable with themselves can reach out to others more easily.

- **Guiding children.** Through effective guidance and discipline, parents help children learn to behave in acceptable ways. Many people think of guidance or discipline only in terms of punishment. But effective **discipline** *helps children learn to get along with others and control their own feelings.* Gradually, children begin to see why certain actions are right or wrong. They learn to manage their own behavior and take responsibility for their actions.

➤ **Children grow and learn through playing.** Why do you think that play is important?

BEING A POSITIVE EXAMPLE TO CHILDREN

Here are some ways to be a positive example:

- Discuss with children the importance of respecting people of all ages, races, and backgrounds.

- Show children healthy ways to deal with anger and frustration.

- Talk with children about the importance of sharing their feelings.

- Set an example to encourage children to read, eat nutritious foods, and get plenty of exercise.

➤ **Love is the most important need of a child. Those who are nurtured learn to nurture others throughout their lives.**

➤ Praise is an important part of guiding children. It makes them feel good about themselves, while encouraging them to do and be their best.

Encouraging Good Behavior

Encouraging good behavior is an important task for parents. Many times, it can be a demanding task. Here are some ways to encourage desired behavior:

- **Set clear limits.** By setting clear limits for behavior, children learn what is acceptable, appropriate, and safe for them to do.
- **Set good examples.** Young children often imitate what adults say and do. Setting the right example by appropriate behavior often works better than long explanations about how a child should act.

➤ Adults must set limits for children to follow. Limits guide children by letting them know what is acceptable and safe for them to do.

- **Give simple explanations.** As children grow, they need simple explanations about expected behavior. When they've done something wrong, children need to know why it's wrong and what should be done instead. Messages must match a child's age and level of understanding. For example, with a younger child you might say, "pet the dog," along with a simple demonstration With an older child you could say, "It hurts the dog when you pull his ears. You have to be gentle to play with him."
- **Give praise.** Children feel good about themselves when they receive genuine praise for appropriate behavior. They're also more likely to continue the desired behavior.

Handling Misbehavior

When children break the rules, caregivers need to respond. Discipline should be immediate and fit the misbehavior. The goal is to help children learn proper behavior. Knowing when to punish misbehavior can be tricky. A mistake is not misbehavior. Don't get angry with a child who drops a glass of milk because she lacks coordination. Instead, teach and help her to clean up the spill. A child who pulls up a plant by its roots may be trying to learn what makes it grow. In this case, you need to explain, not punish. If a child leaves something undone, ask him or her to return to the task to finish it.

Deliberate misbehavior calls for a reaction that fits a child's level of understanding and the misbehavior. Taking away a privilege, such as not allowing a child to go outdoors to play, is one example. Having the child sit quietly without toys or distractions for a few minutes is another way to deal with misbehavior.

Ignoring misbehavior is another form of discipline. Some children whine when they want something at a store. When parents give in, children learn that whining works. If parents decide to ignore the behavior after giving a simple "no," children usually give up whining because it no longer produces results.

PARENTING RESOURCES

Caring for children is demanding both physically and emotionally. Anyone who cares for children needs some time away on a regular basis. Many couples share child care so that the responsibility doesn't fall on only one parent.

Couples need time to themselves, too. If a paid baby-sitter isn't possible, family members and friends may be willing to help. Also, consider taking turns with other parents to care for each other's children.

HANDLING MISBEHAVIOR

Try these tips for handling misbehavior:

- Be consistent in your words and actions.
- Let children know you mean what you say.
- Never allow discipline to be an outlet for your anger or frustration. Self-control is crucial.
- Make sure children understand that you still love them, even when you disapprove of their behavior.

➤ **Teach children the difference between mistakes or accidents and deliberate misbehavior.**

Chapter Summary

- Choosing to become a parent is one of the most important decisions a person ever makes.
- People have children for various reasons, but not all of the reasons are good ones.
- Teen parents often lack the resources, knowledge, and readiness needed to be good parents.
- Children are happiest and healthiest if they are born to parents who want and are ready for them.
- Parenting skills are useful not only to parents, but to relatives, friends, and professional child care workers.
- Caregivers and parents can help children learn by talking, reading, and listening to them from the time the children are born.

Family & Community

With Your Family

Talk to your family about what they learned while caring for children. Which parenting experiences were the most rewarding to them? Which were the most challenging?

In Your Community

Some infants must stay in the hospital for an extended period of time due to illness. Often community volunteers are trained to provide additional cuddling and attention for some babies. As a class, brainstorm ways you could publicize this and recruit volunteers.

- Parents encourage good behavior by setting clear limits, setting good examples, giving simple explanations, and praising children for good behavior.
- Effective discipline is immediate and fits the misbehavior. Taking away a privilege or ignoring misbehavior can be an effective form of discipline.

Reviewing the Chapter

1. What question do couples need to ask themselves before deciding whether to have children?
2. List four questions couples need to ask themselves about *when* to have children?
3. How does parenthood disrupt the lives of teens? Why is teen parenthood hard on children?
4. Name three skills needed for parenting. Who, besides parents, may find parenting skills useful?
5. How can caregivers and parents help children learn?
6. What is nurturing? Why is it important to a child?
7. What is the goal of discipline?
8. Briefly describe four ways parents and caregivers can encourage good behavior.
9. Describe an instance in which effective discipline fits a child's behavior.
10. Give an example of when it may be appropriate for a parent or caregiver to ignore misbehavior.

Thinking Critically

1. **Analyze behavior.** Spend some time at a children's playground observing interactions between caregivers and children. Analyze the ways caregivers provide guidance for behavior. Which methods are appropriate for the age of the children? Which should be changed? Why?

2. **Make a generalization.** When do you think is the ideal time for a married couple to have children? Why?

3. **Fact or fiction.** Think about some of the teen parents in your community. Is it true that the responsibility to raise a child falls mainly on the mother? If so, what steps would you suggest to encourage fathers to accept greater parental responsibility?

Making Connections

1. **Language Arts.** Write a short story about a couple's adjustment to life with a new baby. Be sure to include ways in which the couple's lives have changed.

2. **Health.** Use class, library, or Internet resources to research the nutritional requirements women have during pregnancy.

Applying Your Learning

1. **Demonstrate.** With a partner, prepare brief skits in which one is a caregiver and the other a child. The aim of the skits is to demonstrate caregiver behaviors that will promote the healthy development of the child. Focus on intellectual, physical, social, and emotional development.

2. **Discuss.** Discuss the meaning of the following statements: parenting never ends; parenting is the mother's responsibility. Do you agree or disagree with your classmates? Why?

3. **Describe a good parent.** Complete the following statement: My idea of a good parent is..."

What Would You Do?

Suppose one of your neighbors is a young mother, living with her parents.

When her baby starts to cry, your neighbor frequently gets angry. Today, she confided in you by saying, "Sometimes I feel like shaking him. He makes me so mad when he won't stop crying." You don't want to interfere in your neighbor's life, but you know that shaking a baby can cause brain damage and other serious injury. How would you handle this problem?

Career Network

LANDSCAPE ARCHITECT

Metropolitan park district seeks certified landscape architect to assist with the design, development, and improvement of city park facilities.
• Manage new and renovation projects through all phases.
• Bachelor's degree required.

ENVIRONMENTAL ENGINEER

State government agency has immediate opening for an environmental engineer. Will assess site contamination, prepare reports, and develop solutions related to underground petroleum gas containers.
• Bachelor's degree in environmental engineering, chemistry, or geology required.
• Experience necessary.
• Knowledge of state regulations desirable.

FORESTER

Logging company seeks forester to assist in making land use decisions that comply with environmental regulations.
• Bachelor's degree and forestry research skills required.
• Previous experience preferred.

WASTEWATER TECHNICIAN

County water treatment facility needs technician to collect water samples and conduct tests to determine water safety.
• Associate's degree desired.
• Knowledge of equipment and chemicals required.

AGRICULTURE EXTENSION AGENT

County extension program has opening for agriculture agent to assist landowners through site visits, demonstrations, and educational programs.
• Master's degree in agriculture required.
• Excellent communication skills necessary.

ARCHITECT

Small firm has opening for architect to develop design concepts and manage production of construction plans.
• Bachelor's degree, strong design skills, and AutoCAD experience required.
• Minimum 3 years experience desired.

More Career Options

Entry Level
• Environmental Protection Assistants
• Fish and Game Wardens
• Landscapers
• Heavy Equipment Operators

Technical Level
• Fish and Wildlife Technician
• Surveyor
• Forestry Technician
• Arborist

Professional Level
• Civil Engineer
• Meteorologist
• Wildlife Managers
• Agricultural Scientist

SCIENCE TECHNICIAN

Manufacturing firm seeks science technician for research department. Conduct field tests to measure contaminant levels; monitor pollution sources
- Associate's degree or above required.
- Excellent communication skills necessary.

PARK RANGER

State Department of Conservation has opening for a park ranger responsible for park and visitors' safety.
- Patrol park, register vehicles, and oversee security.
- Two-year college degree and mechanical aptitude required.

URBAN AND REGIONAL PLANNER

Department of Health Services seeks regional planner to oversee the development of waterfront property in growing areas of the state.
- Master's degree desired.
- Knowledge of environmental issues necessary.
- Excellent communication skills and ability to collaborate with other agencies required.

GEOLOGIST

Large oil company has entry-level opening for a geologist to assist in locating oil deposits.
- Bachelor's degree necessary.
- Ability to work as part of team, and good physical stamina required.
- Computer skills a plus.

Linking School to Career

1. Your Career Plan: One form of change is recycling, which is increasingly important--not just for newspapers and aluminum cans, but for YOU. You will almost certainly have to "recycle" yourself by deciding over and over again, "What do I enjoy doing? What do I do best? Where does it fit in the work world? Who needs my skills? How can I benefit an employer? What steps do I take next to prepare for my career?" Think about yourself and write down the answers to these questions.

2. Researching Careers: One thing employers look for in employees is a positive work attitude. What do you think a person with a positive work attitude is like? List the traits that you believe an employee with a positive work attitude has. Do you have any of these traits? Would you want someone like this to be your coworker? How about your boss?

3. Reading: Look up the definitions of the following terms that are found in the want ad listings:
- Renovation projects.
- Contamination or contaminants.
- Environmental regulations.

Managing Your Life

The Balancing Act

YOU WILL LEARN . . .

➤ The importance of balance in your life.
➤ How balance is affected by your values and goals.
➤ Ways to achieve and maintain balance.
➤ Ways to manage time effectively.
➤ How to use work simplification techniques to save time and energy.

TERMS TO LEARN . . .

➤ priorities
➤ work simplification

Imagine ...

... you're walking a balance beam five feet above the ground. In order not to fall, you have to maintain perfect balance. Not only do you need to keep every part of your body in balance, but you also need to keep your mind completely focused.

Think About

• What exercises might you do to develop your body's sense of balance?
• How would you go about keeping your mind focused?
• Can you think of ways in which a sense of balance applies to other areas in your life?

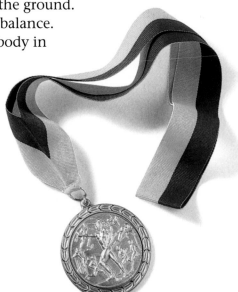

BALANCE IN YOUR LIFE

You may not realize it, but when you decide to make changes in your life, you're often trying to find and maintain balance. Balance involves making intelligent use of your time and energy. You also achieve balance when your values and actions work in harmony.

Troy has a book report to write for his English class. His goal is to finish the assignment before the weekend. One of Troy's **priorities**, or *things most important* to him, is spending time with his dad on Saturdays. Instead of putting off doing his assignment, Troy prioritizes his time, energy, and other resources to meet his goal. As a result, he keeps a sense of balance in his life.

Balance is important in many ways. Finding and maintaining balance gives you strength and confidence to meet life's demands. Without balance, you have less energy and enthusiasm to carry out daily tasks and activities.

➤ Staying focused on your values enables you to accomplish important tasks. You may have to devote more time to studying to receive good grades.

Consider What's Important

Achieving balance isn't easy. A hectic schedule, too many commitments, and unrealistic expectations can sap your energy. The clearer you are about what's important to you, the more able you'll be to use your time and energy wisely.

MAINTAINING BALANCE

"Just when everything was going well, my family was in an auto accident," Amelia says. "It was raining, and the other driver didn't see us. My dad's in the hospital, and my mom got a part-time job to help out. I quit the soccer team so I could take care of my little sister after school."

To stay in balance, you need to keep your values, goals, and priorities in mind. This helps you maintain control whenever expected—and unexpected—situations come your way.

Take Charge of Time

Everything you do takes a certain amount of time. Do you ever say "yes" to activities, then wonder how you'll find the time to do them? When you agree to take part in activities, you give your word you'll spend time accomplishing them.

Having enough time for all you need and want to do isn't easy. Keep your goals and values in mind as you schedule your use of time. You most likely have obligations, such as homework assignments, household chores, or a part-time job. After you finish these obligations, you can spend what time you have left on other activities of your choice. Taking charge of your time helps you achieve balance in your life.

➤ **This teen completes his chores before meeting his friends. He is working to achieve balance in his life.**

GET THE MOST OUT OF YOUR TIME

Take advantage of these tips to make time work for you:

• **Use a calendar.** Write down scheduled activities with family and friends and due dates for school.

• **Eliminate time-wasters.** Don't spend valuable time watching TV. Avoid activities that have little or no connection to your values and goals.

• **Combine activities when possible.** For example, do your homework at the laundromat while waiting for your clothes to dry.

• **Don't schedule every hour of every day.** Set aside some free time to relax and enjoy yourself.

• **Be flexible.** Anticipate possible problems and have backup plans. For instance, if the movie is sold out, have another activity in mind.

• **Maintain self-control when things don't go as you planned.** Losing self-control uses up valuable time and energy. Try to act in a calm, productive manner instead of an emotional one.

Getting Time in Balance

Set Goals

Think about something you want, or need, to achieve—like a major class project or saving money for college. First, set a goal—for a day, a week, a month, or even a year. Then:

- Decide what tasks must be done in order to achieve your goals.
- Estimate how long it will take to complete each task. Allow enough time to do the task correctly.

Make a Daily "To-Do" List

- Write down all the tasks and activities that you intend to accomplish for the day. Don't include more on your list than you'll be able to do.
- Rank the items on your list according to their importance. Place a 1, 2, or 3 after each item, with the most important items rating a 1. Save less important items for another day if you run out of time.
- Cross off each task when completed. You'll be able to see how much you've accomplished in a day.

Don't Procrastinate

- Postponing work on a project makes you feel pressured for time when you finally do it. Schedule it now and then do it. You'll feel good when your task is complete.

Prevent Interruptions

- Interruptions cause you to lose time. Ask that you not be interrupted for a certain length of time. Avoid places where you'll be easily interrupted.

Make Use of Small Amounts of Time

Even 15 or 30 minutes of time are enough to accomplish some tasks or parts of a large project. Think of tasks you can do in 30 minutes or less.

Reward Yourself for Success

After successfully completing a priority task, treat yourself to something you enjoy.

How can you use the above information to get time in balance?

How Do You Use Your Time?

To start taking charge of your time, take a look at how you use it. Keep a record of all your classes and activities for a single day in a small notebook. Include such categories as sleeping, eating, bathing, dressing, studying, working, helping at home, time with friends, participating in sports, etc. As you complete each activity, write down the amount of time you spend on it. Total up the time spent on each activity in a single day to see just where your time goes.

Evaluate how you manage your time. If you find your "to-do" lists include too many things, try to cut out those activities that aren't top priorities. Learn what works and what doesn't to better manage your time.

Time for Learning

If you think about it, you spend at least half of your waking hours at school or doing homework. Because time for education is vital now and for your future, get the most out of your school-related hours by following these suggestions:

- **Get more out of class time.** Do your homework as soon as you can, and make sure you're familiar with your teachers' lesson plans each day.
- **Pay attention.** By listening closely to a teacher and classmates, you have a better chance of understanding what's going on.
- **Take notes.** Writing down important points that are presented and discussed in class will help refresh your memory when you study later. Also, write down assignments, instructions for doing them, and the dates they're due. If you're unclear about any information, ask questions.

THE FINE ART OF TAKING NOTES

- Take notes in outline form. Focus on main ideas.

- Use a few words to write down main ideas and supporting details. Don't try to write down every word a teacher says.

- Abbreviate words when possible. For example, use "w/" instead of "with."

- Double or triple space your notes. That way, you can fill in more details later if needed.

- Review your notes frequently.

- Use different colored pens or markers to emphasize main ideas and supporting details.

- Select a quiet area to review your notes.

- Study the most difficult subject first.

- After you've accomplished a goal, take a 5- or 10-minute break. Walk around, drink a glass of water, or eat a piece of fruit.

➤ Take good notes! Reinforce the class discussion by rewriting or typing your classroom notes. This will refresh your memory and prepare you for future assignments.

MANAGING STUDY TIME

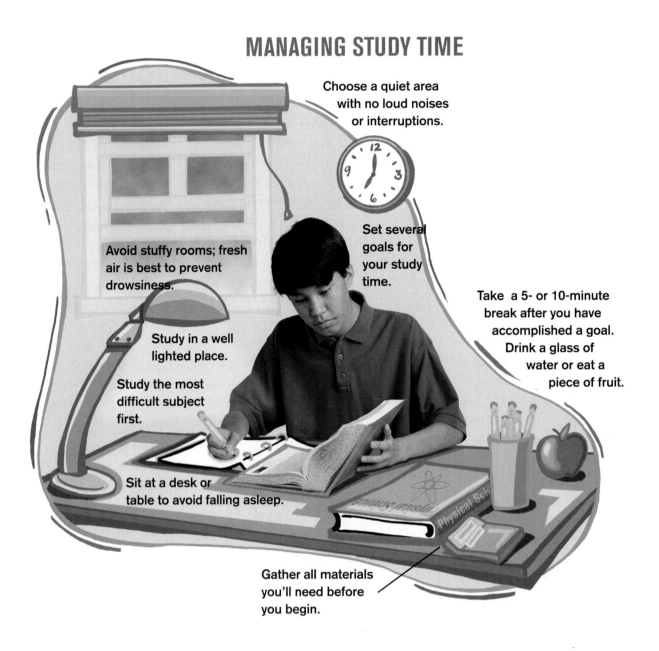

Choose a quiet area with no loud noises or interruptions.

Avoid stuffy rooms; fresh air is best to prevent drowsiness.

Set several goals for your study time.

Take a 5- or 10-minute break after you have accomplished a goal. Drink a glass of water or eat a piece of fruit.

Study in a well lighted place.

Study the most difficult subject first.

Sit at a desk or table to avoid falling asleep.

Gather all materials you'll need before you begin.

• **Review your notes.** As soon as possible after class, take a few minutes to review your notes. Going over your notes while they're fresh in your mind makes it easier to clarify information. You may also find it helpful to rewrite your class notes in a more organized way.

Time for Family, Friends, and Activities

"I wish I could join the drama club, but I work after school. I don't have time to rehearse." Ramon is saving money for college, and can't find time to do everything he'd like.

TRY IT OUT

Division Of Labor

What You'll Need
- Paper
- Pen or pencil

What to Do
1. Work in a small group to create a family. Assign each person a name, age, and specific roles.
2. List jobs that need to be done by family members. Which should be done first and last? How often should each job be done? Who should do each job? Record responses.
3. Consider the importance of each job. Which tasks could be eliminated if time and energy are limited? Which jobs must be done regularly and promptly, even if outside help must be used? Record responses.

To Discuss
- Compare your answers with those of other groups. How were the answers similar? Different? How are values and needs reflected?
- How can considering priorities make it easier to accomplish necessary household tasks? Eliminate unnecessary tasks? Make it possible to divide responsibilities fairly? How can household responsibilities be balanced with career and other responsibilities?

Whether or not you're involved in school activities, there are still many things that you want or need to do. It takes time to be a good family member or friend. You need time for yourself to pursue personal interests. You also need time just to relax. That's why careful time management can help you find balance.

Planning ahead is one way to help manage time. Make plans with your family or friends, and record them on a monthly calendar. To manage your time well, you need to make choices—based on the things that you value—about how to get the most out of it. If you value time with your brother, plan to talk with him, play a computer game, or go hiking. If you and your friend share an interest in sports, make future plans to go to a game.

➤ Planning ahead helps eliminate scheduling conflicts and wasted time. This family is planning ahead for a summer vacation.

Making a DIFFERENCE

DO IT ALL

"Look what I've done," Erika said to her friend Clare, showing her a pocket diary. "I've started keeping daily "to-do" lists."

"Why would you bother?" Clare asked.

"There's so much I want to do, and I can never find the time to do it all. I like being on the student council, but I also want to try out for the talent show. Then there's basketball ..."

"So how does writing everything down help?" Clare asked.

"I prioritize my day," said Erika. "Look, I write down numbers next to each thing I want to do. One is the most important, and three is the least. If I can get the ones and twos done, I'll save the threes for the weekend. Brilliant?"

"Let me see that again," Clare smiled. "I want to try it."

Taking Action

1. How could making a "to-do" list help you better manage your time and maintain balance?
2. What are other ways you might try to manage your time and maintain balance?

➤ **Energy levels vary. You may increase yours by getting plenty of rest, eating healthy foods, and exercising regularly.** How do you practice healthy habits?

Manage Your Energy

Are you an early bird? Do you operate in high gear in the morning and slow down in the afternoon? Maybe you're just the opposite. You may get off to a slow start but pick up steam later in the day and night. Like everyone else, you have a regular energy cycle. Try to schedule tasks that require alertness and energy when you're at your peak.

You can increase your energy level in general by improving your health habits. Eat healthful foods. Exercise regularly, and get enough rest. Chapters 24 and 25 give you more specifics about maintaining your health.

Review & Activities

Chapter Summary

- Balance involves making wise use of your time and energy.
- Keeping your values and priorities in harmony helps you achieve balance.
- Taking charge of your time helps you achieve balance. To take charge of your time, evaluate how you use it each day.
- At least half of your waking hours are spent in school-related activities.
- It takes time to be a good family member.
- Effective time management involves making choices based on what you value, or believe is important.
- Everyone has a regular energy cycle.

Family & Community

With Your Family

Share with family members what you've learned about managing time and energy. Ask each family member to keep track of how he or she balances tasks and other activities for one week. In a family discussion, share problems with one another and discuss possible solutions.

In Your Community

Identify people in your community who spend a great deal of time and energy to improve neighborhoods, schools, and parks. Brainstorm volunteer activities you could do as a class to assist one or more of these individuals. Together:

- Choose one workable activity.
- Develop a plan and carry it out.
- Discuss the results of your action.

Reviewing the Chapter

1. Why is balance important?
2. Why do you need to determine what your priorities are?
3. Briefly explain why maintaining balance is difficult for many people.
4. Why is it important to think of your values and goals when scheduling time?
5. Name three obligations of teens and families that require time and energy.
6. List four suggestions for getting the most out of your school-related hours.
7. How does planning ahead help you manage your time more effectively?
8. Why is it important to understand your regular energy cycle when scheduling tasks requiring alertness and energy?
9. Give three suggestions to increase your energy level.

Thinking Critically

1. **Draw conclusions.** Think about teens and adults you know who have various daily obligations. Which of them seem to balance their lives well—making time for school, work, family, friendships, and community service? What suggestions do you think they might offer to help others balance similar obligations in their lives?
2. **Recognize assumptions.** How might unrealistic expectations affect a person's sense of balance? Think of one or two examples and share them with the class.

Making Connections

1. **Social Studies.** Interview several older adults about how they maintain balance in their lives. How have time and energy demands on their lives changed over the years? Write a summary of your findings to present in class.

2. **Technology.** Study catalogs or visit local stores to research new labor-saving tools, utensils, and storage items. If possible, try out some items and report your results to the class.

Applying Your Learning

1. **Make a "to-do" list.** Make a list of tasks and other activities you want to accomplish in a single day. Prioritize each of them from most to least important. At the end of the day, put a line through the ones you accomplished. Ask yourself: How realistic was my list? Could I have accomplished more? If so, how? Did I accomplish the most important tasks? How can I make "to-do" lists work better for me?

2. **Write an article.** Write an article about problems teens face in maintaining balance in their lives. Give suggestions for managing time and energy. Share your completed article with adult family members. Compare each other's time and energy demands. In what ways are they similar? How are they different?

3. **Describe a time or energy saver.** Briefly write out your typical daily schedule. Think about ways you could save time or energy by rearranging parts of your schedule, or spaces you use for study, storage, dressing, etc. Make a list of your best ideas, and try out several of them.

What Would You Do?

Suppose today's school paper has a notice about auditions for the school play. Several teachers and friends think you'd be perfect for one of the roles. Rehearsals are scheduled after school twice a week for two months—the time you now use to study before going to your part-time job. You want to be in the play, but you also need about two hours each day to study. How would you manage your time and rearrange your daily schedule to try to accomplish these activities?

Managing Money

YOU WILL LEARN . . .

- ➤ The benefits of managing money.
- ➤ How to create a budget.
- ➤ How to write a check and fill out a check register.
- ➤ How to reconcile a checking account.
- ➤ How credit works.

TERMS TO LEARN . . .

- ➤ budget
- ➤ check register
- ➤ credit
- ➤ deposit
- ➤ endorse
- ➤ expenses
- ➤ income
- ➤ interest

Imagine ...

... you get a job with a good salary. It's more money than you thought you'd earn, and after paying all your monthly bills, you have extra money left over to spend in any way you want.

Think About

- What are some things you might do with extra money?
- Where would you keep your money?
- What are some ways to make sure you always have extra spending money on hand?

WHY MANAGE MONEY?

No matter how little or how much money you have, you can learn to make your money work for you—now and in the future. People who manage money well achieve a balance between what they spend and save. They buy what they need and want without wasting money on things they don't care about. Good money managers learn not to spend more than they can afford. They also plan ahead for future spending goals.

➤ Managing your money is easier when you keep a simple financial record. Creating a budget makes it easier to manage your money.

Money and You

Do you think about where your money goes? One way to get a handle on the money you have and spend is to keep simple records. Keep a weekly record for several weeks, then study and compare each week's record. Follow these guidelines to help manage your money:

• **Keep track of what you receive.** First, write down your **income**, or *the amount of money you have coming in.* It may be pay you receive from mowing lawns or babysitting, or an allowance your parents give you. Add up the money you receive from various sources to find the total of your weekly income. This lets you see how much money you have available to use.

• **Keep track of your spending.** Your **expenses** are *the goods and services you spend money on*, such as snacks and meals, school supplies, clothing, and entertainment.

• **Categorize your expenses.** Expenses that must be paid regularly and that don't vary in amount are called *fixed expenses*. Your fixed expenses might include lunch, transportation to and from school, and school activity fees. Divide your fixed expenses into categories. Then record how much you spend in each category.

After your fixed expenses, record *flexible expenses*, those expenses that vary from time to time. They often include items and services that you want rather than need, such as a concert ticket or hobby supplies. Write down these costs by category. You'll probably find your categories change each week.

Compare the totals of your income and your expenses. Do you spend all the money you get, or do you have some left over? Look at your expenses, and ask yourself these questions:

- Do my expenses reflect my values and goals?
- Do I waste money on things or activities I don't really need?
- Am I satisfied with my spending habits?

➤ **Expenses that occur on a regular basis, such as bus fare, are fixed expenses.** What fixed expenses can you name in your daily life?

▼ TRY IT OUT

Money Facts

ACTIVITY

What You'll Need
- Paper
- Pen or pencil

What to Do
1. On a sheet of paper, answer the following questions:
   - How many times each day do you usually spend money?
   - How much do you spend a year for soft drinks?
   - What's your biggest expense item?
2. Compare your answers with those of your classmates. For the first two questions, find the class average. Find the most frequent answer for the last question.

To Discuss
- Which answer did you find the most surprising? Why?
- How might your own answers cause you to reevaluate your spending habits?
- How might comparing your spending habits with those of others be helpful? Why might such comparisons be deceptive?

MAKE THE MOST OF YOUR MONEY

After you've identified how you currently manage money, think about ways to manage it better. Dylan spends less now on extra clothes and shoes, because he's trying to save up for a used car one day. If you want to save money for the future, cut back your spending now.

Create a Budget

To make the most of your money, it's important to create a budget. A **budget** is *a plan for spending and saving the money you have available.* When you make a budget, you set up guidelines for spending money on things that are worth the time and effort you put into earning money.

Make Your Budget a Reality

To make the best use of your budget, first decide what are your most important expenses. List them in order of importance to distinguish between your financial needs and wants. Then take steps to make your budget a reality:

- Record your expected income during the period of your budget. Base your income on what you learned from keeping weekly records.
- Write down what you plan to spend on both your fixed and flexible expenses. The information should reflect your most important goals.
- Review your budget periodically to see how it's working. If you allowed too much or too little for some items, readjust your plan. If you forgot one or more expenses, include these as you update your budget.

➤ Impulse buying is making an unplanned purchase on the spur of the moment. What impulse purchases have you made lately?

USING FINANCIAL SERVICES

Financial institutions, such as banks, credit unions, and savings and loan associations, offer checking and savings accounts. These accounts help you manage your money in a safe, insured place. They also offer you the convenience of being able to withdraw money when you need it and the advantage of earning extra money.

Checking Accounts

Your parents write checks when they pay bills or make various purchases. You may receive checks as payment for work or as gifts. Checks represent money placed in a checking account by the person who writes the checks. A check is a written order to a financial institution to pay a specific amount of money to a person.

Having a checking account is a convenience. It means you can use checks instead of paying bills in cash. You can mail checks rather than pay bills in person. Never send cash through the mail—it can be easily stolen.

➤ A budget helps a family live within its financial limits. There are many new tools, such as self-help books and computer software programs to help in planning budgets.

Opening a Checking Account

When you open a checking account, you agree to follow the terms of a financial institution. One is that you won't write a check for more than the amount of money in your account. Another is that you may have to pay service charges for the handling of your account. Fees on checking accounts vary depending on the type of account and how much money you keep in it. Before opening an account, carefully compare terms at several financial institutions.

Depositing Money

You open a checking account by making a **deposit**, or *putting money into an account.* To make a deposit, you fill out a deposit slip. You receive a supply of preprinted deposit slips and checks when you open an account.

> Accuracy is vital to keep a checking account balanced. Use a calculator to check your statement and check register each month.

Deposits are crucial—checks can only be written up to your balance, or the amount of money in an account. You make deposits in cash or checks. Before depositing a check, you must **endorse** it, or *sign your name on the back*. This transfers your right to the check over to the bank, which deposits it in your account.

Using a Checkbook

You receive a checkbook when you open a checking account. The checkbook contains two important features:

- Checks, which you will fill out in ink, as needed. Write the date and name of the person or business you are paying. Then write the amount first in figures and then in words, and your signature.

- A **check register**, or *small booklet to keep a record of your account*. Each time you make a deposit, write a check, use a debit card, or withdraw cash from an automated teller machine (ATM), record the information in your check register. Write down the date and the amount of the transaction, and the check number when you write a check. After each transaction, add or subtract the amounts so that you know how much money remains in your account. This total is your current balance.

Addition and subtraction are the only math skills needed to use a checkbook and maintain a check register. Check your figures carefully. Accurate recordkeeping is essential.

COMMERCIAL NATIONAL BANK

Member Midwest Financial Group, Inc.
ANYTOWN, USA

DATE *Oct. 22* 20 *07*
DEPOSITS MAY NOT BE AVAILABLE FOR IMMEDIATE WITHDRAWAL.

SIGN HERE FOR LESS CASH IN TELLER'S PRESENCE

JANE SMITH
12235 LAKE FOREST DR.
ANYTOWN, USA

099:5600250000:223 0007 289394

DEPOSIT TICKET
70-4
711

CASH	CURRENCY	15 00
	COIN	
CHECKS LIST CHECKS SINGLY	70-8/711	27 63
TOTAL CHECKS FROM OTHER SIDE		
TOTAL		42 63
LESS CASH RECEIVED		
NET DEPOSIT		42 63

CHECKS AND OTHER ITEMS ARE RECEIVED FOR DEPOSIT SUBJECT TO THE PROVISIONS OF THE UNIFORM COMMERCIAL CODE OR ANY APPLICABLE COLLECTION AGREEMENT.

> Include a deposit slip that is properly filled out with your checking and savings account deposits.

Using Debit Cards and Smart Cards

To pay for purchases, people increasingly use debit cards to transfer money from a checking account to the account of a store or service provider. You can use these cards, which resemble credit cards, at locations where credit card logos are displayed. Since debit cards don't involve borrowing or lending, no credit is involved and no interest is charged. Many people use debit cards in place of cash or checks.

If a debit card is lost or stolen, and is not reported within two days, you may be responsible for all charges made on the card up to $50. If you don't report it within 60 days, you can be liable for all the charges.

Smart cards, which are of plastic credit card size, can also be used instead of checks to make certain purchases up to a specified amount. Phone cards are an example. Each card contains an embedded microprocessor chip and memory, specifying its dollar value. If a smart card is lost, it's the same as lost cash.

➤ Debit cards make shopping easier. They eliminate check writing by deducting the purchase amount from a checking account. The user must be sure to update the checkbook register in order to balance the account properly.

Check Your Financial Statements

Your financial institution will also keep records on your account and send them to you. These records, called statements, are computerized printouts showing which checks have been paid, what deposits have been made, and what fees or service charges have been deducted.

When you receive your statement you need to reconcile your account, or make sure your own records and the bank statement are in agreement. This process, also called balancing your checkbook, is explained on page 290. Some banks return your canceled, or paid, checks along with your statements. Others send copies of the canceled checks. Keep these records as proof of bills you've paid and money you've spent.

If you write checks for more money than you have in your account, the account will be overdrawn. Institutions charge a fee for overdrawn checks. They may also send a check back to the business that presented it for payment, causing you embarrassment and additional charges. For these reasons, keep careful track of your account.

Savings Accounts

You can protect extra money and make it earn money for you by opening a savings account. Many people start savings accounts to save for a major goal, such as a college education or a car. People also save for future vacations and unplanned emergencies.

HOW to...

Reconcile Your Checkbook and Account Statement

Follow these simple guidelines to reconcile your checkbook register with your account statement:

1. Write down the last balance shown on your checking account statement.

2. Total the deposits you've made that don't appear on the statement. Add this total to the amount that appears on your statement.

3. Make a list of checks that you've written that don't appear on the

CHECK NO.	DATE	CHECK ISSUED TO	AMOUNT OF CHECK	✓	DATE OF DEP	AMOUNT OF DEPOSIT	BALANCE 556 48
543	2/8	Pure & Fresh Inc. (bottled water)	16 50	✓			16 50
							539 98
544	2/16	XYZ Center	59 95				59 95
							480 03
	2/18	Deposit				400 00	400 00
							880 03
545	2/20	City Electric	124 63				124 63
							755 40
546	2/21	123 Comm	35 96				35 96
							719 44
	2/22	ATM withdrawal	60 00				60 00
							659 44

statement. These are often called "outstanding" checks. Total all of these checks.

4. Subtract the total of your outstanding checks from the total in Step 2. This amount should agree with the balance in your checkbook register.

➤ **Savings accounts allow you to save money while rewarding you with interest. Always save your deposit slips for your records.**

CHECK OUT FEES

Financial institutions often charge fees for services. Compare fees of different institutions before opening an account. Check to see how much (if any) is charged if:

- Your balance falls below a specific minimum amount.
- You have overdrawn checks.
- You write more than a certain number of checks each month.
- You use a teller rather than an ATM.
- You use another bank's ATM.
- You use online banking from your home computer.

Savings accounts increase the amount you deposit by paying you interest. **Interest** is *the money a financial institution pays at regular intervals for the use of your money*. The interest is a certain percentage of the amount in your savings. Interest rates can vary. Always compare interest rates before opening an account.

Some savings accounts can be opened with a deposit of $100 or less. You may deposit cash or checks, and you need to fill out a deposit slip. When you're ready to use money from your savings, you can withdraw part of it. But you need to maintain a certain amount in the account to keep it open. To take out money, complete a withdrawal slip with your name, account number, signature, and the amount.

You'll receive a record of your savings account showing deposits, withdrawals, and your current balance. This record is usually a printed statement sent at regular intervals.

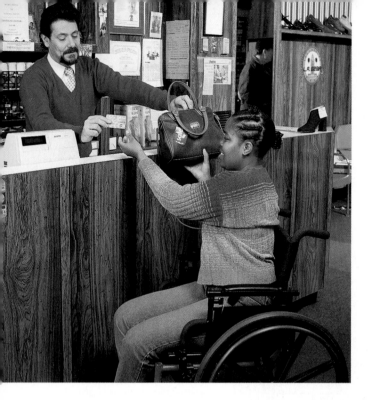

➤ If you are allowed to use credit, use it wisely. Consider the cost and your future credit rating.

Credit

At this stage of your life, you probably pay cash for items and services you buy. In the future, when you'll have more income, you may be eligible to use credit as a tool to help you manage your money. **Credit** is *an arrangement that lets you buy things now and pay for them later.* There are two major types of credit:

- **Loans.** With loans, you borrow money from financial institutions or loan companies. You use the money you borrow to pay for purchases, and then pay back your loan in specific amounts.
- **Sales credit, or charge accounts**. With this type of credit, you receive your purchase now and pay a store or credit card company later for what you owe.

What Does Credit Cost?

Using credit costs money. In addition to money you owe, you also pay the lender a certain percentage of interest. If you use credit cards, you pay interest unless you pay the total of your bill on time each month. The interest will be a percentage of the unpaid balance on your credit card account. Late fees are charged additionally if payments aren't made on time.

Because credit is more expensive than paying cash, use it only when necessary. Interest rates vary, so shop around for credit. You can save money by taking time to find the lowest rate.

To get credit, you must apply for it and prove you're able to pay what you owe. Banks and companies that give you

SAFETY

First

To use an ATM safely:

- Stay aware of your surroundings, especially at night. Only use an ATM in a well-lighted public place.
- Never tell anyone your PIN (personal identification number).
- Fill out deposit forms and have your card ready before approaching the ATM.

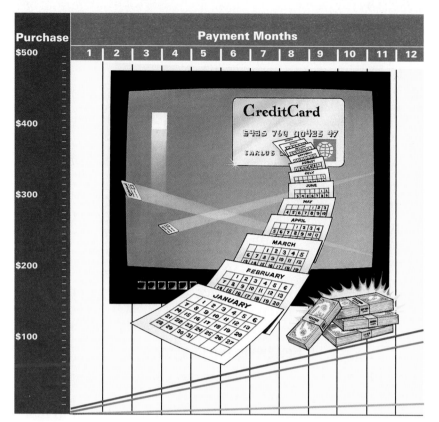

Purchase	Payment Months											
$500	1	2	3	4	5	6	7	8	9	10	11	12

$481.91

■ **Purchase = $500.00**

■ **Payments = $10.00 per month = $120.00 paid over the 12-month period**

▨ **Principal reduction over the 12-month period = $18.09**

■ **Amount of payments that went to interest = $101.91 @ 21% annual**

☐ **Amount owed**

➤ Suppose you bought a $500 wide-screen TV using a credit card. If you paid the $10 minimum due each month with finance charges, you would pay for 119.9 months and spend $1199.00. At the end of 12 months, you would still owe $481.91.

PROTECT YOURSELF FROM CREDIT CARD FRAUD

credit protect themselves against loss. They check your credit application and consider the following:

- **Your credit rating.** Companies called credit bureaus keep track of your record of paying debts. A poor credit rating can stop you from getting more credit in the future. A good credit rating is important throughout your life.
- **Your income and money resources in general.** Will you have enough money to make payments on your credit cards or loan?

Credit is easy to use and misuse. Debts can quickly mount up, and people can get into serious credit trouble. For this reason, it's wise to use credit only when necessary.

To protect yourself from credit card fraud:

- Don't keep your PIN in your wallet or purse. Memorize it instead.

- Use a PIN different from your birthday, address, or Social Security number.

- Report lost or stolen cards immediately to the credit card company. (Write down your account number and company telephone number as soon as you get a card. File the information where it can be quickly found.)

- Save your receipts and compare them with your billing statement.

Review & Activities

Chapter Summary

- Good money management means not spending more than you can afford. It also means planning for future spending goals.
- By keeping simple records, you can see how much money you have and how it's spent.
- Your income includes the money you receive from various sources. Expenses are things you spend money on, such as goods and services.
- Spending can be divided into two categories: fixed expenses and flexible expenses.
- One way to save money for the future is to cut back on your current spending.
- A budget helps you make the most of your money. Review your budget periodically and adjust it when necessary.

Family & Community

With Your Family

With your family members, discuss what might happen if your family won $1,000 in a raffle. Talk about ways the money might be used. Then imagine that the money is divided equally among each family member. Ask each person to make a list showing how his or her part might be used. Share and discuss your lists with each other.

In Your Community

As a class, research community programs that help young people learn to make the most of their money. Think of ways you could inform and encourage teens to participate in some of these programs.

- Checks are often used instead of cash to pay bills or make purchases.
- You agree to certain terms when opening a checking or savings account. Compare terms at several financial institutions before opening an account.
- Credit allows you to buy now and pay later. However, to use credit you must pay interest.

Reviewing the Chapter

1. Describe three characteristics of good money managers.
2. Name three guidelines to follow in managing your money.
3. What is the difference between fixed and flexible expenses? List two examples of each.
4. Why is a budget important? Briefly describe three steps to make a budget a reality.
5. Name three types of financial institutions. Give two advantages of using their services.
6. Why should you send checks, rather than cash, when paying bills by mail?
7. List and explain two important features of a checkbook. Explain how to reconcile your checkbook to bank statement.
8. Name four reasons for opening a savings account.
9. Explain why using credit may cost more than paying cash.

Thinking Critically

1. **Draw conclusions.** Some financial institutions charge a fee for ATM and online banking transactions. Others encourage customers to use electronic banking services by making them available free of charge. How do you think electronic banking benefits the bank? The customer? What drawbacks could exist with electronic banking?

2. **Predict consequences.** Credit cards make buying very easy. What positive and negative consequences might result from using credit cards to make major purchases? What suggestions would you give a friend thinking about using a credit card?

Making Connections

1. **Math.** Some financial institutions pay *simple interest*—interest paid only on money you place in your savings account. The interest earned on the account doesn't earn interest. Use the following formula to calculate simple interest: $I = prt$ (interest = principal × rate of interest × time in years). Figure the interest earned on the following amounts of money: $200 principal at 5% for 1 year; $185 principal at 4% for 6 months; $120 principal at 5.5% for 1.5 years.

2. **Computer Science.** Compare several computer software accounting programs. Consider their ease of use and price. Give reasons for the program you would choose.

Applying Your Learning

1. **Compare financial institutions.** Find ads for checking accounts offered by financial institutions. Make a graph comparing the costs and features of each account. Select one that you think represents the best value, and share your reasons with the class.

2. **Reconcile your checkbook.** Assume you regularly use a checkbook. Reconcile your checkbook with your bank balance using the following information: bank statement closing balance = $244.50; outstanding checks: $21.95, $17.70, $35.15, $23.64, $15.60; service charge = $3.00; deposits not shown on statement = $72.50.

3. **Plan a budget.** Plan a weekly budget for one or more of the following teens: Rico-$25 weekly; Jade-$15 weekly; Anna-$35 weekly; Toccara-$40 weekly. Think about weekly expenses that teens have and then plan your budget. What is the benefit in having a plan for using money?

What Would You Do?

Suppose an elderly neighbor hires you to rake leaves. You agree to work for two hours for a total of $15. But the job takes four hours. How would you handle this situation?

Living with Technology

YOU WILL LEARN . . .

- ➤ How changing technology affects communication, health care, entertainment, and other areas of life.
- ➤ Examples of technology at home, at school, and in the workplace.
- ➤ Ways you may use technology in the near future.

TERMS TO LEARN . . .

- ➤ desktop publishing
- ➤ microprocessors
- ➤ modem
- ➤ technology
- ➤ teleconferencing
- ➤ universal product code

Imagine ...

... you live in a world in which phones, TVs, and computers don't exist. There are no cameras, and no movies. It's not unlike the world a little more than a century ago.

Think About

- If you wanted to communicate with a friend who lived miles away, how would you do it? Would having no phone or computer change your relationship?
- What would you do for entertainment?
- What product of technology would you miss the most?

CHANGING TECHNOLOGY

It's hard to imagine life without technology. **Technology,** *the way in which science and inventions are put to practical use in everyday life,* is everywhere. It includes time-saving, labor-saving, and life-saving devices.

Although new advances continually occur, technology itself isn't new. Technology has been advancing for thousands of years, from simple stone tools to complex spacecraft. What's different today is the rapid rate of change in technology, which sometimes seems faster than the human mind can comprehend.

> Schools rely on computers for creating and grading materials used in today's classrooms. The textbook you are reading was created using a variety of computer software programs.

Communication

One area deeply affected by new technology is communication. As major events unfold around the world, you can learn about them instantly. Technology lets you experience an event as it happens, no matter how far away. The news may be communicated via TV, satellite, or computer.

In the not-so-distant past, it could take weeks for families and friends to exchange written messages. Today, thanks to telephone technology, computers, digital cameras, and the like, you can send and receive messages and images instantaneously.

In the workplace, modern technology has speeded up communication and made it possible to hold virtual meetings. With fax machines, documents can be transmitted in minutes anywhere in the world. **Teleconferencing** *enables people in different locations to see and hear each other at the same time.* This method of meeting is often faster and less expensive than meeting face to face.

Health and Medical Care

Technology triggers almost daily advances in the field of health. From digital thermometers and blood pressure monitors to pacemakers (which help regulate the heartbeat) and dialysis machines (which rid the body of wastes when kidneys no longer function), these new advances play a major role in health care.

For example, dietitians use computers to analyze patients' diets. Health care workers use computer technology to gather data about various illnesses and treatments. With a CT (computerized tomography) scan, for example, several x-ray machines can scan and produce graphic images of a patient's organs. Surgeons use *magnetic resonance imaging*, or MRI (which teams powerful magnets with computers), and lasers (highly focused beams of light) to diagnose and treat health problems. Organ transplants and joint replacements are other medical procedures resulting from changing technology.

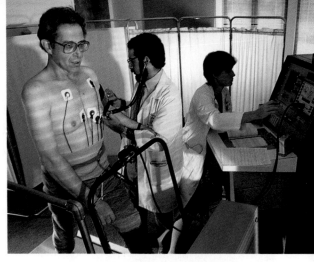

➤ Medical science has been revolutionized through the use of computer technology. Many lives have been saved as a result of these advances.

▼TRY IT OUT

Technology's Reach

ACTIVITY

What You'll Need
- Paper
- Pen or pencil

What to Do
1. Work with a group to make a chart with these headings: At Home, At Work, As a Consumer. Fill in the chart with examples of ways people use technology.
2. Share your ideas with another group. Add additional suggestions to your chart.

To Discuss
- How has technology changed the way people live?
- How has technology changed the way people work?
- What changes have occurred in the way consumers make purchases as a result of technology? How has technology changed the way consumers make financial transactions?

Entertainment

Changing technology has delivered new forms of entertainment into most people's lives. VCRs and DVD players enable people to watch TV programs and movies at home whenever they want. Cable networks and satellite dishes greatly increase viewers' choices. High-definition television (HDTV) makes cinema-quality video and sound available on home TV sets. Interactive software provides games and additional forms of entertainment.

Video arcades, many with virtual reality games, and spectacular amusement park rides are made possible by advanced technology. Technology has even transformed children's toys. With the addition of computer chips, many of today's toys perform in lifelike or highly creative ways.

➤ **Many modern appliances contain internal computers.** What appliances do you know that contain a hidden computer chip?

INFOLINK

See Chapter 27 for more information on safety.

Safety

What kinds of technology do you and your family use to increase your sense of safety? Increasing numbers of homes, businesses, and vehicles employ security systems to protect against intruders. Cars and other vehicles come equipped with sensor-activated air bags. Global positioning satellite equipment informs drivers of their exact location and destination. At home, communication devices are available for the elderly or disabled to call for help during an emergency.

Computer technology also helps make communities safer. For example, police officers' vehicles are often equipped with computers and video cameras to access and record data regarding suspects, stolen cars, and other crimes. National data banks (central computers that store information from around the country) help technicians identify suspects' fingerprints. Computers are also used to analyze fibers, hair samples, and DNA molecules to help solve crimes and identify victims' remains.

Protective technology also plays a vital role in law enforcement and public safety. For instance, bulletproof and flame-resistant clothing helps protect police officers and firefighters from harm.

> Many law enforcement vehicles are now equipped with computer terminals. This officer is using the computer to get driver information during a traffic violation.

TECHNOLOGY AND YOU

Whether you're at home, at school, or in the workplace, technology probably saves you time and energy, and makes life better for you and your family.

At Home

Families use computers for everything from schoolwork and financial planning to entertainment and communicating with others. Computer software for financial planning includes spreadsheet programs that arrange, or "spread," numbers, calculating figures quickly and accurately. Word processing software lets you write and revise papers with ease. With CD-ROM discs, you can access an entire encyclopedia or play an almost unlimited assortment of games.

A **modem**, *a device that connects a computer to a phone line or cable*, lets your computer communicate directly with other computers. It also allows you to use fax machines, e-mail, and the Internet. You can use a scanner to send photos to relatives, incorporate family pictures into newsletters, make birthday cards, or send a drawing to friends.

> Home computers are excellent tools for financial planning. What are some other tasks in which a home computer can be used to simplify home life?

➤ Programmable thermostats that automatically lower the air temperature when you sleep can reduce heating costs.

Hidden Computer Technology

Even if you don't own a personal computer, computer technology may be working in your home. Many new appliances feature hidden **microprocessors**, *tiny single-purpose computers*. Electronic sewing machines contain microprocessors for creating and storing hundreds of designs. Other examples include irons that automatically turn themselves off, microwave ovens, programmable coffee makers, and TVs displaying closed-captioned text for people with hearing impairments.

TAKE NOTE

The Internet

The Internet is a vast network of computer networks which millions of people navigate or "surf." It's a huge communications system developed several decades ago by government agencies, universities, and businesses that wanted to exchange information by computer.

In the early 1990s, the World Wide Web was developed to make the Internet easier to use. The Web consists of millions of computers that can deliver web pages to people with *browsers,* or computer programs that request and display the pages. Web pages include graphics, audio, and even video clips.

You can use the Internet to communicate with people all over the world. You can also use it to gain access to almost unlimited amounts of information. It takes a computer, a modem, a monthly fee, and modest phone or cable charges to get online. Once connected to the Internet, you can:

- Work from your home computer anywhere in the world.
- Transfer files to and from remote computers.
- Search for and retrieve information.
- Purchase goods and services advertised on the Internet without leaving the comfort of home.
- Set up a personal web page.

How could the Internet help you with your studies?

➤ Computer programs exist for studying different subjects. These teens are using a computer program to design a website for their school.

Most home technology aims at convenience, as in the case of computers and VCRs. Motion-sensing and solar-powered lights, as well as automatic garage door openers, provide both safety and convenience. Fully automated home systems control many home functions such as heating, cooling, and lighting.

At School

Computer technology is used throughout many schools today. Teachers use computers to create tests and other materials, as well as multimedia presentations. You may use computers in some classes and in the library, where you have access to the Internet. Also, telecommunications technology is available in some schools, linking students with teachers of specialized subjects many miles away. You may also use a computer to research available college programs or career training opportunities.

In the Workplace

Today most businesses depend on computer technology. More and more companies use cell phones, pagers, voice mail, electronic schedules, fax machines, and document scanners. Workers often use laptop computers while working away from the office.

EARNING MONEY WITH PERSONAL COMPUTERS

You may be able to earn extra money by using your home computer. Consider the following options:

- **Give PC tutoring lessons.** Share your knowledge of computing and software programs with others.

- **Publish newsletters.** Your neighborhood group may need someone to design a newsletter.

- **Write résumés.** You can use simple software to design letters and résumés for friends and neighbors.

- **Create Web sites for family members and friends.** If you have access to a digital camera, use your skills to enhance the Web sites with photos.

INFOLINK

See Chapters 5, 6, and 7 for more information on technology and the workplace.

Computer technology offers businesses, as well as people who work out of their homes, a service called **desktop publishing**, which *uses computers and special software to create professional-looking documents*. Company reports, brochures, newsletters, invitations, greeting cards, and calendars are now commonly created by desktop publishing.

Banking

Technology is now a part of almost every banking procedure. When you go to a teller or automated teller machine (ATM) to make a deposit or withdrawal, a computer manages the transaction. Banks also use technology to calculate checking and savings accounts. Electronic banking lets you use a phone or computer to check on your account, pay bills, and transfer funds to other accounts.

Shopping

Stores use computers for ordering, stocking, and keeping track of merchandise on hand. Scanners at checkout stands read a **universal product code**, or UPC, printed on each product or price ticket. A UPC is *a combination of a bar code and numbers that identifies each product and usually assigns a price*. As a result, checkouts proceed more quickly and with fewer errors.

Credit card and debit card purchases also involve computers. Store clerks use computers to record a credit card or a debit card purchase. The process informs the clerk whether the card is valid.

Many businesses also use video technology. You might see a videotape demonstrating how to apply cosmetics or how to use certain food products. Video cameras are also used for security.

Technology makes it easy to buy products advertised on TV shopping networks or on the Internet. These forms of shopping are convenient, especially to home-bound con-

➤ You can scan the bar code on many products in discount stores to find out their prices. This can save time looking for a salesclerk and lets you decide whether to buy an item.

sumers. However, it's important to get as much information as possible about a product before shopping electronically. Don't assume all the information shown is accurate.

Design

Drafters, architects, engineers, and interior designers frequently use computer-aided design (CAD). It's used to design houses, buildings, bridges, planes, and cars (and even the nuts and bolts that hold them together) before actual construction. CAD allows people to make a design in three dimensions, and then visually "walk" through the space to decide how to use it.

LOOKING TO THE FUTURE

What new technology can you envision for the future? In the near future there will be:
- Wearable computer systems, such as eyeglasses and T-shirts that serve as computer monitors, or shoes that use the body's energy to power a wearable PC.
- Ultrasound that cleans clothes without water.
- Scanning devices that keep inventory of food supplies, print out suggestions for meals using ingredients that you have on hand, and tell you when you are running low on certain supplies.

It's up to you to make the best possible use of present and future technology. If chosen and used wisely, products of technology can give you increased time and energy to meet your goals.

To stay safe on the Internet:
- **Don't give personal information to anyone you don't know. This includes your name, gender, age, phone number, street address, e-mail address, credit card numbers, or Social Security number.**
- **Avoid discussion logs, which may record your conversations.**
- **Inform a parent if online material makes you feel uncomfortable.**
- **When shopping online, make sure you are at a secure site before providing credit card information.**

➤ Computers are used in transportation to navigate or help the captain remain on course. Some computers have the capability of landing a plane without a pilot's help.

Review & Activities

Chapter Summary

- Technology affects many aspects of life, and includes devices that save time, labor, and lives.
- New technology lets people communicate instantaneously with each other around the world.
- Technology has brought about widespread advances in health and medical care.
- New forms of home and commercial entertainment have resulted from advanced technology.
- Many families and communities depend on computer technology for both personal and public safety.
- Microprocessors in today's home appliances increase convenience and safety.
- Computer technology is used extensively by banks and most other businesses.

Family & Community

With Your Family

Think about family activities involving technology products. Talk with family members about some of their favorite products. Discuss why those products are favorites.

In Your Community

Investigate how technology is used in your community to protect public safety. How many different ways is technology used? Brainstorm possible ways that you and your classmates could use technology in your community to make a difference in public safety.

- Desktop publishing allows individuals and businesses to create a variety of professional-looking documents.
- Computer-aided design is used to design houses, buildings, bridges, vehicles, and planes.
- Products of future technology will allow people more time and energy to meet goals.

Reviewing the Chapter

1. What is technology? How has it affected communication between friends and families?
2. Name six products of technology used in health and medical care.
3. List six new forms of entertainment resulting from changing technology.
4. Briefly explain ways that technology can help make homes and communities safer.
5. What is a microprocessor? Name five household products containing microprocessors.
6. Give two examples of hidden computer technology that offer safety and convenience at home.
7. Briefly describe desktop publishing. Name six uses of desktop publishing.
8. What are universal product codes? What three functions do they serve in stores?
9. How is video technology used by businesses?
10. Briefly describe three types of technology expected in the near future.

Review & Activities

Thinking Critically

1. **Compare and contrast.** Think about two occupations that interest you. Compare and contrast the amount of technological knowledge required for each of them. How are they different and how are they the same? How might those requirements affect your choice of an occupation?

2. **Draw conclusions.** Does technology always make life more convenient or safe? Does it always improve communication between people? Explain your answer.

3. **Clarify fact or fiction.** People sometimes think older adults are unable or unwilling to take advantage of new technology. How would you respond to this position?

Making Connections

1. **Language Arts.** New advances in technology help individuals monitor their own health. For example, "smart T-shirts," with optical fibers woven throughout the garment, serve as computers to keep track of a person's vital signs. Find examples of other technological advances in this area and share your findings with the class.

2. **Science.** Lasers are currently used in various areas of healthcare and medicine. Research some current products and procedures now used in ophthalmology, dermatology, and other medical specialties.

Applying Your Learning

1. **Compute the cost of safety.** Use consumer publications to determine the cost of vehicle safety features. List safety features available today. Research safety ratings of vehicles and determine which is safest and which is least safe.

2. **Project the future.** Imagine you're living on earth 200 years from now. Write a short story about the technology available to you. How will it be used?

3. **Design a technology.** Design a product of technology for individuals with a disability. Identify the disability and the challenges it presents. This product should assist these individuals at home, work, or school.

What Would You Do?

Suppose a neighbor paid you to walk her dog while she is away for several days. She gave you the code number to her security system so you wouldn't set off the alarm. One day you turn off the system and forget to reset it. As a result, the house is not monitored for 24 hours. When your neighbor returns, she asks if you made sure the system was on the entire time. You'd like to work for her again, but are afraid if you tell the truth, she'll hire someone else. How would you handle this problem?

Making Consumer Choices

YOU WILL LEARN . . .

➤ Factors that influence consumer choices.
➤ How to be a smart shopper.
➤ Rights and responsibilities of consumers.
➤ Ways to resolve consumer problems effectively.

TERMS TO LEARN . . .

➤ comparison shopping
➤ consumer
➤ impulse buying
➤ marketplace
➤ redress
➤ warranty

Imagine ...

... your parents are helping you shop for a car. You see the car of your dreams, but it is too expensive. Your part-time job does not pay well enough to cover the payments.

Think About

• What would you ask a salesperson about the car?
• If you had just enough money in a savings account to buy the car, what would you do?
• If a salesperson offered you a discount on the car, what would you do?

WHAT INFLUENCES YOUR CHOICES?

To shop safely:

- Try to shop during daylight hours. If you need to shop at night, go with family members or friends.
- Before entering a vehicle, look under the car and check the back seat to make sure no one is hiding there.
- Keep your bag or wallet close to your body at all times. It only takes a minute for it to disappear.
- Stay alert while shopping. Tell a security guard or call your parents if you notice someone following you or acting suspiciously.
- Lock your car doors. Put packages in the trunk or out of sight.

Think of a recent purchase you made. Perhaps you bought a T-shirt or CD, or got a haircut. Any time you pay for something, you're a consumer. A **consumer** is *someone who buys and uses goods and services produced by others.*

How can you determine the right products and services to buy? How can you get the best price? To become a wise consumer, you need to realize that each purchase involves a choice—a choice affected by many factors. These include:

- **Your income.** Whether it's from a paycheck or an allowance, your income is the single most important factor that impacts what you buy.
- **Your job.** Your job also affects what you buy. If you mow lawns on weekends, you need different kinds of clothes than you do if you work in a business office.
- **Your environment.** If you live in a cold climate, you need warm clothing. In a hot climate, you need lightweight clothes.
- **Your personal interests and values.** You choose to spend money on goods and services that you value and that interest you. For instance, your interests may include music, computer software, or playing sports.
- **Your culture.** Each culture has customs and traditions that influence what people choose to spend their money on and how they spend their spare time.
- **Advertising.** When advertising tempts you to buy something, remember that you control your purchasing decisions.
- **Peer pressure.** Keep in mind that you—not your friends—know what you need, want, and can afford.

SMART SHOPPING

Being aware of influences on your purchases can help you make better consumer choices. One way to start is to follow a plan for taking charge of your purchasing decisions.

What Will You Buy?

The most important part of a shopping plan is to figure out what you need to buy. Make your decisions based on your needs and wants—with your values in mind. Max needs a baseball mitt for his recreational baseball league. He knows if he buys the mitt, he won't be able to purchase some CDs he'd like to own. Decide if you can afford to buy a particular item, and still have money left for other things you want and need.

Having a shopping plan helps you resist **impulse buying**, or *making unplanned purchases on the*

> Stores display items designed to encourage impluse buying near the checkout area to increase their sales. Exert your willpower against unplanned purchases.

TRY IT OUT

What's the Message?

ACTIVITY

What You'll Need
- Advertisements from local newspapers
- Paper and pen or pencil

What to Do
1. Working in teams, analyze advertisements from your local newspaper for techniques used to persuade you to buy various products or services. On a sheet of paper, list the persuasive techniques you identified. For each advertisement, note examples of ways that words, people, and emotions are used to persuade you to buy.
2. Share your findings with the class.

To Discuss
- What are some of the persuasive words used in advertisements?
- Which ads use a famous person to endorse the product or service?
- What emotional appeals are used in the ads?
- How do ads influence or persuade you to buy their products or services?

spur of the moment. Kyla saw some earrings she liked and immediately bought them. When she got home, she realized the earrings didn't match the outfits she bought them for. The money Kyla impulsively spent on earrings she really needed for a new pair of shoes.

Stores promote impulse buying with eye-catching displays. Impulse items are often placed close to the front of the store so you notice them as you enter. They're also placed near checkout counters, tempting customers as they wait in line.

Gather Information

Smart shopping involves becoming well-informed about products that you decide to buy. Ask someone you know who owns a product you're interested in buying whether he or she is pleased with the product.

Written material from manufacturers offers consumers another source of valuable information. Use it to compare features of various brands—an important task before choosing which brand to buy. Consumer magazines, such as *Consumer Reports*, are also helpful to compare products. These publications test and rate different brands for quality, safety, and price.

Product advertising in papers, magazines, and on TV and the Internet, can alert you to sales that help save money. However, read ads carefully to make sure they're not misleading. Don't rely on them as your only information source.

➤ **Smart shoppers search for the lowest price before they purchase an item.** What techniques do you use to compare prices?

When Will You Buy?

Knowing when to buy something can be as important as deciding what to buy. Timing your purchases means planning to buy them when it's best for you to do so. For example, some people buy items at end-of-season sales for less money than the items would cost at the start of the season.

Others save credit costs by paying for items with cash they've saved just for that purpose.

Smart shoppers learn about typical sale times and plan their purchases accordingly. For instance, a preseason coat and sweater sale often occurs in July or August. One way to find out about sales is to check out local ads. Then you can get more for your money by buying what you want when prices are reduced.

Where Will You Buy?

Before you decide where to buy a product, it pays to shop around. **Comparison shopping** involves *taking time to compare products, prices, and services*. For example, one store offered Carrie the computer she wanted at a low price. However, it didn't provide the services she thought she would need. You may want the convenience of repair service in case anything goes wrong. One store may offer free repair on the premises. Another store may require you to go elsewhere for service. Still another may charge you for repairs by selling you a service contract. Comparison shopping can help you find the place that offers the best balance of price and services that you want and need.

➤ Keeping a written journal of product information helps you stay organized while comparison shopping. Good organizational skills save time, money, and make you a smart shopper.

Look Before You Buy

It pays to learn as much as you can about a product before you buy it. Once you've gathered information and narrowed your choices, continue your investigation by taking the following steps:

- **Inspect a product's quality.** Check to see how well the item is made. For example, check clothing to see if seams are durable and buttons are attached securely.
- **Look at the price tag.** Is the product worth its cost? Can you find a better buy? Remember, a high price tag doesn't always mean good quality.

- **Find out if it is a name brand or a store brand.** Name brands usually cost more than store brands, mainly because name brands are widely advertised, and the advertising cost is added to the price. You may find the quality of many store brands equal to that of name brands, while the price is usually much lower.
- **Read product labels.** Labels and packages can give useful information that may affect your buying decisions. The federal government regulates information on clothing and food labels. Manufacturers decide what information to include for most other products.
- **Ask about a warranty.** A **warranty** is *a written guarantee that a product will work properly for a specified length of time unless misused or mishandled by the consumer.*

Choosing Where to Buy

Department Stores

They sell a variety of products and may offer a number of customer services, such as free delivery or repairs.

Specialty Stores

They usually sell one type of merchandise, such as sporting goods or shoes.

They offer a wide selection of these products but often charge more than other stores.

Discount Stores

Because they buy in large quantities and limit the number of clerks and customer services, their prices are usually lower than department stores.

Factory Outlets

Manufacturers sell their products directly to shoppers at these stores. Prices may be lower than those at department stores. Some items may be seconds, with slight imperfections, or they may be discontinued.

reduced

Warehouse Clubs

These charge lower prices than most supermarkets or department

club

If the product fails to work properly during that time due to defects in parts, materials, or workmanship, the seller agrees to repair or replace the product, or refund your money. Be sure to read a warranty carefully and fully understand all of its conditions.

YOUR CONSUMER RIGHTS AND RESPONSIBILITIES

In all areas of life, rights and responsibilities go hand in hand. This is especially true in the **marketplace**—*anywhere goods and services are bought and sold.* As a consumer, you have certain rights that are protected by state and federal law, and you have certain responsibilities.

➤ **Many electronic products require a warranty card to be filled out by the consumer. This provides the manufacturer with information needed to make the warranty active.**

stores because they buy in bulk and offer little or no services. They also charge a membership fee.

Mail-Order Companies

These companies feature catalogs of items you can order and have sent to you, thus saving time. When comparing prices among mail-order companies, remember to add shipping and handling fees, or perhaps a sales tax, to items from catalogs.

Electronic Shopping

You can use a TV or a computer to select and buy items without leaving home. Home-shopping channels and the Internet offer a variety of products you can buy with a credit card account.

Other Shopping Alternatives

Garage and yard sales, flea markets, and swap meets provide merchandise often for low prices. There is no customer service, and each item is sold "as is." That means you must shop carefully, because in most cases you won't be able to return items later. Auctions and classified ads also offer a variety of new and used goods for sale.

➤ Your consumer responsibility is to read and follow all instructions before using a product.

PROTECTING YOURSELF FROM CONSUMER FRAUD

- Don't fall for phony prize notifications.

- Never give your family's credit card number over the phone if you didn't place the call.

- Don't send money to any unknown business or organization without checking first to be sure it's reputable.

- Resist sales pressure to "buy today because the price will never be this low again." Take your time to think about what you want and need. The price will probably be the same tomorrow.

What Are Your Rights?

President John F. Kennedy introduced the Consumer Bill of Rights. Additions to the bill were made during the administrations of Presidents Nixon and Ford. These rights include:

- **The right to safety.** Consumers are protected against sales of dangerous products.
- **The right to be informed.** Businesses must give consumers honest and relevant facts about goods and services.
- **The right to be heard.** Consumers have a voice in making laws that affect them.
- **The right to choose.** Consumers have the right to choose from a variety of goods and services at competitive prices. Businesses are forbidden to take actions that limit competition.
- **The right to redress. Redress** is *the right to have a wrong corrected quickly and fairly.*
- **The right to consumer education.** All consumers are entitled to information about consumer issues.

What Are Your Responsibilities?

Rights and responsibilities are intertwined. For example, along with your right to information about products and their safety is your responsibility to learn about products and to use them safely—according to the manufacturers' directions. The same holds true for making wise choices, and seeking redress when goods and services don't measure up to specified standards. Other responsibilities include:

- Taking care of merchandise you handle or try on.
- Being fair and honest with stores. Pay for your purchases. If you don't pay, you're stealing and can go to jail.
- Paying attention while a sales transaction is taking place. Make sure the price registers correctly and you get back the correct change. If you get too much change back, be honest and return it.
- Saving sales receipts, instructions, and guarantees for items you buy. It's your responsibility to furnish these materials as proof of purchase if you return an item.

RESOLVING CONSUMER PROBLEMS

Have you ever bought a product that was damaged or didn't work as it should soon after purchase? Maybe you paid for a service that wasn't performed correctly or a product was sold to you for more than the advertised price. Most consumer problems can be resolved successfully. Businesses want and need satisfied customers and generally do their best to settle complaints fairly.

The majority of consumer problems involve refunding a customer's money or replacing a product that was purchased. Whenever you need to resolve a consumer problem, the following steps may prove helpful:

➤ It is the consumer's right to complain about a product that is damaged or a service when it is not satisfactory.

- **Check your warranty.** If your problem is covered by the product's warranty, follow instructions for service, refunds, or replacements. If the product has no warranty, or if a problem isn't covered in the warranty, take the product and your records to the store's customer service department. If your problem isn't resolved there, politely ask to speak to the manager.

- **State your problem and how you would like it resolved.** Do you want a refund or a replacement? Do you want the item repaired? If your trip to the store does not resolve the problem, put your complaint in writing. Briefly state the problem and the solution you think is fair. Include your name, address, and telephone number, as well as copies of your receipt and warranty. Keep a copy of your letter, along with your original receipt and warranty.

- **Consider further action.** If your letter doesn't bring results, you may contact the Better Business Bureau (BBB) to help resolve your consumer problem. The BBB is an organization of businesses that promise to follow fair business practices. As a last resort, you may choose to go to small claims court. In this type of court, you present your complaint before a judge, and the store or business involved must respond.

Review & Activities

Chapter Summary

- You are a consumer whenever you buy and use goods and services produced by others.
- Every purchase involves a choice that is affected by certain factors.
- A shopping plan can help you resist impulse buying.
- Smart shoppers get informed about products that they decide to buy.
- By timing your purchases, you can often buy items for less money.
- Comparison shopping lets you find the best balance of price and services that you want and need.
- Consumers have certain rights and responsibilities that are protected by law.
- Most consumer problems can be resolved successfully.

Family & Community

With Your Family

Think about some of the major purchases made by your family. Then talk to family members about factors they considered when making the purchases. Are they satisfied with their purchases? Discuss what changes, if any, they would suggest when making future purchases.

In Your Community

Some people are often unsuccessful at resolving legitimate consumer complaints for a variety of reasons. Think of volunteer activities you could do as a class to help individuals and families learn how to solve consumer problems effectively.

Reviewing the Chapter

1. Briefly describe seven factors that affect a consumer's choices.
2. Define impulse buying. How can a shopping plan help you resist buying on impulse?
3. List four sources of information about products you decide to buy.
4. Explain what it means to time your purchases to save money.
5. What is the purpose of comparison shopping?
6. Why do name brands usually cost more than store brands? Are name brands usually of better quality than store brands? Explain your answer.
7. What is a warranty? Why is it important to read a product's warranty?
8. List six consumer rights and six consumer responsibilities.
9. Briefly describe three steps you might take to resolve a consumer problem.

Review & Activities

Thinking Critically

1. **Assess outcomes.** Do you think most advertisements are helpful and reliable sources of information about products you are thinking of buying? Give examples to support your answer.

2. **Draw conclusions.** What are some ways that advertisers attempt to appeal to different cultural groups? Which advertisements do you feel are the most successful at attracting specific cultures? Explain your answer.

3. **Make generalizations.** What advice would you give consumers thinking of making purchases on the Internet? Why?

Making Connections

1. **Language Arts.** Write an imaginary letter of complaint that is sure to be poorly received by a businessperson or company. Read the letter to the class and discuss reasons why the letter would be unsuccessful. Rewrite the letter, following suggestions in this chapter, so that it's likely to get results.

2. **Art.** Select a newspaper or magazine advertisement that you think makes the most effective use of art to sell a product. Give reasons for your selection.

Applying Your Learning

1. **Write a skit.** Write and present a skit showing how peer pressure can influence people's buying decisions. Afterwards, brainstorm ways to deal with pressure to buy things you don't want or need.

2. **Role-play.** With a partner, role-play a situation in which a teen is returning a garment to a store. The garment faded when it was laundered according to the care instructions. Perform the skit before the class, with one person playing the part of the teen and the other the part of the store manager. Have the first part of the skit illustrate an unsuccessful meeting with the manager. In the second part of the skit, how the problem is resolved successfully. Point out steps a consumer should follow for success.

What Would You Do?

Suppose you go clothes shopping with some friends. At one store, the dressing room attendant is away on break while you and your friends try on clothes. As you leave the dressing area, you notice a red shirt (that one of your friends tried on) isn't in the dressing area. You're almost certain she stuffed the shirt in her bag. You know that shoplifting is wrong, but you don't want to accuse your friend or get her into trouble. How would you handle this problem?

Conserving the Environment

YOU WILL LEARN . . .

➤ Examples of renewable and nonrenewable resources.
➤ The importance of resource management.
➤ Ways to conserve resources.
➤ The importance of precycling, reusing, and recycling.

TERMS TO LEARN . . .

➤ conservation
➤ natural environment
➤ natural resources
➤ nonrenewable resources
➤ precycling
➤ renewable resources

Imagine ...

... you have to give a speech to your community on the state of the local environment. You have to explain some problems and progress about the environment in your community.

Think About

• How much do you know about the environment in your community? What could you do to find out more?
• What problems would you focus on?
• What good news might you present?

THE STATE OF EARTH

Each year, the president of the United States delivers a State of the Union address. In the speech, the president presents a summary of the condition of the country and its citizens. What if you had to give a State of the *Community* speech, describing the condition of your community's environment? How much do you know about it, and what would you say?

Today, many challenges face the **natural environment**—*the living and nonliving elements around you.* Polluted air, overflowing landfills, and toxic waste are a few of the environmental problems that communities everywhere need to solve. Fortunately, increasing numbers of people have become aware of environmental problems and are making positive changes. Perhaps you're among those who are making a difference.

➤ Food scraps can be placed in a compost bin. Natural resources must be protected against waste and harm. What steps can you take to conserve natural resources?

Earth's Natural Resources

Air, water, and trees are some of Earth's **natural resources**. These are *resources that occur in nature.* Imagine what life would be like without forests, rivers, lakes, and blue skies. The air you breathe and the water you drink help keep you alive and healthy. Other natural resources include coal and natural gas, fuels that are used to provide heat and light and run machines. Some natural resources, such as minerals and trees, are made into everyday products like household items and paper.

The Supply of Natural Resources

Only nature creates natural resources. Some resources, called **renewable resources**, *replace (renew) themselves over time.* Plants renew themselves by producing seeds, which in turn produce new plants. Air, water, and soil are also replaced through natural cycles. Supplies of fresh air, water, and soil are always being produced unless something interferes with their natural cycles.

Nonrenewable resources *do not replace themselves,* and their supply is limited. For example, once current world supplies of oil, copper, iron and other minerals are used up, no more will be available. Supplies of nonrenewable resources could last a long time, but only if people use them wisely.

Resources such as farmland, wilderness areas, and rain forests are also threatened. Large areas of land in many countries are being cleared so that growing populations will have a place to live. Clearing forests and vegetation in this way can have wide-ranging consequences.

YOU CAN HELP TO CONSERVE RESOURCES

Everyone has the responsibility to help manage Earth's natural resources. Management of natural resources involves **conservation**, or *protecting resources against waste and harm.*

Water

Imagine waking up one morning to find no more fresh water. Severe water shortages exist in many parts of the world. In other areas, water supplies are polluted and unusable. No matter where you live, clean, fresh water is a precious resource. Helping to conserve water means not wasting it. Here are simple ways to conserve water:

➤ Collecting rainwater is a natural and healthy way to water your plants and garden. It saves water and your plants will flourish.

- Turn faucets completely off after use, and repair plumbing leaks promptly. A leaky faucet can waste 650 gallons a year.
- Install aerators on your faucets and shower heads. They use less water but supply the same water pressure.
- Take quick showers instead of tub baths.
- Run the dishwasher or washing machine with full loads.
- Use fruit and vegetable scraps as compost for plants or a garden instead of putting them down garbage disposals. Disposals require running water.

Making a
DIFFERENCE

BETTER DAYS

"I think it's time for a new electric drill and power lawn mower," Ezra's dad said as they cleaned out the garage. "They've seen better days. We can check out some new ones later today."

"What will you do with these?" Ezra said.

"Toss them," his dad replied.

"There's a guy in town who repairs old household machines and tools," Ezra said. "He donates them to Habitat for Humanity for people who need them. Why don't we give them to him?"

"How'd you find out about him?"

"In class. We were studying how to help protect the environment. If you toss these out, they'll just end up in a landfill. Somebody else might get some use out of them.

"Good idea," said Ezra's dad. "Better days for someone else."

Taking Action

- Are there any items at home you're planning to discard? What could you do with them that would help protect the environment?
- What "environmentally friendly" tips could you give Ezra's dad for buying a new drill or lawn mower?

Heating and Cooling

It takes natural resources to heat and cool a home. Some heating requires nonrenewable fuels. Other kinds of heating and air conditioning depend on electricity—often produced by burning a nonrenewable fuel. For fuel supplies to last, it's important to minimize use. Here are some ideas to help conserve heating and cooling resources:

- Set a heater no higher than 68°F (20°C) during the day to save fuel. Turn the thermostat down at bedtime.

- Use weather stripping and caulking to stop heat from escaping around windows and doors.
- If your climate is cold, install storm doors and windows in the winter. These keep heat in and cold drafts out, thus conserving fuel.
- Close shades and draperies at night in cold weather to keep in the heat and keep out the cold. On sunny days, open shades and draperies. This lets you use the sun's energy to heat your home.
- Set your air conditioner no lower than 78°F (26°C) during the summer months. Have your air conditioner checked yearly. Coolant leaks can damage the planet's atmosphere.
- Use fans instead of an air conditioner. Fans use less electricity.

Lighting and Appliances

Lighting and appliances use Earth's reserves of fuel. You can help stretch fuel resources by the way you light and use appliances in your home.

- Clean lamps and lighting fixtures regularly.
- Replace high-wattage light bulbs with lower-wattage ones or fluorescent lights, which use less electricity.
- Turn off lights, TV sets, and stereos when you leave a room.
- Use an appliance that requires the smallest amount of energy for any task you do. For example, use a toaster to heat a bagel rather than heating it in an electric range.
- Don't open an oven door unnecessarily when cooking. This lets heat escape.
- Don't leave the refrigerator door open.
- Run a clothes dryer only as long as necessary to dry laundry. Consider air-drying clothes instead of using a dryer.

➤ **You can help with laundry duties and conserve energy by keeping the lint filter clean. This also helps to prevent dangerous fires.**

Transportation

Most vehicles are powered either by gasoline or diesel fuel. These fuels are made from crude oil, or petroleum, which is a nonrenewable resource. To cut fuel use and still meet your transportation needs:

• Use transportation that doesn't require fuel, such as biking, walking, or inline skating.

• Use public transportation, such as buses and subways.

• Join a carpool. Sharing rides is an efficient use of fuel.

• Keep your car maintained so it makes the best possible use of gas. Change the oil, keep tires at the correct air pressure, and have regular tune-ups.

• Eliminate unnecessary car trips. For example, call ahead to make sure a store has what you want.

➤ Cars with engines that are assisted by an electric motor during acceleration save energy and conserve natural resources. These cars can travel 70 miles on one gallon of fuel.

Consumer Goods

Most manufacturers are responsible corporate citizens. They follow government regulations to produce products in a way that reduces waste and minimizes the impact on the environment. Most products that you buy are manufactured using natural resources as raw materials. Paper, for example, is made from wood pulp, a substance from the wood of trees.

Some of these raw materials, such as trees, are renewable. Others can only be used once. The manufacturing process itself requires energy and may also produce materials that can pollute the environment.

While government regulations restrict pollution, you, the consumer, also play a role. Think before you buy. Your choices today make a difference in what the world will be like tomorrow.

➤ Paper products can be recycled and made into gift wrap and greeting cards. Look for the recycled paper symbol when making your purchases.

Making Wise Consumer Decisions

As a consumer you can help conserve resources by making wise consumer decisions at home and in the marketplace. Consider the following suggestions and add others as you read through the list.

• Ask yourself if you really need or want the item. Many items may not be worth the use of resources or the space they eventually take up in landfills.

• Buy products that feature the recycling symbol. This symbol is on packages that can be recycled and packages made from recycled materials.

Doing Your Part

ACTIVITY

What You'll Need
- Notebook paper
- Pen or pencil

What to Do
1. On a sheet of paper, list five nonfood products you use regularly, such as notebook paper, shampoo, and batteries. Describe how you use each product, how often you use it, the product's packaging, and whether or not it can be recycled.
2. Working in a group of four students, share your lists and descriptions. Discuss how these products and their packaging affect the environment.

To Discuss
- Does your use of these products show that you are doing your part to protect the environment? How?
- How might you reduce, reuse, or recycle these products and their containers?

➤ **Recycling is a method of replenishing resources.** What are some items that can be recycled?

➤ **Fighting pollution requires responsible action.** How can you and your friends help fight pollution in your community?

- Choose items that last as long as possible. Examples include rechargeable batteries and long-lasting light bulbs.
- Select items with little or no packaging. It takes resources to make wrappers and boxes.
- Reuse plastic bags when you shop and carry groceries and other products home.
- When buying appliances, compare their use of electricity or gas. EnergyGuide labels will help you choose appliances that make good use of fuels.
- When purchasing a vehicle, compare the miles per gallon of various models. Select a model that gets excellent mileage, using as little fuel as possible.

PROTECTING THE ENVIRONMENT

It's never too soon to do your part to protect the environment. Your actions to conserve precious natural resources and reduce waste can have a far-reaching effect. By taking time to be aware of environmental issues, inform others, and make sound consumer decisions, you can help make the world a better place to live.

REDUCING WASTE

- Consider reuse when you buy a product. If you can't use the container now, store it for use later.
- Try to repair broken items instead of throwing them away.
- Donate things you no longer want or can't use to people who can use them.
- Reuse ribbons, packaging cartons, and shipping materials.
- Look for nontoxic household cleaners to avoid ingredients that may cause pollution.

Taking Action against Trash

You can do your part to reduce the amount of garbage in the environment by precycling, reusing, and recycling materials. Look at the following examples of ways to get involved.

Precycling

Precycling is one way of conserving resources before you use them. You can precycle as you shop when you:

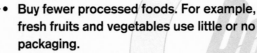

- Buy fewer processed foods. For example, fresh fruits and vegetables use little or no packaging.

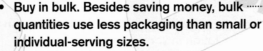

- Buy in bulk. Besides saving money, bulk quantities use less packaging than small or individual-serving sizes.

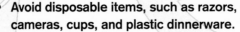

- Avoid disposable items, such as razors, cameras, cups, and plastic dinnerware.

- Select refillable computer printer toner cartridges.

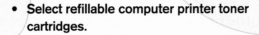
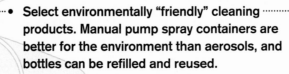

- Select environmentally "friendly" cleaning products. Manual pump spray containers are better for the environment than aerosols, and bottles can be refilled and reused.

Reusing

Many things you throw away can be reused to satisfy everyday needs. How can you add to the following list of ways that trash can be reused?

- Reuse plastic containers for food storage.

- Use containers or glass jars to organize small items.

- Reuse wrapping paper, plastic bags, boxes, and lumber.

- Cut old towels and sheets into small pieces to clean and dust.

- Give books and magazines you no longer need to your school library, or community centers.

Recycling

Recycling is the treating of waste so that it can be reused—rather than buried in landfills. Most large-scale recycling requires energy and water, plus fuel to transport materials to recycling facilities. However, fewer resources are used than in the original manufacturing process. For example, recycled aluminum products use 95 percent less energy than the same products made from raw materials. Materials that you and your family can recycle include:

- Newspapers and other paper products.

- Aluminum cans and other aluminum containers such as pie pans and frozen food trays.

- Cardboard.

- Glass bottles and jars.

- Motor oil. Take motor oil to a service station or oil change shop for proper disposal.

- Recyclable steel products.

- Tires. Many states require service stations to recycle worn tires that are removed from cars when new tires are purchased.

- Kitchen waste and yard clippings. Compost heaps or bins store organic waste that decays naturally to form fertilizer for trees, plants, and gardens.

Chapter Summary

- Air, water, and trees are some of the earth's natural resources.
- Unless something interferes with natural cycles, renewable resources replace themselves over time. Nonrenewable resources do not replace themselves.
- You can protect natural resources by conserving water and fuel used for heating and cooling.
- Tomorrow's trash often comes from what you buy today, so make wise consumer decisions.
- EnergyGuide labels can help you choose appliances that are fuel-efficient.

Family & Community

With Your Family

Talk about some of your favorite outdoor places. Gather past photographs of some of these places. If possible, take new pictures of these places and compare them with the old pictures. Have they changed or stayed the same? Summarize your findings.

In Your Community

Many communities are concerned about the current and future capacity of their landfills. Questions about what to do with increasing amounts of trash remain unanswered. Brainstorm some volunteer activities you could do as a class to inform citizens of these problems.

- Fewer resources are used to recycle products than in the original manufacturing process.
- Kitchen waste and yard clippings can be composted to form fertilizer.

Reviewing the Chapter

1. What is the natural environment? Name three environmental problems that communities need to solve.
2. Give three examples of renewable resources.
3. Give two examples of nonrenewable resources.
4. List six ways you can conserve water.
5. Give seven suggestions for conserving heating and cooling resources.
6. What are four ways you can cut fuel use and still meet your transportation needs?
7. Give two examples of items that are long-lasting and help conserve resources.
8. What is the purpose of EnergyGuide labels?
9. Briefly describe five ways you can precycle and conserve resources.
10. Give seven examples of materials you and your family can recycle.

Thinking Critically

1. **Draw conclusions.** Why do you think recycling has more supporters today than it did in previous years? In what ways has your community (or your family) changed its recycling efforts?

2. **Make generalizations.** How would keeping a vehicle a few extra years be a good example of precycling? In what ways do you precycle, reducing the amount of trash discarded?

3. **Clarify fact or fiction.** Some household trash may contain hazardous materials. What are some of these products? Why should they not be mixed with nonhazardous waste in landfills not designed for such materials?

Making Connections

1. **Science.** Investigate the use of carpools in your community, the miles-per-gallon estimates of current models of vehicles sold, or the amount of gasoline your family uses each week. How could each impact the environment?

2. **Science.** Conduct a classroom experiment involving a battery-powered radio, flashlight, or toy to contrast the life of disposable batteries with rechargeable ones. Then compare the actual operating costs. Discuss the effect of discarded batteries on landfills and drinking water.

Applying Your Learning

1. **Create a display.** Create a display to encourage students to conserve and recycle. With permission, set up the display in your school.

2. **Write letters.** Compare two products: one that has a minimum amount of packaging and one with an excessive amount. Write a letter to each manufacturer: commend the company with minimal packaging; encourage the other to reduce its packaging.

3. **Keep a log.** Keep a log of everything you throw away for one week. Circle the items that could have been reused or recycled. At the end of the week, think about how the environment would be affected if everyone threw away the same amount of garbage as you do.

What Would You Do?

Suppose you live in a neighborhood with some beautiful trees and a small pond. It saddens you to see your neighbors throw trash along the edge of the street. You care about the environment and want to keep it clean. You also don't want to get into disputes with any of your neighbors. How would you handle this problem?

Career Network

INSURANCE SALES AGENT

Growing insurance company needs licensed sales representative with proven sales ability.
- Excellent income potential.
- Salary and commission for six months, then commission only.
- College degree preferred.

CONSUMER JOURNALIST

Small weekly newspaper has entry-level opening for consumer journalist. Research and write articles related to family issues such as education and health.
- Self-discipline in meeting deadlines essential.
- Four-year degree in journalism required.

ADVERTISING DIRECTOR

Advertising agency seeks director to create and oversee development of effective ads for clients.
- Must work well under pressure.
- Supervisory experience necessary.
- Four-year degree required.

ACTUARY

Large insurance company is seeking actuary for entry-level position.
- Bachelor's degree and high math skills required.
- Candidates must have passed two or more Society of Actuaries exams.

LOAN OFFICER

First City Bank seeks entry-level loan officer for consumer loan department.
- Bachelor's degree and computer skills required.
- Must work well with people and pay close attention to detail.
- Training program provided.

RETAIL MANAGER

Large retail store needs manager for toy and sporting goods departments. Will supervise employees and manage daily activities.
- Good customer service skills needed.
- Associate's degree required.
- Formal training provided.

More Career Options

Entry Level
- Cashier
- Retail Salesperson
- Bank Teller
- Market Researcher
- Credit Checker

Technical Level
- Demonstrator
- Technical Support Specialist
- Home Appliance Repairer
- Library Technician

Professional Level
- Financial Analyst
- Benefits Administrator
- Controller
- Marketing Manger
- Consumer Specialist

PERSONAL BANKING REPRESENTATIVE

Enthusiastic sales rep needed to sell bank products and provide customer service.
• Should have strong sales aptitude.
• Bachelor's degree and banking experience preferred.

TAX PREPARER

National tax service is looking for experienced tax preparers for seasonal positions.
• Bachelor's degree required.
• CPA preferred.
• Comprehensive training provided.

HUMAN RESOURCES DIRECTOR

Expanding company seeks organized human resources director to oversee employee relations, benefits, and compensation programs.
• Degree in human resources desired.
• Previous supervisory experience required.

TRAVEL AGENT

Entry-level opening for travel agent to work in a fast-paced office.
• Technical training provided.
• Excellent communications and customer service skills needed.

Linking School to Career

1. **Your Career Plan:** Many careers require that you relocate or "go where the jobs are." Some jobs can only be found in certain places , such as large cities or in particular areas of the country. Think of five jobs that interest you. Could you find work in the jobs you listed in your community? Can you think of any jobs that do not exist in your area? Would you be willing to move for your career?

2. **Researching Careers:** Many careers in consumer and resource management demand math skills. Research some of the jobs listed on this page to determine what other skills they call for. Which jobs interest you? How could you go about building the skills they require?

3. **Reading:** Look up the definitions of the following terms that are found in the want ads:
• Entry-level
• Commission
• Self-discipline
• Aptitude
• Compensation

Your Health and Wellness

Good Health

YOU WILL LEARN . . .

➤ The importance of physical, mental, emotional, and social health.
➤ The benefits of maintaining physical health.
➤ The contribution good grooming makes to your health.
➤ The role stress plays in your life.

TERMS TO LEARN . . .

➤ acne
➤ dandruff
➤ decibel
➤ dermatologist
➤ grooming
➤ health
➤ plaque
➤ wellness

Imagine ...

... a vintage guitar. It was made before you were born, yet the instrument is in excellent shape. The wood is polished, with no cracks or warps. The strings have just the right amount of tension, each one in tune. Notes sound sweet and clear. You marvel at the craftsmanship that produced such a fine guitar and the care that keeps it playing so beautifully.

Think About

• Do you think this guitar is played regularly?
• What would happen if the strings were too tightly strung?
• What does the condition of the guitar tell you about its owner?

HEALTH AND WELLNESS

Good health is like a fine instrument. Your body and mind are in tune with one another. Maybe you've never thought of well-being that way before. What exactly does good health mean to you? Some of your friends might reply "not being sick" or "feeling good." Another person might say "being happy." They'd all be partly right. Actually, **health** is *the condition of your body and your mind*. It includes:

- **Physical health**—the condition of your body.
- **Mental and emotional health**—as reflected in your thinking, attitudes, and feelings.
- **Social health**—as reflected in your relationships with others.

Physical, mental, emotional, and social health are inter-related, like the parts of a fine, well-tuned instrument. All are affected by your day-to-day actions and decisions. For instance, one night Gary didn't get very much sleep. The next day he felt down and irritable. He didn't perform as well on the math test or race as fast at track practice as he could have. He argued with his best friend, who avoided him the rest of the afternoon. How would you rate Gary's overall health that day?

Wellness is *a way of living based on healthy attitudes and actions*. When you're feeling good, you may not think about what you do to make that attitude happen. If you take care of your body and keep a positive attitude, you're more likely to enjoy good health.

YOUR PHYSICAL HEALTH

Your everyday activities—sleeping, grooming, eating, and exercising—all contribute to your physical health. When you enjoy physical health, you have enough energy for all the things you need and want to do every day. You also look and feel your best.

It makes good sense to seek regular medical checkups. This gives you the chance to talk to a doctor about any health problems or questions you have. Doctors can usually identify and handle small problems before they turn into major ones.

➤ Proper rest, a well-balanced diet, and exercise affect your health. Why do you think these are important contributors to a person's wellness?

➤ Sleep is your body's way of revitalizing itself. Most people require 7-9 hours of sleep each night. Lack of sleep can lead to health problems.

For example, physicians have issued warnings about decibel damage. The **decibel** *measures the loudness of sound.* Any noise above 85 decibels can damage your hearing. When sound levels are too high, the sound can destroy hearing receptors (hair cells) and cause hearing loss. Using headphones to listen to blaring music or standing near amplified speakers at concerts exposes you to a range of 115-120 decibels. Lowering the volume or wearing ear plugs offers protection.

Sleep and Rest

You've heard experts say that sleep is important. While you sleep, your body repairs itself, removes waste products from cells, and builds a supply of energy for action the next day.

You may think that you can get more done if you sleep less. But when you don't get enough sleep, everything feels like an effort. It's hard to concentrate, and you're more likely to make mistakes. Teens need to aim for about eight hours of sleep a night. You'll feel a lot better the next day—and will be more likely to get done everything you want to do!

➤ **Practicing healthy habits now will reduce the chance for problems as you age. Eating right will improve both your physical and mental health.**

INFOLINK

See Chapters 28 and 29 for more information on good nutrition.

➤ **When do you feel most self-confident? When you practice good grooming habits, you get a head start on making yourself a more attractive person.**

Exercise and Nutrition

Exercise and good nutrition are a powerful combination. Do you have the exercise and nutrition edge? It's been proven that people who are more physically active and maintain a healthy weight have trimmer bodies, fewer health problems, more energy, a better mental outlook, and better coordination.

In some ways, your body is similar to a machine. Machines need oil in order to run smoothly. Your body needs nutritious food in order to function efficiently. Eating a variety of foods keeps you well-nourished and gives you the energy you need to keep on top of your schedule.

Good Grooming

Grooming means *the personal care routine you follow to keep yourself clean and attractive.* Everyone isn't born with natural good looks, but anyone can be attractive by making the most of what he or she has.

HOW to...

Protect Your Skin and Enjoy the Sun

Why protect your skin in the sun? Studies show that too much exposure to the sun's rays damages your skin. The greatest threat of too much sun is skin cancer.

What can you do to protect your skin? Doctors recommend using *sunscreen* for protection. Sunscreens provide a barrier between your skin and the harmful ultraviolet rays of the sun. Sunscreens have an SPF (sun protection factor) number. This number indicates the amount of protection you receive from the sun. For example, an SPF of 10 allows a person who would normally burn after 30 minutes of exposure to be in the sun safely 10 times longer than usual.

Here are some tips to help you select and use sunscreen:

- Choose a sunscreen with an SPF of 15 or higher, especially if you burn easily.
- Apply sunscreen liberally over your entire body. Some people get sunburned even through their clothing.
- Apply sunscreen at least 30 minutes before you go out in the sun. This allows time for the sunscreen to be absorbed into your skin, making it less likely to be washed away by perspiration.
- Reapply sunscreen if you go into the water often or perspire heavily.

Cleanliness is vital for your health and appearance. As you read about grooming and cleanliness, think about how your routine measures up.

Caring for Your Skin

Your skin is like fabric that covers and protects your body. It warns you about heat, cold, and pain. It produces oils to keep itself soft and moisture (perspiration) to help regulate your body temperature.

As a child, how many times did someone remind you about being clean? "Don't forget to wash behind your ears." Take a daily bath or shower as part of your routine. If you can't shower or bathe every day, fill a bowl or basin with water and wash yourself from head to toe. Soap and water wash dirt away and remove dried skin, extra oil, and surface bacteria that can cause body odors and infections.

► Clean skin leads to healthy skin. Bathe or shower daily. What should you do if you develop allergies to cleansing products?

Everyone perspires—TV commercials won't let you forget it. Perspiration is a natural body process that regulates your body temperature. Your body contains a lot of sweat glands under your arms. When you perspire, skin bacteria react with the perspiration and produce an odor. How do you control the odor? Use a deodorant or antiperspirant every day. Antiperspirants also help to keep your skin drier.

Acne

Acne is *a skin problem that develops when glands below the pores (tiny openings) in the skin become blocked.* The oils that normally move through the pores to soften the skin are trapped beneath it. As more oil becomes trapped, blackheads and whiteheads develop. Often these areas become irritated or infected and develop into pimples. Despite what you might think, no medical evidence links your diet—chocolate, cola drinks, or potato chips—to the cause of acne.

If you have acne, you're not alone. About 80 percent of all teens develop acne. Acne is most common on the face, upper chest, and back. The best treatment for mild cases of acne is to wash your face twice daily. You can also blot your face with a tissue between washings to remove the oil. Over-the-counter acne medicine that you buy without a doctor's prescription may help. Try not to use oily makeup on problem areas. The worst thing you can do

► Stress and strong emotions can trigger acne. What are some ways, besides medication, to treat it?

is pick or squeeze the acne. This injures the skin, spreads bacteria, and can leave lifelong scars.

Serious cases of acne need to be treated by a **dermatologist,** *a doctor specializing in skin problems.*

Caring for Your Hair

Did you know that hair reflects your general health? Attractive hair begins on the inside. A poor diet, emotional stress, or even a bad cold can alter the appearance of your hair.

How often do you need to shampoo your hair? Many teens have so much natural oil in their hair that they need to shampoo it every day. Others need to shampoo it less often. Wash your hair often enough to keep it looking good.

Dandruff, or *scales and flakes on the scalp*, is a problem for many teens. To help control dandruff, keep your hair clean. Special dandruff shampoos can often be effective. Keep combs, brushes, and other hair-care equipment clean. Change your pillowcases often. Avoid scratching your scalp with sharp combs or finger nails. If your dandruff is severe and doesn't improve, a dermatologist may help.

BUYING SHAMPOO

Are you confused by the many different types and brands of shampoo on store shelves? These facts may help you choose:

- Shampoos do one thing only—clean hair—regardless of advertised promises.

- Shampoos containing protein can make your hair look and feel fuller and less limp temporarily. Eating enough protein in your diet is the only way to get it in your hair.

➤ Because people have different types of hair, proper hair care varies for each individual. Think about your friends and the differences in their hair.

Caring for Your Teeth

"Look ma, no cavities." Now there's a phrase to make you smile. Good dental hygiene is important for healthy teeth and an attractive smile.

Brushing your teeth after eating and before going to bed helps remove decay-causing plaque. **Plaque,** *a sticky film that clings to your teeth*, is formed by the food, bacteria, and air in your mouth. Together, plaque and sugar combine to form acid. In turn, the acid eats away your tooth enamel and forms a cavity. Any sugary or starchy food will feed the bacteria in plaque.

How do you fight plaque? Following some simple tips can help you prevent tooth decay:

- **Brush your teeth after eating.** Bacteria start to work within minutes after you eat.

- **Floss regularly between your teeth.** Dental floss removes food particles between your teeth that a toothbrush can't.

- **Eat starchy and sugary foods at mealtime rather than snacktime.** The liquids you drink at meals, along with your saliva, help rinse sugar from your mouth.

- **See a dentist regularly.** A dentist can check out minor problem areas before they become major ones.

➤ **"Brushing each day keeps decay away."**
Keep your smile beautiful.

YOUR EMOTIONAL AND SOCIAL HEALTH

When you turn on your sound system to listen to your favorite music, you adjust the controls until the sound is just right. You try to strike a good balance of sound.

In your everyday activities, you also want to strike a balance between your emotional, social, and physical health. If one of these areas is seriously out of balance, the other areas often suffer, too.

When Jolene neglected taking care of her teeth, she developed a toothache. That made her feel irritable. When her close friend Samantha kidded her after school, they got into an argument. That ruined their basketball game. When you balance the physical, emotional, and social parts of your life, you feel positive about yourself. You're able to get along with others and manage problems and stress in a mature way.

➤ Everyone experiences stress. It can be good if it pushes you to work harder. Too much stress can lead to health problems. Learn to balance your stress.

Stress

Stress is the physical or emotional strain or tension that is the body's natural response to conflict. Everyone has to deal with stress. Anyone who moves to a new city or school experiences stress. Family problems can trigger stress. Trying to meet a deadline for school can cause stress. You may never be completely free of stress, but you can definitely learn how to manage it.

Stress isn't entirely negative. When you get ready for a major sports event or test in class, it's natural to feel a certain amount of stress. The stress you feel compels you to work harder to succeed. When the event or test is over, the stress you felt usually vanishes. On the other hand, too much stress can cause emotional strain and even lead to physical health problems.

➤ Have you ever felt these signs of stress? How did you overcome it?

Signs of Stress

How do you know when you're suffering from an overload of stress? Your body gives you physical and emotional signals. For example, a racing heart if you get scared and sweating hands if you're nervous are physical clues to stress. Other signs of stress can include headaches, tightness in your shoulders or neck, and feeling overly tired, which can lead to irritability.

Signs of stress are like warning lights. They could be warning you of serious problems. When you see signs of stress in yourself, try to find healthy ways to reduce the stress in your life.

What Can You Do?

Much of the time, it's your attitude about an event, not the event itself, that results in stress. For example, if you have to stand in a long line, your attitude about waiting will determine how stressful the situation will be. You can become frustrated and angry over the delay. Or you can choose not to be upset. Which attitude is more likely to create stress?

Try some of these tips the next time you feel stressed:
• Think about the positive side of a situation.
• Choose the problems you decide to meet head on.
• Learn to be more accepting.
• Be open to other points of view.
• Try to relax or work off your stress with a physical activity.

Juggling Act

ACTIVITY

What You'll Need
- 5 tennis balls

What to Do
1. Ask a partner to catch the tennis balls as you toss them to him or her one at a time. Throw the balls slowly so your partner can catch most of them.
2. Retrieve the balls and repeat the activity, but this time toss the balls fast enough that your partner has trouble catching most of them.
3. Retrieve the balls again and repeat the activity, but this time toss all the balls to your partner at once.

To Discuss
- What can this activity tell us about the effects of stress in our lives?
- What are some positive and negative ways to handle stress?

Setting goals may help you reduce or manage stress. If you have a goal to work toward, extra tasks and responsibilities will be more meaningful. A goal will also help you measure your work. You'll be able to see how much you have accomplished and how much remains to be done. It makes handling stress easier and helps you strike a better balance in your physical, emotional, and social health—like a well-tuned instrument!

➤ Setting realistic goals and planning activities enable you to meet your expectations. Being organized leads to less stress.

Review & Activities

Chapter Summary

- Your health is a reflection of the condition of both your body and mind.
- Your physical, mental, emotional, and social health are interrelated.
- Sufficient sleep, exercise, and nutrition all contribute to good physical health.
- Following accepted grooming practices helps you to achieve a healthier life.
- Skin protects your body and requires regular care.
- Good dental care helps to prevent dental cavities from developing.
- Learning to recognize and handle stress is important to your overall health.

Reviewing the Chapter

1. Identify the three main components of health.
2. Why is sleep important to your health?
3. How do you benefit from exercise and good nutrition? Give two examples.
4. Explain why good grooming practices are important to your health.
5. What causes acne?
6. Identify four steps you can take to help prevent tooth decay.
7. Describe how stress can be both harmful and helpful.
8. List four signs of stress.
9. Describe at last four ways you can handle stress.

Family & Community

With Your Family

Talk with family members about your family health practices and habits. In what areas do you think you could make improvements? Identify one or two specific practices that you would like to change and improve. Try out your ideas to see how they work.

In Your Community

Work with your classmates to develop a school wellness campaign. Use eye-catching posters. Obtain the approval and cooperation of school authorities.

- Select a theme.
- Develop motivational posters.
- Assess the effectiveness of your campaign.

Thinking Critically

1. **Predict consequences.** What would happen if you were not able to balance all parts of your life? How would it affect your relationships with family and friends?

2. **Draw conclusions.** How can poor grooming practices affect other areas of your life? Why does society place importance on being well groomed? How does good grooming relate to a healthy self-concept?

3. **Analyze the situation.** How would you react if a friend said, "I'm all stressed out"? What would you say to your friend? Why is it important for teens to recognize and learn to handle stress?

Making Connections

1. **Language Arts.** Select a good grooming practice. Write an article for a teen column in a school newspaper explaining the importance of this practice.

2. **Science.** Talk to a dentist for suggestions about how teens can improve their dental hygiene. Explain in class why these pointers are important. Support your information with research.

Applying Your Learning

1. **Achieve balance.** Make a list of five people you know who demonstrate balance in their physical, mental, and social life. Explain why you selected these people.

2. **Take a survey.** Develop a questionnaire to survey teens in your school about their health practices. What practices are important to include? Summarize your findings.

3. **Share ideas.** In small groups, brainstorm a list of common stressful situations teens face. Offer suggestions about how to handle these situations in a healthful manner. Share your suggestions with the class.

What Would You Do?

Your best friend has been very moody lately, and always seems too busy to get together. He or she is trying out for the basketball team, working to improve grades, participating in the school play, and now wants to get a part-time job on Saturdays. Should you talk to your friend about his or her busy schedule? If so, what would you say?

YOU WILL LEARN . . .

➤ The benefits of exercise.
➤ The factors affecting weight.
➤ Strategies for maintaining healthy weight.
➤ The risks associated with eating disorders.

TERMS TO LEARN . . .

➤ aerobic exercise
➤ anorexia
➤ basal metabolic rate
➤ binge eating disorder
➤ bulimia
➤ muscular endurance
➤ sedentary

Imagine ...

... watching a muscular track star in a race. How did the runner's body get so fit and full of energy? The athlete trained and exercised daily, ate healthful foods, and treated her body like a valuable possession. No wonder the runner easily won her track event.

Think About

• What would have happened if the runner did not take such good care of her body?
• How does a runner know just how much time to spend on exercise?
• What might happen to the runner if she overdid her exercise?

> Lack of physical activity is a risk factor for heart disease. Participating in regular activity greatly reduces the risk for heart disease and many other illnesses. What is your exercise routine?

WHY EXERCISE?

Do you ever look at well-known athletes, film and TV personalities, or fashion models, and wish you were like them? Maybe you've even daydreamed about having a total make-over.

What's the difference between you and the personalities you admire? At one time, they were exactly like you. If you could find out what made them successful, what do you think it would be? Most of them would tell you that they set goals. An important part of their plan was making a commitment to be physically fit. You can make fitness your priority, too.

Why not exercise? Exercise helps you become physically fit. You'll have more energy, and end up more mentally alert. You'll feel good about yourself and gain more self-confidence. You'll reduce stress, or how your body reacts to change. You'll improve your muscle tone and your overall appearance. So why isn't everyone exercising?

Make Your Program a Habit

In order to get the most benefit from exercise, make it a regular habit. Your program should include the four elements of fitness described on page 356. However, you don't need to work on all four elements every day. Follow the tips that some experts suggest to plan a personal exercise program:

- Include a strength-building session two times a week. Work all the major muscle groups: chest, stomach, back, legs, and arms. Allow at least 48 hours between strength workouts to rest your muscles and build new tissue.
- Perform stretching exercises several times a week. You might do them before and after your workouts, or before going to bed.
- Do some type of aerobic exercise at least three times a week. Most health experts recommend performing aerobic exercise for 30 minutes each session.

It's easier to stick with an exercise program if you're active and have fun at the same time. Make a date with a friend to play tennis, go hiking, run track, shoot baskets, or go line dancing. Get a workout tape, exercise to music, or organize an exercise group that works out together at least two times a week. Exercising, playing sports, or walking with friends combines two important parts of your life— socializing and physical fitness.

Keeping Workouts Safe

Just as important as doing exercise is to do it safely. If you overdo your workouts or develop an injury, you'll be sidelined and miss out on the fun and benefits of your exercise program. Also, remember to drink plenty of water before, during, and after any vigorous exercise.

Pick a safe place and time to exercise. Surfaces with some cushioning, such as a track, are better for running than hard surfaces, like concrete. On hot days when you may get dehydrated, try to exercise in the early morning or early evening when it's cooler.

Developing an Exercise Program

You need a variety of activities to benefit your body in different ways. A total exercise program works on all four of these elements:

Muscular Endurance

The ability of your muscles to work continuously over a long time is called **muscular endurance**. Most aerobic activity improves your muscular endurance.

Muscular Strength

Strength enables your muscles to push or pull with force. Having strong muscles can also improve your posture and help prevent injury. Exercises such as weight lifting, leg lifts, and push-ups are examples of weight-bearing exercises. They increase the strength of your muscles, bones, and joints.

Heart and Lungs

Your heart, lungs, and blood vessels deliver oxygen to every part of your body. You can train them to work more efficiently with regular aerobic exercise. **Aerobic exercise** is any vigorous activity that causes your heart to beat faster for a sustained amount of time. Jumping rope, running, cycling, swimming, and walking at a fast pace are healthful aerobic exercises.

Flexibility

You should be able to move your muscles and joints easily, without pain or stiffness. Slow, gentle stretching exercises help improve flexibility.

Start each exercise session with a warm-up period. It prepares your body for more vigorous activity and helps prevent injury. March in place for a few minutes to warm up your muscles, and then do stretching exercises. Finally, begin a "light and easy" version of the activity you're planning to do.

After you've exercised, end each session with a cool-down period. This allows your heart rate to slow down and return to normal. Think about driving a car 60 miles per hour and suddenly hitting the brakes. You'd feel quite a jolt. A cool-down lets you gradually slow down your body, rather than feel as if you screeched to a sudden halt. Then stretch again to help prevent soreness.

MANAGING YOUR WEIGHT

Second to infancy, your teen years are the fastest growth stage of life. As a teen who's still growing, your body is in the process of developing. It's natural for you to gain weight. You can't change your natural development, but you can determine the direction it takes.

➤ Exercise uses up your body's supply of fluids. Fluids are replaced through foods and beverages. Drink 6-8 glasses of water per day to maintain a proper fluid balance.

What Affects Weight?

Your weight isn't the result of any single factor or any one thing you do. One person can eat an unbelievable amount of food every day and never seem to gain a pound. Another person has to struggle to even stay at the same weight.

Your weight is affected by your metabolic rate, your genetic makeup, your body composition, your physical activity, and the food you eat. Each of these factors influences the number of pounds that registers when you step on a scale.

- **Your basic energy needs.** Your **basal metabolic rate** (BMR) is *the rate at which your body uses energy when you're inactive.* Your body is always working for you. It needs energy for your heartbeat, for breathing, and keeping your

Making a DIFFERENCE

RUNNING STRONG

"Both of us would rather watch TV after school than exercise," Cass said to Diana, her best friend. "And we both complain all the time that we feel out of shape."

"So?" Diana asked, suspiciously.

"So, I have an idea," Cass replied. "What if we made a pact. We could jog together twice a week, and see if we like it."

"What makes you think we'll like it? I won't!"

"Diana, you don't even know yet. We haven't tried. We'll be together, and you might even have fun. The best thing is, we'll feel better about ourselves for trying."

Diana shrugged. "Well, as long as you promise we do it together."

"Promise," Cass laughed. And they slapped hands to cement their pact.

Taking Action

1. If you don't exercise regularly, what exercise could you think of to do regularly with a friend?
2. What other reasons could Cass give Diana to convince her of the healthful benefits of exercise?

body warm. It also cools your body down, sends messages to your brain, and produces thousands of body chemicals. Your basal metabolism consumes about 60 percent of your body's energy needs.

- **Genetic makeup.** Your genetic makeup is what you inherit from your family. It helps to determine your skin and hair color, your height and size, as well as your body shape. Genetics also affect your basal metabolism.
- **Body composition.** Your body is made up of lean tissue (muscle and bone) and body fat. Exercise develops muscles. Muscles burn up more calories than fat tissue, but take up less space. So if you develop muscles through exercise, you can improve your body and appearance.

➤ Genetic traits can be predicted by the past history of your relatives. What are some of the genetic traits shared by your family?

- **Physical activity.** When you move your body, you use energy. Very active people use more energy than **sedentary** (*inactive*) people. Physical activity generally accounts for 30 to 40 percent of your energy needs. When you're physically active, you increase your basal metabolic rate for at least 24 hours after exercise. So while sleeping, your exercise routine is still working for you.
- **Food.** Nutrients in food supply energy, so it's important to make eating healthful foods a natural part of your exercise program.

Keep a Fitness Record

You may keep a record of how you spend your money, so you'll be able to save for some new clothes or a class trip. Why not keep a record of your eating and exercise habits? Habits evolve, or develop, over time. Sometimes you may not even realize an activity has become a habit. For instance, one day after school you might turn on the TV out of boredom. Gradually, you develop a habit of watching TV for hours after school every day.

Are you always aware of the habits you've developed? A journal can help you check out your habits, both good and poor ones. It's been shown that people who keep a food and exercise diary are more successful at staying fit than those who don't keep any records at all.

➤ Having too much or too little body weight is hard on your body and leads to health problems. Check with your doctor or look at a current weight chart to see if you are at a healthy weight.

Make exercise and physical activity fun, not work. You can be more active and still have fun at the same time.

- Try a variety of activities to exercise different muscles, including your heart!

- Exercise to stay fit but don't overdo it. You don't need to do a heavy workout every day.

- Exercise adds up. If you can't do 30 minutes at one time, try smaller segments that add up to 30 minutes: a 10-minute brisk walk, 10 minutes jumping rope, or vacuming 10 minutes at home.

- If you watch TV, exercise at the same time.

It takes commitment and a few minutes a day, but keeping a fitness record is fairly easy. Each day for at least a week do the following:

- List the foods and beverages you eat and drink, and the amounts you consume.
- Write down the time and place where you eat or drink
- Comment on how you feel when you eat, your mood, and how hungry you are.
- List your physical activities and the amount of time you spend doing them.

After a week or two, take a close look at what you've written. You'll probably notice some clear patterns. Maybe you snack on chips in front of the TV at night or eat when you have nothing to do. Maybe you skip meals and later grab fast food on the run. Check out your physical activities and see whether you're getting enough exercise.

Are you satisfied with the patterns you see in your diary? What changes could you make to be more physically fit? Are you willing to make these changes?

A Weight Management Plan

You can use the information in your diary to set personal weight management goals. Make realistic and specific goals you can measure. Instead of saying, "I'm going to exercise more," say, "I'm going to join the intramural soccer team after school."

➤ **Healthy eating and exercise habits lead to better health and wellness.** What healthy habits do you practice? **Keeping a fitness record for one week can help you study your behaviors.**

If you want to lose weight, do it gradually. Successful weight-loss programs prove that a weight loss of one-half to one pound a week is a realistic goal. It's much easier to stick with your plan over a longer period of time. "Quick-fix" diets don't work. People who lose weight quickly often gain it right back.

If you want to gain weight, you'll have to take in more calories than you burn. You can:
- Add some snacks between meals.
- Spread out your food during the day
- Choose food higher in calories. Some nutritious examples include granola, bagels, dried fruit, peanut butter, dried peas and beans, starchy vegetables, pasta and grains, low-fat cheese, and low-fat ice cream.

Eating Disorders

It's normal for teens to be concerned about their weight, but sometimes those concerns get out of control. Obsession about food, combined with mental and emotional problems, may indicate an eating disorder. Eating disorders are extreme and serious eating behaviors that can lead to sickness and even death.

There are three main types of eating disorders:
- **Anorexia** is *an eating disorder characterized by self-starvation.* People with this disorder have a strong fear of being overweight. They eat very little and become extremely thin, yet still think they weigh too much.
- **Bulimia** is *a condition in which people eat large quantities in a short period of time and then purge.* They induce vomiting, abuse laxatives, or over-exercise in order not to gain weight.
- **Binge eating disorder** is characterized by *compulsive overeating.* People eat unusually large amounts of food, can't stop eating when they are full, and become extremely overweight.

Anyone can develop an eating disorder, but teens—especially teen girls—are particularly at risk. The disorders may be triggered by low self-esteem, poor body image, or other psychological factors. People who develop eating disorders cannot usually get better on their own. They need professional psychological help.

SAFETY First

A safe weight-loss plan:
- Is based on real foods, not pills, powders, or special liquids.
- Has enough calories to maintain energy.
- Includes a variety of foods from all the food groups.
- Doesn't promise weight loss without exercise.
- Doesn't promise weight loss of more than one-half to one pound a week.

Chapter Summary

- A varied exercise program promotes overall fitness.
- If you enjoy exercise, you are more likely to make it a habit.
- Exercising safely is important in continuing an ongoing exercise program.
- Your weight is based on your basal metabolic rate, family genetics, body composition, and exercise and eating habits.
- A successful weight management plan needs realistic and specific goals.
- Eating disorders are extreme and serious eating behaviors that can lead to sickness and even death.

Family & Community

With Your Family

Talk with members of your family about what you can do together to make fitness a family goal. Try out several of your ideas to see how they work.

In Your Community

Along with your classmates, identify youth groups in your community and share information about staying fit.

Reviewing the Chapter

1. Why is it important to follow a good exercise program?
2. What type of exercise program should you follow?
3. Identify the four elements of a good exercise program.
4. List at least four ways to keep exercise workouts safe.
5. Name five factors that affect a person's weight. Briefly explain each factor.
6. How can keeping a fitness record help you evaluate your eating and exercise habits?
7. What are two important points to consider when developing a weight management plan for yourself?
8. What are the three main types of eating disorder?
9. Which segment of the population is particularly at risk for developing an eating disorder?

Thinking Critically

1. **Predict consequences.** If you don't get enough exercise as a teenager, how do you think it might impact your life now? How might it affect your life 10 or 20 years from now?

2. **Analyze the situation.** Why do you think people who lose weight often gain back the weight they lost? What suggestions can people follow to maintain their weight loss?

3. **Draw conclusions.** Why do you think teens are particularly at risk for developing an eating disorder? What aspects of the teen years might cause teens to become obsessed with their weight?

Making Connections

1. **Health.** Choose an exercise you'd like to learn more about, and research articles about it in a library. Search for additional information about how to do the exercise safely without injury. Present a report in class.

2. **Math.** Compare the costs of membership in different health programs in your community. What activities do they have that you could do at home on your own?

Applying Your Learning

1. **Create an announcement.** Develop a one-minute public service announcement for a radio program about the importance of exercise.

2. **List questions.** Write three questions you'd ask a health and fitness consultant about exercise and fitness.

3. **Keep a record.** Record your food and exercise habits for a week. Use the suggestions on page 360. At the end of the week, decide which practices you'd like to continue and which you want to change.

What Would You Do?

You've been studying about the importance of eating a healthy diet and exercising regularly. If you had a good friend who spent all of his or her spare time in front of the TV eating snack foods, how would you encourage your friend to develop healthier habits?

YOU WILL LEARN . . .

- ➤ The dangers of drugs.
- ➤ How you can benefit from avoiding the use of drugs and alcohol.
- ➤ The importance of avoiding sexually transmitted diseases and early pregnancy.

TERMS TO LEARN . . .

- ➤ abstinence
- ➤ acquired immunodeficiency syndrome (AIDS)
- ➤ addiction
- ➤ depressants
- ➤ hallucinogens
- ➤ inhalants
- ➤ marijuana
- ➤ sexually transmitted diseases (STDs)
- ➤ stimulants

Imagine ...

... meeting someone who makes you feel like you can do no wrong. Everything you say is brilliant. Everything you do is outstanding. Deep down, you know your words and actions aren't that remarkable. But the person makes you feel so special it's hard to resist such admiration, especially on days you feel so ordinary. You're spending more time with this person and less time on homework and with other friends. Lately this person has pressured you to take risks you've never even thought about. You don't want to lose this person in your life, and you're confused by the situation.

Think About

- Does this new acquaintance have your best interests in mind?
- What might happen to your grades and friendships if you continue the relationship?
- What personal qualities can help you leave this relationship and avoid similar ones?

KEEPING YOUR BEST INTERESTS IN MIND

When Justine first met Darryl, she felt flattered by his interest in her. He was popular, intelligent, and seemed sure of himself. Most of all, Darryl kept telling Justine how extraordinary she was. One night at a friend's party, Darryl asked her if she wanted an alcoholic drink.

Justine had to think twice. She'd never tried alcohol before. She knew alcohol is considered a drug. If she said no, Darryl might lose interest in her. But then, Justine thought, if not drinking could change his opinion of her, maybe Darryl wasn't someone worth having in her life.

Drugs that are prescribed by doctors often help people fight disease or control pain. Physicians are aware that the positive effects of prescribed medication outweigh negative risks to the body. They carefully regulate the dosage of drugs they prescribe to patients. But what about drugs that aren't prescribed by doctors, or that are illegal?

Making wise decisions is a critical part of becoming an adult. It's hard enough to make certain choices when you're alert and in control. But it's much harder if you use illegal drugs, which can alter your judgment, emotions, and self-control. Under the influence of illegal drugs, teens are more likely to do things they normally wouldn't dream of doing and take deadly risks.

What drugs are frequently abused? Tobacco, alcohol, marijuana, stimulants, and inhalants are among the most commonly abused drugs. They all have one thing in common. These drugs affect the user's feelings, behavior, and outlook. They also can injure your physical health.

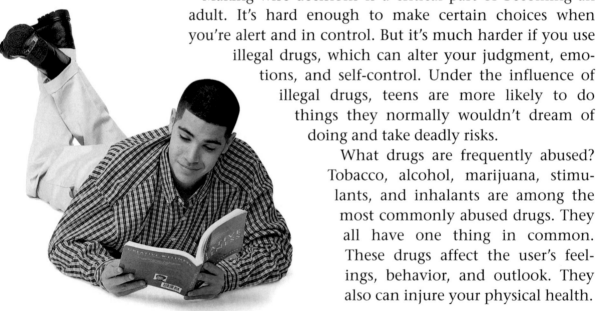

➤ It's in your best interest to learn to think about how your own actions affect you today and tomorrow.

Tobacco

Think about the following statement. "If someone tells me not to smoke, I'm out of there. No one's going to tell me what's good for me." What's the difference between someone telling you not to smoke, and an advertisement that glamorizes smoking? Both seek to influence your behavior.

You can choose to ignore what someone says about the dangers of smoking. On the other hand, you can also choose not to be influenced by manipulative messages about smoking. In order to make an intelligent decision, take a look at the facts.

- Cigarettes, cigars, pipes, and chewing tobacco (smokeless tobacco) all contain nicotine, which is an addictive drug. Most tobacco users crave greater amounts of nicotine and, as a result, they smoke or use more tobacco products.

- Many studies prove beyond a doubt that tobacco causes cancer and is related to various other health problems. Each year tobacco use kills more people than AIDS, alcohol, drug abuse, car crashes, murders, suicides, and fires combined.

- Some people claim that smoking calms their nerves. Actually, smoking releases a substance that creates physical stress rather than relaxation.

- Secondhand smoke is dangerous to your health, too. Secondhand smoke is the smoke given off by a burning cigar, cigarette, or pipe. That's why laws have been passed to make many public areas smoke-free. Secondhand smoke in a crowded room can produce *six times* the pollution of a busy highway.

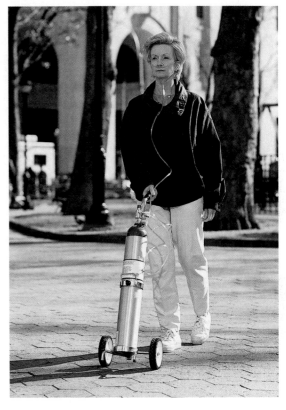

➤ **This person never thought this would happen to her when she smoked her first cigarette. It happened!**

Alcohol

Why is it against the law for anyone under the age of 21 to drink? As a teen, you risk serious harm to your health if you drink. Teens can become more rapidly addicted to alcohol than adults because their bodies are still developing. Drinking alcohol interferes with a person's natural growth and development. Excessive use of alcohol can cause serious damage to nearly every part of the body.

Alcohol is a depressant that reaches the brain in a matter of minutes. Drinking over time destroys brain cells, which can't be repaired or replaced like other cells in the body. As

> These teens are having fun playing a game. It's a fact—teen life is more fun and healthy without alcohol.

a result, the brain can't function properly, and movements, speech, vision, and good judgment are dramatically altered.

People have many ways of persuading you to drink.

- "You'll be more grown up."
- "You'll relax and forget your problems."
- "Everybody does it. It's cool."

The truth is, drinking doesn't make anyone look or act like an adult, but it *can* make a person look foolish. Drinking doesn't help anyone forget problems, but it *can* create more problems.

Inhalants

Inhalants are *substances with dangerous fumes that are sniffed to produce a mind-altering high.* Glue, hair spray, nail polish, and spray paints, are a few examples of inhalants. What's wrong with inhaling these products? Plenty!

TRY IT OUT

Influences on Your Abilities

ACTIVITY

What You'll Need
- A pair of gloves
- A needle with a large eye
- A two-foot strand of sewing thread

What to Do
1. In a group of four, take turns threading the needle, then removing the thread and passing the needle to the next person.
2. Repeat, competing with other groups in your class.
3. Repeat, but this time the person threading the needle must wear gloves.

To Discuss
- How did the pressure of competing against others affect threading the needle? How did wearing gloves affect your ability to thread the needle?
- What can this activity tell you about the effects of alcohol and other drugs? How do alcohol and other drugs affect your abilities?
- How might a person under the influence of alcohol or drugs react under pressure? What behaviors might result from the pressure the impaired person feels?

When these products' fumes are inhaled through the nose or mouth into your body, the effects are extremely dangerous. They can cause dizziness, loss of coordination, and memory loss. Death can occur, even the first time one of these products is abused, because they can cause fatal breathing and heartbeat patterns. Every year over 1,000 teens die from using inhalants.

➤ **Take precautions when using products with fumes that can cause dizziness or breathing problems.**

369

Other Drugs

Tobacco and alcohol aren't the only drugs that cause serious health and social problems. The use of illegal drugs and the misuse of prescribed medications are also problems.

Other Illegal Drugs

Illegal drugs are just that—*illegal*—and for good reasons. They're not prescribed for medical purposes, and they're dangerous to use. You don't know how your body will react when you take them. Equally important, they're addictive.

Why do some teens experiment with illegal drugs? You may hear people offer many different reasons, but the truth is there are *no* good reasons to use illegal drugs.

Stimulants, depressants, marijuana, and hallucinogens can all lead to *dependence*, or **addiction**.

Avoid Using Drugs

What is your best defense in avoiding drug use? Be prepared! Think of some ways *ahead* of time to deal with this pressure. As you read the following suggestions, think of other ways you can avoid the use of illegal drugs:

- Choose your friends carefully. Choose friends who don't use or approve of using illegal drugs.

- Avoid situations in which people might use drugs. If you know ahead of time that a parent or guardian will not be at Saturday's party, stay away. Find another fun activity to do with your friends that won't jeopardize your health or safety.

- Leave a situation if people start using drugs. Drug use can cause violent, dangerous behavior. Since drug use is illegal, you and others also could be arrested just for being there while drugs are used.

- Use your voice and say a firm "NO." For some, this little word packs a lot of power. Others may need a reason for your action. You might say, "Why should I do something that will hurt me?" or "If you're *really* my friend, you wouldn't pressure me to do drugs!" or "I respect myself too much to use illegal drugs."

- **Stimulants** *increase heart rates, speed up the central nervous system, increase breathing rates, and raise blood pressure.* Illegal stimulants, such as cocaine and crack cocaine, produce an initial rush of energy, followed by depression as the drug wears off. The short "fix" isn't worth the "crash" that follows.
- **Depressants** *reduce blood pressure, and slow down heart and breathing rates.* They result in a loss of coordination, poor attention span, mood changes, and extreme anxiety. Examples of depressants include barbiturates, or sleeping pills, and tranquilizers, or anxiety-reducing drugs.
- **Marijuana** is *a drug made from the hemp plant.* It can be eaten or smoked. Marijuana is addictive and interferes with a person's ability to learn. Marijuana smoke contains more harmful substances than tobacco. It is extremely damaging to the lungs and respiratory system.
- **Hallucinogens** are *street drugs that distort the user's thoughts, moods, and senses.* PCP and LSD are hallucinogens. The effects of taking hallucinogens are extremely unpredictable. Some people using them have *died* believing they could fly out of a window or do other impossible stunts.

➤ How many lives might be saved by using this dog to locate illegal drugs? It may save someone you know.

Prescription and OTC Drugs

Prescription and OTC (over-the-counter, sold without a prescription) drugs are beneficial in treating many health conditions. Doctors will tell you that everyone responds to these drugs differently. That's why it's important to follow your doctor's and pharmacist's directions for prescription and OTC drugs. What do you need to know to avoid misusing medicine?
- Don't use a drug prescribed for someone else—you don't know how your body will react to it.
- Take the amount prescribed by your doctor or listed on the OTC drug label, not more or less.
- Don't mix any drug—prescription or OTC—with alcoholic drinks. Alcohol can severely change the beneficial effects of *any* drug. For example, mixing acetaminophen

Anabolic steroids are illegal drugs that are dangerous to your health (although some have prescribed medical uses).

- Steroid use can cause increased aggressiveness and severe mood swings, and may be linked to certain forms of cancer.
- Steriod use is dangerous and illegal in all organized sports because of the health risks.

➤ **Although some herbal products can be healthful, many can be dangerous. Consult your doctor before using any herbal products.**

(Tylenol®) and alcohol over time can damage your kidneys and liver.

- OTC products such as diet pills and herbal supplements can also be dangerous to your health. Don't use these products unless advised by your doctor.

SEXUALLY TRANSMITTED DISEASES

Sexually transmitted diseases (STDs) are *diseases passed from one person to another through sexual contact.* There are over 30 STDs, including chlamydia, gonorrhea, and herpes.

- STDs are dangerous, even deadly. Symptoms and complications can range from feelings of discomfort to permanent physical and mental damage.
- No vaccines or treatments exist to prevent STDs. Your body can't build up an immunity (resistance) to STDs. The *only* way to avoid contracting an STD is by practicing sexual **abstinence,** *not engaging in any sexual activity.*
- **AIDS (acquired immunodeficiency syndrome)** is *a life-threatening disease that interferes with the body's natural ability to fight infection.* The virus that causes AIDS is called HIV (human immunodeficiency virus). There is no cure for AIDS. HIV is spread from one person to another by the exchange of body fluids. It is also transmitted by unclean needles used to inject illegal drugs. *You have no idea who is an HIV carrier.* For your own protection, it's important to guard against getting AIDS by practicing sexual abstinence and not using illegal drugs. Why take the risk for even one moment!

AVOIDING EARLY PREGNANCY

Teen pregnancy can create harmful health risks for both young mothers and their children. A teen girl's body is still developing, and may not be able to support and nourish an unborn child. One third of all pregnant teens receive inadequate prenatal care, or care received during pregnancy. Their children are often born with low birth weights, which lead to health problems later on, as well as other physical and mental disabilities. Yet every year in the U.S., teen girls give birth to more than 500,000 babies. Over 75 percent of teenage mothers are unmarried.

Most teen mothers choose to keep their babies, despite the fact that they lack money, education, and emotional maturity. Parenting children is a great challenge for mature adults. For teens, the demands of parenting often prove disastrous! Many teen mothers and fathers are unable to pursue higher education, or learn skills to gain higher-paying jobs. While their friends are enjoying the freedom and fun of being teenagers, teen parents often feel trapped by having become parents too soon.

STAY HEALTHY—AVOID HEALTH RISKS

Saying "no" to illegal drugs or sexual activity is one of the most important decisions you'll ever make. You show that you value your health and that you are in charge of your own life. By refusing to use drugs or have sex, you won't suffer any negative consequences:
- You won't be any less popular.
- You won't be any less loved.
- You won't be any less attractive.

You will be making an important choice. People who abuse drugs or become involved in sexual activity often hurt family members and friends who care about them. Even more important, they hurt themselves.

Chapter

26

Review & Activities

Chapter Summary

- Making the choice not to use drugs is an important decision in your life.
- Tobacco is an addictive drug that is harmful to your health.
- Alcohol is a drug that harms your development and affects your judgment.
- Common household products used as inhalants are dangerous and deadly.
- Stimulants, depressants, marijuana, and hallucinogens are illegal drugs that can lead to dependence.
- Misusing prescription and over-the-counter drugs can be dangerous to your health.
- Abstinence is the safest way to avoid sexually transmitted diseases and early pregnancy.

Reviewing the Chapter

1. Identify three problems resulting from tobacco use.
2. Explain why drinking alcohol is dangerous for teen health.
3. What are inhalants and why are they dangerous?
4. Describe the harmful effects of illegal drugs.
5. Identify at least three guidelines for using prescription and over-the-counter drugs.
6. What are sexually transmitted diseases and what is the only way to avoid contracting an STD?
7. Why is it in your best interest to avoid teen pregnancy?

Family & Community

With Your Family

Have a discussion with your family about alcohol and other drug-related problems teens face in your community. How could you get involved to help teens avoid alcohol and drugs?

In Your Community

In small groups, research local programs that encourage students to remain drug free. Use the telephone book, talk with a guidance counselor, or check out the Internet for community resources. Present your findings to the class.

Thinking Critically

1. **Compare and contrast.** How would you describe the difference in values of a person who is a drug abuser and one who chooses to avoid drug use? What are the long-range consequences of each person's decisions?

2. **Analyze behavior.** Think about the ways you have seen tobacco products used. What motivates people to buy, smoke, or chew tobacco? How can an effective case be made for not using tobacco?

3. **Draw conclusions.** What conclusions can you draw about the physical, social, emotional, and financial readiness of teens for parenthood? Why is sexual abstinence in the best interests of teens?

Making Connections

1. **Health.** In small groups, take turns role-playing situations in which you and your friends need to deal with saying "no" to the pressure to use drugs.

2. **Language Arts.** Make a list of at least six ways that you can say "no" to sexual pressure.

Applying Your Learning

1. **Compile a directory.** Make a list of local contact groups that assist with alcohol and other drug-rehabilitation programs. Include the organization's telephone number and the type of assistance offered.

2. **Suggest alternative activities.** Brainstorm a list of activities in your community that offer alternative choices to help teens stay drug free.

3. **Interview a counselor.** Talk to a counselor working in a drug abuse rehabilitation program. What information does this person have that can be helpful to share with other teens?

What Would You Do?

Assume you have a friend whom you believe has started drinking alcohol. You've been close friends for a long time. You have a responsibility to try to talk with your friend about his/her drinking. What would you say to your friend?

Personal Safety

YOU WILL LEARN . . .

➤ How to be safety-conscious.
➤ Ways to be safer at home and away from home.
➤ What to do when an emergency happens.

TERM TO LEARN . . .

➤ crime

Imagine ...

... you're a painter, and you've just completed your best painting yet. You're thrilled when a local gallery wants to display it. You're concerned, though. You've heard the gallery was recently broken into, and some artwork was stolen.

Think About

• What security measures would you look for at the gallery?
• Why don't you just keep your painting at home for friends and family to enjoy?
• What would happen if every artist was afraid to display his or her work?

WHY THINK ABOUT SAFETY?

To help stop crime and make your community a safer place:

- Make sure you follow the rules and laws of your community.
- Choose friends who want to make your community a better place to be, not a worse one.
- Take action. Report any criminal activity you see.
- Know your neighbors and where they live. Some could provide a safe haven in case of emergency.
- Help set up a neighborhood crime watch program that encourages people to look out for one another.

You may not be a painter concerned about the safety of an art gallery, but every day you make important decisions that affect your safety. You also make decisions that affect the safety of others at home, at school, and maybe at an after-school job. The great majority of people around you are law-abiding citizens who care about the safety of their family and others in the community. They're ready to help someone in trouble.

Why think about safety? A small minority of people do commit criminal acts. A **crime** is *an illegal act committed against someone or something.* Why does someone commit a crime? Many factors may play a role in a criminal act, including economics, emotional problems, and alcohol or drug abuse.

Some experts believe that endless violence on TV series and in movies encourages criminal and violent acts. They think the media makes crime seem acceptable and even glamorous. Others feel that traditional family life has been so weakened that moral values are no longer stressed. Still others offer evidence that easy access to weapons contributes to the number of crimes committed every year in the U.S. So what can you do to keep yourself safe?

➤ These girls have been taught how to safely carry their purses. Think about safety in all situations and you'll be less likely to be a victim of crime.

Three Rules of Safety

Safety officials suggest you follow three basic commonsense rules:

1. **Stay alert.** Be aware of your surroundings wherever you are. Don't be taken by surprise.
2. **Trust your instincts.** Your instincts or gut reactions tell you what you think you should do. If you feel uncomfortable in a place or situation, leave. Get help if necessary.
3. **Act confident.** Don't show fear. Don't act like a victim. Stand tall and walk confidently.

➤ **Locking your car doors as you travel keeps you and your possessions safer. What** might happen at an intersection if the car doors were unlocked?

TRY IT OUT

Choosing Safety

ACTIVITY

What You'll Need
- Paper
- Pen or pencil

What to Do
1. On a sheet of paper, write down what you would do in the following situations:
   - You and a friend are walking home after a late movie. Your friend wants to take a shortcut through a dark neighborhood instead of staying on the well-lighted sidewalk.
   - When shopping in a mall, you become aware that a stranger appears to be following you.
2. Compare your answers with those of your classmates. As a class, determine the safest way to deal with the situations.

To Discuss
- Why is important to think ahead about unsafe situations that you might encounter?
- What kinds of unsafe situations are you most likely to encounter in your day-to-day life?
- How can you prepare in advance for these situations?

Safety at Home

Your home is a place where you should be able to feel secure. Clearly, some neighborhoods are safer than others. But even in the safest areas, law enforcement authorities suggest you and your family take "safety-smart" precautions:

- Don't give your phone number or address to someone you don't know well.
- If a stranger needs to come inside your home, have an adult come to the door. If you're alone, ask to see and check the identification of repair workers and community employees.
- Keep doors and windows locked when no one is home. Deadbolt locks are the best choice. When you turn the key from inside or outside the door, a strong metal bar slides into the door frame.
- Use ventilation locks on windows through which someone can easily enter. Ventilation locks are inexpensive metal stops you can adjust to any level for air to enter. You can find them at hardware stores.
- Make sure the area around outside doors is well lighted. That makes your home safer.
- Use available security devices and techniques. Some, like home alarm systems, can be costly. Other alternatives, such as forming a neighborhood volunteer patrol system, are free. Neighbors make it a point to look out for each other and report any suspicious activity.

STOCKING A FIRST AID KIT

Every first aid kit should include these basic items:

- Adhesive strip bandages in a variety of shapes and sizes.
- Sterile gauze pads.
- Gauze rolls.
- Adhesive tape.
- Medicated soap.
- Antibiotic ointment.
- First aid manual.
- List of emergency telephone numbers.

➤ **There are many phone scams across the country. Never follow the requests of strangers to press any numbers or give any personal information.**

- Have your house key ready when you enter or leave your home. If you witness suspicious activity near your home, contact the police. Be prepared to explain why you're concerned. Accurate descriptions of people, cars, and license plates are helpful.
- If you're using a computer chat room, don't give a stranger your address, phone number, or other personal information.

INFOLINK

See Chapter 48 for more information on home safety.

Safety Away from Home

Being safety-conscious is equally important when you're away from home. Juanita decided to start jogging. One night at dusk, she was running in her neighborhood when she became aware someone was following her. She got scared but wasn't sure what to do. She'd always felt safe in her own neighborhood. What advice would you give Juanita?

Whether you're alone or with friends in a crowd, keep safety in mind. Let someone at home know where you are when you're out at night. Carry identification and phone numbers of people to contact in case of an emergency. Getting to know the neighborhood where you live means learning where police and fire stations are located.

When you're out with your friends, enjoy yourself but follow commonsense safety tips for an even better time. Wear a safety belt when riding in a car or truck. At night, walk in well-lighted areas whenever possible. What other suggestions could you add to this list?

➤ When you and your family are staying overnight in an unfamiliar building, plan ahead by locating emergency escape routes. A few minutes may save your life.

Sports Safety

When exercising or playing a sport, remember—safety first. Then you can really enjoy yourself and avoid being sidelined by an injury.

- Follow the rules of any sport. When bicycling, ride on the right side of the road with traffic, not against it. When skating, avoid parking lots, streets, and areas with traffic.

▶ This skateboarder is a trained professional. Protective gear is not the only precaution to take in some sports. Training and knowledge must be acquired before attempting high-skilled feats.

- Wear protective gear and helmets when bicycling or skateboarding. Wear bright clothing during the day and reflective clothing at night—and carry a flashlight. Wear a life jacket in a boat.
- Use the buddy system, a plan where two people watch out for each other, and get help in case of an emergency.

Making a DIFFERENCE

SAFE CALL

Walking home from a friend's house one evening, Lea sensed something unusual. She knew her neighbor Mrs. Chang was out of town, but Lea heard noises coming from the house. Her neighbor's lights were out, but she could see a side window was wide open. For a moment, Lea didn't know what to do. She made a quick decision. Lea ran inside her home and dialed 911.

When Mrs. Chang returned home the next day, she gratefully thanked Lea for stopping a robbery in its tracks.

Taking Action

1. If Lea had made a mistake, and no crime had taken place, did she still make a safe call? Why or why not?
2. What would you do in a similar situation?

WHEN EMERGENCIES HAPPEN

Emergencies are never planned. They just happen. How can you be better prepared to handle emergency situations?

At home, post emergency phone numbers near the phone in view of everyone. Post the following emergency numbers:

- Police, fire, and ambulance (911 or dial 0).
- A poison control center.
- A doctor or clinic.
- Parents' or guardians' work numbers.
- Nearest relative.
- Friend or neighbor.

➤ Communities plan for emergency disasters with warning sirens and media directions. Take them seriously. Have you and your family discussed your emergency plans? If not, do so.

If you need to make an emergency call, stay calm. Wait for the dial tone, then dial 911 or 0 for an operator. Speak clearly and tell the person what's wrong. Give your name, address, and phone number. If you're not at home, give your exact location. Don't hang up the phone until told to do so. Follow any instructions the person gives you.

In case of fire, get outside the house. Call from the nearest phone. Never go inside a burning building. If someone is on fire, remember to immediately have him or her "stop, drop, and roll" to put out the flames.

Know the basic principles of first aid. You can get first aid information from the American Red Cross or an authorized instructor. Every emergency situation is different, and it's critical to know when and how to act.

In an emergency, every minute counts. Don't walk away from an emergency. You can always do something. Others may be depending on your actions.

GETTING HELP

All communities offer services you can contact for help. Your local telephone book lists important emergency numbers. Call the local police department to help you or refer you to services you may need. Try to get help before a situation becomes a crisis. Don't be afraid to speak to people at the police department or an emergency hot line. People who work at these locations are trained to help out.

Review & Activities

Chapter Summary

- Everybody makes decisions that affect personal and public safety.
- You and your family can help to make your home and neighborhood a safer place to live.
- It is important to be safety-conscious when away from home.
- You can prevent injuries by being safety-minded when playing a sport.
- Being prepared helps you to handle emergencies when they occur.

Family & Community

With Your Family

Develop a fire escape plan for all rooms in your house. Practice the plan with your family. Work together to make the plan a better one.

In Your Community

If your neighborhood doesn't already have a neighborhood watch program, investigate the possibility of starting one. Contact your local police department and obtain some information.

Reviewing the Chapter

1. List three basic rules to follow to help ensure personal safety.
2. Identify at least five safeguards you can follow to help keep your home secure.
3. What safety precautions would you observe when you are away from home?
4. What safety guidelines can you follow when participating in sports?
5. Identify the emergency telephone numbers that should be posted near your home phone.
6. Describe what you should do if you need to call for emergency assistance.

Thinking Critically

1. **Analyze the situation.** Remember a time when you felt as if you were in an unsafe situation. What made it seem unsafe to you? How could the situation have been prevented or made safer?

2. **Predict consequences.** Consider this statement, "Some people don't think in an emergency. They lose their cool." What can happen when someone does not remain calm in an emergency situation?

3. **Compare and contrast.** Why are some people greater risk-takers than others? What are the advantages and disadvantages of taking risks? What are the advantages and disadvantages of being more cautious?

Making Connections

1. **Health.** Contact a representative of the American Red Cross to have a volunteer demonstrate simple first aid procedures.

2. **Math.** Select a sport you enjoy. Calculate the total cost of buying safety equipment for your sport of choice.

Applying Your Learning

1. **Post telephone numbers.** Write out a list of emergency phone numbers and post it next to your phone at home. Check to be sure all of the important numbers are included.

2. **List dos and don'ts.** Work with your classmates to develop a list of safety dos and don'ts for home, school, and sports. Which items on the list are the easiest and least expensive to follow?

3. **Discussion.** Discuss the following statement with your classmates: "No matter what your problem may be, there are positive solutions to the problem. Committing a crime is never one of them." Support your opinions.

What Would You Do?

You and a friend are walking home at dusk. You've always felt safe in your neighborhood. But lately you've heard about a few robberies. What precautions would you take?

Career Network

PHARMACIST

Customer-oriented, licensed pharmacist needed to join the staff of a major retail chain.
• Must provide patient counseling and drug information, and supervise associates.
• Work weekends and evenings.

MEDICAL RECORDS TECHNICIAN

Healthworks physician's organization has immediate opening for a medical assistant in our family practice.
• High school diploma and knowledge of medical terminology and procedures required.
• Completion of medical assisting program preferred.

REGISTERED NURSE

Residential facility has full and part-time openings for caring RN's who enjoy working with senior citizens.
• Associate's degree required.
• Second shift only.
• Signing bonuses available.

MEDICAL ASSISTANT

Healthworks physician's organization has immediate opening for a medical assistant in our family practice.
• High school diploma and knowledge of medical terminology and procedures required.
• Completion of medical assisting program preferred.

RADIOGRAPHER

Children's hospital seeks certified radiographer to assist radiologists.
• Must work well with children.
• Prepare patients for exams, assist during testing, and operate equipment.
• Good benefits package.

HEALTH SERVICES ADMINISTRATOR

Long-term health care facility has immediate opening for administrator to coordinate daily business activities and supervise staff.
• Bachelor's degree required, master's degree preferred.
• Licensed with proven success in health care management a plus.
• Excellent salary and benefits package.

More Career Options

Entry Level

• Nursing Assistant
• Aerobics Instructor
• Emergency Medical Technician
• Dietary Assistant

Technical Level

• Pharmacy Technician
• Paramedic
• Medical Secretary
• Phlebotomist

Professional Level

• Optometrist
• Physician
• Medical Scientist

MEDICAL ILLUSTRATOR

Medical college needs illustrator to draw human anatomy and surgical procedures for audio-visual presentations used in teaching.
- Bachelor's degree necessary
- Exceptional artistic ability required.

PERSONAL TRAINER

Health club seeks energetic personal trainer to plan and supervise fitness regimes for clients on an individual basis.
- Must be physically fit, health conscious, and personable.
- Two-year degree preferred.

DENTAL HYGIENIST

Opening available for an organized dential hygienist with excellent people skills to join our team.
- Bachelor's degree and x-ray certification required.
- Experience preferred.
- Must work one Saturday per month.

PHYSICAL THERAPIST

Licensed physical therapist needed for growing outpatient rehabilitation center.
- Strong interpersonal skills desired for working with patients who have diverse range of ailments.
- Degree required and/or volunteer experience preferred.

Linking School to Career

1. **Your Career Plan:** What kind of work have you done so far, with or without pay. Make a list from the following: volunteer activities, school projects, family chores, part-time jobs, church groups, sports, music, school assistant, and scout troop. How will this work help in preparing you for your future career?

2. **Researching Careers:** The American medical system has undergone a number of changes in recent years and continues to evolve. Find out about anticipated future trends. What effect do you think these changes will have on careers in health and medicine?

3. **Reading:** Look up the definitions of the following terms that are found in the want ad listings:
- Nourishment management.
- Nutrition education.
- Medical terminology.
- Fitness regimes.

Unit 8

Food and Nutrition

Chapter 28

How Nutrients Work

YOU WILL LEARN . . .

➤ Six types of nutrients and their functions in the body.
➤ Symptoms of nutrient deficiencies.
➤ How you can meet your energy and nutritional needs.

TERMS TO LEARN . . .

➤ amino acids
➤ calories
➤ carbohydrates
➤ cholesterol
➤ deficiency
➤ fiber
➤ nutrient density
➤ nutrients
➤ proteins

Imagine ...

... that parts of your body are suddenly able to tell you how they feel. Your stomach cries, "You forgot to feed me breakfast. Your body can't work to capacity without fuel." Your skin and hair speak up: "We're too dry. Please drink some water before we wither away!" Your teeth exclaim, "Good job with the milk. We're feeling strong today."

Think About

• What have you eaten during the past week? How did your food intake impact your performance in school?
• If your body could talk, what might it say to you?
• How does a person's body "tell" things without words?

THE NUTRIENT TEAM

The food you eat is a source of **nutrients,** *the substances found in food that keep your body in good working order.* That's why it's important to choose the right foods on a regular basis.

Your body needs nutrients to fuel your energy and to help you grow. It also needs nutrients to repair itself and to maintain basic functions. Six key nutrients work together for you as a team. They include carbohydrates, proteins, fats, vitamins, minerals, and water.

Carbohydrates

Carbohydrates are *the body's main source of energy.* They're the sugars and starches in foods. There are two kinds of carbohydrates. Sugars are *simple carbohydrates.* Starches are *complex carbohydrates,* because their structure is more complicated. Starch is broken down into sugar when digested.

The fruits, vegetables, and milk you eat all contain natural sugars, plus other important nutrients. Candy and soft drinks have sugar, too, but they often don't provide you with other nutrients.

Breads, cereals, pasta, rice, dry beans, and some vegetables, such as potatoes and corn, contain starch. All of these foods are rich sources of other nutrients, too.

Many complex carbohydrates also contain fiber. **Fiber** consists of *plant material that doesn't break down when you digest food.* It's an important part of healthful eating. Fiber helps your body eliminate waste.

Proteins

Proteins are *nutrients used to build, maintain, and repair body tissues. Protein foods are made up of chemical compounds* called **amino acids.** Amino acids make up the body's

➤ This is your body's nutrient team. Each needs the other to "win" your good health.

"building blocks." Every type of protein food contains a different combination of amino acids that perform different and vital functions in your body.

The body makes all but nine of the amino acids that you need. Those nine are called *essential amino acids*. They have to be supplied by the food you eat. Your body can't make them.

Foods from animal sources (meat, fish, poultry, milk products, and eggs) are called *complete proteins*. These foods have all of the nine essential amino acids.

Plant foods (grains, dry beans and peas, nuts, seeds, and vegetables) also contain proteins. They're called *incomplete proteins* because they lack one or more of the essential amino acids.

When eaten in combination, incomplete proteins fit together like the pieces of a puzzle to form complete proteins. For example, eating beans and rice adds up to complete protein. You can also make complete proteins by eating a complete and an incomplete protein together. When you add milk to cereal, the complete proteins in the milk fill in for missing amino acids in the cereal. The best way to give your body complete proteins is to eat a wide variety of foods throughout the day.

➤ **This bowl of cereal and orange juice can provide you with enough energy and brain power until lunch time.** What do you supply your body with to get to lunch?

Fats

Fats are the most concentrated form of food energy. They provide substances the body needs for normal growth and healthy skin. Fat also helps make foods taste better.

Fat works as a partner with other nutrients. Just as sugar dissolves in water, some vitamins dissolve in fat and are carried where needed in your body. Fat also helps you feel full after eating.

Foods, such as butter, margarine, sour cream, and salad dressing, are fats you can easily see. Fats you may not see as easily are called hidden fats and are found in meat, fish, egg yolks, whole milk, cheese, bakery items, and nuts.

There are two main types of fats:

- **Saturated fats** are fats that are solid at room temperature. They're found in animal foods such as meat, poultry, egg yolks, and whole milk dairy products. Saturated fats are also found in tropical oils—coconut, palm, and palm kernel.
- **Unsaturated fats** are fats that are usually liquid at room temperature. They're found mainly in vegetable oils, with the exception of tropical oils.

Cholesterol and Saturated Fats

Cholesterol is *a fat-like substance that's part of every cell in the body. It helps the body make necessary chemicals and aids in digestion.* The body manufactures all the cholesterol it needs. You also get cholesterol from foods you eat. Cholesterol is found in foods from animal sources.

Physicians can measure the amount of cholesterol in the bloodstream. When cholesterol levels are high, there's a greater risk for heart disease. Health professionals advise people to eat foods lower in fat and cholesterol, especially foods from plant sources.

Vitamins

Vitamins trigger many body processes. They work like spark plugs in an engine. They set off chemical reactions in your body cells. Each vitamin regulates a different process. Their roles are so specific that one can't substitute for another. Your body requires at least 13 vitamins each day. Generally, you get all the vitamins you need if you eat a variety of healthful foods. (See the charts on pages 396 and 397 for more about vitamins needed for good health.)

COMBINING COMPLEMENTARY PROTEINS

Although plant proteins are incomplete, they can supply your body with the protein it needs if used in the right combination. Grains and dry beans, peas, and peanuts are complementary proteins. This means each supplies amino acids that the other lacks. Try including the following combinations in your meal plans:

- Whole wheat bread and peanut butter.
- Meatless chili with beans and cornbread.
- Pinto beans and rice.
- Split-pea soup and bagel.

➤ Fats supply energy and promote absorption of the fat-soluble vitamins A, D, E, and K. Some dietary fat is needed for good health. **Identify foods that supply good fats and those that are too high in fat.**

Vitamins are grouped into two categories:

- **Fat-soluble vitamins.** Vitamins A, D, E, and K are absorbed with the help of fats. The body can store fat-soluble vitamins. However, getting too much of these vitamins can be harmful.
- **Water-soluble vitamins.** Vitamin C and the B-complex vitamins dissolve in water and easily pass out of the body as waste. As you can imagine, you need a frequent supply of these vitamins. Very large doses may be harmful.

Minerals

Minerals also work like spark plugs in the body. Like vitamins, each mineral has certain jobs to perform. They are also an essential part of bones and internal organs. To work efficiently, your body requires at least 16 minerals daily.

If you eat a variety of foods every day, you'll normally get the minerals you need. Calcium is especially important to you as a teen. It makes up the structure of your bones and teeth. Sometimes it's hard to think about the future, but if you develop a solid bone structure now, you'll have strong bones later in life. Drinking and eating dairy products is a good way of getting the right amount of calcium. The chart on page 398 tells you more about minerals.

Water

You can live longer without food than without water. One-half to three-quarters of your body weight is water. As one of the essential nutrients, water carries nutrients to your cells and carries waste from your body. Water also helps to regulate your body temperature.

Do you drink the recommended six to eight glasses of liquids every day? Foods with a high water content, such as soups, fruits, and vegetables, provide some of the water you need. Liquids you drink, like milk, juice, and water, provide the rest.

FAT-SOLUBLE VITAMINS

Vitamin	Where It's Found	What It Does
Vitamin A	Dark green, leafy vegetables (spinach, kale); deep yellow and orange fruits and vegetables (cantaloupe, carrots, sweet potatoes, apricots); liver; milk, cheese, and eggs	Helps keep skin and hair healthy; aids night vision; builds strong bones and teeth
Vitamin D	Milk with vitamin D; egg yolk; salmon; liver	Helps build strong bones and teeth; helps the body use calcium and phosphorus.
Vitamin E	Whole-grain breads and cereals; dark green, leafy vegetables; dry beans and peas; nuts and seeds; vegetable oils, margarine; liver	Helps form red blood cells, muscles, and other tissues
Vitamin K	Dark green, leafy vegetables; cabbage	Helps blood to clot

DEFICIENCIES IN NUTRITION

When your body doesn't get enough nutrients, a **deficiency,** or *shortage,* occurs. The symptoms, or effects, depend on how serious the deficiency is.

At first the symptoms of nutrition deficiency may not seem very serious. They may include tiredness, difficulty sleeping or concentrating, frequent colds, weight gain, or weight loss. A more serious nutrition deficiency can affect certain parts of the body, such as the skin, eyes, tongue, or bones.

The way to avoid nutrition deficiencies is to eat a variety of foods. Each food has nutrients you need for good health.

WATER-SOLUBLE VITAMINS

Vitamin	Where It's Found	What It Does
B-complex vitamins (riboflavin, niacin, B_6, B_{12}, thiamine)	Whole-grain and enriched breads and cereals; dry beans and peas, peanut butter, nuts; meat, poultry, fish; eggs; milk	Helps the body use carbohydrates, fats, and proteins; helps produce energy in cells; helps maintain healthy nervous system, muscles, and tissues
Folate	Fruits; enriched and whole wheat breads; dark green, leafy vegetables; liver; dry beans and peas	Helps build red blood cells and genes
Vitamin C	Citrus fruits (oranges, grapefruit), strawberries, broccoli, tomatoes, potatoes, etc.	Helps maintain bones, teeth, and blood vessels; helps heal wounds

➤ **Drinking water feeds and cleanses your body. Water is an important element for all forms of life.** How do you supply your body with sufficient water each day?

IMPORTANT MINERALS

Mineral	Where It's Found	What It Does
Calcium	Milk and milk products; dark green, leafy vegetables; dry beans and peas; sardines, salmon (eaten with bones)	Builds and maintains strong bones and teeth; helps heart, muscles, and nerves work properly; helps blood to clot
Phosphorus	Meat, poultry, fish, and eggs; dry beans and peas, nuts; milk and milk products	Builds and maintains strong bones and teeth; helps body use carbohydrates, fats, and proteins
Iron	Red meats, liver, egg yolk; dark green, leafy vegetables; dry beans and peas, nuts; whole-grain and enriched breads and cereals; dried fruits (raisins)	Helps red blood cells carry oxygen to all parts of the body; helps cells use oxygen
Sodium	Salt; many foods	Helps maintain fluid balance in body; helps muscle and nerve action
Potassium	Oranges, orange juice; bananas, dried fruits; dry beans and peas, peanut butter; meats	Works with sodium to help maintain fluid balance in body; helps heart and muscles work properly; helps regulate blood pressure

DIGESTION

In order to use the nutrients in food, your body must first digest the food. When your body digests foods, it uses nutrients from almost everything you eat. Digestion begins when the thought, sight, smell, and taste of food starts the flow of saliva. The chemicals in saliva, along with chewing, begin to break food down. The path that food takes through the digestive system is illustrated on the facing page. Any undigested food is eliminated as body waste.

THE DIGESTIVE SYSTEM

Food moves from the mouth through the esophagus to the stomach, where digestive juices break it down further. Food remains in the stomach about three to five hours. From the stomach, food moves to the small intestine, where nutrients are absorbed into the bloodstream. Unneeded nutrients and undigested food become body waste.

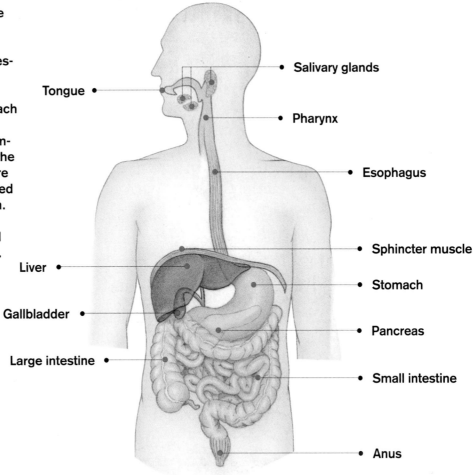

Tongue

Salivary glands

Pharynx

Esophagus

Sphincter muscle

Liver

Stomach

Gallbladder

Pancreas

Large intestine

Small intestine

Anus

ENERGY AND CALORIES

Food supplies the body with energy. Some energy is needed for normal body processes, such as breathing and pumping blood. You also need energy for all your activities.

Calories are *units for measuring energy,* just as inches measure length. Calories are used to measure both the energy you take in from food and the energy you use up.

How many calories you need daily depends on several things, such as your age and your activity level. Getting more calories than you need causes weight gain, while getting fewer calories than you need causes weight loss.

INFOLINK

See Chapter 25 for more details about weight management and fitness.

Making a DIFFERENCE

BETTER CHOICES

Elise and Jackie sat at their local burger hangout with friends. One of them, Lonny, had gone to pick up their orders.

"Look at Lonny," Elise said. "He takes great care of himself. We ordered cheeseburgers with everything on them, fries, and soda. He ordered a plain burger, a salad instead of fries, and a glass of milk."

"Well, he's an athlete," Jackie shrugged. "What do you expect?"

"It's true," said Elise. "But why don't we start eating like Lonny? We'll probably feel better—and best of all, look better."

"How do we do that?" Jackie asked.

"Let's make a deal," Elise said. "Next time we order the same as Lonny."

Taking Action

1. What are three ways you could improve your own diet?
2. How does eating healthful foods make you feel and look better?

MEETING YOUR ENERGY NEEDS

The source of your calories is important. The energy in foods comes from fats, carbohydrates, and proteins. Vitamins, minerals, water, and fiber don't provide energy.

Fat is the most concentrated source of energy, with 9 calories per gram. Carbohydrates and proteins have 4 calories per gram. (A gram is a metric unit of weight.)

Healthcare experts suggest that you get approximately:

- Fifty-five to sixty percent of your calories from carbohydrates (mainly complex carbohydrates).
- About fifteen percent of your calories from protein.
- Thirty percent (or less) of your calories from fat (mainly unsaturated fat).

➤ **Your body's needs for calories and nutrients change as your body ages.** How might a teen's nutritional requirements differ from those of an older adult?

Nutrient Density

When you choose foods, consider nutrient density. **Nutrient density** is *the amount of nutrients in a food relative to the number of calories.*

Foods such as candy, potato chips, and sugary soft drinks have low nutrient density. They add to your calorie intake, but contribute few important nutrients.

Foods such as fruits, vegetables, whole grains, lean meats, and low-fat milk have high nutrient density. They do more than just help meet your energy needs. They also supply proteins, vitamins, minerals, and fiber, all contributing to good health.

Chapter Summary

- Six nutrients—carbohydrates, proteins, fats, vitamins, minerals, and water—work together to help your body function effectively.
- Carbohydrates supply energy and should be the major part of your diet.
- Proteins are important for growth and repair of your body.
- Fats help to supply energy but should be eaten in moderation.
- Vitamins and minerals assist in regulating different body processes.
- Water is important for normal body processes.
- Nutritional deficiencies may cause tiredness and difficulty in sleeping or concentrating.
- You can meet your energy and nutritional needs by eating a balanced diet of nutrient-dense foods.

Family & Community

With Your Family

With your family, make a list of the foods high in fat that your family eats. Think of substitutes that are lower in fat. Try one or two of the substitutes for a week. Decide whether you could make the temporary changes permanent ones.

In Your Community

It's a generally known fact that American diets are higher in fat than is recommended. What could your class do to help create a greater awareness in your school and in the community about eating less fat?

Reviewing the Chapter

1. What are the two types of carbohydrates? Give an example of each type.
2. Explain what amino acids are. Why are they important?
3. What is the difference between saturated and unsaturated fat?
4. Define cholesterol and explain what role it plays in your body.
5. What is the major difference between vitamins and minerals?
6. Briefly describe the body's digestive process.
7. What is the suggested percentage distribution of calories for carbohydrates, fat, and protein?
8. Explain the difference between foods having low nutrient density and those with high nutrient density.

Thinking Critically

1. **Analyze fat content.** Identify a list of foods high in fat that are popular with teens. What lower-fat substitutes would you suggest?
2. **Draw conclusions.** Why do carbohydrate foods have a negative image among some teens? How could you convince others that eating carbohydrates is beneficial?
3. **Clarify fact or opinion.** Do you agree or disagree with this statement, "Taking a vitamin pill gives you all the vitamins you need." How would you support your answer?

Making Connections

1. **Science.** Research some of the well-known nutritional deficiency diseases, such as scurvy, rickets, night blindness, or beriberi. What were the major causes of these nutritional diseases? How were the diseases cured?

2. **Math.** Keep track of the amount of fat (in grams) and calories that you eat in foods for one day. Use the following formula to determine the percentage of fat calories you've eaten in one day:
   a. Multiply the total grams of fat by 9 (the number of calories in 1 gram of fat). This gives you the number of calories from fat.
   b. Divide the total calories from fat by the total calories you ate in one day.
   c. Multiply the answer from step b by 100 to determine your percentage of calories from fat.

Applying Your Learning

1. **Write a cheer.** In the chapter, find examples of how nutrients work together to perform related functions in the body. Use your examples to write a cheer about nutrient teamwork. Present your cheer to the class.

2. **Plan a skit.** Identify important nutrients often found lacking in the teen diet. Develop a skit stressing the importance of these nutrients and offering suggestions for ways that teens could include more of these nutrients in their diets.

3. **Create a display.** Develop a display to encourage people to eat more complex carbohydrates. Include attention-getting slogans.

What Would You Do?

A friend of yours says, "I don't have enough time to eat right. Why not just take a couple of vitamin pills instead of eating?" How would you convince your friend of the importance of eating a variety of foods that include carbohydrates, proteins, fat, vitamins, and minerals?

Guidelines for Healthy Eating

YOU WILL LEARN . . .

> The Dietary Guidelines for Americans.
> How to recognize the food groups and the recommended servings in the Food Guide Pyramid.
> How to recognize standard serving sizes.

TERMS TO LEARN . . .

> Dietary Guidelines for Americans
> Food Guide Pyramid
> obesity

Imagine ...

... that you're showing a curious child how to construct a pyramid. You explain that the bottom has to be bigger than the rest so it can hold up other layers. The top has to be lightest of all, you explain. Like many young children, this one asks his favorite question. "Why?"

Think About

- How would you answer this young child's question?
- Why do you think fats, oils, and sweets are at the top of the Food Guide Pyramid?
- Why might happen if someone put fats and sweets at the foundation of his or her eating plan?

EATING AND GOOD HEALTH

What's the relationship between the way you eat and good health? Plenty, according to health experts. They've found that poor eating habits play a big role in serious health problems, such as heart disease, high blood pressure, diabetes, and some forms of cancer. The good news is that developing good eating habits now can reduce the future risk of these diseases. You can use the Dietary Guidelines for Americans and the Food Guide Pyramid to make healthful eating a part of your everyday life.

DIETARY GUIDELINES FOR AMERICANS

The **Dietary Guidelines for Americans** includes *nine simple suggestions for making healthful food choices*. These guidelines consider what you eat over time—not just in a single day. Remember, however, that the guidelines are suggested for healthy people age two and older. They're not for infants and young children, since their food needs are different. The Dietary Guidelines include:

Aim for Fitness
- Aim for a healthy weight.
- Be physically active every day.

Build a Healthy Base
- Let the Pyramid guide your food choices.
- Choose a variety of grains daily, especially whole grains.
- Choose a variety of fruits and vegetables daily.
- Keep food safe to eat.

Choose Sensibly
- Choose a diet that is low in saturated fat and cholesterol and moderate in total fat.
- Choose beverages and foods to moderate your intake of sugars.
- Choose and prepare foods with less salt.

Healthy Weight and Physical Activity

In today's world, it's not easy to decide what weight is best for you. Do you think your weight is about right? The weight that's best for you isn't necessarily the lowest weight you think you can be. Your healthy weight depends on several factors:

- Your age, height, and whether you're male or female.
- How much of your weight comes from body fat compared to muscle, bone, and other lean tissue. (Muscle weight is preferable.)
- A family history of weight-related health problems.

Remember that maintaining a healthy weight requires balancing good nutrition with physical activity. If you're concerned about your weight, talk with a health professional to help you identify your healthy weight range.

➤ For successful weight management, eat well-balanced meals and exercise regularly. Making these gradual changes will encourage a permanent lifestyle change and allow you to maintain your desired weight.

The Food Guide Pyramid

Follow the guidelines in the Food Guide Pyramid to ensure that your body gets the nutrients it needs daily. Remember that different foods provide different nutrients. No single food can supply all of the nutrients in the amounts you need. Choose the recommended number of daily servings from the five major food groups. Make sure to select sensible portion sizes. See pages 409-411 for more information.

Grains, Fruits, and Vegetables

Grains, fruits, and vegetables are good sources of carbohydrates, fiber, vitamins, and minerals. How can you eat more of these nutritious foods? Wake up to a bran muffin and a glass of fruit juice in the morning. Get extra vegetable toppings on your slice of pizza. Eat a vegetable or fruit salad. Or, choose a side dish made from rice, pasta, or another whole grain.

Food Safety

Keeping foods safe from harmful bacteria and other hazards is vital to healthful eating. This means washing your hands before preparing and eating food, cooking food to safe temperatures, and refrigerating food that perishes easily. Chapter 34 talks more about ways to keep food safe.

INFOLINK

See Chapter 25 for more information on fitness and managing your weight.

Low Fat, Saturated Fat, and Cholesterol

Fat is an important nutrient for your health. It helps to supply energy and is important for many body functions, so eating some fat is a good idea. Eating too much fat contributes to **obesity**—or *being seriously overweight due to an excess of body fat.* High-fat diets are also linked to other health problems, including heart disease and some cancers.

Moderate Sugars

Do you have a sweet tooth? Many popular foods, such as ice cream, candy, and sweetened cereals, contain sugar. Some sugar is fine, but you don't need it in large amounts. Eating too many sugary foods often limits other more nutritious foods. Gaining weight is also a possibility.

Moderate Salt and Sodium

Do you shake salt on your food before you even taste it? Most Americans eat more salt and sodium than they need.

Salt and seasonings containing sodium are added to many processed foods. Check out food labels for the sodium content of foods, such as canned soups, snack foods, and frozen pizza. You may be surprised at the amount of sodium in these foods.

Sodium helps the body keep a balance of fluids. It also helps regulate blood pressure. In some people, too much sodium is linked to high blood pressure.

➤ Throw a nutrition party! Dare to be different. Serve raw fruits and vegetables and health grain snacks to munch on. Low-fat sour cream and yogurt can be used to make a dipping sauce for these snacks.

➤ Are these teens practicing good nutrition? **You may be surprised that the answer is "yes", they are eating low-fat sugar-free yogurt.**

Lower the Fat

Health experts agree that no more than 30 percent of your calories should come from fat. This doesn't mean you have to give up eating your favorite foods. Try these ideas that lower the fat in the foods you eat:

- Drink skim or low-fat milk instead of whole milk.
- Eat meat in moderation.
- Choose lean cuts of meat when buying meat. Look for the "Select" or "Lean" label on meat.
- Limit the use of luncheon meats, bacon, and sausage.
- Trim the fat off meat before cooking or eating.
- Cut the skin off chicken or turkey before eating. White meat is lower in fat than dark meat.
- Buy tuna packed in water or rinse the oil off oil-packed tuna.
- Eat broiled, baked, or steamed foods. Limit your intake of fried foods.
- Substitute plain low-fat yogurt for sour cream in dips and on potatoes.
- Use less butter, margarine, mayonnaise, and gravy on foods. Use naturally fat-free seasonings, such as lemon juice and herbs.
- Limit the use of cheese, nuts, and peanut butter. They're nutritious, but high in fat.

➤ Substituting herb seasoning for salt offers flavor without excess sodium.

THE FOOD GUIDE PYRAMID

The **Food Guide Pyramid** shown on page 410 is *an eating plan that outlines what to eat each day.* It's designed to give you a better sense of your overall eating habit goals. How? Think of any food you eat. It fits somewhere in the pyramid. The Food Guide Pyramid can help you and your family put the Dietary Guidelines for Americans into practice.

The Food Groups

Each group provides specific nutrients necessary for good health. You can see that the Pyramid calls for eating a variety of foods. If you eat the recommended servings of foods from each of the food groups every day, you'll probably get all of the nutrients you need.

FOOD GUIDE PYRAMID
A Guide to Daily Food Choices

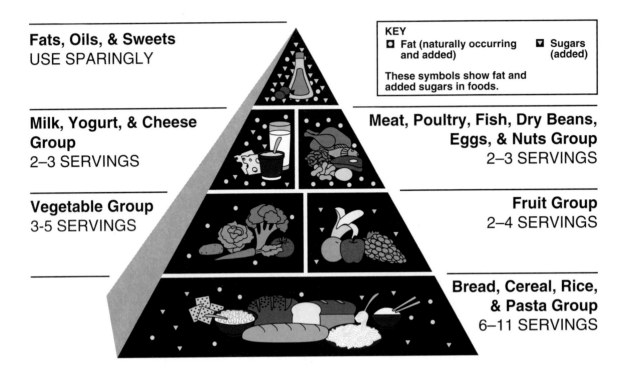

Fats, Oils, & Sweets
USE SPARINGLY

KEY
☐ Fat (naturally occurring and added)   ☑ Sugars (added)

These symbols show fat and added sugars in foods.

Milk, Yogurt, & Cheese Group
2–3 SERVINGS

Meat, Poultry, Fish, Dry Beans, Eggs, & Nuts Group
2–3 SERVINGS

Vegetable Group
3-5 SERVINGS

Fruit Group
2–4 SERVINGS

Bread, Cereal, Rice, & Pasta Group
6–11 SERVINGS

Food Examples for One Serving

Milk, Yogurt, and Cheese Group
- 1 cup milk or yogurt
- 1½ ounces ripened cheese
- 2 ounces processed cheese

Vegetable Group
- 1 cup leafy raw vegetables (lettuce, spinach)
- ½ cup other vegetables, cooked or raw
- ¾ cup vegetable juice

Meats, Poultry, Fish, Dry Beans, Eggs, and Nuts Group
- 2 to 3 ounces of cooked lean meat, poultry, or fish
- 1 cup cooked dry beans
- 2 Tbsp. peanut butter—equivalent to 1 ounce of meat

Fruit Group
- 1 orange, apple, banana, or pear
- ½ cup chopped, cooked, or canned fruit
- ¾ cup fruit juice

Bread, Cereal, Rice, and Pasta Group
- 1 slice bread
- ½ cup cooked cereal, rice, or pasta
- 1 ounce ready-to-eat cereal

The peak of the Pyramid suggests using fats, oils, and sweets sparingly. Fats and sugars (shown as circles and triangles) are in all of the food groups, not just in the tip. This is to show you that some foods in the other groups could also be high in fats or added sugars. For example, although croissants are part of the bread group, they are also high in fat.

How Many Servings?

Notice that the Food Guide Pyramid gives the recommended number of servings from each food group as a range. You should have at least the lowest number of servings in the range. If you're physically active, have a large body frame, or are a growing teen you may need to eat the larger number of servings.

➤ Pizza is a favorite teen food. While it can be basically nutritious, do not count on it to be your total source of nutritional servings.

What Counts as a Serving?

Serving sizes differ among foods. Look at the examples of one serving of food listed at the bottom of the Pyramid. If your portion size is bigger than a recommended serving, it counts as more than one serving. If it's smaller, it's part of a serving. You can get a quick estimate of portion size by using these tips:
- Three ounces of meat, poultry, or fish is about the size of a deck of cards.
- One-half cup of a fruit, a vegetable, pasta, or rice is about the size of a preschool child's fist.
- One ounce of cheese is about the size of your thumb.

PUTTING IT ALL TOGETHER

What have you learned from the guidelines in this chapter? In general, it's important to develop healthful eating habits. The food you eat daily may not always fit perfectly into the categories of the Food Guide Pyramid. What counts is your eating pattern over several days.

Review & Activities

Chapter Summary

- The Dietary Guidelines for Americans are nine suggestions for making healthful food choices.
- The Dietary Guidelines include: aim for a healthy weight; be physically active daily; let the Pyramid guide your food choices; choose a variety of grains, fruits, and vegetables daily; keep food safe to eat; choose a diet low in fat, saturated fat, and cholesterol; choose beverages and foods to moderate your sugar intake; choose and prepare foods with less salt.
- The Food Guide Pyramid is an eating plan that shows you how to plan healthful food choices each day.
- Eating the recommended servings of foods from each of the food groups will help you get all the nutrients you need.

Reviewing the Chapter

1. What are the three main messages of the Dietary Guidelines for Americans?
2. Identify three factors that help determine whether your weight is a healthy one for you.
3. Why is it important to eat plenty of grain products, vegetables, and fruits?
4. Why is choosing a low-fat meal plan a good idea?
5. What's the benefit in choosing a diet moderate in salt and sodium?
6. What is the purpose of the Food Guide Pyramid?
7. Identify the Food Guide Pyramid's five food groups.

Family & Community

With Your Family

Discuss with your family how food choices and serving sizes have changed since older family members were your age. How do your family members think the Food Guide Pyramid and the Dietary Guidelines for Americans have influenced their food choices?

In Your Community

Select an ethnic cuisine that is represented in your community. Where do the foods from this culture fit into the Food Guide Pyramid? Illustrate the pyramid and display it in your school cafeteria.

Thinking Critically

1. **Fact or fiction.** Some advertisements or food labels may include such phrases as "low cholesterol," "reduced fat," or "high fiber." Identify examples that you've seen or heard. How can these statements be misleading to consumers? How are they helpful? How can you judge the reliability of this information?
2. **Draw conclusions.** Although food is plentiful, many Americans don't get the nutrients they need. What factors contribute to poor nutrition in the U.S.?
3. **Compare and contrast.** Think about the food choices that you make now in comparison to those you made when you were younger. How do your choices compare? What are the similarities and differences? Do you make better choices now? Why or why not?

Making Connections

1. **Health.** Interview healthcare professionals, such as physicians, nurses, and dietitians. Ask them for their suggestions to help people live healthier lifestyles.
2. **Social Studies.** Different sections of the country have regional food favorites. Investigate one area of the United States. Identify its regional foods. What factors make these foods popular? How do these foods help meet the requirements of the Food Guide Pyramid and the Dietary Guidelines for Americans?

Applying Your Learning

1. **Create menus.** Use the Food Guide Pyramid to develop a three-day menu plan for yourself. Include the minimum number of servings from each of the food groups. Be sure to use foods you like and would enjoy eating.
2. **Compare serving sizes.** Using your favorite breakfast cereal, fill a cereal bowl with the portion size you'd typically eat. In a second bowl, use a measuring cup to measure out the portion recommended on the cereal box label. How do the two portions compare? Next, compare them to the serving size identified on the Food Guide Pyramid. What conclusions can you draw?
3. **Compare menus.** Gather menus from several of your favorite restaurants. Compare the food choices available at each restaurant. How can these food choices help you meet your daily needs according to the Food Guide Pyramid?

What Would You Do?

Suppose you had a friend who wanted to improve his diet but had no idea about where to begin. Your friend has asked you for help. Keeping in mind that habits are sometimes difficult to change, what suggestions would you offer?

Making Food Choices

YOU WILL LEARN . . .

➤ What influences food choices.
➤ How to identify accurate information about food and nutrition.
➤ How individual needs affect nutrition.
➤ Nutritional needs for athletes.

TERMS TO LEARN . . .

➤ additives
➤ irradiated foods
➤ myth
➤ organic food
➤ vegetarian

Imagine ...

... that your Saturday job is bagging groceries at the supermarket. One customer buys 20 cans of mushroom soup and a package of cut-up chicken. The next person in line has a cart full of salad greens and an assortment of fresh vegetables and fruits. As you work, you wonder what meals these shoppers have in mind.

Think About

• How would working around food impact your food choices?
• Does your knowledge about nutrition enable you to make good choices?
• If you were in charge of meal plans for your family, how would you decide what to cook every day?

WHAT INFLUENCES FOOD CHOICES?

Have you ever thought about why you and your family eat certain foods? Perhaps your family serves special foods on holidays and family celebrations. Some of the following factors have probably influenced the way you feel about food.

- **Family and culture.** A lot of people tend to follow their family's traditional food customs.
- **Friends.** Eating is a social event. When you go out with friends, you're all likely to eat the same foods.
- **Religious beliefs.** Many of the world's religions include guidelines on food and eating.
- **Emotions.** People often associate certain foods with feelings of comfort or love.
- **Geographical area.** Different regions or countries often feature their own food traditions.
- **Advertising.** Food-related businesses spend millions of dollars each year to convince you to buy their products.
- **Lifestyle.** The amount of time you have for meals and how important good health is to you make a difference in the foods you choose.

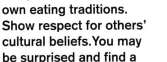

➤ Many families have their own eating traditions. Show respect for others' cultural beliefs. You may be surprised and find a new favorite food.

GETTING THE FACTS

Sometimes it's hard to separate truth from questionable claims. When the topic of food comes up, should you believe all of the claims made? How would you evaluate the following statements?

- An apple a day keeps the doctor away.
- We're born with a preference for rich, fatty foods.
- Health food stores have the healthiest foods.

Food Myths

You've probably heard many myths in your lifetime. A **myth** is *an untrue statement that people believe.* Sometimes myths become widely circulated.

The previous three statements about apples, fatty foods, and health foods are myths. What are the facts?

* Apples are a low-calorie, high-fiber snack food. Eating one every day isn't a bad idea, but it won't prevent illness.
* Preference for fat is actually acquired.
* "Health food" printed on a package doesn't necessarily mean that what's inside is healthful. You can find nutritious foods in supermarkets and foods with little nutritional value in health food stores.

Questions to Ask

You get information about food and nutrition from many sources. However, not all sources of information are reliable. How can you be sure you're getting the facts? Here are some questions you can ask:

* Who wrote or made the statement? What are the person's qualifications in regard to nutrition?
* Why was the statement made? Is balanced coverage given? Was this meant to advertise or inform?
* Are the claims supported by credible or believable sources such as a government agency or health organization?
* What do registered dieticians or doctors say?

Health Foods

Have you ever wondered what the terms "good for you" and "healthy" mean? Many "health" foods aren't any more or less nutritious than regular food products. There is one difference, however. Health foods usually cost more.

Before you buy a product, read the label carefully. Compare it with other products. Then decide whether the product is worth the extra cost.

➤ Myths about foods are commonly spread. Don't believe everything you hear!

GETTING THE MOST NUTRIENTS

Vitamins and minerals are key to all body processes—they work as a team. Keep the following preparation techniques in mind to maintain high nutrient levels:

* Leave edible skins on vegetables and fruits whenever possible. Most vitamins and minerals are found just below the skin.

* Eat vegetables and fruits raw or steam them just until they're tender-crisp.

* Cook vegetables in small amounts of water.

* Cut vegetables into large pieces before cooking to lose fewer nutrients.

* Save liquid from cooked vegetables and add it to soups, stews, and sauces.

Dietary Supplements

You probably know people who take vitamins every day. Maybe you've heard people debate the pros and cons of taking vitamins. You may have wondered who was right.

Most health experts agree that you don't need a daily vitamin or mineral supplement if you eat a variety of foods from the Pyramid. An exception may be if a physician recommends taking a supplement because of a health condition.

Some people think that taking megadoses, or large amounts, of a vitamin or mineral will cure disease. This isn't only untrue, it's often dangerous. Taking too much of any nutrient can be harmful.

➤ Vitamin and mineral supplements can benefit some people. Check with your physician before taking suppliments.

Food Additives

Why does the oil separate from some peanut butters and not from others? What makes ice cream so smooth and creamy? The answer lies in **additives,** or *substances added to food for a specific purpose.*

Additives keep peanut butter from separating and ice cream smooth. They're also used to boost the nutritional value of popular foods and increase freshness. All additives must pass rigid governmental tests for safety.

➤ Food additives keep foods fresher longer. For example, homemade breads will mold much more quickly than store bought breads that contain food additives.

Irradiated Foods

Some stores advertise **irradiated foods.** These *foods have gone through a process that destroys bacteria, mold, and insects by passing them through a field of radiant energy similar to x-rays.* This process makes foods safer to eat and maintains the quality of foods. It also extends the shelf life of these foods. Irradiated foods are just as nutritious as foods that aren't irradiated. Irradiated foods must be labeled on the package according to law.

The irradiation process is controversial. Many believe that irradiated food is radioactive. However, this isn't the case. Most of the radiant energy used in food passes through the food, in much the same way as microwaves pass through food.

INFOLINK

See Chapter 28 for more information on how nutrients work.

TRY IT OUT

How Preservatives Affect Food

ACTIVITY

What You'll Need
- 1 slice store-bought bread
- 1 slice homemade bread
- 2 plates, 2 labels, and plastic wrap

What to Do
1. Place each slice of bread on a plate. Label and date each plate and cover with plastic wrap. Leave out at room temperature.
2. Observe the bread slices daily. Record the date that mold appears on each slice of bread.

To Discuss
- How many days did it take for mold to appear on each slice of bread?
- What preservatives are listed on the store bread label?
- What conclusions can you draw about the value of preservatives to the food supply?

SAFETY First

Avoiding Dehydration

When you exercise, you sweat or lose body fluids. You need to replace body fluids by drinking liquids to avoid dehydration. Try drinking an eight-ounce glass of water before and after you exercise. Be on the alert for these conditions that cause dehydration:

- High temperatures can cause you to sweat more.
- Harder workouts can cause you to sweat more.
- Body size can affect how much you sweat. Smaller bodies tend to sweat less than larger bodies.
- Long workouts can cause you to lose more body fluids.

Organic Foods

Another word that you might see when shopping for food is "organic." **Organic food** is *food that is produced without manufactured chemicals.* There's no difference in nutritional value between foods grown with organic fertilizers and those grown with chemical fertilizers. However, some people buy organic fruits and vegetables out of concern for health and the environment.

INDIVIDUAL NUTRITIONAL NEEDS

Different people have different nutritional needs. Their needs are based on their size, activity level, age and other factors.

Nutrition for Medical Conditions

Nutrition is an important concern when someone is ill. Good nutrition, along with rest and proper care, can help someone regain strength and get well. However, a person who's ill may not want or be able to eat normally. Long-term medical conditions (such as diabetes) can also affect food needs. It's best to follow a physician's advice about what a patient should eat.

➤ You can purchase foods that have been organically grown at farmers markets and at some supermarkets. Check your local store's produce department for these products.

Nutrition for Vegetarians

What is a vegetarian? A **vegetarian** is generally *someone who does not eat meat, poultry, or fish.* Vegetarian meals are typically made up of vegetables, fruits, grains, nuts, and sometimes eggs and dairy products. If vegetarians eat a wide selection of food, they're eating in a way that fits today's nutritional guidelines. Vegetarian meals feature plant foods rich in fiber and complex carbohydrates. Well-planned vegetarian eating patterns are often lower in fat and cholesterol than nonvegetarian ones. It's important to get nutritional counseling before following a strict vegetarian diet.

➤ Medical conditions affect the body's nutritional needs. Former Miss America, Nicole Johnson, is a diabetic. She wears an insulin pump to regulate her body's need for insulin.

Nutrition for Athletes

Good nutrition is important for you to reach peak performance in any sport. Are the nutritional needs of competitive athletes any different from those of people who exercise for health and enjoyment? The answer is no. Athletes need carbohydrates, protein, fat, vitamins, minerals, and water. However, competitive athletes may need more of these nutrients.

Quenching Thirst

You sweat when you're physically active—everyone does. Perspiration evaporates from your skin, and you need to replace the fluid you lose. Drink fluids before, during, and after activities even when you aren't thirsty. Thirst is a sign of dehydration. But what should you drink? If you work out for 60 minutes or less, drink water. For longer, strenuous activities, you can also dilute fruit juices to half-strength.

Fuel for Your Body

Carbohydrates are the best source of energy. If you are an athlete, you should plan on getting 60 to 65 percent of your energy needs from carbohydrates. Eating foods rich in complex carbohydrates increases your athletic fitness and endurance. By using carbohydrates as your body's main fuel, you should be able to keep up strenuous activity for a longer time.

➤ A well-planned vegetarian diet is healthful, nutritionally adequate, and may provide health benefits in the prevention and treatment of diseases.

Review & Activities

Chapter Summary

- A variety of different factors influences people's food choices and eating habits.
- Evaluate the accuracy of information made about food claims before you follow new advice.
- Nutritional supplements are not usually necessary if you eat a balanced diet.
- Food additives are used to make food more appealing and nutritious.
- Irradiation extends shelf life and makes foods safer to eat.
- Well-planned vegetarian eating patterns fit today's nutritional guidelines.
- It's important to drink fluids during any athletic workout to replace lost water.
- Carbohydrates are the best source of energy for athletes and should supply 60 to 65 percent of total energy needs.

Reviewing the Chapter

1. Identify at least four factors that influence people's food choices.
2. How can you check out the accuracy of information about foods and nutrition?
3. Explain why most people don't need to take dietary supplements.
4. How can you be sure that food additives are safe to eat?
5. What are the advantages of irradiating foods?
6. What are organic foods and why do some people prefer them?
7. What health benefit does a well-planned vegetarian eating pattern provide?
8. How can eating food high in complex carbohydrates benefit an athlete?

Family & Community

With Your Family

Work with another family member to plan and prepare a vegetarian meal for your family. Discuss what you liked about the meal and what you'd change. What other vegetarian meals would you be willing to try?

In Your Community

Investigate the food customs of ethnic groups represented in your community. How do the climate, available transportation, and economic conditions influence available food choices?

Thinking Critically

1. **Draw conclusions.** Why do some people believe questionable claims made for food? What might be some of the consequences for people who don't examine these claims? Why is it important to obtain accurate information about the food you eat?

2. **Analyze food additives.** If you were going to develop a totally new food additive to improve the appearance, stability, or nutritive value of food, what would you investigate? What benefits would it offer?

3. **Compare and contrast.** Do you think athletes are more likely to believe claims made for special food supplements than nonathletes? Explain your answer.

Making Connections

1. **Math.** Obtain several cans or bottles of different sports drinks. Compare the costs of these drinks per ounce. Conduct a taste comparison to see which of the drinks seems most appealing.

2. **Science.** Obtain several different food labels from packages, cans, and jars. Read the list of ingredients. Try to find more information about any ingredients that are unfamiliar. What is their function? What do you think the product would be like without these ingredients?

Applying Your Learning

1. **Make recommendations.** Investigate reliable sources of information about nutrition in your library and on the Internet. Which of these would be of particular interest to teens? Share your recommendations with others.

2. **Survey the market.** Identify at least five food products in your supermarket that are advertised as being healthy or good for your health. Examine the labels carefully. What makes these foods especially healthful?

3. **Plan menus.** Develop several high-carbohydrate menus you would recommend for athletes. Try to prepare at least one of your recommendations. Have others evaluate your selections.

What Would You Do?

Suppose you overheard someone trying to sell your next-door neighbor, a good family friend, a food supplement. The seller was saying that the supplement increases energy and makes people happier. You know that's an exaggerated claim. What would you say to your neighbor?

Buying and Storing Food

YOU WILL LEARN . . .

➤ How to prepare for shopping and shop for food.
➤ How to store food safely.

TERMS TO LEARN . . .

➤ food product dating
➤ homogenized
➤ legumes
➤ pasteurized
➤ staples
➤ unit price

Imagine ...

... that you've been asleep for one hundred years. You open your eyes and you're standing in the middle of a large, bright supermarket. What is that noise? It can't be music! What in the world are all these packages?

Think About

• What might startle you most about the food available today?
• Which items would be familiar? Would you know what pizza was?
• How might the way food is stored be different?

GETTING READY TO SHOP

Food shopping can be a chore. It can also be fun, but even fun activities take some planning. If you take time to plan ahead for the meals you'll have during the week, you'll be a lot happier with the results of what you buy.

Making a List

Have you ever gone to the supermarket and forgotten some of the things you intended to buy? It's easy to do. That's where a grocery list helps out.

Keep a running list of grocery items your family needs to prepare the meals you plan on having. Keep track of the **staples** that you need. These are *foods that you are likely to use often,* such as milk, eggs, and bread. To organize your list, group each food category together, such as dairy products, produce, meats, breads, and canned goods.

➤ Newspaper ads and coupons can save you money only if products are what you usually buy. How can you benefit from comparing prices?

The Family Food Dollar

Most families have a food budget. Being organized helps you stay within the amount your family has to spend. What are some things you and your family can do?

• Check supermarket specials in the newspaper. Many families plan menus around these specials.

• Clip coupons from newspapers, magazines, and stores for items your family needs and uses. Coupon items may not always be the best buys.

• Shop on a full stomach. If you're hungry when you shop, you're more likely to buy extra food, whether or not you need it.

Deciding Where to Shop

If you live in a city, you'll likely have your choice of where to shop. If you live in a small town or rural area, your choices may be limited.

For many people, shopping choices include supermarkets, warehouse stores, specialty stores like bakeries, seasonal farmer's markets, and convenience stores. Most carry a variety of food products at varying prices.

Online computer shopping is a convenience available in some areas. You need a computer and a modem to place your order. Your food is then delivered to your home. These services add to the cost of the food.

SHOPPING FOR FOOD

If helping to shop is your job, how are you going to organize your grocery shopping? First of all, keep your shopping list handy. As you select items, cross them off the list. Some people use a calculator to keep track of spending.

Store Layouts and Displays

Food stores use a number of techniques to encourage impulse buying. Bright, colorful packaging and displays are designed to catch your eye. Special displays are often placed in the middle of or at the end of an aisle. The items on display are sometimes on sale, but not always.

Popular items are often placed at eye level so you'll be more likely to see and buy them. Slow, relaxing music encourages shoppers to take their time and buy more. Some stores offer food samples to encourage consumers to try new products. By sticking to your shopping list and being aware of these techniques, you'll be less likely to make impulse purchases.

Comparison Shopping

Instead of picking up the first package you see, take the time to comparison shop. When you compare different items, you can be sure you're getting what you want at a fair price. Your comparison shopping will be easier if you know more about labels, pricing, freshness, and quality.

➤ Planning your meals in advance saves time and money. Some people take recipes to the store to ensure they get the ingredients they need.

INFOLINK

See Chapter 22 for more information on impulse buying.

Comparing Brands

When you shop, compare national brands, private labels, and generic products.

- **National brands.** Major food companies produce many products you see on supermarket shelves. They're sold across the country and advertised nationally.
- **Private label, or store brand, products.** These products are packaged for a particular chain of stores. Prices are usually lower than for national brands. There may be differences in quality, but the nutritional value is usually the same as for national brands.
- **Generic products.** Identified by their plain packaging, generic products are less expensive. Their nutritional value compares to other products, but the quality and appearance may not be as appealing.

➤ Farmers' markets sell fresh produce at a low price. For the best selections, plan to shop early.

Reading Labels

Would you buy any package without knowing what was inside? Probably not. Food labels give you an insight to what's in a package. On almost every packaged food you'll find important consumer and nutrition information. Food labels tell you the name of the product, the weight of the contents, ingredients listed from most to least, and often the name and address of the manufacturer.

Take a look at the nutrition facts panel, too. (See the diagram on page 430.) It can help you make healthful food choices.

Using Unit Pricing

The **unit price** is *the price per ounce, pound, or other unit of measure.* Unit pricing makes it easy for you to compare the cost of products in different-sized packages. Look for unit prices posted on the shelf near the item. The total price for the package is also given.

Some stores don't list unit prices. You can calculate them yourself. Divide the total cost of the package by the number of units (ounces or pounds) to get the cost per unit.

Checking the Food Product Dating

Food product dating is *a date used to indicate product freshness.* You'll see three types of dating stamped on product packages:

- "Sell by" or "pull date" is the last day a product should be sold if the food is to remain fresh for home storage.
- "Pack date" is when the food was processed or packaged.
- "Best if used by date" tells when the food should be used for best quality.

What's the best way for you to use these dates? Try to purchase food that will be fresh when your family is ready to eat it. If the "sell by" date has passed, don't buy the product.

➤ **When selecting packaged meat, check the "sell date" for product freshness. Don't buy foods with expired dates.**

TRY IT OUT

Product Comparison

ACTIVITY

What You'll Need
- 3 cans of a fruit or vegetable: a generic, a store brand, and a name brand
- Paper and pen or pencil

What to Do
1. Working in a group of four students, create a chart that compares the three products for color, size, shape, flavor, texture, amount of liquid, price, and nutrition information.
2. Compare the three products and record your findings on the chart.

To Discuss
- Which product would you choose to serve as a side dish? Why? Which product would you choose if you were using it as an ingredient in a recipe? Why? Which would you choose if your funds were limited?
- What generalizations can you make based on your findings? How would you decide if and when you would use each of these products?

NUTRITION FACTS

Calories.
The number of calories from a single serving are listed.

Nutrient amounts.
Only the nutrients related to today's most important health issues are listed.

Daily values footnote.
Figures show the maximum amounts recommended for fat, saturated fat, cholesterol, and sodium.

Nutrition Facts

Serving Size 1/2 cup (114g)
Servings Per Container 4

Amount Per Serving	
Calories 90	Calories from Fat 27

	% Daily Value*
Total Fat 3g	5%
Saturated Fat 0g	0%
Cholesterol 0mg	0%
Sodium 300mg	13%
Total Carbohydrate 13g	4%
Dietary Fiber 3g	12%
Sugars 3g	
Protein 3g	

Vitamin A	80%	• Vitamin C	60%
Calcium	4%	• Iron	4%

*Percent Daily Values are based on a 2,000 calorie diet. Your daily values may be higher or lower depending on your calorie needs:

		Calories	2,000	2,500
Total Fat	Less than		65g	80g
Sat Fat	Less than		20g	25g
Cholesterol	Less than		300mg	300mg
Sodium	Less than		2,400mg	2,400mg
Total Carbohydrate			300g	375g
Fiber			25g	30g

Calories per gram:
Fat 9 • Carbohydrates 4 • Protein 4

Serving size and number of servings. Servings are based on an average size and aren't always the same size as those in the Pyramid.

Percent of daily values. These percentages give you a general idea of how much one serving contributes nutritionally to a 2,000-calorie daily diet.

Calories-per-gram conversion. Figures state the number of calories in one gram of fat, carbohydrate, and protein.

➤ Produce is perishable. For best results, eat it soon after it's purchased.

Food Quality

As you shop for groceries, one major challenge is to choose the freshest and best quality products you can find.

Buying Produce

Knowing some signs of quality will help you buy the best quality produce.

• **Avoid bruised and wilted produce.** It's a sign that produce has passed its peak of freshness or hasn't been handled properly. It's also a sign that nutrients have been lost.

• **Handle some produce to get a better idea of its quality.** Head lettuce and cabbage should feel solid. Citrus fruit, squash, cucumbers, and tomatoes should feel heavy for their size. Celery, asparagus, and green beans are best when crisp.

➤ Although it may be less expensive per ounce to purchase a larger quantity, food not eaten is a waste. Be a smart shopper, plan your meals carefully.

- **Avoid buying root vegetables with sprouts.** When root vegetables, such as potatoes and onions, begin to show sprouts, it's a sure sign of age.
- **Handle fruits and vegetables gently.** Fresh produce is easily bruised with careless handling.

Buying Protein Foods

Protein foods are perishable, meaning they spoil quickly. The following suggestions can help you.

- Color is a sign of freshness in meat and poultry. Look for bright red beef and grayish pink pork. Poultry should be creamy white to yellow, without bruises or torn skin.
- Fish should smell fresh (not ammonia-like) and be firm to the touch. Fresh fish should be iced and refrigerated.
- The percentage of lean on ground beef packages is a clue to the fat content. Ground round is usually the leanest.
- When buying eggs you'll have the choice of size and grade. Stores often sell grades AA and A eggs in medium, large, extra large, and jumbo sizes. Open egg cartons to check for cracked eggs before you buy.
- **Legumes** are *plants in which seeds grow in pods, such as beans, peas, and lentils.* When buying legumes, buy only as much as you'll use within six months. Beans are available dried or canned and ready to use. Look for firm, clean legumes of uniform size and color. If sizes are uneven, they won't cook evenly.

SAFETY First

When buying packaged and convenience foods:

- Avoid packages with holes, tears, or open corners. It's a sign that someone has either tampered with the package, or it's been mishandled.
- Never buy cans that are swollen, damaged, rusted, or dented. These are warning signs of bacteria that causes botulism, a serious food-borne illness.
- Check safety seals and buttons on containers to be sure they're intact. You'll often find safety seals on milk, yogurt, cottage cheese, and glass jars of food that are vacuum-sealed for safety. If seals are broken, avoid the product.

Buying Dairy Products

Fresh milk is sold as whole milk (at least 3.25% milk fat) and milk with lower fat content (skim, .5%, 1%, 1.5%, and 2% milk fat). Except for the fat, the nutrient content of all milk is about the same.

When you shop for fresh milk, you'll see the words "pasteurized" and "homogenized." **Pasteurized** means that *the milk has been heated to destroy harmful bacteria.* **Homogenized** means that *the fat particles in the milk have been broken up and distributed throughout the milk.*

Check safety seals on milk, yogurt, and cottage cheese. If seals are broken, don't buy the product. Many kinds of cheeses are available in the dairy case. Check cheese labels carefully and choose low-fat varieties whenever possible.

➤ Cheese is made with varying amounts of milk fat. Farmer's cheese, Mozzarella, and low-fat Swiss cheese are made with skim milk and contain less fat. Read the label before buying cheese. You may be surprised by the nutritional variations.

Buying Grain Products

Grains are the seeds or fruits of cereal grasses. Grain products include cereal, rice, pasta, and bread. The products are made from a variety of grains—wheat, oats, corn, barley, and rye. The following tips can help you shop for grain products:

- Read labels carefully to buy the type of grain best suited to your needs.
- Select grain products that contain whole grain or bran for more nutrients and fiber. Also, look for grain products that are enriched.
- Check cereal labels for sodium, sugar, and fat content.
- Check out the varieties of pasta and rice. Pasta comes in a variety of shapes and sizes. Rice is available in brown and white forms, instant or regular, and short, medium, or long grain. The length of cooking time varies with the type of rice you choose. Most pasta is dried and sold in boxes or bags. Fresh pasta is often available in the refrigerated section.

Buying Packaged and Convenience Foods

Many foods are available in a variety of convenience forms. You can buy main dishes, side dishes, snacks, and entire meals already prepared. Some are frozen, while others can be stored at room temperature. Many can be heated in the microwave oven for quick meals.

Convenience foods can be part of a healthful diet. However, many convenience foods are high in fat, sugar, and sodium, so it's important to read labels carefully.

STORING FOOD

When you're ready to store food after grocery shopping, store it at the right temperature. Put frozen foods away first to prevent thawing. Next, put away refrigerated foods. Then put cans and boxes in cabinets or on shelves.

Is your refrigerator cold enough to keep food fresh? Ideally, refrigerator temperatures should be between 32° and 40°F (0°to 5°C). Freezer temperatures should be 0°F (-18°C) or below. An inexpensive refrigerator thermometer can help you check on temperatures.

➤ Grains such as barley, rye, and wheat are excellent sources of soluble fiber, protein, and B vitamins. Grains can be added to soups, casseroles, and various other foods. **What grains do you eat most often?**

➤ Always put the new food products behind the older ones. Use older or opened packages first.

Chapter Summary

- Organizing grocery shopping helps families spend grocery money wisely and adds to shopping satisfaction.
- Consider the advantages and disadvantages of shopping in different types of food stores.
- If you are aware of the techniques grocery stores use to encourage shoppers to buy, you will be less likely to make impulse purchases.
- When you comparison shop for food, look at different brands, read labels, and compare prices.
- Reading the labels on food products provides you with important consumer and nutrition information.
- You can select the best quality foods by knowing the signs of freshness, the terms appearing on labels, and other important packaging information.
- Storing food properly will keep it fresh and safe to eat.

Reviewing the Chapter

1. List four things you can do to organize grocery shopping before you go to the store.
2. What techniques do food stores use to encourage impulse purchases?
3. Compare the advantages and disadvantages of national and store brands, as well as generic products.
4. Tell how unit pricing can help you when you shop for food.
5. Explain the differences between the following types of product freshness dating: "sell by" date, "pack date", and "best if used by" date.
6. Identify four signs of quality to look for when buying fresh produce.
7. List three points to look for when buying dairy products.
8. What guidelines should you follow when storing the food you purchase?

Family & Community

With Your Family

Brainstorm ideas with your family about how you could help the family to buy and store groceries. Select one or two ideas to try. Talk with your family about how successful these ideas were.

In Your Community

Identify one or more organizations in your community that help to distribute food to people in need. Find out what you can do individually or as a class to help.

Thinking Critically

1. **Analyze decisions.** If you shop in supermarkets that advertise the lowest prices, why should you be concerned about comparison shopping? When is the lowest price not always the best buy?

2. **Draw conclusions.** In your experience, what is the biggest mistake people make when shopping for food in terms of spending time and money? Why?

3. **Compare and contrast.** How do your experiences in shopping for food differ from those of people in previous generations? Is shopping for food easier or more difficult now compared to previous years? Explain your answer.

Making Connections

1. **Math.** Collect several cents-off coupons for different items. Compare the cost of similar items without the coupons. Which are the best buys and why?

2. **Language Arts.** Compose a one-minute public service announcement offering suggestions about how to save money when shopping for food. Try out your announcement with your classmates to get their reactions.

Applying Your Learning

1. **Identify strategies.** Think about the times you've been shopping for food. What strategies have stores used to encourage shoppers to make impulse purchases? In each of these cases, what motivates people to make a purchase?

2. **Develop a checklist.** Select several popular fresh produce items that your family enjoys. Develop a checklist of pointers to look for when buying these items.

What Would You Do?

Imagine you were shopping for food and saw someone open a package, take a cookie out, eat the cookie, and put the package back on the shelf. How do these behaviors affect the store and other shoppers? What do you think your reaction would be?

Chapter

32

Eating Together

YOU WILL LEARN . . .

- ➤ Different ways to serve food.
- ➤ How to set a table correctly.
- ➤ Tips for good table manners.
- ➤ The proper behavior for eating out in a restaurant.

TERMS TO LEARN . . .

- ➤ à la carte
- ➤ appetizer
- ➤ courses
- ➤ entrée
- ➤ etiquette
- ➤ flatware
- ➤ place setting
- ➤ tableware

Imagine ...

... that you've invited some new friends over to your home on Saturday. Your uncle stops by uninvited, as he often does, just in time for lunch. Your friends seem surprised. You feel obligated to invite your uncle to have lunch with you.

Think About

- What will you tell your friends? Will they understand?
- What is your opinion of people who just "stop by" at mealtime?
- What do you think about when you hear the term "good manners?"

SERVING FOOD

Mealtimes give family members an opportunity to spend time together and catch up on each other's news. Each family has its own approach to meals. Some families are spontaneous and welcome friends or relatives dropping by for a casual meal. Others prefer quiet meals at set times. The way food is served often depends on the menu, the number of people eating, and the space available.

Some different ways food is served include:

- **Family-style service.** Dinner plates are placed at each person's seat. Foods are served in dishes on the table, which are passed around so people can help themselves.
- **Plate service.** Individual plates are prepared in the kitchen and taken to the table.
- **Head-of-table service.** For special occasion meals, the person seated at the head of the table serves food on plates and passes them down the table to each person.
- **Buffets.** This is a good way to serve food when there are too many people to seat around the table. Dishes, flatware, napkins, and serving dishes of food are placed on a table or counter and people help themselves.

➤ Buffets allow you to eat a variety of different foods when you want them. Always use a clean plate when returning to the food line.

Making a DIFFERENCE

BIRTHDAY TREAT

"It's Mom's birthday next week, and we should do something special for her," Lynne said to her brother Jesse. "Things haven't been easy for her lately."

"What can we do?" Jesse said. "We're both short on money."

Lynne thought a minute. "How about taking her and her sisters out to dinner?"

"That could be steep," Jesse said. "I've got an idea. You love to cook. Let's do a surprise dinner at home. Nothing fancy."

"Great. I'll do a simple buffet dinner—a pasta dish, salad, garlic bread. And it won't cost a lot. But guess what? You're doing the grocery shopping."

Taking Action

1. What options would you consider to celebrate a family member's special occasion?
2. How can celebrating special events help strengthen family ties?

TABLE SETTING

When you go out to eat, are you ever confused about the arrangement of plates, glasses, and flatware on the table? A lot of other people feel the same way, but table settings aren't as complicated as they first seem.

Except at picnics and buffets, most tables are set with individual place settings. A **place setting** is *the arrangement of tableware and flatware for each person.* The tableware at each person's place has a logical organization. **Tableware** includes *dishes, glasses, and* **flatware,** or *the eating utensils.* Each place setting usually has at least one plate, glass, fork, knife, spoon, and napkin. Depending on what food is being served, other tableware may be used. The photos on page 440 show two typical place settings.

The Place Setting

An attractively set table brings pleasure to mealtime. Setting the table according to a set standard is designed for the convenience of eating. Before you get started setting each place setting, put placemats or a tablecloth on the table. Then decide what tableware will be needed for each person to eat the meal. Here are some simple guidelines to follow for setting the table. Informal styles are shown at left and formal styles below.

1. Put a dinner plate in the center of each place setting about 1 inch (2.5 cm) from the edge of the table.

2. Place the dinner fork to the left of the plate. If more than one fork is needed, place the fork you'll use first farthest from the plate. For example, if you are serving a salad before the entrée, you would place the salad fork to the left of the dinner fork.

3. Put the dinner knife to the right of the plate, with the blade facing the plate.

4. Place the spoon to the right of the knife. If more than one spoon is needed, place the spoon you'll use first farthest from the plate.

5. Line up the handle end of each piece of flatware with the lower edge of the plate.

6. Place the salad plate above the forks.

7. Put the water glass just above the tip of the knife. If you're serving another beverage besides water, put the glass to the right and slightly in front of the water glass.

8. Place the cup and saucer (or mug) to the right of the spoon. The handle should be parallel with the edge of the table.

Activity:
With a partner, practice setting the table for a typical family meal of your choice.

TABLE MANNERS

Have you ever been confused about **etiquette,** or the *accepted rules of behavior* at a meal? Knowing basic etiquette guidelines will give you confidence in different social situations. Although it seems like a lot to remember, once you start to follow some of these tips, they'll become automatic:

- Place your napkin on your lap.
- If you're not sure which piece of flatware to use, observe what the person at the head of the table uses.
- Use serving forks and spoons to serve your food.
- Cut one bite of food at a time and then eat it.
- Eat quietly. Chew with your mouth closed. Avoid talking while you have food in your mouth.
- You can use your fingers to eat foods such as sandwiches, bread, carrot and celery sticks, and pizza.
- If food is too hot to eat, wait until it cools.
- After eating, put your knife and fork across the center of your plate and your napkin to the left of your plate.

➤ Most restaurants assign an employee who is responsible for providing you a table in a specified area of a restaurant. You might have the option to specify a preference for a table or a booth.

EATING OUT

When someone says, "Let's eat out," do you think of going to a fast-food restaurant or a restaurant with table service?

Some restaurants require that you phone ahead to reserve a table. If you haven't been to the restaurant before, it's also a good idea to find out about the price range and dress code. If you have a reservation, try to get to the restaurant on time. If you can't get there as planned, telephone to cancel the reservation or to tell them you'll be late.

At many restaurants, someone will greet you when you come in. The person will probably ask how many are in your party and where you prefer to sit. If you have a reservation, give the name of the person who made the reservation. When your table is ready, someone will lead you to it. If you go to a restaurant where no one greets you, go ahead and seat yourself.

Ordering from the Menu

Menus are often divided into sections for different types of food or different **courses,** which are *parts of the meal.* For example, the menu might include appetizers, soups, salads, entrées, desserts, and beverages. An **appetizer** is *an optional first course.* The **entrée** is *the main course.*

The food on a menu will probably be listed and priced in one of two ways:

- Items may be listed separately, or **à la carte.** In this kind of listing, *each item has an individual, or separate, price.*
- The menu may list a complete meal for a certain price. Be sure to notice what's included in the meal.

Behaving in a Restaurant

Have you ever been to a restaurant where a group of people was loud and disruptive? You probably know how annoying that kind of behavior can be to others. Most people want to eat, talk quietly, and enjoy themselves.

If you need anything during the meal, politely ask your server. Your server will generally stop at your table while you eat to check on your needs. If a problem is urgent, get the server's attention by raising your hand.

Paying the Bill and Tipping

At the end of the meal, it's time to pay. If the check isn't given to you, ask for it. Who pays? Try to agree before you get to the restaurant. If you invite someone out, be clear about who's paying. If you're invited out and it's not clear who's paying, bring enough money so you can cover your own bill just in case.

Before paying, check the bill to be sure it's accurate. Remember, a sales tax is usually added to restaurant bills. It's customary to leave a tip for your server. The amount is usually 15 to 20 percent of the bill before tax. A tip is for service, not for food. Whether the food was good or bad, if the service was good, leave a tip.

UNDERSTANDING MENU LANGUAGE

You might see the following words on a menu:

- **au gratin.** Browned and buttered bread crumbs with cheese. Mostly used on vegetables.

- **au jus.** French for "in juice." Describes meat served in its own juices.

- **alfredo.** Pasta served in a white sauce made with cream, butter, and cheese.

- **cacciatore.** Italian for "hunter style." Chicken cooked in a spicy tomato sauce.

- **vinaigrette.** French for "vinegar." A sauce made of oil, vinegar, and seasoning to flavor meats and as a salad dressing.

> A tip or gratuity is your way of rewarding your server for service they provided you. Always treat your server with respect.

Some restaurants automatically add a service charge to your bill when a large group dines at the same table. In this case, you don't have to leave a tip. The service charge is the tip.

Some checks read at the bottom: "Pay the cashier." In that case, leave a tip at the table, and pay the cashier on the way out. Often the server will take your money and check to the cashier. When you get the change from the server, leave a tip.

Knowing what to expect in different kinds of restaurants will help you feel more comfortable in any situation. If you're not sure what to do, just ask someone. Most people are very willing to help you.

32

Review & Activities

Chapter Summary

- The type of food service used depends on the menu and number of people eating.
- Place settings, which include the arrangement of tableware and flatware for each person, follow a logical order.
- Knowing the correct mealtime etiquette will help you feel confident in social situations.
- Restaurant menus are generally organized according to courses, such as appetizers, entrées, and desserts.
- Familiarize yourself with what to do and expect at different types of restaurants so that you will feel more comfortable when eating out.

Reviewing the Chapter

1. Identify and describe at least three different types of family food service.
2. Describe how to properly set the table for a typical evening meal.
3. Suggest at least five tips about manners to keep in mind when you are eating with others.
4. Explain each of the following terms: appetizer, entrée, and à la carte.
5. Explain the general procedure you would expect to follow when eating out in a restaurant with table service.
6. How can you avoid embarrassment over who should pay the bill in a restaurant?

Family & Community

With Your Family

Offer to set the dinner table at home for a week. Try to make the table as attractive as possible.

In Your Community

People in retirement homes appreciate thoughtfulness and contact with others. Work with your classmates to make individual placemats or centerpieces for the tables or trays of people living in retirement homes.

Thinking Critically

1. **Recognize points of view.** Assume you have a friend who says that eating is meant to be enjoyed and trying to use good table manners gets in the way of having a good time. Do you agree or disagree with your friend's opinion? Explain your answer.
2. **Predict consequences.** How could using poor table manners impact relationships with others?
3. **Analyze the situation.** If you were going to a restaurant that you had never been to before and wanted to feel comfortable there, what would you do beforehand?

Making Connections

1. **Language Arts.** Write a paragraph describing a humorous experience you've had while eating at home or dining out. Share your experiences with others.
2. **Math.** Obtain a menu from a local restaurant. Compute the total cost of a meal you might order. Remember to include the sales tax and tip.

Applying Your Learning

1. **Set the table.** Write one or more menus for family meals. Exchange your menus with other classmates. Arrange place settings for one of the menus you've received. Have others check out your place settings.
2. **Manners check-up.** Role-play eating a meal. Make several intentional errors with manners. See if others can identify the errors and correct them.
3. **Learn the terms.** Obtain menus from a variety of restaurants in your community. Look for menu terms you don't understand. Research what the terms mean.

What Would You Do?

Imagine you're eating out with a group of friends. One of your friends takes the tip someone left on the table next to yours. You know that the tip was intended for the server. You don't want to create a scene, but on the other hand, you know it's wrong. What would you do or say?

REGISTERED NURSE

Residential facility has full and part-time openings for caring RN's who enjoy working with senior citizens.
• Associate's degree required.
• Second shift only.
• Signing bonuses available.

ASSISTANT RESTAURANT MANAGER

National restaurant chain has several openings for assistant managers.
• Associate's degree in hospitality services or previous experience preferred.
• Must be willing to relocate after completing training program.

DIETITIAN

Large hospital seeks *licensed* dietitian.
• Responsible for therapeutic menu, nourishment management, and consumer nutrition education.
• Bachelor's degree and experience required.

PERSONAL TRAINER

Health club seeks energetic personal trainer to plan and supervise fitness regimes for clients on an individual basis.
• Must be physically fit, health conscious, and personable.
• Two-year degree preferred.

CHEF

Large banquet facility needs experienced chef to oversee dining room and special events.
• Responsible for menu planning and staff management.
• Post-secondary technical training required.

PHYSICAL THERAPIST

Licensed physical therapist needed for growing outpatient rehabilitation center.
• Strong interpersonal skills desired for working with patients who have diverse range of ailments.
• Degree required and/or volunteer experience preferred.

More Career Options

Entry Level
• Cafeteria Worker
• Nursing Assistant
• Food Preparation Worker

Technical Level
• Food Scientist
• Food Technologist
• Recipe Tester

Professional Level
• Food Service Manager
• Health Educator
• Pharmacist
• Sports Medicine Specialist

CATERING MANAGER

Food service company seeks creative, customer-oriented catering manager.
• Associate's degree and supervisory experience required.
• Evening and weekend assignments are common.

FLAVORIST

Manufacturer of flavors and fragrances seeks creative flavorist to work on the Sweet Goods team.
• Excellent project manager who enjoys working as part of a team.
• Experience in developing flavors in confectionery and oral care.
• B.S. degree in food science or chemistry preferred.

REHABILITATION SPECIALIST

Full, part-time, flexible hours, and live-in opportunities available. Will work with developmentally disabled adults.

• Requires direct care and assisting with daily living skills in home environments.
• Must be at least 18 years old, have valid drivers license, and high school diploma.

MEDICAL ILLUSTRATOR

Medical college needs illustrator to draw human anatomy and surgical procedures for audiovisual presentations used in teaching.
• Bachelor's degree necessary.
• Exceptional artistic ability required.

Linking School to Career

1. **Your Career Plan:** Hobbies and interests can often lead to careers. How do you spend your time? What activities do you enjoy? Make a list of three hobbies or interests that you have. Can you translate these into future jobs? Name some jobs that you think are related to your hobbies and interests.

2. **Researching Careers:** Many people who work in nutrition and wellness enjoy the reward that comes from helping people look or feel better. Interview someone who works in this field to learn of other rewards. Ask, too, about the demands and challenges of the job. What are some of the hardest aspects to deal with? Share your findings with the class.

3. **Reading:** Look up the definitions of the following terms that are found in the want ads:
• Hospitality
• Signing bonus
• Therapeutic
• Audiovisual presentation
• Interpersonal skills

Unit 9

Working in the Kitchen

Kitchen Equipment

YOU WILL LEARN . . .

- ➤ Names and uses of various kinds of utensils.
- ➤ Names and uses of various types of cookware.
- ➤ Small kitchen appliances that make cooking time more productive.

TERMS TO LEARN . . .

- ➤ cookware
- ➤ immersible
- ➤ utensils

Imagine ...

... that your family is going tent camping. You've been put in charge of packing kitchen supplies. "Just bring the necessities," your dad says. "It's only for the weekend."

Think About

- In deciding what to bring, what would you need to know?
- What equipment could be used for more than one purpose?
- Which conveniences from your kitchen would you miss? Why?

UTENSILS

Your home kitchen doesn't need dozens of supplies for you to be a successful cook in almost any situation. Most kitchens are stocked with basic equipment that lets you perform an amazing number of cooking tasks.

Small kitchen tools are called **utensils.** If you've already done some cooking, you know how helpful utensils can be. Without them, it would be hard to measure, mix, or prepare food. Sturdy, well-made utensils last a long time. If you have a dishwasher or microwave oven, it's helpful to have utensils that are dishwasher-safe or can be used in the microwave.

➤ Cooking utensils are sold in sets as well as individually. Select utensils that are safe to use with your cookware. Use nylon utensils with nonstick pans.

Measuring Utensils

Measuring utensils help you accurately measure ingredients for recipes. Some popular measuring utensils are shown here.

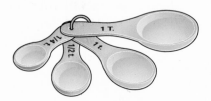

Dry measuring cups, used to measure dry ingredients such as flour and sugar, usually come in sets: ¼ cup, ⅓ cup, ½ cup, and 1 cup. Sizes found in a set of metric dry measures include: 50 mL (milliliters), 125 mL, and 250 mL.

Measuring Spoons are used for measuring smaller amounts of liquid and dry ingredients. The most common sizes are ¼ teaspoon, ½ teaspoon, 1 teaspoon, and 1 tablespoon. A set of small metric measures includes 1 mL, 2 mL, 5 mL, 15 mL, and 25 mL.

Liquid measuring cups have a spout for pouring and measurements marked on the side in cups, ounces, and milliliters. Common sizes are 4 cups, 2 cups, and 1 cup (1000 mL, 500 mL, and 250 mL in metric).

Mixing Utensils

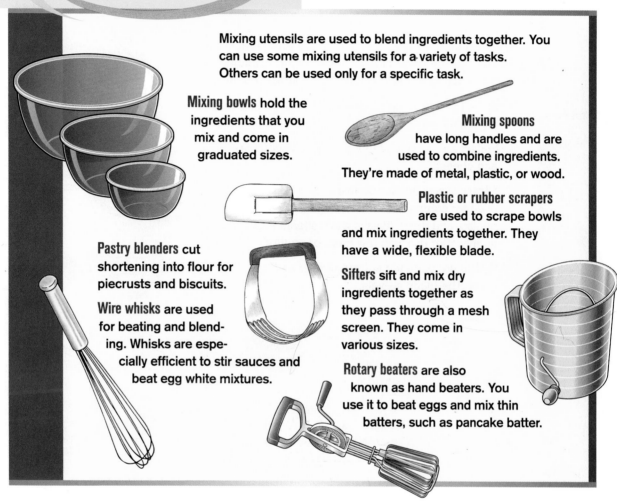

Mixing utensils are used to blend ingredients together. You can use some mixing utensils for a variety of tasks. Others can be used only for a specific task.

Mixing bowls hold the ingredients that you mix and come in graduated sizes.

Mixing spoons have long handles and are used to combine ingredients. They're made of metal, plastic, or wood.

Plastic or rubber scrapers are used to scrape bowls and mix ingredients together. They have a wide, flexible blade.

Pastry blenders cut shortening into flour for piecrusts and biscuits.

Wire whisks are used for beating and blending. Whisks are especially efficient to stir sauces and beat egg white mixtures.

Sifters sift and mix dry ingredients together as they pass through a mesh screen. They come in various sizes.

Rotary beaters are also known as hand beaters. You use it to beat eggs and mix thin batters, such as pancake batter.

Cutting and Chopping Utensils

Cutting and chopping tools are used to cut food into smaller pieces. Keep safety in mind when you use cutting tools.

- *Paring knives* are good for peeling fruits and vegetables.
- *Utility knives* are all-purpose knives for cutting and slicing foods.
- *Chef's knives* are used for cutting, mincing, and dicing.
- *Bread knives* come in handy for slicing bread or baked goods.

Paring Knife

Utility Knife

Chef's Knife

Bread Knife

Other Kitchen Utensils

A variety of other tools can help make your work in the kitchen easier. Several examples are shown here. In addition to these, what other utensils does your family find helpful?

- **Cutting boards** serve as a base for your cutting work, keeping knife blades sharp and counters in good shape.

- **Graters** are used to shred and grate vegetables and cheeses.

- **Kitchen shears** are sturdy scissors used for cutting vegetables, pastry, poultry, and meat. Always wash shears thoroughly after use with raw meat or poultry.

- **Peelers** are used to peel vegetables and fruits. The blade swivels.

Cutting Board

Kitchen shears

Grater

Peeler

Colander

Strainer

Slotted spoon

Spatula

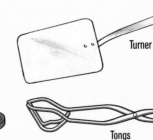

Turner

Tongs

- **Colanders** are bowls with holes for draining foods, such as cooked pasta.

- **Strainers** are wire mesh baskets with handles, used to strain liquids from solid foods, such as water from steamed vegetables.

- **Slotted spoons** are helpful for lifting solid food from liquid, like pasta from water.

- **Spatulas** have dull, narrow metal blades. They're useful in leveling dry ingredients, such as flour, in measuring cups.

- **Turners**, or wide spatulas, are used to lift and turn foods, such as pancakes or hamburgers.

- **Tongs** grasp or hold foods, such as a chicken drumstick or a corncob.

  - **Ladles** are helpful when serving hot soup and stews.

  - **Cooling racks** are made of wire and allow air to circulate around hot baked products.

Ladle

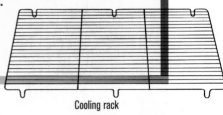

Cooling rack

Cookware

Cookware includes pots, pans, and other containers for use on top of the range, in the conventional oven, or in the microwave oven. Cookware items are made of metal, glass, or plastic.

- **Saucepans and stockpots** are deeper than skillets. They come in a variety of sizes, usually measured in quarts or liters. Some have covers. Saucepans have one handle, while stockpots have two, one on each side.

- **Cake pans** are round, square, or rectangular. They can be used for baking many foods in addition to cakes.

- **Loaf pans** come in different sizes and are used for breads and meat loaves.

- **Casseroles**, or baking dishes, come in a variety of shapes and sizes. They're deep enough to hold a main-dish mixture and often have covers.

- **Skillets** are shallow and have long handles. They come in assorted sizes and sometimes have covers.

- **Baking sheets** are rectangular, low-sided pans. They're most often used for baking cookies.

- **Pie pans** are round with sloping sides and come in different sizes.

- **Muffin pans** have from six to twelve individual cups to hold muffins and cupcakes.

- **Custard cups** are made from heatproof glass. You might use them to bake custard or microwave eggs.

Stock pot

9" x 13" Cake pan

Loaf pan

Saucepan

Round cake pan

Casserole

Skillet

Baking sheet

Custard cups

Pie pan

Muffin pan

Small Kitchen Appliances

Small kitchen appliances are pieces of equipment that are generally powered by electricity. They can be set on a table or counter and can be moved easily from place to place.

- **Toaster.** Holds slices of bread for toasting. Some can adjust for thicker breads.

- **Blender.** Has push-button speed controls for a variety of mixing and chopping tasks, such as blending fruit drinks.

- **Hand-held mixer.** Can be used for whipping cream, mixing cake batter, or even whipping potatoes. It's lightweight, easy to manage, and convenient to store.

- **Food processor.** Different blades and disks can be used to perform a number of cutting and mixing tasks.

- **Electric skillet.** Electric skillets have a thermostatic control on the handle to regulate cooking temperatures. Use it to fry, roast, simmer, or bake.

SMALL APPLIANCES

Using small appliances can help make your cooking time more productive. There are hundreds of small appliances available today. Before buying one, ask yourself how often you'll use it. Is it worth the cost? Do you have enough space to store and use it?

Comparison shop to get information about various appliance brands you're considering. Find out about safety features and the kind of warranty each brand offers. Look for the Underwriters Laboratories (UL) seal on the appliance. This seal tells you an electrical appliance is safe to use.

Some appliances are **immersible,** which means that *the entire appliance can be safely put into water to be washed.* On these appliances, the electrical unit has been sealed so no water can enter. Immersible appliances will have the term "immersible" on them. If you don't see the term, don't put the appliance in water. See page 456 for some common small appliances.

LARGE KITCHEN APPLIANCES

Most kitchens are equipped with basic large appliances, such as a range (gas or electric) and a combination refrigerator-freezer. Additional large kitchen appliances include microwave ovens, dishwashers, freezers (upright or chest type), trash compactors, and garbage disposals.

Appliances such as these are major purchases. The costs will vary depending on the style, size, and features you choose, and whether you buy new or used appliances. When shopping for large kitchen appliances, compare the EnergyGuide labels and look for safety and performance seals.

Be sure to read and keep the owner's manual for all appliances. Each manual contains a lot of valuable information about using and caring for your appliances.

To operate electrical appliances safely:

- Read all instructions before using appliances.
- Complete and mail warranty cards to receive safety notifications or recall notices.
- Use an appliance only for its intended use.
- Dry your hands before using any appliance.
- Avoid touching any moving parts of an appliance.
- Don't allow power cords to hang over the edge of a counter.
- Keep power cords away from heat.
- Unplug power cords from outlets when not in use and before cleaning or attaching any parts.

INFOLINK

See Chapter 37 for more information about microwave ovens.

Review & Activities

Chapter Summary

- Kitchen utensils are helpful when you mix, measure, and prepare food.
- Use standard measuring cups and spoons to measure recipe ingredients accurately.
- Mixing utensils are useful for blending ingredients together.
- Cutting and chopping utensils are important for cutting food into smaller pieces.
- Different types of cookware containers are used to cook food on top of the range and in the oven or microwave.
- Small kitchen appliances are convenient to use and often use energy more efficiently.

Family & Community

With Your Family

With your family members, inventory the kitchen utensils, equipment, and small appliances that you have. Discuss which items are used most often. Based on your discussion, what equipment do you think seems most important?

In Your Community

Community service organizations often operate resale shops where household items and clothing are sold. Profits fund the organizations' assistance programs. Help to organize a drive to collect kitchen utensils and small appliances for a local organization.

Reviewing the Chapter

1. Identify the standard dry measuring cups and measuring spoons that come in a set. Give an example of foods you'd measure with each.
2. What are four different mixing utensils commonly found in kitchens? How are they used?
3. List three different types of knives used for food preparation. Explain when each is most useful.
4. Explain the differences between the following utensils: colander, strainer, slotted spoon, and ladle.
5. What are the differences in the design of skillets, saucepans, and stockpots? Give an example of a food you could cook in each.
6. What are three important questions to ask before buying a small kitchen appliance?

Thinking Critically

1. **Analyze decisions.** If you could buy twelve kitchen utensils to equip your first kitchen, what twelve would you select? Explain your choices.
2. **Predict consequences.** Think about what might happen if someone attempted to work in a kitchen without knowing the names and uses of the different pieces of kitchen equipment. How could being familiar with equipment be helpful?
3. **Justify choices.** Select one small kitchen appliance that you consider the most useful and can be used in a variety of different ways. Defend your choice.

Making Connections

1. **Science.** To experiment with measuring, measure one cup of flour into a two-cup liquid measuring cup. When you think you have the right amount, carefully pour the flour from the liquid measuring cup into a one-cup dry measuring cup. How do the measurements compare? What does this tell you about using the right piece of equipment for each task?
2. **Language Arts.** Write a paragraph explaining why it's helpful for experienced and inexperienced cooks to understand different pieces of kitchen equipment and how to use them.

Applying Your Learning

1. **Do a demonstration.** Select one kitchen utensil and think of how many ways it could be used in the kitchen. Demonstrate some of the uses to the class and ask them for additional ideas.
2. **Design a kitchen utensil.** Design a new type of kitchen utensil that you think would be useful. As an alternative, design an improved version of an already existing kitchen utensil. Use words, pictures, or both to describe your invention, its use, and how it works.
3. **Survey consumer publications.** Locate surveys or studies in consumer magazines that compare the safety, features, and performance of a small kitchen appliance. Based on your reading decide which model you'd select. Explain your decision.

What Would You Do?

Assume your older brother is moving into his first apartment away from home. He doesn't have very much cooking experience, and he owns no kitchen equipment. He's on a tight budget. What basic utensils would you suggest he buy?

Safety and Sanitation

YOU WILL LEARN . . .

➤ How to prevent injuries from occurring in the kitchen.
➤ What you can do to control foodborne illness.

TERMS TO LEARN . . .

➤ bacteria
➤ cross-contamination
➤ foodborne illness
➤ sanitize

Imagine ...

... that you once became very ill after eating a friend's party food. It had tasted fine but had been sitting out at room temperature for a long time. Now you're planning a backyard get-together after your sister's graduation. You want the food to taste delicious, but you're also concerned about food safety.

Think About

- Do you think it would it be safer to buy prepared foods rather than make them yourself?
- Should you serve food inside rather than outside?
- Is it okay to have nacho chips and cheese on a picnic table throughout the party? Burgers? Cake?

SANITATION IN THE KITCHEN

The American food supply is one of the safest anywhere in the world. Food safety is the responsibility of food producers and the government. However, once you buy food and take it home, food safety becomes your responsibility.

Health experts estimate that every second of every day in the year, someone in the United States becomes stricken with **foodborne illness.** Also known as food poisoning, it's *an illness caused by eating spoiled food or food containing harmful bacteria.* **Bacteria** are *one-celled living organisms so small they can be seen only with a microscope.*

Under certain conditions (heat, moisture, and right temperature), bacteria double in number every 20 to 30 minutes. With just a little carelessness, you can create ideal growing conditions for bacteria in your own kitchen. For example, if utensils and hands are not washed properly, **cross-contamination**—*when harmful bacteria are transferred from one food to another*—can occur.

However, the flip side is that simple precautions prevent foodborne illness. Experts say that 85 percent of all foodborne sickness is avoidable if you take proper precautionary steps. Taking time to **sanitize**—or *clean to getting rid of bacteria*—is the first step in preventing foodborne illness. See pages 464-465 for more information on steps you can take to prevent foodborne illness.

➤ **Washing knives promptly after use and returning them to their proper storage makes the kitchen a safer place.**

WORKING SAFELY IN THE KITCHEN

Along with food safety, cooking safety is also important. More accidents take place in the kitchen than in any other room in the home. Prevent accidents by thinking ahead and working safely in the kitchen. Following are some guidelines to help you make the kitchen a safe place to work. What other safety rules can you add to the list?

TRY IT OUT

How Fast Do Bacteria Grow?

What You'll Need
- 4 petri dishes with growing medium

What to Do
1. Contaminate the growing medium in three petri dishes with the following samples from your body: scrapings from under fingernails, a hair, and scrapings from your face. Label each petri dish with the contaminate each contains.
2. As a control, wash your hands thoroughly using soap and warm water. Then rub your fingers across the growing medium in the fourth petri dish. Label this petri dish as the control.
3. Allow the bacteria to grow at room temperature for 24 hours. Check your results.

To Discuss
- On which samples did the bacteria grow?
- Did any bacteria grow on the control dish?
- Draw several conclusions about the importance of cleanliness in the kitchen.

Preventing Cuts and Bruises

It's very easy to cut yourself in the kitchen because of the sharp utensils you use. To prevent cuts and bruises:
- Wash knives and other sharp objects separately. Never put a sharp knife in a sink of sudsy water to soak.
- Store sharp knives separately from other utensils.
- Keep knives sharp to avoid slipping while cutting.
- Use a cutting board. Keep fingertips away from the knife.
- Unplug a garbage disposal before retrieving an object from it.
- Close cabinet doors and drawers when not in use. Otherwise, someone can walk into them and be injured.
- Use a ladder or step stool for reaching hard-to-get items.
- Wipe up spills from the floor right away.

Sanitation in the Kitchen

To avoid foodborne illness, use the following tips:

Always wash your hands with warm soapy water before you handle food. Also wash your hands after handling raw meat, poultry, and fish, and after using the bathroom.

Wear clean clothes when you work with food.

Use separate towels for drying hands and dishes. It's also a good idea to use a clean sponge for cleaning and a fresh towel for drying dishes every day.

Wash cutting boards after cutting raw meat, poultry, or seafood. Sanitize cutting boards with a solution of two teaspoons of chlorine bleach and one quart of water for at least 30 seconds.

Thoroughly wash all utensils you use to prepare food to avoid cross-contamination.

Use a clean spoon every time you taste food during cooking.

Keep all kitchen surfaces clean.

Wash raw fruits and vegetables thoroughly under cold running water. It's a good idea to wash prepackaged salad mixes, even if the label says they're prewashed.

Thaw frozen foods in the refrigerator or in a microwave oven.

Cook hamburgers, poultry, fish, and eggs thoroughly to kill any harmful bacteria.

Keep hot food hot and cold food cold. Serve cooked and cold foods immediately.

Refrigerate or freeze leftovers within two hours of serving.

Making a
DIFFERENCE

FIREFIGHTER

"Watch out!" Brian called to his younger brother Ronny. Ronny had been frying a hamburger patty on the kitchen stove. Now the grease flamed.

"Oh no!" Ronny cried. "What do I do?"

Brian raced over to a kitchen cabinet and pulled out some baking soda. Quickly he poured it over the flaming pan, then used the pan cover to smother the flames.

Wide-eyed, Ronny stared at his older brother. "Where'd you learn that trick?"

"In class," Brian said. "Hope you like baking soda-burgers!"

Taking Action

1. Have you ever had a kitchen accident at home? What did you do?
2. What does Ronny need to learn about kitchen cooking safety?

Preventing Burns

> Some ranges exhaust oven heat at the base of the range top. Use caution. Items left on the range may become very hot when the oven is in use.

You can't be too careful when working around gas and electric appliances. Here are some ways to prevent burns:

- Be careful not to touch the heating units on a range.
- Use flat-bottomed cookware and well-balanced cooking utensils on the range so they won't tip over easily.
- Turn handles of cooking utensils inward on the range so they won't be knocked off. Be sure handles don't extend over another heating unit that's hot.
- Use thick, dry potholders when handling hot cookware.
- Remove a pan cover by lifting the far side of the cover first. In that way, the steam flows away from you.
- Dry food thoroughly before placing it into a pan full of hot oil. Water causes oil or fat to spatter.
- Use kitchen tongs to remove food from hot water and to turn frying food.

Preventing Fires

Fires can start very easily at a kitchen range. If a grease fire starts, don't throw water on flames—they'll spread. Instead, smother the fire with the pan cover or with salt or baking soda. Keep a fire extinguisher in the kitchen and learn how to use it. To prevent a kitchen fires:

- Avoid wearing dangling jewelry or loose-fitting clothes. They can get caught in appliances or catch fire.
- Keep towels and electrical cords away from the range.
- Don't use an oven as a heat source to warm the kitchen.
- Avoid using a dishtowel to handle hot cookware. Towels can catch fire. Damp towels can cause steam burns.
- To avoid overloading circuits, never plug more than two appliances into an electrical outlet at one time.

➤ **Keep appliances unplugged when not in use. A toaster left plugged in can be a fire hazard.**

Preventing Electrical Shock

Electrical equipment should be in good working order and used properly. Water and metal are powerful conductors of electricity. To prevent electrical shock:

- Use dry hands when touching electrical equipment.
- Never plug in an appliance while standing on a wet surface.
- Don't put an electrical appliance in water unless it's marked "immersible."
- Always unplug a cord from the wall outlet before removing it from the appliance.
- Disconnect an appliance by pulling on the plug. If you pull on the cord, it can become damaged.
- Keep forks and knives out of electric toasters. If bread gets stuck, disconnect the toaster and try to shake the bread loose.

Preventing Poisoning

Many household chemicals contain dangerous substances that can be poisonous if swallowed, inhaled, or splashed on the skin. Keep the number of the nearest poison control center by the phone and call it in an emergency. See the safety feature on this page for ways to prevent poisoning.

SAFETY *First*

To prevent poisoning in the kitchen:

- Keep drain cleaners, household cleaners, and other poisons in their original containers. Read all label warnings and directions. Follow them exactly.
- Store household chemicals out of the reach of children and away from food.
- Don't mix household chemicals together. Some mixtures cause toxic chemical reactions.

Chapter Summary

- Every family member is responsible for kitchen safety and sanitation.
- Foodborne illnesses can be avoided by following proper sanitation procedures.
- Thinking ahead and working safely in the kitchen can prevent accidents.
- Handle knives and other sharp objects carefully to avoid being cut with sharp edges.
- Prevent burns by avoiding hot surfaces, using potholders, and following other safety precautions.
- Prevent electrical shock by drying your hands before using appliances, and by following other safety precautions.
- Handle and store household cleaning materials carefully to prevent poisoning.

Reviewing the Chapter

1. What causes foodborne illness?
2. Why should you wash your hands thoroughly when working with food?
3. How can you prevent cross-contamination when handling food products?
4. List four precautions to follow when handling knives.
5. What are three guidelines to observe when using cookware on the range?
6. Describe what you should do if there is a grease fire at the range.
7. Why should you dry your hands before touching an electrical appliance?
8. Explain why household cleaning products are dangerous.

Family & Community

With Your Family

Work with other family members to survey your home kitchen for potential safety hazards. Decide how you can correct the problems you find. Work with others to eliminate the safety problems.

In Your Community

Develop a kitchen safety program to present to younger children in elementary school, scouting groups, or other after-school programs. Plan how to hold their attention and to emphasize your message.

Review & Activities

Thinking Critically

1. **Cause and effect.** Think of a time when you or someone you know had a serious kitchen accident. What contributed to the accident? What effect did the accident have? How could the accident have been prevented?

2. **Analyze meaning.** What is meant by the expression, "It's an accident waiting to happen?" Give examples to illustrate your answer.

3. **Compare and contrast.** Compare a kitchen where foodborne illness is likely to occur with one where it is less likely to occur. How are these kitchens different?

Making Connections

1. **Science.** Obtain additional information about foodborne illnesses. How do they develop? What precautions should be followed to minimize risks?

2. **Social Studies.** Identify federal, state, and county organizations responsible for food safety. Contact one of these departments about what role they play in community food safety.

Applying Your Learning

1. **Conduct interviews.** Contact restaurant owners or food service managers of commercial kitchens to find out precautions that they follow to ensure food safety. How can the public be assured that the food they eat when they are out is safe?

2. **Write slogans.** Hold a kitchen safety slogan writing contest. Publicize the winning slogans.

3. **Obtain information.** Call the poison control center listed in your phone directory. Obtain more information about how to prevent poisoning from occurring and how to handle poisoning emergencies.

What Would You Do?

Assume you're eating out in a fast-food restaurant. While you wait in line to place your order, you notice some workers using poor sanitation practices. Is it your responsibility to do something about this? If so, what action would you take?

Recipes and Measuring

YOU WILL LEARN . . .

➤ How to select and interpret a recipe.
➤ How to measure ingredients in a recipe.
➤ What recipe terms mean.
➤ Ways to alter a recipe and substitute ingredients.

TERMS TO LEARN . . .

➤ abbreviation
➤ equivalents
➤ recipe
➤ yield

Imagine ...

... that you have a weakness for white chocolate and for macadamia nuts. Whenever you buy a bakery cookie, that's what you choose. You're excited to see a recipe for chocolate macadamia cookies in a local weekly newspaper. As you assemble the ingredients, something strikes you as odd. The recipe calls for ½ cup baking soda. That seems like a lot...

Think About

• Would you trust the recipe? Why or why not?
• Would you have more faith in a cookbook recipe?
• How much baking soda would you expect to use in a batch of cookies?

CHOOSING A RECIPE

A **recipe** is *a set of directions used in cooking.* Recipes list the amounts of ingredients needed and tell you what to do with those ingredients. Look at the sample recipe below.

You can find recipes in cookbooks, magazines, newspapers, on computer software, and on the Internet. Try comparing recipes by asking yourself these questions:

- Does this recipe sound good? Consider the likes and dislikes of others.
- How long will the recipe take to prepare? Do I have enough time?
- Do I understand all the steps? Do I have the needed skills?
- Do I have all the necessary equipment? Will I be able to find all the ingredients?

If you haven't had very much cooking experience, look for recipes with fewer ingredients and steps. They're usually easier to prepare.

➤ Recipes provide you with information you need to prepare foods. You may get best results from a favorite cookbook, or recipes from your family and friends. Does your family share a special recipe?

DILLED GREEN BEANS WITH ALMONDS

Amount	Ingredients
2 cups	Green beans, frozen
1½ tsp.	Butter or margarine
1 tsp.	Dill weed
¼ cup	Slivered almonds

Directions
1. Simmer green beans according to package directions until tender-crisp.
2. Drain liquid from green beans.
3. Stir in butter or margarine and dill weed until well blended.
4. Mix in slivered almonds. Serve hot.

MEASURING INGREDIENTS

Are you experienced in measuring ingredients? Much of your success in preparing food depends on the way you measure and combine ingredients. If you know abbreviations, equivalents, and measuring techniques, you'll be off to a good start.

Abbreviations and Equivalents

The chart on page 474 shows abbreviations and units of measure commonly used in recipes. An **abbreviation** is *a short form of a word.* Recipes often use abbreviations of terms to save space.

Some recipes are written using customary measurements, such as cups and tablespoons. Others use metric measurements, such as milliliters. Generally, it's best to use the correct measuring equipment, customary or metric, for the recipe you're following.

You'll also find it helpful to know some basic equivalents. **Equivalents** are *amounts that are equal to each other,* such as twelve inches and one foot. Equivalents come in handy when you double or halve a recipe or when you don't have the right measuring equipment. Look at the equivalents chart to become familiar with basic equivalents.

Measuring Dry Ingredients

Dry ingredients include sugar, flour, salt, and baking powder. To measure ¼ cup (50 mL) or more, use a dry measuring cup. Hold the cup over waxed paper, a paper towel, or the ingredient's container. Spoon the ingredient into the cup and heap it a little over the top. Then level off the ingredient with the straight edge of a spatula. For smaller amounts, use a measuring spoon in the same way. Some dry ingredients call for special techniques:

- Flour has tiny granules that pack together. If the recipe calls for sifted flour, sift it first, then measure in the usual way. Don't tap the cup. Tapping packs down the flour and gives you too much.

➤ Sifting flour before mixing helps to remove any lumps it may have. Measure the sifted flour before adding it to the other ingredients.

UNITS OF MEASURE

Type of Measurement	Customary Units and Abbreviations	Metric Units and Symbols
Volume	teaspoon (tsp.) tablespoon (Tbsp.) fluid ounce (fl. oz.) cup (c.) pint (pt.) quart (qt.) gallon (gal.)	milliliter (mL) liter (L)
Weight	ounce (oz.) pound (lb.)	gram (g) kilogram (kg)
Temperature	degrees Fahrenheit (°F)	degrees Celsius (°C)

EQUIVALENTS

Dash	Less than ⅛ tsp.	Less than 0.5 mL
¼ tsp.		1 mL
½ tsp.		2 or 3 mL
1 tsp.		5 mL
1 Tbsp.	3 tsp.	15 mL
1 fluid oz.	2 Tbsp.	30 mL
¼ cup	4 Tbsp. or 2 fluid oz.	50 mL
⅓ cup	5 Tbsp. + 1 tsp.	75 mL
½ cup	8 Tbsp. or 4 fluid oz.	125 mL
⅔ cup	10 Tbsp + 2 tsp or 6 fluid oz.	175 mL
1 cup	16 Tbsp. or 8 fluid oz.	250 mL
1 pt.	2 cups or 16 fluid oz.	500 mL
1 qt.	2 pt. or 4 cups or 32 fluid oz.	1 L (1000 mL)
1 gal.	4 quarts or 16 cups or 128 fluid oz.	4 L
1 lb.	16 oz. (weight)	500 g
2 lb.	32 oz. (weight)	1 kg (1000 g)

- Pack brown sugar firmly into a measuring cup and level it off. It should keep the shape of the cup when turned out of the cup. (Other types of sugar aren't packed.)

Measuring Liquid Ingredients

Liquid ingredients, such as milk, water, or oil, are measured in clear, liquid measuring cups. For accurate measurements, place the cup on a flat surface and read the measurement at eye level.

You can measure small amounts of liquids in measuring spoons. Just fill the spoon to the brim.

Measuring Fats

Sticks of margarine or butter have measurements marked on the wrapper. One stick equals ½ cup (125 mL). If you need just part of a stick, cut through the wrapper on the appropriate marking.

You can measure solid fats, such as shortening, in a dry measuring cup. First, pack the fat into the cup and level it off. Use a plastic (flexible) scraper to remove the fat from the cup.

UNDERSTANDING RECIPE TERMS

Some words have a special meaning when used in food preparation. When reading a recipe, pay attention to the exact term used. It's your clue to the tool you need and the technique to follow.

➤ Fats are easier to work with if they are at room temperature.

Mixing Terms

A number of recipe techniques are used to describe different ways of combining ingredients. Here are some of the most common ones.

- **Stir.** Use a spoon to make circular or figure eight motions, as in stirring soup when it warms.

- **Blend, mix, combine.** Use a spoon to stir two or more ingredients together thoroughly.

- **Beat.** Use this technique to smooth a mixture, as in mixing a cake batter. Use a quick, over-and-under motion with a spoon or wire whisk, or a rotary beater or electric mixer.

- **Whip.** Use this technique to beat ingredients very rapidly to bring in air and increase volume, as in whipping cream. Use a wire whisk, rotary beater, or electric mixer.

- **Cream.** Use a spoon, beater, or mixer to combine ingredients until soft and creamy, as in combining fat and sugar together for a cake.

- **Cut in.** Use a pastry blender or two knives and a cutting motion to mix solid fat with dry ingredients, as in cutting fat into flour for a piecrust.

- **Fold.** Use a rubber scraper to gently combine ingredients in a delicate mixture, such as folding beaten egg whites into a mixture.

Cutting Terms

Do you know the difference between mincing and chopping or between cubing and dicing? Some of these techniques may seem minor at first glance, but they can make a big difference in the appearance or texture of a dish.

- **Chop.** Cut food into small, irregular pieces, as in chopping green peppers.

- **Mince.** Chop food into pieces that are as small as possible, as in mincing an onion.

- **Cube.** Cut into evenly shaped pieces about ½ inch (13 mm) on each side, as in cubing bread.

- **Dice.** Cut into evenly shaped pieces about ¼ inch (6 mm) on each side, as in dicing ingredients for a salad.

SAFETY First

To safely use knives:
- Use sharp knives. They're less likely to slip and cause an accident.
- Always use a cutting board. Never hold the food in your hand while cutting or cut toward yourself.
- When using one hand to hold the food steady, tuck your fingers under. That way your knuckles, not your fingertips, are closest to the knife.

- **Pare.** Cut off the outside covering of a fruit or vegetable, as in paring a carrot.

- **Grate.** Rub food over a grater (the side with small holes) to get fine particles, as in grating cheese.

- **Shred.** Cut or tear food into long, thin pieces. Depending on the food, you might use a knife, two forks, a grater, or a food processor.

Other Cooking Terms

You'll probably read some of the following terms as you look through recipes:

- **Baste.** Moisten foods, such as meat, while cooking. Basting adds flavor and helps keep food from drying out.

- **Brush.** Use a brush to lightly cover the surface of one food with another, as in brushing barbecue sauce on meat.

- **Coat.** Cover the surface of a food with a dry ingredient, such as flour, cornmeal, dry bread crumbs, or sugar.

- **Garnish.** Decorate a food dish with a small food item, such as a sprig of parsley, a carrot curl, or an edible flower.

- **Grease.** Rub lightly with fat, such as butter, margarine, oil, or shortening, as in greasing a baking sheet.

- **Season.** Add seasonings, such as salt, pepper, herbs, or spices to add to the flavor of a food.

- **Drain.** Remove excess liquid by placing food in a colander or strainer, as in draining pasta.

ALTERING RECIPES

You don't have to follow every recipe exactly as it's written. You may want to change the number of servings, as many people do. You may need to substitute another ingredient for one that you don't have. The following guidelines may help you alter, or change, recipes successfully.

Changing the Yield of a Recipe

The amount of food or number of servings a recipe makes is called the **yield.** If you want more or fewer servings, you need to alter the recipe. To do this, put your math skills and knowledge of equivalent measurements to work. See below for more information on changing the yield of a recipe.

Making Substitutions

It's no fun to be in the middle of preparing a recipe and suddenly discover that you're missing an ingredient. Before you begin, read through the ingredients list and make sure you have all the items on hand.

➤ Making substitutions, such as applesauce in place of oil in cakes or brownies, can reduce the fat content.

HOW to...

Change the Yield of a Recipe

Suppose you're going to prepare a favorite casserole recipe. You want to make four servings, but the recipe yields eight. Follow these simple steps to cut your recipe in half.

- **Divide the number of servings you want by the original yield.** The answer is the number you'll use to calculate the new amount for each ingredient. In this example, $4 \div 8 = \frac{1}{2}$.

- **Multiply the amount of each ingredient by ½.** If the recipe calls for 2 pounds of ground beef, you'd use 1 pound ($2 \times \frac{1}{2} = 1$).

- **Convert measurements as needed.** As you multiply, you may need to convert from one unit of measurement to another. If a recipe calls for ¼ cup grated cheese, the new amount would be ⅛ cup ($\frac{1}{4} \times \frac{1}{2} = \frac{1}{8}$). If you don't have a ⅛ cup utensil, use the chart on page 476 to help you figure out an equivalent measure.

- **Calculate the new amount for each ingredient in the recipe.** Write the new amounts down so you don't forget to change an amount.

To double a recipe, simply multiply the amount of each ingredient by 2. Doubling a recipe requires a pan that's twice as large or two pans of the original size.

The baking or cooking time may also have to be adjusted. If you double the recipe and pan size, you'll likely need to bake the mixture a little longer.

USING HERBS AND SPICES

Herbs grow in temperate climates and are the fragrant leaves of plants. Spices grow in tropical climates and come from the bark, buds, fruit, roots, seeds, or stems of plants and trees. When cooking with herbs and spices, keep this in mind:

- Avoid too many herbs and spices in one dish. A few herbs and spices accent the flavor and taste of food.

- Substitute dried for fresh herbs in a recipe by using the following equivalents: 1 tsp. dried herb = 1 Tbsp. fresh herb.

- Crumble dried herbs between your fingers before adding to other ingredients to release more flavor and aroma.

- If a recipe calls for a long cooking time (soups and stews) add herbs and spices toward the end of cooking.

- Add spices and herbs to liquid ingredients. The moisture brings out the flavor.

- Chop fresh herbs very fine. Cut surfaces release more flavor.

If you don't have an ingredient, you may be able to make a substitution. Experience shows that some ingredients can be used in place of others with good results. Some of these substitutions are listed in the chart on page 481. You may find others listed in cookbooks.

Making Creative and Healthy Changes

A recipe is your guide to success. At first, it's a good idea to do exactly what the recipe tells you to do. After you've used the recipe several times, you may want to try some variations.

Seasonings can often be changed. For example, chili is a spicy food. If you and your family believe "the hotter, the better," then add extra chili powder for the desired taste!

You may decide that you want to cut back on the fat you eat and work toward a more healthful diet. You could use lean ground beef or ground turkey in place of regular ground beef in a casserole. If a pasta sauce recipe calls for ¼ cup of oil, you might try using half the amount without changing the taste too much. Lowfat yogurt can take the place of sour cream in dips. What other things could you do to decrease the amount of fat in the foods you eat?

Remember that chefs and test-kitchen food experts change recipes all the time. You can modify recipes in your own "test kitchen." If you use your understanding of measuring ingredients, common sense, and a dash of creativity, you'll quite likely be pleased with the results.

➤ Altering recipes can be fun. However, baked goods are not as flexible as other recipes. A slight change can severely damage your final product.

SUBSTITUTIONS THAT WORK

Ingredient	Substitution
2 Tbsp. (30mL) flour (for thickening)	1 Tbsp. (15 mL) cornstarch
1 cup (250 mL) sifted cake flour	1 cup – 2 Tbsp. (220 mL) sifted all-purpose flour
1 cup (250 mL) whole milk	½ cup (125 mL) evaporated milk + ½ cup (125 mL) water
1 cup (250 mL) sour milk or buttermilk	1 cup (250mL) fresh milk + 1 Tbsp. (15mL) vinegar or lemon juice
1 square (1 oz. or 28 g) unsweetened chocolate	3 Tbsp. (45 mL) unsweetened cocoa powder + 1 Tbsp. (15 mL) butter or margarine
1 cup (250 mL) granulated sugar	1 cup (250 mL) packed brown sugar or 2 cups (250 mL) sifted powdered, or confectioners, sugar

➤ **Creative chefs use garnishing methods to prepare beautiful food displays.** What cutting methods have you used?

Chapter Summary

- Familiarize yourself with recipes before you begin preparing them.
- Learning recipe abbreviations and equivalents will contribute to successful food preparation.
- Accurate measurements are important in food preparation.
- Understanding recipe terms helps you to combine and handle recipe ingredients.
- Many recipes can be successfully altered to change the number of servings or make ingredient substitutions.
- You can use your creativity in making many recipe changes to add variety and to prepare healthier meals.

Family & Community

With Your Family

Select some recipes that are family favorites. Look over the recipes with other family members and think of ways the recipes could be altered to make them even more healthy to eat. Try out and evaluate some of your selections.

In Your Community

Fresh herbs are popular culinary ingredients and are used in home kitchens and restaurants. Grow some herbs in individual containers. Market the herb plants and donate the proceeds to a community organization of your choice.

Reviewing the Chapter

1. What are three questions you would ask before deciding to prepare a new recipe?
2. Why is it important to know how to measure ingredients for a recipe?
3. Explain what cooking abbreviations and equivalents are.
4. Describe how to measure a cup of flour.
5. What is the most accurate way to read the correct amount of liquid in a liquid measuring cup?
6. Tell how you would measure solid fat in a dry measuring cup.
7. Define the following recipe terms: cream, mince, fold, cube, pare, baste, coat, and season.
8. If you divided a recipe in half, what would the new measurements be for each of the following: 1½ lb. ground beef, ½ tsp. salt, 12 oz. canned tomatoes, ¾ cup diced green pepper, 1 cup minced onions?

Thinking Critically

1. **Predict consequences.** Suppose you approximated measurements for the recipes that you prepared. Which type of recipes would be the most and least successful? Explain your expected results.

2. **Analyze recipes.** What makes some recipes more interesting or inviting to prepare than other recipes? How could nutritional recipes be made more appealing?

3. **Draw conclusions.** What successes have you had in altering or changing a recipe? What changes have been less successful? What have you learned from these experiences?

Making Connections

1. **Math.** Find a recipe with at least eight ingredients. Alter the recipe in two different ways. Divide it in half and double it.

2. **Social Studies.** Herbs and spices are important recipe ingredients. Retrace the history of spice trading over the past 2,000 years. Where are the sources of most of our spices and herbs today?

Applying Your Learning

1. **Evaluate recipes.** Select five nutritious and appealing recipes that you think would be good choices for less experienced cooks to prepare. What criteria did you use to select these recipes?

2. **Demonstrate measurements.** Show how to measure different ingredients to your class. Ask your classmates to identify any mistakes you make and tell how the measurements should be done correctly.

3. **Improve directions.** Find examples of confusing or poorly written recipe directions. Explain how you would rewrite them to make them clearer and easier to follow.

What Would You Do?

You have always been interested in food and are thinking of entering a recipe contest. Contest guidelines state that you can use no more than five ingredients (excluding seasonings). The dish must be prepared within 30 to 45 minutes, and it must be nutritious. What recipe would you propose?

Quick Meals and Snacks

YOU WILL LEARN . . .

- ➤ Ways that the elements of meal appeal impact meal planning.
- ➤ How meal patterns and resources impact meal planning.
- ➤ Ideas for planning quick meals and snacks.
- ➤ How to work efficiently and safely in the kitchen.

TERMS TO LEARN . . .

- ➤ convenience foods
- ➤ dovetail
- ➤ graze
- ➤ meal pattern

Imagine ...

... that you've just come home from school, and you're starving. Fortunately, your mom stocked up on groceries yesterday. You can pop popcorn, munch an apple, have a cup of yogurt or even a piece of pizza. There's also a pan of brownies your sister just made for the cheerleaders' bake sale. Would they miss just one?

Think About

- Which snack would you choose? Why?
- What might happen if you helped yourself to a brownie?
- Does it bother you to eat certain foods at an unusual time, like cereal at 8 p.m.?

IT'S TIME TO EAT!

Think of the foods you like to eat. Do you like them because they taste good? Surveys have shown that the main reason people choose one food over another is—you guessed it—taste!

Today's family life is often hectic. Classes at school, sport practice, job responsibilities, volunteer work, and even travel cut into family mealtime. Dinner at your house may mean buying take-out foods at the supermarket and eating at home. You might order a pizza and make a salad to solve a mealtime problem. Or you or someone else in the family may cook a full meal on the spur of the moment. Somehow your family finds inventive ways to make meals work, even when everyone's schedule seems impossible.

Did you know the number of meals people eat away from home increases every year? According to one survey, the average American eats out at least four times a week. Since you usually have lunch at school, the number of meals you eat away from home is probably even higher.

Even though families usually have some type of menus planned, you have the responsibility to select foods that you like and that are healthy for you when you're not at home. The Food Guide Pyramid can be your personal guide for making healthful food choices.

➤ **Bagels are low fat and versatile for a quick, easy meal.**

INFOLINK

See Chapter 29 for more information about the Food Guide Pyramid.

PREPARING MEALS AND SNACKS

One or more family members may be responsible for planning and preparing meals and snacks at home. Some of the time it may be your responsibility entirely. How are you going to rate yourself?

Planning Meal Appeal

The smell of good food is hard to turn down. The appearance of food and the way it looks on the plate are also important. Have you ever heard the remark that people eat with their eyes?

Think of a meal you especially like. Does it have foods with different colors, shapes, flavors, and textures? All of these elements paint a picture. Does the picture look good enough to eat? When you're putting a meal together, think about some of the following elements:

- **Color.** Try combining different colors together in a meal. Green lettuce, orange carrots, yellow corn, brown hamburgers, and red strawberries add color contrast.
- **Shape.** Carrot strips, bow-tie pasta, and round peas offer contrasting shapes.
- **Flavor.** Experiment with different flavors in a meal. A baked potato with sour cream, corn-on-the-cob, and barbecued chicken combine different flavors together.
- **Texture.** Crunchy foods contrast with soft ones. Visualize the contrast of a green salad and mashed potatoes.

➤ **Presentation of food makes eating more pleasurable.** What can you do to perk up the looks of a meal?

Meal Patterns

How do you and your family organize your meals? Do you have three meals a day or do you **graze,** or *eat several mini-meals throughout the day?* Do you eat a light lunch and a big evening meal—or the reverse? Over time, most people establish a **meal pattern,** or *way of grouping daily food choices into meals and snacks.*

There's no one way to eat smart. As you decide on what to eat, keep the Food Guide Pyramid in mind. Try eating more of the foods at the base of the Pyramid.

Are you a meal skipper? What are your excuses—not hungry, no time, no food, nothing interesting? Skipping meals once in awhile can happen, but skipping meals as a habit isn't healthy. You pay the price with fatigue, poor concentration, and being physically run down.

When people skip meals, they often overeat later. They may omit foods from some food groups. If you skip a meal, try to make up for it with a healthy snack or small meal later. Guard against going overboard on foods high in fat and sugar.

➤ **Eating breakfast provides energy that helps you feel better every day.** Some high school cafeterias offer nutritional breakfast products before school.

Here are some quick tips for packing a fresh, safe lunch:

- Wrap sandwiches well or use an airtight container.

- Try freezing sandwiches (except those with raw veggies, mayonnaise, or eggs). Pack the frozen sandwich in your lunch to keep other foods cold.

- Pour steaming hot soups into a vacuum bottle and seal the bottle tightly.

- Pour chilled beverages into a chilled vacuum bottle and seal tightly.

- Pack dairy products, such as chilled yogurt, in airtight containers.

- Use an insulated lunch bag with a freezer gel pack to keep foods cold until you're ready to eat.

➤ Omelets can be stuffed with leftover meats, or vegetables. They can make a quick, nutritious meal any time of day.

Meal Tips

Over time, families have found ways to make mealtime easier on everyone. Spending the day in the kitchen isn't a luxury most families have anymore. Many families still emphasize good food and good nutrition, but have found ways to save time and energy. Would any of the following ideas be helpful to your family?

- Keep easy-to-fix foods handy. Possibilities include rice, pasta, frozen foods, canned foods, prepared pasta sauce, salad ingredients, bread, deli meats, cheese, and yogurt.

- Buy **convenience foods,** or *prepared or partially prepared foods*. These are real time savers. Possibilities include washed salad greens, precut stir-fry vegetables, chicken and beef strips, and grated cheese. One drawback to prepared foods is their higher cost.

- Use fast-cooking methods such as microwaving, stir-frying, and broiling. Cutting food in small pieces also helps it cook faster.

- Create one-dish meals. Try a chef's salad. Stuff a pita pocket with tuna fish and chopped vegetable salad. Wrap chicken, beef, or pork in a soft taco for a fajita.

- Try assembling ingredients for a make-your-own meal. Sandwich ingredients with a store-bought salad or fixings for quick English-muffin pizzas are possibilities.

- Make extra servings of food when you do cook. Pasta sauce freezes well. Chicken and many meat dishes taste good warm or cold.

Snack Attacks

When you hear the word snack, what comes to mind? Snacking has become part of our lifestyle. Think of how often you see people eating ice cream at the mall, dropping coins in a food vending machine, and buying a quick snack fix at a convenience store.

Snacking can be both a healthy habit and an unhealthy one. It's unhealthy when soda always replaces milk. It's also unhealthy when snacks high in fat and sugar replace meals high in complex carbohydrates and other nutrients.

Snacking is good if you're an active teen who sometimes needs extra energy. When snacking comes to mind, consider this idea: When you eat isn't as important as what and how much you eat.

- **Build snacks into your personal meal plan.** Think about them as part of the food groups in the Food Guide Pyramid, especially those found at the pyramid base.
- **Eat snacks only when you're hungry.** Substitute another activity for snacking when you're bored. Take the dog for a walk. Exercise. Practice basketball lay-ups.
- **Munch snack-size portions.** Snacks aren't meant to replace an entire meal. Match snacks to your calorie needs. If you're active, higher calorie snacks are okay. If you're less physically active, try lighter snacks.
- **Plan ahead for snacks.** Try to keep nutritious snack foods (fruit, air-popped popcorn, low-fat cheese and crackers, fruit juice, snack-size carrots) on hand.
- **Substitute fresh fruit or fruit juice for candy bars and soda.** Try crackers and peanut butter with fruit juice.

The best kinds of snacks are tasty and nutritious. What other good snacking tips would you add to the list above?

BUDGETING FOR FOOD

Whether you're buying snacks or food for a meal, you'll probably have to watch your spending. Food costs can eat up a large part of a family budget. By making wise choices, you can buy foods that make tasty, nutritious meals without overspending.

One way to save money is to plan for leftovers. Sometimes they're called "planned-overs." Leftover meat can be used the next day to make sandwiches. You can heat up leftover pasta for a second meal. Extra rice can be turned into fried rice. Planned-overs save time and money, and reduce food waste.

➤Your teen years are an important period of peak bone mass formation. Eating foods high in calcium will help you build the strongest bones possible. What foods do you eat that have a high calcium content?

➤ Teamwork saves time and allows for better organizational skills.

SHARING KITCHEN SPACE

Most of your work in the school's food lab is in groups. Working with others gives you a chance to learn about teamwork. Each person in the group is important. You're each responsible for certain jobs. When one member of the team doesn't do a job correctly or on time, everyone else is affected. Success results when groups work together.

Planning Your Work

➤ Planning ahead ensures you'll have the ingredients needed to prepare a meal. Take time out to list the items you'll need to purchase for your menu.

All groups need a plan. Each part of the plan is important. For example, your teacher may ask you to list the ingredients and the amounts of the foods you need. Your supplies will be added to the total grocery list for the lab. If your list isn't accurate, your group may not have the needed ingredients.

When you're in a food lab, you'll often work against the clock. Lab times are usually short, so you'll have to plan to use time wisely. Work out a schedule by listing major jobs in the order they need to be done. Estimate how long it will take to do each job.

Be sure your schedule allows time for getting ready to cook. Before you begin making the recipe, you will need to:

• Wear a clean apron, tie back long hair, roll up dangling sleeves, and wash your hands.

• Set out all the ingredients and equipment you'll need.

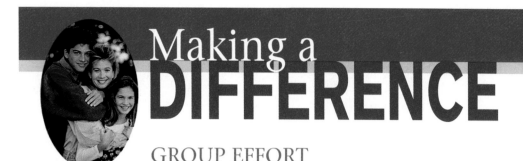

Making a DIFFERENCE

GROUP EFFORT

"I'll just watch you two cook," Bert said to Lloyd and Donna. The three classmates were assigned to make fajitas in the school cooking lab.

"That's what you think," Donna said, laughing. "While I'm preparing the stuffing, you wash and dry the frying pans, and grease them."

"What's the point? This is one big waste of time."

"Hey, hold on," Lloyd said, chopping vegetables. "One day you *just* might have a family. And the more you learn now about how to cook, the more prepared you'll be."

"That's right," said Donna, "and to make sure you're prepared, after you grease the pans, you can wash these utensils, garnish the plates, and set the table."

Bert made a face.

"Believe me," said Donna, "one day you'll thank me."

Taking Action

1. How do you think learning to cook in a group could improve your adult life?
2. Would you rather cook a meal or do the preparation work and cleanup? Why?

- Complete tasks you need to do before combining ingredients. These may include preheating the oven, greasing baking pans, measuring ingredients, peeling or chopping foods, heating water, or melting fat.

  After you've listed all the tasks, decide who'll do each job. Divide the work fairly so that everyone shares responsibility.

Carrying Out Your Plan

When you go into the lab, know your assigned job. Post the time plan where it can be seen. Follow rules about dress, behavior, and lab procedures for your safety.

When you complete your work, volunteer to help someone else who's behind. If you see something that needs to be done, do it.

Cleaning Up

Cleaning up as you go along helps you at the end of class. If food spills on the counter or floor, wipe it up right away. Have a sink of warm, sudsy water ready. When you finish using a utensil, soak it in water (except for sharp knives). Whenever you have a few minutes while waiting for something to cook, wash and rinse the utensils.

Remember to wipe off tables and counters and sweep the floor. Leave the food lab clean and ready for the next group.

Evaluating Your Work

Evaluation is an important part of the lab experience. When you evaluate your work, you judge its quality. Your teacher may have you use a rating sheet. You can also evaluate your teamwork by asking yourself some important questions: Did everything work as planned? What did we do well? How could we have improved? Your answers build on your success in future labs.

Working in Your Home Kitchen

In many ways, preparing food at home is similar to working in the food lab. In both situations, you probably have limited time.

At home as well as at school, it helps to write out a time plan or schedule. Allow a little extra time for unexpected delays. Often two or more family members work together. Decide how you'll divide tasks.

When you work alone, you can still be efficient. Look for ways to dovetail tasks. **Dovetail** means *fitting tasks together to make the best use of time.* For example, wash salad greens during the time it takes water to boil for cooking noodles.

HOW to...

Organize A Meal

Timing is everything, especially at mealtime. With some thought and practice, the meals you prepare will be "timely." The following plan is an example of how to organize a simple meal using convenience foods.

Pasta with Tomato Meat Sauce
Green Salad   Italian Bread
Canned Fruit   Packaged Cookies
Milk

6:00   Assemble utensils and ingredients. Set table.
6:10   Brown ground meat and drain fat. Add bottled tomato sauce. Simmer on low heat.
6:20   Put pasta water on to boil. Wash and dry salad greens.

Assemble salad in bowl. Put salad bowl in refrigerator. Slice bread. Warm in oven.
6:35   Cook pasta to al dente. Put fruit in bowls and cookies on plate.
6:50   Drain pasta and toss with sauce.
6:55   Serve meal. Enjoy!

Here are some tips to keep in mind as you work in the kitchen:

- First, put out the utensils and foods you'll need.
- Begin by working on the recipes that take the longest to prepare.
- Dovetail tasks whenever possible.
- Allow a few extra minutes in your timetable for the unexpected.

Planning a schedule is especially important when you're preparing an entire meal. You want all the food to be ready at the same time. Begin your schedule with the foods that take the longest to prepare and cook. It may take 20 minutes to put a casserole together and another 45 minutes to bake. If you were also having a canned vegetable and a tossed green salad, you'd need to begin the casserole first. With more experience, you may not need to write out a schedule every time.

Family meals don't just happen. They require planning and preparation. Being organized can give you more time to eat well and to enjoy yourself.

Review & Activities

Chapter Summary

- The appearance of food on a plate contributes toward making a meal more appealing to eat.
- No one type of meal pattern is best as long as you eat a variety of healthy foods.
- Families have found a variety of ways to simplify meal preparation.
- Snacks can make a nutritional contribution to a healthy diet.
- Working as a group member in the food lab helps you to develop your skills as a team member.
- Making and following a plan when working in the food lab and at home helps you to accomplish your goals.

Reviewing the Chapter

1. Identify four elements that help to make a meal appealing to eat.
2. What are some of the problems resulting from skipping meals?
3. How can convenience foods help to save time in meal preparation? What is the disadvantage of using convenience foods?
4. List five tips for healthy snacking.
5. Name at least three steps you can take when working in a food lab to save time and help the lab go smoothly.
6. Explain why evaluation is an important part of a food lab experience.
7. What are the similarities of working in a school food lab and at home?
8. Define the term dovetailing and give an example.

Family & Community

With Your Family

Discuss the "Meal Tips" on page 488 with your family members. Which ideas might help your family save time and energy in meal preparation? In what other ways might such time-saving ideas benefit your family?

In Your Community

Contact a local or national organization that helps families by providing tips for stretching a food budget. What tips do they share? Volunteer to help, perhaps by making posters to display in community centers.

Review & Activities

Thinking Critically

1. **Recognize values.** Consider this idea, "The family that prepares meals together builds stronger family ties." Do you agree or disagree? Support your answer.

2. **Analyze snacks.** Why are snack foods so popular with teens? Do you consider the snacks you eat nutritious? How could you improve the nutritional quality of your snacks?

3. **Analyze behavior.** When you work in the kitchen at home, in what ways are you most and least organized? How could you improve your organization?

Making Connections

1. **Math.** Plan a simple menu. Calculate how much time it would take to prepare the menu if you were working alone, with one other person, or with two other people. What can you conclude?

2. **Social Studies.** Find an example of a country in which the typical meal pattern differs from the one you're used to. At what times of day do people in that country usually eat? What is typically served at each meal or snack?

Applying Your Learning

1. **Meals with appeal.** Plan a nutritious meal that includes variety in color, shape, flavor, and texture. describe what specific elements give the meal eye and taste appeal.

2. **Compare meal patterns.** Write two daily menus, one that includes breahfast, lunch, dinner, and a snack and the other following a different meal pattern. Make sure both menus provide enough Food Guide Pyramid servings (see page 410). Explain how the menus compare in nutrition and convenience. When might you choose each pattern and why?

3. **Snack shopping list.** Make a shopping list of nutritious snacks that appeal to you. Explain why each is a healthful choice.

What Would You Do?

Your family used to eat together often, but now everyone's on a different schedule. You miss having family meals. How might you bring up tour concern to family members? What suggestions might you offer?

Chapter

37

Basic Cooking Techniques

YOU WILL LEARN . . .

- ➤ Various techniques for cooking foods.
- ➤ Guidelines for using a microwave oven.
- ➤ Guidelines for preserving nutrients when cooking.

TERMS TO LEARN . . .

- ➤ baking and roasting
- ➤ boiling
- ➤ braising
- ➤ broiling
- ➤ deep-fat frying
- ➤ frying
- ➤ pan frying
- ➤ sautéing
- ➤ simmering
- ➤ steaming
- ➤ stir-frying

Imagine ...

... that everything must be moved out of your kitchen while it's being remodeled. Your family will use a makeshift kitchen in a tiny laundry area for at least a week. There's room for either the microwave oven or the range, but only for one of them. Which would be your choice?

Think About

- Do you feel more comfortable using the microwave oven or the range?
- If you had only a microwave, what wouldn't you be able to do?
- Have you ever been without the refrigerator, range, or kitchen sink? How did your family adapt?

CHOOSING COOKING TECHNIQUES

If you look through cookbooks and recipes in magazines, you'll find lots of ideas about different methods to cook foods. All cooking methods fall into one of several categories: dry-heat methods, moist-heat methods, cooking with fat, or microwave cooking.

DRY-HEAT COOKING

Dry-heat methods require that food be cooked uncovered without adding liquid. Foods cooked by dry-heat methods may be cooked on the range top or in the oven. Naturally tender foods are best cooked by dry-heat methods. For example, you might cook a lean pork roast or a whole chicken by using dry-heat methods of cooking.

Cooking WITH Dry Heat

Broiling. In this method, food is cooked directly over or under the source of heat. The heat source may be the broiler in an oven or a grill. In both cases, fat drains away from the food during cooking. Broiling is often used for cooking tender meats such as hamburgers, steaks, and chicken and for cooking some vegetables.

Baking and Roasting. These methods describe food cooked uncovered in an oven. "Roasting" most often refers to large pieces of meat or poultry. Many foods you eat are baked— meat, poultry, fish, breads, pies, cakes, and cookies.

Broiling. In this method, *food is cooked directly over or under the source of heat.* The heat source may be the broiler in an oven or a grill. In both cases, fat drains away from the food during cooking. Broiling is often used for cooking tender meats such as hamburgers, steaks, and chicken and for cooking some vegetables.

Baking and Roasting. These methods describe *food cooked uncovered in an oven.* "Roasting" most often refers to large pieces of meat or poultry. Many foods you eat are baked—meat, poultry, fish, breads, pies, cakes, and cookies.

HOW to...

Check Food for Doneness

Judging when food is done cooking can be a challenge. Your first guide to checking doneness will be the cooking time listed in the recipe. Actual cooking times can vary for many reasons. That's why experienced cooks also rely on other methods for checking doneness. Try these tips for checking doneness:

- **Use a thermometer.** You can check foods such as meat and poultry with a meat thermometer. Insert the thermometer in the thick muscles for meat and poultry, away from any bone, to get an accurate reading. You can also use a thermometer to check other foods such as liquid fats and candy.

- **Use a toothpick or metal tester.** To check the doneness of cakes and breads, use a wooden toothpick or metal tester. When inserted into the center of cakes and breads, the tester should come out clean when the product is done.

- **Pierce foods with a fork.** Foods such as potatoes, carrots, green beans, and fish can be easily checked with a fork. When vegetables are done, the fork goes in and out easily. When fish is done, it flakes apart easily with a fork.

- **Taste a food sample.** Remove small pieces of pasta or a vegetable, cool it slightly, and taste it. Pasta should be slightly chewy, not mushy; vegetables should be tender-crisp.

- **Check out the color and feel of foods.** You can tell the doneness of many foods by the way they look or feel. If you press lightly on the center of a cake and it springs back, the cake is done. Fully cooked meat and poultry should not be pink inside.

MOIST-HEAT COOKING

Moist-heat methods require the use of added liquid or steam to cook and tenderize foods. Moist-heat methods often take a longer cooking time than dry-heat methods. The combination of longer cooking time and added moisture helps to tenderize meat and vegetables that contain lots of fiber. Water, broth, and even vegetable or fruit juices can be used in moist-heat cooking. The amount of liquid varies depending on the type of food and your recipe.

Moist-heat cooking methods involve using liquids or steam to cook the food. They include:

Boiling. In this cooking method, you bring food to a boiling point (212°F) or plunge food into boiling water. **Boiling** involves *heating liquid at a high temperature so that bubbles rise and break on the liquid surface.* You might bring a sauce to a boil or cook noodles in boiling water.

Steaming. This is a method of *cooking food over boiling water rather than in it.* A metal basket or other utensil holds food over boiling water. This cooking method is most often used for vegetables.

Simmering. When a recipe calls for **simmering,** it means *heating a liquid to a temperature just below the boiling point until bubbles barely break on the liquid surface.* Simmering is usually preferable to boiling because fewer nutrients are lost in the method. Foods that can be simmered include vegetables, meat, poultry, and fish.

Braising. This cooking method involves *browning food in a small amount of fat, then simmering in very little added liquid.* Less tender cuts of meat are often braised.

Stewing. This cooking method is similar to braising, but the food is cut into small pieces before it's stewed. Poultry and less tender cuts of meat are often stewed.

COOKING WITH FAT

Frying, or *cooking with fat,* is another cooking method. You can use melted fat, such as shortening or butter, or liquid fats, such as vegetable oil. Eat fried foods in moderation for good health. See page 502 for more information on cooking with fat.

Cooking WITH Moist Heat

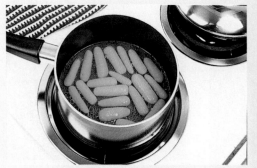

Boiling. In this cooking method, you bring food to a boiling point (212°F) or plunge food into boiling water. Boiling involves heating liquid at a high temperature so that bubbles rise and break on the liquid surface. You might bring a sauce to a boil or cook noodles in boiling water.

Simmering. When a recipe calls for simmering, it means heating a liquid to a temperature just below the boiling point until bubbles barely break on the liquid surface. Simmering is usually preferable to boiling because fewer nutrients are lost in the method. Foods that can be simmered include vegetables, meat, poultry, and fish.

Steaming. This is a method of cooking food over boiling water rather than in it. A metal basket or other utensil holds food over boiling water. This cooking method is most often used for vegetables.

Braising. This cooking method involves browning food in a small amount of fat, then simmering in very little added liquid. Less tender cuts of meat are often braised.

Stewing. This cooking method is similar to braising, but the food is cut into small pieces before it's stewed. Poultry and less tender cuts of meat are often stewed.

Cooking
WITH Fat

Deep-fat frying. In this cooking method, food is completely covered in fat. Foods such as french fries and chicken are deep-fat fried.

Pan frying. In this cooking method, foods such as tender cuts of meat, fish, and eggs are fried in a skillet with a smaller amount of fat. When thinly sliced vegetables such as onions are cooked in a very small amount of fat, it's called sautéing.

Stir-frying. This is a cooking method in which small pieces of food are stirred and cooked very quickly at high heat in very little fat. This method is used for vegetables, meat, poultry, and fish. You may use a skillet or a wok.

Deep-fat frying. In this cooking method, *food is completely covered in fat.* Foods such as french fries and chicken are deep-fat fried.

Pan frying. In this cooking method, *foods such as tender cuts of meat, fish, and eggs are fried in a skillet with a smaller amount of fat.* When *thinly sliced vegetables such as onions are cooked in a very small amount of fat,* it's called **sautéing.**

Stir-frying. This is a cooking method in which *small pieces of food are stirred and cooked very quickly at high heat in very little fat.* This method is used for vegetables, meat, poultry, and fish.

MICROWAVE COOKING

Why do people microwave foods so often today? Your first answer is probably that it saves time. Did you also realize that microwaving preserves more nutrients than many other cooking methods?

In microwave cooking, electricity is converted into microwaves. A fan moves microwaves around the inside of the oven. Microwaves pass through glass, ceramic, paper, and plastic but bounce off metal. That is why metal pans made for conventional ovens shouldn't be used in microwave ovens.

You'll also want to avoid using brown paper bags and towels made of recycled paper that can burn when heated. Plastics that aren't microwave-safe can melt from the heat or transfer chemicals to food.

Preparing Foods for Microwaving

Preparing foods properly and using correct cooking containers is essential for successful microwave cooking. Be sure a container fits into your microwave oven without touching the walls, top, or door of the oven. Many manufacturers suggest using round containers because they help food cook more evenly. Here are other additional tips for successful microwave cooking:
• Use a container two or three times larger than the amount of food you cook when heating liquids such as soups. This helps prevent runovers.

To safely fry foods:
• Be sure food is dry before putting it in fat or oil. Moisture can cause hot fat to spatter and burn you.
• Put food into fat slowly and carefully so it won't spatter. Use a spoon or tongs, not your fingers.
• If a grease fire starts, smother the flame with the pan cover or with salt. DON'T throw water on the fire. Putting water on a grease fire can spread flames.

To safely microwave foods:

- Pierce foods with skins, such as potatoes, with a fork before cooking to allow steam to escape.
- Don't microwave eggs in the shell. They may explode during cooking.
- If you cover a dish with plastic wrap, fold back a corner or an edge about an inch.
- When removing plastic wrap, open it away from you to avoid being burned by steam.

- Cut pieces of food into uniform sizes for even cooking.
- Arrange foods as indicated in your instruction manual to ensure even cooking. For example, some foods, such as chicken drumsticks, should be arranged in a ring or spoke pattern. Place the parts of the food that take the longest to cook toward the outside of the container.
- Cover foods to prevent drying out and spattering.
- Follow package instructions on microwave convenience foods. For example, you may need to remove part of the packaging to cook the food.

Setting Microwave Controls

Accuracy is essential in microwave cooking. Set the power level and cooking time as indicated in the recipe or package instructions. Even a few extra seconds or minutes of cooking can overcook your food, making it too tough to eat.

Some recipes will give you a range of cooking time, such as 6 to 8 minutes. Use the shortest time suggested, or set the timer for a few seconds or minutes before you think the food will be done. You can always increase cooking time if needed.

During Cooking Time

To ensure even cooking, your recipe directions may tell you to use one or more of the following techniques during cooking time:

- **Rotate the food.** Turning a cooking container ensures even cooking. Your instructions may tell you to give the food a ¼ or ½ turn. This means the part of the dish that had been facing the door of the microwave oven should now face the side or back.
- **Stir.** Stir food from the outside edges of the container toward the center.
- **Rearrange.** Move food around in the container. Move outside pieces of food to the center, and foods on the bottom to the top.
- **Invert.** Turn the food over in the dish.

Standing Time

After cooking time is finished, many directions may tell you to let food stand. During standing time, the food continues to cook. Leave the food covered for the specified recipe time, then check for doneness. If necessary, add more cooking time.

CONSERVING NUTRIENTS

During cooking, foods can lose some of their nutrients. You can help preserve as many nutrients as possible by following these guidelines:

- Consider nutrition when considering cooking methods. Baking and roasting, broiling, microwaving, and simmering in a small amount of water generally conserve more nutrients.
- Avoid overcooking food. Carefully follow directions for cooking temperature and time.
- Leave the skins on fruits and vegetables when possible. The skin contains vitamins, minerals, and fiber.
- Save liquid in which food is cooked. It contains valuable nutrients. If liquid will not be eaten with the food, save it for making soup.

Now that you know some cooking methods, you're off to a good start. You may find that cooking is enjoyable, even exciting.

MICROWAVING SUCCESS

As you already know, microwaving is different than cooking on a gas or an electric range. The following tips can help you cook efficiently and safely in a microwave.

- Place the thicker or tougher parts or irregularly shaped foods toward the outside of the container. Try this with chicken legs or broccoli spears.

- Keep foods covered while cooking to keep them moist. For safety, allow a little space for steam to escape.

- Check for doneness at the shortest cooking time given in a recipe. You can always add more cooking time if needed.

- When you use a microwave oven to cook, follow the recipe guidelines carefully, especially the first time you try a recipe.

- Don't expect foods to brown in a microwave oven like they do in gas or electric ovens.

Chapter Summary

- Learning about different methods of cooking enables you to prepare a variety of recipes.
- The dry-heat method of cooking is often used for naturally tender foods.
- The moist-heat method of cooking is often used to help tenderize foods.
- Cooking with fat adds flavor to foods but should be used in moderation.
- Microwave cooking is time-saving and helps to preserve nutrients.
- When cooking food, use cooking techniques that preserve nutrients.

Reviewing the Chapter

1. Identify two methods of dry-heat cooking and briefly explain each.
2. Name four methods of moist-heat cooking and briefly explain each.
3. What is the difference between stir-frying and deep-fat frying? Briefly describe each.
4. Explain how food is cooked in a microwave oven.
5. List six helpful guidelines to follow when microwaving foods.
6. What are four steps you can take to help preserve nutrients when cooking food?

Family & Community

With Your Family

Learn more about a cooking method you and your family frequently use. Find additional recipes using this cooking method. Decide whether your family would enjoy trying these foods.

In Your Community

What community organizations prepare food for hungry people? Try to find out more about these organizations. How do they prepare food? How can you and other people in the community help them?

Thinking Critically

1. **Compare and contrast.** Which cooking method is the easiest for beginners to follow? Which would be the most difficult? Explain the basis for your choices.
2. **Draw conclusions.** How might your experiences in using different cooking methods as a teen be different from your parents' experiences? What do you think accounts for these differences?
3. **Analyze the situation.** What guidelines are important for young children to follow when using a microwave oven safely? Why are these guidelines important?

Making Connections

1. **Science.** Contrast the way food is cooked in a microwave oven versus a conventional oven. Explain the different methods of transferring heat to the food.
2. **Social Studies.** Research the origin and history of one cooking method that particularly interests you. Where did it originate? What were the local conditions that helped to popularize this method?

Applying Your Learning

1. **Compare cooking methods.** Find recipes that give directions for both conventional and microwave cooking. What are the differences in utensils, ingredients, amounts of ingredients used, and techniques? What are the reasons for these differences?
2. **Make safety first.** Identify important safety pointers to keep in mind for each of the different cooking methods. Which cooking methods seem to present the greatest safety risks? Why?
3. **Complete a statement.** Complete the following statement: "The most healthful cooking method is . . . " Explain your reasoning.

What Would You Do?

You are interested in expanding your repertoire of cooking techniques. How would you begin to do this? What resources would you use to reach your goal? How would you chart your progress?

Preparing Grains, Fruits, and Vegetables

YOU WILL LEARN . . .

- ➤ Which nutrients are supplied by grains, fruits, and vegetables.
- ➤ How to buy, store, prepare, and cook grains, fruits, and vegetables.

TERMS TO LEARN . . .

- ➤ al dente
- ➤ bran
- ➤ endosperm
- ➤ enriched
- ➤ germ
- ➤ leavening agent

Imagine ...

... your mom has left a note asking you to start cooking supper at about 4 o'clock. That's strange, you think. Heating leftovers only takes a few minutes. Then you notice a big bag of fresh green beans and a basket of peppers. They must be from Mr. Kelly's garden. But what in the world are you supposed to do with them?

Think About

- What would you do if your Mom couldn't be reached?
- Which veggies do you like? Does it matter to you if they're fresh, frozen, or canned?
- Are you open to trying foods prepared in different ways?

NUTRIENTS IN GRAINS

Why are grains such an important part of healthful eating? Grains, especially whole grains, are excellent sources of complex carbohydrates and fiber. They contain B vitamins and iron. When combined with animal protein or legumes, they also provide high-quality protein. Most important, since they're plant foods they don't contain saturated fat or cholesterol. You need six to twelve servings of grain foods per day.

Grains are the seeds and fruits of cereal grasses. Each part of the grain kernel contributes different nutrients. Here are the three parts found in every type of grain kernel:

- **Bran.** The **bran** is *the grain kernel's outside covering.* It contains mostly fiber, many B vitamins, and about 20 percent of the grain's protein.
- **Endosperm.** The **endosperm** is *the largest part of the grain kernel, mostly composed of carbohydrate.* It also contains about 75 percent of the grain's protein.
- **Germ.** The **germ** is *the sprouting section of the grain kernel.* It contains vegetable oil and is a rich source of vitamins. Perhaps you've heard of some people adding *wheat germ* to foods for added nutrition.

When grains are processed for flour and cereals, the bran and germ are often removed. Only the carbohydrate and protein found in the endosperm remain. Federal law requires that processed grains be **enriched,** or have *nutrients added back after processing.* Food labels explain how products are enriched.

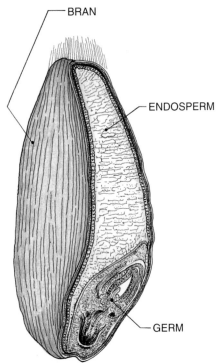

BRAN

ENDOSPERM

GERM

➤ **A kernel of grain.**

PREPARING GRAINS

Probably many grain products you like are ready-to-eat. It's hard to top the convenience of dry cereal and packaged breads. However, some grain products require you to do at least some of the preparation. So, if you enjoy eating them, why not learn to prepare them?

Buying Grain Foods

Here are some guidelines for buying various types of grains:

- **Cereals.** Some types of cereals are ready-to-eat, while others require cooking. Some are made from whole grains; others are enriched. Cereals that are *heavily* enriched or have added dried fruit and nuts can be costly. It's impossible to get all your nutrients from one bowl of cereal. For best nutrition, eat a variety of foods at regular intervals.

- **Rice.** Rice is available in several types: brown rice, enriched white rice, pre-cooked rice (often known as "instant" rice that comes in brown or white forms), and converted rice, which is partially cooked before the bran is removed to retain nutrients. Each type of rice requires a different cooking time. Follow package directions for best results.

- **Pasta.** An excellent source of carbohydrates, pasta, or macaroni and noodle products, comes in many shapes and sizes. Some pasta has added eggs for extra nutrition and tenderness.

- **Flour.** The most common type of flour is *all-purpose flour.* You can use it in most recipes. Other types of flours include cake flour (which has a lighter texture), self-rising flour (which contains a leavening agent), and whole-grain flours, such as whole wheat, oat, and rye. Be sure to use the type of flour called for in your recipe. Substituting different types of flour can lead to poor results in baked products.

Which grain foods might be best to prepare for quick meals?

Cooking Pasta and Rice

Are pasta and rice among your favorite foods? When you cook pasta and rice in water, the starch absorbs water, becomes soft, and increases in size. Pasta generally doubles in volume, and rice expands up to three times its original volume. Choose a pan large enough for grain products to expand as they cook. Also, allow additional space for water to boil when cooking pasta. Rice usually absorbs all or most of the cooking water. Pasta needs to be drained.

> Never rinse pasta after it has been cooked. Just drain the cooking water off the pasta. Rinsing washes away pasta's valuable nutrients.

STORING GRAIN FOODS

Here are some tips for storing grain foods:

• Store grains in a cool, dry place.

• Keep packages and containers of grain foods tightly sealed to retain freshness. This also helps keep grains free of insect contamination.

• Store most bread at room temperature. In hot or humid weather, refrigerate bread to keep it from getting moldy.

> Quick breads can be baked in greased loaf pans. They usually crack on top while baking.

Follow the package directions for cooking grain products. Remember that cooking times given for pasta are only approximate. Sample the pasta near the end of the cooking period to determine doneness, so it doesn't overcook. How do you know when it's finished? Experienced pasta makers cook pasta only until it's "**al dente**" *(tender but firm to the bite).*

Making Muffins and Biscuits

Muffins and biscuits are called quick breads. Why? Quick breads use a short-action **leavening agent,** such as baking power or baking soda, that *causes baked products to rise.* They take less mixing time and require less time to rise than yeast breads do.

General cookbooks usually offer directions for several types of muffins and biscuits. You'll mix most quick breads in one of two ways, the muffin method, or biscuit method.

Mix Muffins

2. Mix wet ingredients (usually eggs, oil, and milk) together.

The muffin method, used for most muffins and corn bread, follows three easy steps:

1. Mix dry ingredients (usually flour, salt, sugar, and baking powder) together.

3. Stir together the dry and wet ingredients. The trick in making great muffins is not to overmix the batter. It should be somewhat lumpy, not smooth.

The biscuit method is a little different from that used for making muffins. It also has three steps:

1. Dry ingredients are mixed thoroughly, as you do for muffins.
2. Fat (usually shortening) is *cut into* dry ingredients. Cutting in means breaking the solid fat into pea-size pieces in dry ingredients.
3. Wet ingredients are mixed into the dry. The dough is rolled out, and the biscuits are cut.

Nutrients in Fruits and Vegetables

INFOLINK

For more information on serving sizes, see Chapter 29.

What makes fruits and vegetables so good for you? Plenty! For the number of calories they provide, most fruits and vegetables are packed with generous amounts of vitamins and minerals. Although amounts may differ generally, fruits and vegetables are good sources of carbohydrate, vitamin A, vitamin C, and minerals, such as calcium and potassium.

Color is the clue to nutrients in fruits and vegetables. For example, fruits and vegetables that are deep yellow or dark green are better sources of vitamin A than those with pale color. Choose yams, apricots, cantaloupe, carrots, broccoli, collard greens, kale, or green peppers for good nutrition.

Citrus fruits, such as oranges and grapefruit, are outstanding sources of vitamin C. Other good sources include tomatoes, strawberries, red sweet peppers, and white potatoes. For good health, you need two to four servings of fruits and three to five servings of vegetables each day.

Oatmeal Muffins

Amount	Ingredient
¾ cup	Whole-wheat flour
¾ cup	All-purpose flour
1 cup	Uncooked rolled oats
1 Tbsp.	Baking powder
3 Tbsp.	Sugar
½ tsp.	Cinnamon
¼ tsp.	Salt
1	Egg
1 cup	Milk
¼ cup	Oil

Yield: 12 muffins

DIRECTIONS
Pan: Muffin pan
Temperature: 400°F (200°C)
1. Grease and flour muffin pan.
2. Combine flours, rolled oats, baking powder, sugar, cinnamon, and salt. Mix well.
3. Beat egg in a separate bowl.
4. Add milk and oil to egg. Stir well.
5. Add liquid mixture to flour mixture.
6. Stir until just blended. Batter should be lumpy.
7. Fill muffin cups ⅔ full.
8. Bake 15 to 20 minutes or until muffins spring back when touched.

Nutrition Information
- **Per serving (approximate):** 150 calories, 4 g protein, 20 g carbohydrate, 6 g fat, 19 mg cholesterol, 135 mg sodium
- **Good source of:** thiamine, calcium, phosphorus

PREPARING FRUITS AND VEGETABLES

Depending on the time of year, your family may use fresh, frozen, canned, or dried fruits and vegetables. You'll need to cook fresh and frozen vegetables, and only heat canned ones thoroughly.

Handling Fresh Produce

Wash fresh fruits and vegetables thoroughly under cold running water. Use a brush to clean firmer vegetables, such as potatoes and carrots. Pare, slice, or cut fruits and vegetables just before you use them. Water-soluble nutrients (B vitamins and vitamin C) are destroyed by air. You also lose water-soluble nutrients when you soak produce in water.

Cut fresh fruits, such as bananas, apples, peaches, and pears, just before serving. They darken when cut and exposed to the air. If you cut fruits before serving, squeeze lemon, orange, lime, or grapefruit juice on them to prevent browning. The wax coating on some fruits and vegetables, such as apples and cucumbers, is safe to eat. It's put on after they're picked to keep them moist and to protect them from bruising.

➤ A food dehydrator removes water from foods, making them easier to store. Dehydrated fruits and vegetables make nutritious snacks.

Making Salads

Do you and your family enjoy salads? If you do, you have a wide choice of ingredients, including meat, fish, cheese, vegetables, fruits, pasta, grains, and legumes. How many of these ingredients have you ever used to make a salad?

Salad greens taste best when crisp. Keep greens in the refrigerator until you're ready to use them. Remove discolored leaves and rinse greens thoroughly in cold water. Dirt clings to some greens, such as spinach, and escarole. Put them in cold water, move them around a little, and lift them out of the water. The dirt settles on the bottom. You may need to rinse some greens more than once.

Buying Fruits and Vegetables

Here are some guidelines for buying various forms of fruits and vegetables:

- **Fresh fruits and vegetables.** Buy fresh fruits and vegetables *in season* for the lowest cost. Avoid buying fruits and vegetables that are wilted, discolored, or have soft spots. These are signs of age and poor quality. What should you look for? Head lettuce and cabbage should feel solid. Citrus fruits, squash, and tomatoes should feel heavy for their size. Celery should be crisp, not limp. Potatoes and onions shouldn't have sprouts.

- **Frozen, canned, or dried fruits and vegetables.** Read labels to find out whether these items are whole, halves, slices, or pieces. Labels also list seasonings, preservatives, and other added ingredients. When buying juices, remember that only those labeled "juice" contain 100 percent juice. Cans and packages of fruits and vegetables should be in good condition. Avoid dented or bulging cans—they may carry harmful bacteria. Ice crystals on frozen packages show poor storage.

On your next shopping trip, try to pick out the best fruits and vegetables according to the above guidlines.

Dry greens in a salad spinner or clean towel before adding them to a salad. This helps the dressing cling to the leaves. If you make a tossed salad, tear the greens into bite-size pieces. When adding other vegetables or fruits to a salad, be sure they are thoroughly clean. Pour salad dressing on just before serving time to keep greens from wilting.

➤ Salads are a healthy addition to a meal. Be sure to keep them cool until mealtime.

Cooking Fruits and Vegetables

Fruits and vegetables change quite dramatically when cooked. Their starch and fiber soften, and they become less crisp. Careful cooking can help you save nutrients. Some water-soluble nutrients dissolve in water, and others are destroyed by heat. Use the following ideas to prepare fruits and vegetables:

- Leave the skin on fruits and vegetables whenever you can. (The skin acts as a seal.) If fruits and vegetables are cooked whole or in large pieces, less of the nutrients are lost in the water.
- Cook fruits and vegetables only until just tender. Slightly crisp is better. Remember that fruits and vegetables cut into larger pieces are going to take longer to cook than small pieces.
- Use as little water as possible to cook vegetables. (Starchy vegetables, such as potatoes, are an exception and need to be cooked in more water.) Steaming vegetables over water or microwaving them in very little water conserves nutrients.
- Follow package directions when you cook frozen vegetables. You'll end up with better flavor and nutrition if the food is still frozen when placed into boiling water. Separate frozen pieces with a fork after cooking begins so they cook more evenly.

STORING FRUITS AND VEGETABLES

Here are some tips for storing fruits and vegetables:

- Store fresh fruits and vegetables unwashed in the refrigerator.
- Store potatoes and onions in a cool, dry, dark place
- Keep canned fruits and vegetables in a cool, dry place.
- Use frozen fruits and vegetables within a few months of purchase.

Carrot Slaw

Amount	Ingredient
4 medium	Carrots
½ cup	Celery, diced
2 Tbsp.	Onion, diced
3 Tbsp.	Raisins
⅓ cup	Apple, diced
½ tsp.	Lemon juice
⅓ cup	Mayonnaise, lowfat
	Salt and pepper, to taste

Yield: 4 servings

DIRECTIONS
Equipment: Mixing bowl, paring knife, grater, or food processor

1. Grate carrots in a food processor or by hand on a grater.
2. Dice the celery, onion, and apple.
3. Toss the diced apple with lemon juice.
4. Add celery, onion, raisins, and apple to carrots and mix.
5. Add mayonnaise, stir until combined.
6. Cover and chill before serving, if possible.

Nutrition Information
- **Per serving (approximate):** 151 calories, 1 g protein, 18 g carbohydrate, 9 g fat, 0 mg cholesterol, 105 mg sodium
- **Good source of:** vitamin A, vitamin C

Chapter Summary

- Grains are sources of complex carbohydrates, fiber, B vitamins, and iron. They don't contain saturated fat or cholesterol.
- Pasta and rice absorb water when cooked and increase in volume.
- Quick breads are easily assembled and are mixed using either the muffin or biscuit method.
- Fruits and vegetables provide a variety of nutrients including vitamins, minerals, and carbohydrates.
- When preparing fresh fruits and vegetables, it's important to use techniques that help to preserve nutrients.
- Salad greens should be thoroughly cleaned and are best when served crisp.

Reviewing the Chapter

1. How many daily servings of grains are recommended for healthful eating?
2. What are enriched grains?
3. Describe the similarities and differences in cooking pasta and rice.
4. What are quick breads? Give an example of two different types of quick breads.
5. How is the color of fruits and vegetables a guide to their nutritional value?
6. Why do some fruits darken when cut and what can you do to prevent the browning?
7. List three steps you would take with cooking fruits and vegetables to preserve the nutrients.

Family & Community

With Your Family

Think about some fruits and vegetables your family doesn't usually eat. Try to prepare one or two fruits or vegetables your family has agreed to sample. If this is successful, talk with your family about trying other fruits and vegetables.

In Your Community

Plan and give a demonstration for younger children to encourage them to include more healthy whole grains in their snacks and meals. Look for appealing ideas. Stress the benefits of eating whole grains.

Thinking Critically

1. **Analyze meaning.** What do you think is meant by the expression, "Grain is the staff of life"? Explain your answer.

2. **Draw conclusions.** Some people consider salads to be "rabbit" food. What factors do you think contribute to this viewpoint? Why is this viewpoint a limited one?

3. **Identify evidence.** In your opinion, are people eating the variety of fruits and vegetables suggested in the Food Guide Pyramid? Cite evidence to support your opinion.

Making Connections

1. **Social Studies.** Investigate a lesser known grain such as kasha, couscous (KOOS koos), bulgur, millet, or quinoa (KEEN wah). In what area of the world is the grain most commonly found? Why? How is this grain most often prepared?

2. **Math.** Make a cost comparison of equal-size portions for three different fruits or vegetables. Compare the cost per serving for as many forms as possible (fresh, frozen, canned, and dried). What factors contribute to the difference in cost per serving?

Applying Your Learning

1. **Brainstorm ideas.** Why is it difficult to get people to eat a greater quantity and variety of vegetables? How can vegetables be made more appealing so people will include more of them in their meals?

2. **Make a comparison.** Cook a pasta product following the package directions. Sample the pasta two minutes before the suggested cooking time is reached, at the suggested time and two minutes after the suggested time. Compare the taste results.

3. **Develop a recipe.** Select a fruit or vegetable and develop a new recipe using it. Prepare the recipe. Have others sample it and give their opinions.

What Would You Do?

Imagine you are with a group of friends at school. One of the people in the group begins to make negative comments about the unusual ethnic grain foods that another student's family eats. Your family has always respected cultural differences. What would you do in this situation?

Preparing Protein and Dairy Foods

YOU WILL LEARN . . .

➤ Nutrients provided in protein and dairy foods.
➤ How to buy, store, and prepare protein and dairy foods.

TERMS TO LEARN . . .

➤ freezer burn
➤ marbling
➤ salmonella
➤ scorch

Imagine ...

… that your family is hosting a family reunion this year. With your family and other relatives, there will be 14 to 16 of you. Your parents' hectic schedule means they're counting on you to help. You've cooked before, but never helped plan a meal for so many! Your parents also want to serve turkey.

Think About

• Would you know what size turkey to buy?
• How would making lists make the day go smoothly?
• Are there ways you could ease the workload for your family?

NUTRIENTS IN PROTEIN FOODS

What do foods in the Meat, Poultry, Fish, Dry Beans, Eggs, and Nuts Group have in common? All are good sources of protein. Meat, poultry, fish, and eggs provide *complete protein.* Dry beans and nuts contain *incomplete protein* that can be combined with other plant and animal protein to meet your protein needs.

Along with protein, the foods in this group also supply the following nutrients:

- Meat supplies iron and B vitamins.
- Poultry contains iron, B vitamins, and phosphorus.
- Fish and shellfish are often good sources of iron and vitamins A and D. Most saltwater fish and shellfish also supply iodine.
- Legumes are rich in carbohydrates and fiber. They also supply iron, calcium, phosphorus, B vitamins, and vitamin E.

All sources of protein are nutritious, though they vary in fat content. The Dietary Guidelines recommend eating foods low in fat. Two forms of fat are found in meats. The large sections of fat around meat edges can be trimmed away before cooking. **Marbling,** or *tiny veins of fat throughout the meat muscle,* adds tenderness and juiciness to meat. Lean meats are also flavorful and juicy if cooked properly. Choosing leaner meats lowers the fat and can save you money. See page 523 for more information on choosing lowfat protein foods.

➤ Proteins are important nutrients for building and repairing body tissues. Eating a variety of protein foods is essential to good health.

PREPARING PROTEIN FOODS

When you cook protein foods, try to use low to moderate cooking temperatures. Lower temperatures help keep protein tender, whereas higher temperatures make it tougher. Of course, broiling is an exception. In this case, high temperatures seal in juices over the heat.

HOW to...

Buy Protein Foods

When buying protein foods, skillful shopping is essential, since most of these foods are expensive. To make good choices, consider nutrition, quality, and money-saving options. For example, buying low-cost legumes gives you a good source of lowfat protein. Another way to save is to combine small amounts of protein foods with other foods, as in soups or stews.

To find the best buy for your money, consider the *cost per serving* of protein foods. The package labels tell you the cost per pound, the number of pounds, and the price you pay. To find the cost per serving, divide the cost-per-pound by the number of servings per pound. Here are some additional tips for buying protein foods:

- **Meat.** Beef, pork, and lamb are types of meat. Meat is made up of muscle (the lean portion), connective tissue, fat, and bone. Connective tissue holds the muscles together. Meats with less connective tissue are usually more tender than other meats. The tenderest cuts are usually the most expensive. Meats are divided into different "cuts." The cuts you find in the supermarket are called *retail cuts*. Meat labels will tell you the type of meat and the specific retail cut. Meats are graded for quality: *Prime, Choice, and Select.* All are nutritious, but the *Select* grade is lowest in fat and the least expensive.

- **Poultry.** Chicken and turkey are the most common types of poultry. You can buy poultry fresh, hard chilled—0° to 26°F (-18° to -4°C), or frozen—below -18°F (-28°C). To get the best buy on poultry, check out the cost per serving of different forms. Usually larger, whole forms of poultry cost less per pound, and you get more meat. Poultry is also available in packages of pieces, such as leg and breast portions, and boneless, skinless pieces.

- **Fish.** Fish and shellfish can be purchased fresh, frozen, and canned. Frozen and canned fish are available all year. The supply and cost of fresh fish varies with the season of the year. Fish spoils easily. If you notice any unpleasant odor (often an ammonia-like odor), don't buy it. Also, consider the cost per serving when buying fish.

- **Eggs.** Eggs are a low-cost source of protein and other nutrients. Eggs come in a variety of sizes and grades. Stores most often sell the higher grades AA and A in medium, large, extra large and jumbo sizes. As a general rule, the larger the egg and the higher the grade, the more money you'll pay. Most recipes are tested using large eggs. Before you buy eggs, open the carton to check for cracks and broken eggs.

- **Legumes.** Legumes can be purchased canned, in boxes or bags, or from large bins or sacks by the pound. Some can be purchased canned and ready to use. When buying dry legumes, look for firm, clean legumes that are uniform in size and color. If sizes are uneven, they won't cook evenly.

Cooking Meat, Poultry, and Fish

You can get a lot of ideas for cooking protein foods from cookbooks. You may also want to look over the basic cooking methods discussed in Chapter 37.

For your safety, always thaw meat, poultry, and fish in the refrigerator, or use a microwave oven for defrosting. Don't thaw protein foods at room temperature. They spoil easily and can cause you to become ill. Food defrosted in the microwave must be cooked right away, since microwave thawing begins to cook the food.

Tenderness is the key for choosing a cooking method. Tender cuts of meat usually are cooked by one of the dry-heat methods—roasting, broiling, sautéing, or frying. It's preferable to cook less tender cuts of meat with a moist-heat method (braising or stewing).

Cook poultry labeled "broiler-fryer" just as the name states. You can microwave as well. Broil, bake, or fry fish because it's naturally tender.

Ground meat and poultry can harbor bacteria, which cause foodborne illness. Only thorough cooking destroys the bacteria. Use a meat thermometer to check the internal temperature at the center of meat and poultry to be sure it's completely cooked. Ground meat should be at least 160°F (71°C), poultry pieces 170°F (77°C), and whole poultry 180°F (82°C).

➤ Cooking meat at a low temperature for a long period of time makes it more tender. Plan ahead to allow ample cooking time, as the meat must reach safe temperatures to kill bacteria.

Because fish is tender, it requires a shorter cooking time. Allow 10 minutes of cooking time for every inch of thickness. Fish is done cooking when it separates easily with a fork.

Cookbooks give guidelines for suggested cooking times based on weight and size. Remember that these are only guidelines. Brownness on the outside of hamburgers and poultry isn't a guarantee of doneness. It's important that you cook poultry and ground meat until no pink shows inside and juices run clear.

Cooking Eggs

You can cook eggs in a variety of ways. Whatever method you use, be sure to cook eggs thoroughly, until the yolks are firm. If you undercook eggs, you may not destroy the **salmonella,** *bacteria that can cause foodborne illness,* found in some eggs.

Southwest Tortilla Pizzas

Amount	Ingredient
4	Flour tortillas, 10-inch size
4 tsp.	Vegetable Oil
2 16 oz. cans	Red kidney beans, drained and mashed
5	Green onions, minced
¼ c.	Salsa
1½ c.	Shredded, low-fat cheddar cheese

Yield: 4 servings

DIRECTIONS
Pan: Cookie sheet, 1-quart bowl
Temperature: Broil
1. Preheat the broiler.
2. Sprinkle 1 tsp. of oil on one side of each tortilla. Place tortillas on a cookie sheet, oiled-side down.
3. Combine mashed red kidney beans, green onions, and salsa in a 1-quart bowl.
4. Spread one-fourth of the bean mixture on each tortilla.
5. Sprinkle one-fourth of the shredded cheddar cheese on each tortilla.
6. Place tortillas under the broiler about 10 inches from the broiler unit.
7. Broil for 8 to 10 minutes or until the beans are heated through and the cheese has melted.
8. Serve hot.

Nutrition Information
• **Per serving (approximate):** 466 calories, 32 g protein, 70 g carbohydrate, 12 g fat, 7 mg cholesterol, 1080 mg sodium
• **Good source of:** phosphorus, iron, calcium, and vitamin B$_6$

➤ Simmering gently reduces the chance for mushy beans with broken skins. Cooking beans is a long process, so plan your time accordingly.

Cooking Legumes

Dry beans are usually soaked in water before cooking. This softens them and shortens cooking time.

To soak, cover the beans with water and simmer for two minutes. Take the pan off the heat, cover it, and let the beans stand for one hour. Drain and rinse the beans. Then follow your recipe directions.

Storing Protein Foods

Except for legumes, refrigerate or freeze all protein foods. Protein foods are highly perishable. The length of time they stay fresh in the refrigerator varies as follows:

- Fresh meat and poultry: 2 to 3 days.
- Ground meat: 1 to 2 days.
- Fresh fish: 1 to 2 days. Cover tightly to keep odors from transferring to other foods.
- Eggs: up to 5 weeks. Store them in the carton in the coldest part of the refrigerator.

TAKE NOTE

Buying Milk, Yogurt, and Cheese

Be a smart consumer when buying milk, yogurt, and cheese. Read package labels to be sure you get the product you want. Check the date on the package for the last date on which a product should be sold. Here are other helpful tips for buying milk, yogurt, and cheese:

- **Milk.** All fresh milk has been pasteurized, or heated to a certain temperature to destroy harmful bacteria. This process increases the length of time you can store milk. Milk can also be homogenized. Homogenized means the fat particles have been broken up and evenly distributed throughout the milk. If milk is not homogenized, the fat—or cream—rises to the top.

- **Yogurt.** Yogurt has a smooth, thick texture with a tangy flavor. It's available plain or flavored. Frozen yogurt is a popular substitute for ice cream because it's often lower in fat. Because yogurt products vary in calories and fat, check labels carefully.

- **Cheese.** Cheese is another popular dairy product available in dozens of varieties. To make cheese, milk is first thickened. The solid part, or *curd,* is separated from the liquid, or *whey.* Some cheese is aged or ripened. Cheddar and Swiss cheese are examples. Cream cheese and cottage cheese aren't aged. Processed cheese (such as American) is made by combining different aged cheeses. Check labels carefully, and choose lowfat versions when possible.

How can you keep fat to a minimum when buying dairy products?

Protein foods can be frozen for longer storage. Use freezer-safe wrap or airtight containers to prevent **freezer burn** *(a white discoloration on a food that lowers quality and nutrition)*. Store legumes in a cool, dry place in a tightly covered container.

NUTRIENTS IN DAIRY FOODS

> ➤ **Your teenage years are important growing years for your body. A nutritious diet helps provide the nutrients your body needs.**

Dairy foods from the Milk, Yogurt, and Cheese Group are good sources of nutrients. Milk, yogurt, and cheese provide the best sources of calcium and riboflavin—one of the B vitamins. Dairy foods are also good sources of protein, phosphorus, and vitamins A and D. You need nutrients provided by dairy foods throughout life.

The Food Guide Pyramid recommends at least two or three servings of milk, yogurt, or cheese per day. It's also recommended that you choose lowfat versions of dairy foods when possible. Although these products have fewer calories and less fat, they still contain the same important nutrients.

PREPARING DAIRY FOODS

A lot of dairy products you eat are convenience foods that don't require cooking. You can pour milk into a glass, eat yogurt, or snack on a cube of cheese.

However, you may decide to make a melted cheese sandwich, macaroni and cheese, or a cup of cocoa, which all need to be cooked. What should you keep in mind?

- Use low heat when cooking dairy food. High heat will **scorch,** or *burn,* heat-sensitive proteins in dairy foods.
- Cover the pan when you're heating milk to prevent a film from forming on top. If you don't use a cover, stir it often.

- Follow directions for cooking time and temperature when heating milk in a microwave oven. As you know, microwaves cook very fast. Turn off the power as soon as milk starts to foam. Then stir the milk after heating to distribute heat evenly.

Storing Milk, Yogurt, and Cheese

Here are some helpful tips for storing milk, yogurt, and cheese:
- Keep fresh milk in the refrigerator in its original container.
- Store unopened canned, nonfat dry, or UHT (ultra high temperature) milk in a dry, cool place. Store opened canned and UHT milk in the refrigerator.
- Transfer nonfat dry milk to an airtight container after opening.
- Refrigerate nonfat dry milk after mixing with water.

Corn and Potato Chowder

Amount	Ingredient
2 cups	Whole kernel corn, frozen
2 cups	Potatoes, frozen, diced or shredded
1½ cups	Chicken broth, lowfat
1 12 oz. can	Evaporated skim milk
2 Tbsp.	All-purpose flour
½ tsp.	Garlic salt
¼ tsp.	Pepper

Yield: 4 servings

DIRECTIONS
Pan: 3-quart saucepan with cover
Temperature: Low heat
1. Combine corn, potatoes, chicken broth, garlic salt, and pepper in a 3-quart saucepan; bring to a boil.
2. Reduce heat to a simmer and cook, covered, for 5 minutes or until vegetables are tender. *Do not drain liquid from the vegetables.*
3. Gradually stir the milk into the flour in a small bowl.
4. Add the milk mixture to the saucepan.
5. Cook and stir over low heat until mixture becomes thick and bubbly. Then cook and stir one more minute.
6. Ladle chowder into serving bowls and serve hot.

Nutrition Information
- **Per serving (approximate):** 230 calories, 15g protein, 44 g carbohydrate, 1 g fat, 2 mg cholesterol, 230 mg sodium
- **Good source of:** calcium, phosphorus, vitamin D, potassium, riboflavin, and niacin.

Chapter Summary

- Meat, poultry, fish, dry beans, eggs, and nuts are protein foods that contain varying amounts of fat.
- Use low to moderate cooking temperatures when cooking protein foods.
- The best way to comparison-shop for protein foods is to consider the cost per serving.
- Tender cuts of meat are usually cooked by a dry-heat method and less tender cuts by a moist-heat method.
- You can determine whether meat is thoroughly cooked by checking the internal temperature using a meat thermometer.
- Dairy foods are good sources of calcium and protein and also contain several important vitamins.
- The protein in dairy products is heat-sensitive at high temperatures.

Reviewing the Chapter

1. Give two examples of complete protein and two examples of incomplete protein foods.
2. Where are the two places fat is often found on cuts of meat?
3. Why is it best to use low to moderate temperatures when cooking protein foods?
4. Explain why it's risky to thaw meat, poultry, and fish at room temperature.
5. Why is it important to cook poultry and ground meat thoroughly, and what is a safe internal temperature for cooked ground meat and poultry?
6. Identify four ways to lower the fat when selecting and eating protein foods.
7. Why are dried beans usually soaked in water before cooking?
8. Describe what happens when you use high heat to cook dairy foods.

Family & Community

With Your Family

Talk with your family about ways you can lower the fat content of the protein foods you generally purchase and eat. Try one or more of the suggestions and decide whether you would like to continue using these ideas.

In Your Community

Your school board has asked that more milk products be included in school lunches. Your committee assignment is to help plan lunch menus for two weeks, including at least six different milk product dishes each week.

Review & Activities

Thinking Critically

1. **Determine reliability.** If you read an advertisement stating that a new product contained higher quality protein than meat, poultry, fish, or eggs, how would you determine the reliability of the statement?

2. **Analyze the situation.** Why do you think many people make meat the centerpiece of their meal planning? What suggestions would you offer to highlight other foods during meal planning?

3. **Compare and contrast.** Which protein food do you consider the most underrated one? Why do you think this is the case? What could be done to make this protein more popular?

Making Connections

1. **Social Studies.** In general, protein foods are more expensive than foods in other food groups. Investigate the major protein sources of foods in different areas of the world. What factors have influenced the importance of these proteins in different cultures?

2. **Language Arts.** Compose a one-minute radio bulletin about the importance of cooking chicken and ground meat thoroughly to prevent foodborne illness.

Applying Your Learning

1. **Explore ideas.** Look for recipes in which dairy foods could be added to increase the nutritional value of the dish. Try one or two of these ideas and evaluate the results.

2. **Get more for less.** Discuss ways of choosing and preparing protein foods economically to get good nutritional value for less money. Try at least one suggestion and discuss its merits.

3. **Foods lab.** Prepare scrambled eggs using whole eggs, an egg-substitute product, and egg whites. Compare the nutritional value and taste of each.

What Would You Do?

You have a 75-year-old neighbor who has found out that she has brittle bones that can be easily broken, a condition called osteoporosis. She has been told to include more calcium in her diet. What suggestions could you offer her?

Career Network

ENGINEERING AND INDUSTRIAL

DRAFTER

Manufacturing company seeks drafter to develop drawings.
- Post-secondary technical training required.
- Strong problem-solving abilities needed.
- Computer-aided drafting and design (CAD) experience necessary.

ROBOTICS TECHNICIAN

Large manufacturing firm seeks robotics technician with technical skills in electronics, computer programming, and numeric control.
- Must set-up, operate, and perform maintenance on robotics equipment.
- Post-secondary technical training required.

PRODUCTION ASSOCIATES

Window manufacturer seeks production associates to work second shift in state-of-the-art factory.
- Heavy lifting required.
- High school diploma, good work record necessary.
- Hourly wage and benefits provided.

INDUSTRIAL ENGINEER

Fiberglass manufacturer has a challenging opportunity for an industrial engineer. Conduct time studies, design experiments, and improve work procedures in home building products division.
- Bachelor's degree and experience required.
- Excellent problem solving and communications skills needed.

ELECTRONICS TECHNICIAN

Growing aerospace manufacturing company has immediate opening for electronics technician to assist in developing and testing electronic circuits for use in aircraft equipment.
- Computer programming skills desired.
- Bachelor's degree required.

MANUFACTURING TECHNICIAN

Machine tool manufacturer needs technician to work closely with engineers and operators.
- Responsible for keeping equipment running and integrating new machinery into production.
- Associate's degree in electronics required.
- Knowledge of mechanics and hydraulics needed.

More Career Options

Entry Level
- Computer Support Specialist
- CNC Operator
- Hydraulic Repairer
- Cable Splicing Technician

Technical Level
- Aircraft Mechanic
- Fiber Optic Technician
- Laser Technician
- Automobile Technician
- Local Area Network (LAN) Specialist

Professional Level
- Quality Assurance Technician
- Mechanical Engineer
- Safety Inspector
- Materials Engineer
- Aerospace Engineer

MIS ADMINISTRATOR

Electronic supply company seeks highly motivated MIS administrator to support and maintain computer hardware and software applications.
• Requires ability to set up new systems and troubleshoot problems.
• Associate's degree required, bachelor's degree preferred.

COMPUTER PROGRAMMER

Consulting firm seeks qualified programmer to update and change software products used in the construction industry.
• Bachelor's degree in computer science required.
• Must be comfortable working in a small, team environment.
• Tuition reimbursement available.

SYSTEMS ANALYST

Home and auto insurance company has opening for an experienced systems analyst. Evaluate current computer systems and propose new systems.
• Bachelor's degree a must.
• Excellent communications skills required.
• Non-smoking environment.

NETWORK ANALYST

Expanding office needs analyst to manage, install, and upgrade networking software.
• Must also maintain web site and provide technical support to staff.
• Excellent communication skills necessary.
• Associate's degree and experience required.

Linking School to Career

1. Your Career Plan: There is more computer power in today's automobiles than in rockets that carried people to the moon in the 1970s. Computers have not only changed the way automobiles operate; they have also changed the way most businesses operate. For example, list all of the jobs you can think of that are found at an automobile dealership. Do these jobs require the use of computers? Were computers used in these jobs 30 years ago? Does the career you are considering require computer skills?

2. Researching Careers: Most manufacturing companies in the past required employees to work in hot, dusty plants. How have the following changed the manufacturing environment: addition of robots and computers, increase in the number of plastic parts, decrease in the number of metal parts, new health and safety laws, and concern for the environment?

3. Math: Many manufacturing and industrial careers require the heavy use of math skills. Identify several manufacturing and industrial careers that interest you. Research which require math skills. Then examine your own skills. What are your strengths and weaknesses regarding math? Make a plan to improve your math skills.

Unit 10

Clothing

Clothing That Suits You

YOU WILL LEARN . . .

➤ How to develop a wardrobe plan.
➤ Ways to select attractive clothes using the elements and principles of design.
➤ Guidelines for shopping for clothes.

TERMS TO LEARN . . .

➤ accessories
➤ clothing inventory
➤ elements of design
➤ fads
➤ fashions
➤ illusion
➤ multipurpose clothes
➤ principles of design
➤ silhouette

Imagine ...

... you notice an outfit in your favorite color pictured in a department store's sale flyer. It would be perfect for the school dance on Friday. You can't wait to get to the store. Studying your reflection in the dressing room, your excitement dims. It doesn't look as nice as you'd hoped. But you have enough money with you and it's a very good deal.

Think About

• Have you ever had this experience?
• What would you do in this situation?
• If a parent or friend offered his or her opinion about the outfit, would you listen?

PLANNING YOUR WARDROBE

When you look around at a group of people, do the clothes they wear tell you anything about them? Someone may have on jeans or a shirt with a designer label. Another person may appear not to have given much thought to his or her clothes at all. Still another may sport a well-coordinated outfit. Although everyone dresses differently, clothes convey messages about how a person wants to be seen by others.

A wardrobe that works well for you doesn't just happen. It takes time and effort to find clothes that you enjoy wearing and that mix and match well together. When you make that effort, you feel better about the way you look. When you look good, your self-esteem improves and you feel more able to cope with life's challenges.

➤ **This teen is taking a clothing inventory of his closet to determine his clothing needs. How** do you determine your clothing needs?

Taking an Inventory

The best way to begin planning your wardrobe is to take a look at what you already have. Making *an organized list of your clothes* is called taking a **clothing inventory.** A clothing inventory helps you decide what clothing you need to fill the gaps in your wardrobe. When taking your clothing inventory, sort your clothing into the following groups:

- Clothing you like and wear regularly.
- Clothing you don't want.
- Clothing you're undecided about.

Now look again at the clothing items in your "undecided" pile. Would repairing or updating some clothes make them workable in your wardrobe? If so, add these garments to your inventory list. What about the clothes in the "don't want" pile? Perhaps you could give them to someone else—a sibling, friend, or charitable organization.

➤ **Many charitable organizations accept donated clothes.** What do you do with your unwanted clothes?

Planning New Purchases

After you complete your clothing inventory, look over your lists. Do you see any gaps? You should have the greatest amount of clothing for the activities you're involved in most often.

Planning helps you make choices that will improve your wardrobe. Keep the following tips in mind:

- **Needs and wants.** Which items do you really need? Which do you want but could get along without? Needs are usually more important than wants.
- **Budget.** How much money do you have to spend on clothes? Which clothing needs are most important?
- **Versatility.** To stretch your wardrobe, look for **multi-purpose clothes,** or *clothes that can be used in a variety of situations.* For example, a sweater could be both casual and dressy, depending on how you combine it with other clothes. Shop for separates. Shirts, pants, jeans, skirts, sweaters, vests, and jackets are all separates. These garments can be combined to make several outfits. Select colors that go with clothing you already own, so you can match them up to make several different outfits.
- **Fashion.** Be aware that advertising, fashion, and fads can influence what you want. **Fashions** are *styles that are*

You can actually dress in a way that saves energy. Just remember these guidelines:

• Dark colors can help you stay warm by absorbing heat from the sun. Light colors help you feel cooler in sunlight.

• Close-fitting clothes trap body heat to keep you warmer. To feel cooler, wear clothes with large neck, arm, and leg openings, open-type shoes, and fewer accessories.

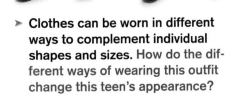

➤ **Clothes can be worn in different ways to complement individual shapes and sizes.** How do the different ways of wearing this outfit change this teen's appearance?

currently popular. Some fashions are considered **fads,** or *fashions that last only a short time.* It's usually not wise to spend a lot of money on fads, because you won't wear them very long. Fashion-wise people usually invest in classics, styles that are fashionable over a longer period. Classics you might consider are jeans, slacks, white or neutral-colored shirts, or solid-colored sweaters.

• **Accessories.** Using **accessories,** *small items of clothing that complete an outfit,* is an inexpensive way to update your wardrobe. Belts, ties, scarves, and jewelry can give a new look to the clothes you already own.

INDIVIDUALIZING YOUR CLOTHING

Every person is a unique individual with a different personality, a specific body shape, and certain hair and complexion characteristics. Your clothing can also work for you as another part of individualizing your look.

How can you make your clothes work for you? One way is to use **illusion,** which influences or leads the eye to see *something that doesn't actually exist.* Illusion can make a short person appear taller and a tall person shorter. You can use illusion to make yourself look slimmer or heavier, or to draw attention to your best features. You can create your own illusions by using the basic elements and principles of design.

Elements of Design

You can use the **elements of design**—*line, color, texture, shape, and pattern*—to your advantage in dressing. Understanding how these elements work will help you choose styles that look good on you. See pages 542–543 for more information on the elements of design.

• **Line.** Line guides eye movement up and down or across an area. An important line in a garment is the *outline,* or **silhouette.**

- **Shape.** Shape is the form created when lines are combined. Shapes within a garment might include sleeves, cuffs, pockets, and pant legs.
- **Pattern.** The arrangement of lines, shapes, and colors in a fabric, garment, or outfit makes a pattern.
- **Texture.** Texture is the surface characteristic that you see or feel in a fabric.
- **Color.** Color is one of the most important design elements. The best colors for you are the ones that flatter the color of your hair, skin, and eyes. One good clue is to think about which of your clothes bring you the most compliments. Try holding up different colors to your face and looking in a mirror. Which colors are most flattering? Do you look better in bright or soft colors? Do certain colors seem to make your eyes and hair shine?

Principles of Design

Just as the principles of baking tell you how to combine the ingredients for cookies, the **principles of design**—*proportion, emphasis, harmony, scale, balance, and rhythm*—help you combine the ingredients, or elements, of design to fit you and your personality. See page 548-549 for more information on the principles of design.

SHOPPING FOR CLOTHES

What are your shopping experiences usually like? No one is born with total shopping savvy. You can learn to be a smart consumer and a satisfied one, too. Armed with a plan and some thought, you'll probably be happier with your choices.

SELECT QUALITY CLOTHING

Signs of quality are:
- Machine stitching that is straight and even.
- Seams are smooth and straight, and stitches are even without signs of puckering, edges are finished.
- The garment hem is even and parallel to the floor.
- Plaids and stripes are matched at the seams.
- Areas of strain are reinforced.
- Buttonholes are closely stitched and reinforced; openings fit the buttons and lie flat when closed.
- Zippers zip easily. When closed, zippers lie flat and are covered by the fabric.

➤ **Fabrics require different methods of care.** What methods do you know about caring for your clothes?

Using the Elements of Design

Vertical lines run lengthwise. These lines can make the body seem taller than it is.

Horizontal lines run from side to side. These lines can lead the eyes across the body, making it seem broader.

Bulky textures, such as the fluffy yarn in this sweater and the corduroy in the slacks, tend to add apparent size. Smooth textures produce the opposite effect.

Shiny textures, as in the fabric of this shirt and slacks, tend to give the illusion of increased size.

Subtle patterns can blend to give the illusion of a solid color.

Bold patterns can draw attention and give the illusion of increased size.

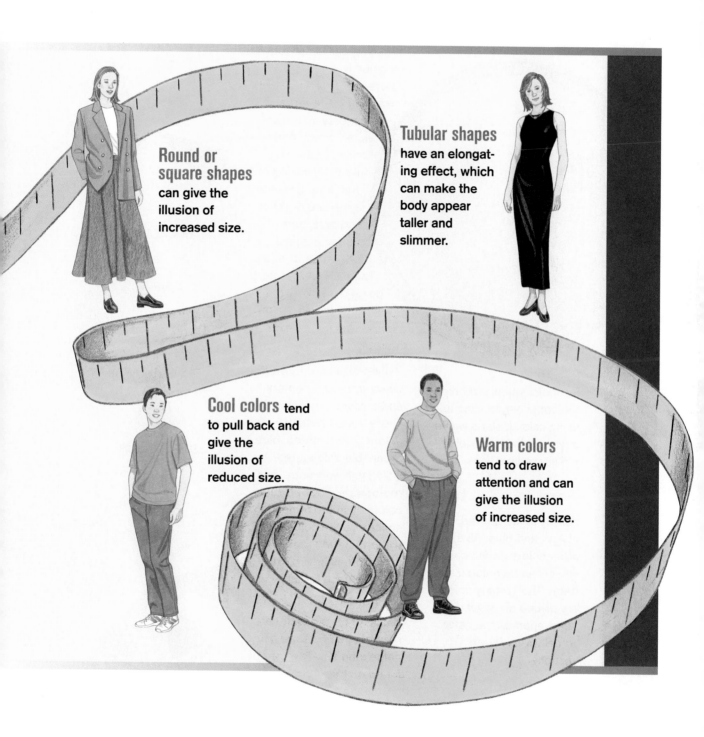

Round or square shapes can give the illusion of increased size.

Tubular shapes have an elongating effect, which can make the body appear taller and slimmer.

Cool colors tend to pull back and give the illusion of reduced size.

Warm colors tend to draw attention and can give the illusion of increased size.

Using Color

The color wheel image shows all twelve colors labeled: YELLOW, Yellow-Orange, ORANGE, Red-Orange, RED, Red-Violet, VIOLET, Blue-Violet, BLUE, Blue-Green, GREEN, Yellow-Green.

Secondary colors are formed when two primary colors are mixed in equal amounts. The three secondary colors are violet, green, and orange. Violet is made by mixing red and blue. Green is a mixture of yellow and blue, and orange is made from red and yellow. The secondary colors go on the color wheel halfway between the primary colors from which they are made.

Tertiary colors are formed when you mix a primary and a secondary color. There are six tertiary colors: yellow-green, blue-green, blue-violet, red-violet, yellow-orange, and red-orange. These tertiary colors fill in the remaining spaces on the color wheel. (Note that the primary color comes first in the name of each tertiary color.)

Black, gray, and white are neutral colors, as are ivory, beige, and tan. They're not found on the color wheel.

The color wheel is a helpful tool for understanding and using color. It starts with a circle divided into twelve pie-shaped sections.

The Color Wheel

Primary colors are red, yellow, and blue. All the other colors on the color wheel can be made from them. The primary colors are placed an equal distance apart on the color wheel (every fourth section).

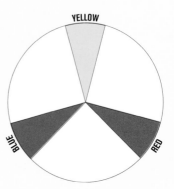

PRIMARY COLORS

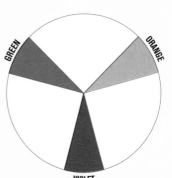

SECONDARY COLORS

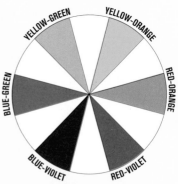

TERTIARY COLORS

Color Schemes

There are a number of color schemes, or combinations, that are pleasing to the eye. As you can see, each one is based on the color wheel.

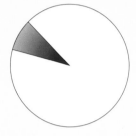

Monochromatic scheme uses variations of only one color. For example, you could combine light and dark, dull and bright greens.

Complementary scheme is made up of two colors directly opposite each other on the color wheel. Examples are blue and orange, red and green, and yellow and violet.

Triadic color scheme uses three colors the same distance from one another on the color wheel. For example, the primary colors—red, blue, and yellow— form a triadic scheme.

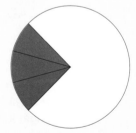

Analogous color scheme is made up of two or more colors next to each other on the color wheel. Blue-green, green, and blue, for example, form an analogous color scheme.

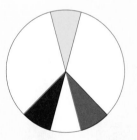

Split-complementary scheme results when a color is combined with colors on each side of its complement. Blue, red-orange, and yellow-orange form a split-complementary scheme.

The Effects of Color

In the study of color, it's important to understand and control the effects of color. The qualities shown here can make a difference in your appearance.

Value is the lightness or darkness of a color. Compare the lightest value of red, pink, with its darkest value, maroon. Light values are called tints and dark values are shades. Value also can make things look larger or smaller. For example, dark pants can make the lower half of the body appear slimmer.

Intensity describes how bright or dull a color appears. A color at full intensity, such as bright red, tends to stand out. Colors with lower intensity, such as dusty rose, are less obvious. In general, low-intensity colors are often used for large pieces, such as jackets and pants. Bright colors are better for accents, such as tops and accessories.

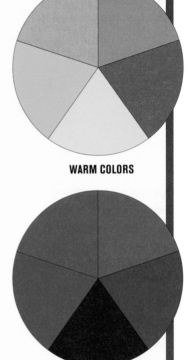

WARM COLORS

COOL COLORS

DARK VALUE

LIGHT VALUE

LOW INTENSITY

HIGH INTENSITY

Colors can make you feel **warm or cool**. Yellow, orange, and red colors are associated with warmth. Warm colors also make areas appear larger and closer to you. Green, blue, and violet colors may remind you of cool water, trees, and sky. Cool colors tend to make areas look smaller and farther away.

Getting Ready to Shop

Develop a game plan before your next shopping trip. After you've taken a clothing inventory, you have a good idea about what clothes you need. Do your needs fit into your family's budget or will you use your own money? Then prioritize your "needs" list and buy the highest priority items first.

Shopping Strategies

Stick with your list. Purchase the clothing you need to fill out your wardrobe. You may not always be able to locate the exact item you want. If not, decide what would be the best substitute.

Some other checkpoints to keep in mind when you shop include:

- **Check the care label.** Make sure you can give the garment proper care. A "dry clean only" garment means continuing costs.
- **Check the price tag.** Will the price of the the clothing fit into your budget? Remember, a sale item is only a good buy if it meets your needs.
- **Check the fit.** Try the garment on to be sure it doesn't pull or wrinkle or feel uncomfortable when you move around.
- **Check the quality.** Buy the best quality you can afford. Remember, the garment will have to stand up to the strain of being worn and laundered frequently.

Deciding to Buy

After checking the care instructions, price, fit, and quality, you should have a good idea whether a garment is right for you. Don't buy anything if you have doubts about it.

Check the exchange or return policies before you buy. If a store's policy is "exchanges only, no returns," you know you won't get your money back. Instead, you're able to exchange an item for one of equal value. Keep the sales receipt until you're absolutely certain you won't return the item.

RESPONSIBLE SHOPPING

Here are some tips for responsible shopping:

- Avoid wearing jewelry that could snag or catch on clothing.
- Carefully remove clothes from hangers when you try them on. Unbutton buttons and unzip zippers.
- If you wear makeup, be careful not to get it on the clothes. Make sure your hands are clean.
- Tell a salesclerk if you find a damaged garment.
- When you're through trying on a garment, return it to the rack or a salesclerk if you don't buy it.
- Don't shoplift. Shoplifting is illegal. Most stores turn shoplifters over to the police.

Using the Principles of Design

The principles of design have been tested for centuries and apply to all art forms. The drawings on these pages demonstrate how the design principles of proportion, emphasis, harmony, scale, balance, and rhythm are used to enhance clothing.

Proportion involves the relationship of one part to another and to the whole. If you make one section of your body look long, wide, or large, then another section will appear shorter, narrower or smaller. With a shirt tucked in, slacks seem to lengthen the leg. Wearing a longer shirt creates the illusion of shorter-looking legs.

Emphasis is the point of interest that the eyes see first. Emphasis can be used to draw attention to your best features. A splash of color in a tie or scarf highlights the face. A bright belt could emphasize a slim waist.

Harmony is the feeling that all parts of a design belong together. That doesn't mean that everything has to match. Variety is interesting if the design details grouped together have something in common, such as style, shape, color, or size.

Rhythm is the feeling of movement, leading the eye around the garment or outfit. Repeating one or more design elements creates this movement. For example, there's rhythm in repeating the colors of an outfit in a coordinating scarf or in choosing square patch pockets to repeat a jacket's boxy shape.

Balance gives a feeling of equal weight among all parts of a design. Balance can be symmetrical or asymmetrical. Symmetrical balance occurs when one side of a garment or outfit seems like a mirror reflection of the other. Asymmetrical balance occurs when the two sides of the garment or outfit are different in size, form, texture, or color. Think of a jacket that buttons to one side rather than down the center front.

Scale refers to the overall size of a design detail or its size compared to other details. For example, a very large plaid seems even larger in a short, slim skirt on a small person. The two are considered out of scale with each other.

Review & Activities

Chapter Summary

- Taking a clothing inventory is a good first step in organizing your wardrobe.
- Planning your clothing purchases can help you make choices that will improve your wardrobe.
- Use the elements and principles of design to choose styles to individualize your clothing.
- The best colors for your wardrobe are the ones that complement your hair, skin, and eyes.
- Developing a shopping plan will help you to be more satisfied with your purchases.
- Examine the labels, price, construction, and fit of clothes carefully before you purchase them.
- Check the store's exchange or return policy before you buy.

Reviewing the Chapter

1. How can taking a clothing inventory help you plan your wardrobe?
2. List four points to keep in mind as you plan your clothing purchases.
3. Identify five elements of design. Briefly explain each one.
4. How can you determine the colors that look best on you?
5. Identify six principles of design. Briefly explain each one.
6. What are two important steps you can take before you get ready to shop for clothes?
7. List four important points to consider before you make a clothing purchase.
8. Suggest four ways you can be a more responsible clothing shopper.

Family & Community

With Your Family

Talk with your family about your clothing wish list. Discuss how your wish list fits into the larger family clothing budget.

In Your Community

Find out what local or national organizations hold clothing drives for needy families. When are these drives held? How can you and other community members offer assistance?

Thinking Critically

1. **Determine reliability.** How can catalogs and magazines be useful in planning your wardrobe purchases? In what ways are they not helpful?

2. **Analyze meaning.** Consider this statement, "Clothing is what you need for school, work, and leisure. Fashion is the icing, the nonessential." Do you agree or disagree? Explain why.

3. **Analyze the situation.** How does your current lifestyle affect your clothing needs? Which activities require special clothes? What lifestyle changes, such as taking a part-time job, might change your clothing needs?

4. **Draw conclusions.** Why is it helpful to understand the color wheel, color schemes, and the effects of color when purchasing your clothes? Give an example to illustrate your thoughts.

Making Connections

1. **Art.** Find a clothing design that would minimize one of the following: wide shoulders; long, thin legs; short arms; large hips; small chest.

2. **Math.** After you take a clothing inventory, look carefully at the clothes you are undecided about. Estimate how much it would cost to repair or update them to include in your wardrobe.

Applying Your Learning

1. **Collect examples.** Use magazines, catalogs, and newspapers to find examples of clothes that are fads and classics. Discuss the reasons for your choices. Which would you choose for your wardrobe? Why?

2. **Role-play buying influences.** Develop a role-play that illustrates how peer pressure influences teens' clothing choices. Discuss the impact of peer pressure in clothing choices. How easy or difficult is it to dress in your own individual style?

3. **Focus on a basic.** Describe, find a picture, or draw a versatile basic outfit you would like. How many different looks could you create by combining it with clothes and accessories you already own?

What Would You Do?

Imagine you're shopping with a group of friends. One of your friends shoplifts an inexpensive item. You don't believe anyone else saw the incident. Personally, you know shoplifting is wrong, but what would you do about your friend's actions?

Fibers and Fabrics

YOU WILL LEARN . . .

➤ The features of natural and manufactured fibers.
➤ Characteristics of common fibers.
➤ The different methods of making fabric.
➤ Why fabric finishes are important.

TERMS TO LEARN . . .

➤ fibers
➤ generic name
➤ manufactured fibers
➤ natural fibers
➤ trade name

Imagine ...

... that you're an old cotton T-shirt that's had a long life. You've been squished in a basket for days on end, washed at least 300 times, and tumbled around with a perfume-scented scrap of tissue for hours on end. Your color has faded, but your fibers remain fairly strong. Sometimes you think it would be a relief to go to the rag bag.

Think About

• Do you have a favorite garment that you've worn forever?
• What makes it such a favorite?
• Why do you think so many people like cotton garments?

FIBERS

Fibers are *hairlike substances that are twisted together to make yarns and fabric.* Just as each of your friends has unique personality traits, different fibers have unique characteristics. The characteristics of fibers include traits such as moisture absorbency, strength, stretchability, and heat sensitivity. There are two groups of fibers—natural and manufactured.

- **Natural fibers.** From plant and animal sources, **natural fibers** are *produced by nature.* They include cotton, linen, ramie, wool, and silk, among others.
- **Manufactured fibers.** Made from substances such as wood pulp, petroleum, and coal, **manufactured fibers** are *produced in laboratories through chemical processes.* Chemical engineers have designed these fibers to have special characteristics.

Natural Fibers

Cotton, linen, and ramie are natural fibers that come from plants. Natural fibers have been used for thousands of years. Your favorite cotton jeans are made from the same type of cotton fiber that people made their clothes from in the fourth century. Of course, the fabric construction and style are different, but the fiber is the same.

- **Cotton.** As the most widely used natural fiber, the characteristics of cotton have contributed to its popularity. It absorbs moisture, which makes it comfortable to wear in hot weather. It's strong, easy to launder, and dyes well, which makes it suitable for many uses. Its negative features, such as wrinkling and shrinking, can be corrected with special finishes. Garment tags will inform you about this.
- **Linen.** A product of the flax plant, linen is strong, absorbent, and can be laundered. Because linen wrinkles easily, it's either used in garments featuring the "wrinkled look" or has a wrinkle-resistant finish applied.

- **Ramie.** From the stalks of a shrub-like plant, ramie is grown mainly in Southeast Asia. It's very strong and durable. Ramie absorbs moisture and dries quickly. Since it's brittle when dry and wrinkles easily, ramie is often combined with other fibers, such as cotton or linen.

- **Wool.** Made from the fleece of sheep, wool is valued for its warmth. Wool fibers trap air and prevent the loss of body heat. Wool wears well, resists wrinkling, absorbs moisture and still feels dry. It shrinks when washed in hot water, so wool is usually dry cleaned or washed in cold water. When exposed to very high heat, wool burns easily. Wool can also be damaged by insects, such as moths, so it's sometimes treated for moth resistance.

- **Silk.** Spun by silkworms, silk is the strongest of the natural fibers. It's comfortable to wear because it absorbs body moisture and resists wrinkles. It's usually dry cleaned, but some silks can be hand washed. Silk drapes well and can be dyed with bright colors.

Manufactured Fibers

Many manufactured fibers now mimic popular natural fibers because they look, feel, and act like them. Manufactured fibers have many desirable qualities. They're generally strong. They have the ability to spring back to their original shape, so they don't wrinkle and are easy to maintain. Almost all manufactured fibers repel water rather than absorb it. As a result, they dry quickly and shrink very little. Because they don't absorb water, however, they feel hot and uncomfortable to wear on warm days. Newer manufacturing processes have helped to make them more absorbent, and as a result, more comfortable to wear.

➤ **Liquid nylon is forced through a spinnerette and then hardens into fibers.** What items can you make with this manufactured fiber?

You may have some of the following manufactured fibers in your wardrobe. Your favorite shirt may have some polyester, which resists wrinkles and looks neat when you wear it. Your active sportswear could be made from spandex, which stretches and springs back into shape. All of these favorable characteristics are possible because of manufactured fibers.

You've heard the names. Now learn what these fabrics are and how they are used:

- **Broadcloth.** Closely woven plain-weave fabric; mostly cotton; used for shirts and sportswear.

- **Burlap.** Rough-textured fabric; made of jute; used for accessories.

- **Flannel.** Soft, napped fabric; made of cotton, wool, or rayon; used for shirts, nightwear, and sheets.

- **Fleece.** Thick, lightweight nap; used for warm jackets and sweatsuits.

- **Madras.** Plain-weave cotton in plaids, checks, or stripes with noncolorfast dyes that "bleed"; used for shirts and sportswear.

- **Seersucker.** Plain weave with puckered stripes; made of cotton or a blend; used for sportswear and summer suits.

- **Acetate.** With its high luster and slick surface, acetate is commonly used for evening wear and as lining fabric. It's comfortable to wear, but acetate doesn't wear well because it's a weak fiber.

- **Acrylic.** Known for warmth without weight, acrylic fabric can be woven or knitted. It's machine washable and wrinkle-resistant, but it also pills, or forms small matted balls on the surface.

- **Nylon.** Noted for its strength and durability, nylon's ability to repel water makes it useful for clothing and various commercial uses. You'll find nylon made into hosiery, swimwear, carpets, and car tires.

- **Polyester.** One of the most popular manufactured fibers, polyester is used alone or blended with other fibers. It's most often mixed with cotton to make easy-care shirts, pants, sheets, and tablecloths. You may have found it as a filler in parkas, jackets, and comforters. Why? Because it stays fluffy even when wet.

- **Rayon.** The first manufactured fiber, rayon is used in a variety of clothes and household textiles. It's comfortable to wear and is often combined with other fibers. Rayon is specially treated to minimize wrinkling and shrinking.

- **Spandex.** Another high-performance fiber, spandex stretches and can easily recover its original shape. It's made into elastics, undergarments, sportswear, and swimwear.

Each manufactured fiber has two names, a generic name and a trade name. The **generic name** is *a common name for a group of similar fibers.* A **trade name,** or *the manufacturer's name,* is given to a specific fiber that a company produces. Every manufactured fiber is put into a group depending on the materials from which it's made. For example, Dacron®, Fortrel®, Kodel®, and Trevira® are all trade names for polyester fibers. All members of the polyester family have similar characteristics and need the same type of care. Labels on garments and fabrics may carry both names, but they're more likely to include the generic term only.

The newest manufactured fiber, however, is known only by its trade name, Tencel®. Produced from wood pulp, Tencel's generic name is lyocell. It's a strong fiber and it makes soft, fluid machine-washable fabrics. It's popular for casual shirts, pants, and skirts.

Blends

Every fiber has good qualities. But no fiber is perfect. As a result, manufacturers have developed fabric blends, fabrics containing two or more fibers. Blends combine the best qualities of each fiber. As an example, mixing cotton and polyester provides the moisture absorbency and comfortable wear of cotton, and the quick drying, wrinkle- and shrink-resistance of polyester.

FABRIC CONSTRUCTION

Fibers are twisted together to make yarns. These yarns are usually about the thickness of sewing thread. Yarns are then put together to form fabric. The final yarn arrangement affects the wear you can expect from the fabric. It also affects the care a fabric needs. Three common methods of making fabric from yarn are weaving, knitting, and bonding.

TAKE NOTE

Microfibers

Microfiber is a new textile term for superfine manufactured fibers. It's said that the fibers are four times finer than a spider's thread. Nylon microfiber fabrics are used mostly in activewear. Polyester microfibers are popular for luxurious blouses, skiwear, and rainwear. The fabric repels water, yet it's comfortable to wear. Polyester microfibers have the look and feel of fine silk, but they wear better, are less expensive, and can be washed like other polyesters.

When you shop, examine garment labels. How many contain microfibers?

➤ Fabric blends contain two or more fibers. This shirt resists wrinkles because it is a blend of cotton and polyester. Name some commonly blended fabrics.

Weaving

In weaving, lengthwise and crosswise yarns are laced together at right angles. The tightness of the weave determines the firmness of the fabric and affects how it will wear. Generally, tightly woven fabrics wear better than loosely woven fabrics. Four basic types of weaves are used to make fabric.

PLAIN

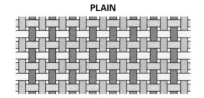

TWILL

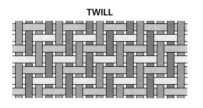

SATIN

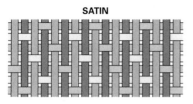

- **Plain weave.** Each crosswise yarn passes over and under each lengthwise yarn in a plain weave. Broadcloth, chambray, and canvas are examples of plain weave fabric.
- **Twill weave.** The lengthwise yarns pass over two and then under two crosswise yarns in twill weave. You can see the diagonal ridges made by yarns on the surface of the fabric. The twill weave produces a stronger fabric than other weaves. Denim and chino are twill weaves.
- **Satin weave.** The lengthwise yarns in a satin weave pass over four or more crosswise yarns and generally under one crosswise yarn. The satin weave is shiny but not as strong as the twill or plain weave.
- **Pile weave.** Three sets of yarn are used to make the pile weave. Pile fabrics, such as velvet and corduroy, are first woven in a plain, twill, or satin weave. Then an extra set of yarns is woven in so that loops or cut ends are produced on the fabric surface.

➤ Hand-knit wearables are time-consuming to construct. Most people who knit by hand follow a pattern when making a garment.

Knitting

Another way of making fabrics is by knitting. Knitted fabrics are stretchy and comfortable. They're made by interlocking loops of yarn row after row. Yarns of various fibers, weights, and textures are knit by machine or hand. Knits are more easily snagged and pulled than woven fabric. Clothing made from knitted fabrics allows free movement. It generally holds its shape well. As with woven fabrics, knitted fabrics may be made by several different methods.

- **Single knits.** These are often used for T-shirts and simple dresses. Also called jersey, single knits have a flat, smooth appearance on the front side and horizontal loops on the backside.
- **Rib knits.** Made with two sets of needles, rib knits feature obvious vertical "ribs" on both sides. Because they're

TRY IT OUT

Weave It!

ACTIVITY

What You'll Need
- 10 strips each of two different colors of felt or construction paper
- 1 sheet of paper
- Staples and stapler

What to Do
1. Staple ten strips of one color of felt or construction paper evenly across the top of a sheet of paper with sides touching.
2. One at a time, weave strips of the second color horizontally over and under the first set of strips, following the pattern for one of the three basic weaves: plain, twill, or satin.
3. Undo your weave and repeat the steps, following the pattern for each of the other two remaining basic weaves.

To Discuss
- Describe the basic characteristics of each weave.
- Which weave was simplest to make? Which was the most difficult? Which has a distinctive diagonal pattern? Which would snag the easiest?
- For what uses would you suggest each weave? How would the tightness of the weave affect its durability?

very stretchy, they're used for close-fitting tops and stretch trims.

- **Interlock knits.** A variation of the rib knit, interlocks have an identical smooth surface on both sides. They have much less stretch, so they're used for soft casual garments of all types.

- **Double knits.** These knits are made with two interlocking layers on the front and back that can't be separated. Double knits are durable and wrinkle-resistant.

- **Tricot knits.** Narrow vertical ribs on the front and crosswise ribs on the back characterize tricot knits. They have plenty of stretchability and are run-proof, snag-resistant, and nonraveling. Undergarments and nightgowns are made of tricot knits.

➤ Weaving, knitting, and bonding are common methods of making fabric from yarn. This teen is wearing clothing from the three fabric methods. **What method of fabric construction is used most often in the clothes that you wear?**

Bonding

Bonding is a method used for making nonwoven fabrics. Fibers are mechanically or chemically joined together with steam or heat used with an adhesive. Bonding gives shape to nonwoven fabrics used for interfacing, blankets, carpet, and disposable diapers.

FABRIC FINISHES

Finishes are one of the final touches put on yarns and fabrics. Finishes change some natural characteristics of fabrics to make them more appealing and useful. A variety of finishes are applied to fabrics.

➤ **Piece-dyeing is the most common method of coloring fabric.** What are some other ways to add color and design to fabrics?

Color

Adding color to fabric is an age-old art. It's also as new as the most complex computer. Some dyes come from nature and some are developed in the lab. The way dye is applied varies. Sometimes yarn is dyed before it's woven into fabric. The most common method of dyeing is called piece dyeing. The dye is applied after the yarn is made into fabric.

Color can also be applied by using a printing process. Patterns, such as flowers or other designs, can be rolled onto fabric by using rollers or cylinders. Sometimes patterns are applied by screen printing, in which dyes are forced through a screen onto the fabric. This process is similar to stenciling.

Weaving patterns out of pre-dyed yarn is another way to create a design in fabric. Plaids and stripes are patterns that can be formed this way.

Other Finishes

A number of fabric characteristics can be changed by finishing processes. Some finishes are permanent, and some are not. It's best to check the label. Here are some finishes you'll see when you read the labels on textile products.

- **Flame-retardant.** Helps fabric resist burning.
- **Permanent or durable press.** Requires little or no ironing after washing.
- **Sanforized.** Prevents fabric from shrinking more than 1%.
- **Stain- and spot-resistant.** Helps fabric resist stains and spots.
- **Waterproof.** Prevents fabric from absorbing water.
- **Water-repellent.** Protects fabric from absorbing water but doesn't shed it completely.

Many fabric finishes can be destroyed if fabrics aren't cared for properly. Check the care labels and follow the manufacturer's directions carefully.

INFOLINK

See Chapter 42 for more information about caring for clothing.

➤ Screen printing is one method manufacturers use to add color to fabrics.

Caring for Clothing

YOU WILL LEARN . . .

➤ How to care for clothes.
➤ Ways to store clothing.
➤ How to launder and press clothes.
➤ How to make simple clothing repairs.

TERMS TO LEARN . . .

➤ dry clean
➤ ironing
➤ pressing
➤ pretreatment

Imagine . . .

. . . that the weather has turned cold and you need some warmer clothes to wear. Yours have worked their way to the back of your overcrowded closet. A few garments have funny looking yellow spots on them. Everything is wrinkled and needs to be ironed or washed again. You close your eyes and wish for a bigger closet.

Think About

• If wishing doesn't improve your closet situation, what do you think would help?
• How might you relieve the overcrowding in the closet?
• Why do you think you should check clothes at the end of a wearing season?

ROUTINE CARE

You can prevent wrinkles, stains, shrinkage, and repair problems with your clothes by taking routine, or regular, care of your clothes. This takes only a little extra time. Then, when you want to wear your favorite clothes, they'll be ready to wear and you'll look your best. Make the following steps part of your clothing care routine:

- Open all the fasteners, such as buttons, zippers, and snaps when dressing or undressing to help prevent rips and tears.
- Take your shoes off before getting in and out of pants and shorts.
- Check for stains right after taking off your clothes. Remove stains as soon as you can. The longer stains remain in clothing, the harder they are to remove.
- Check for needed repairs, such as ripped seams and loose or missing buttons. Directions for making simple repairs are at the end of this chapter.
- Put clothes that need to be washed in a laundry basket away from clean clothes.
- Hang up or fold clothes that don't need washing.

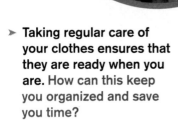

➤ **Taking regular care of your clothes ensures that they are ready when you are.** How can this keep you organized and save you time?

STORING CLOTHES

Most people complain that they never have enough storage room. You may have this problem, too. What's the solution? Organizing your belongings can make a little space seem like a lot more space.

Drawers

Use drawer dividers or drawer-size boxes to help keep your smaller items in place. Avoid packing too many clothes into a drawer. Sweaters, T-shirts, and other clothes will be less likely to wrinkle when you allow enough storage space. If drawer space is very limited, look for plastic storage containers or covered boxes that fit under a bed.

Closets

It's easy for a closet to become disorganized because you can close the door, and then you don't see the mess. The illustration below shows you how organization can come to your rescue again.

WASHING CLOTHES

Because of busy schedules, many families share the responsibility for doing the laundry. How often have you helped? It's not a difficult job, but it's not effortless. Taking time to prepare clothes for washing will help make the job easier.

Care Labels

Care labels sewn into garments are your best source of information about clothing care. If a garment is washable, the label will tell you what steps to follow in washing and drying. Care labels also tell you what *not* to do, such as "Do not bleach."

Fold pants over hangers or hang them by the bottom of the legs to keep their shape.

Hang skirts by the waist.

Hang similar clothes together, such as pants and shirts, so they're easier to find.

Shelf space is useful for hats, shoes, and folded sweaters and T-shirts.

Keep shoes in pairs to prevent them from getting jumbled together on the floor.

Sort Clothes

Sorting your clothes is important to get clothes clean, to prevent colors from running together, and to keep garments in good condition. Not all clothes can be treated the same way.

Using the care labels, sort the clothes to be machine washed into separate piles as follows:

- Delicate fabrics that require warm water and a gentle cycle.
- Sturdy white and light-colored clothing.
- Permanent press and knit fabrics.
- Dark-colored clothes.
- Heavily soiled garments that should be washed separately.

As you sort the clothes, empty all pockets. Also, close all zippers and fasten snaps, hooks, and buttons.

➤ Stains must be removed as quickly as possible. The longer a stain remains on fabric, the harder it becomes to remove.

Pretreat Clothes

Pretreatment refers to *any special attention you give a garment before laundering.* Pretreatment helps remove heavy soil and stains. Necklines and the cuffs of long-sleeve shirts often need special attention. Washing alone may not be enough to get such areas clean. Rub undiluted liquid detergent on the soiled or stained area or use a special pretreatment product. Follow label directions.

Choose Laundry Products

Many different types of products are available for doing laundry. Detergents, bleaches, and fabric softeners each have special jobs to do.

- **Detergents.** The primary job of detergent is to remove dirt from clothes. Be sure to put in the recommended amount. If too little is used, clothes won't get clean. If too much is used in an automatic washer, it's difficult to rinse out all the suds.

TRY IT OUT

Effects of Chlorine Bleach on Stains and Fabrics

ACTIVITY

What You'll Need
- 6 stained fabric samples obtained from your teacher
- Chlorine bleach
- Water
- Pan
- Tongs

What to Do
1. Observe the stains on the fabric samples. Try to identify the cause of each stain.
2. Carefully make a solution of 1 quart water and 2 tablespoons bleach.
3. Place fabric samples in the pan for 5 to 10 minutes and observe the results.

To Discuss
- Which stains did the bleach remove?
- Which fabrics were damaged by the bleach?

- **Bleaches.** Bleaches are used along with detergents to remove stains, whiten, and brighten 100 percent cotton fabrics. Nonchlorine bleach is safe to use on all washables and helps maintain whiteness if used regularly.
- **Fabric softeners.** These will reduce static cling, make fabrics softer, and reduce wrinkling. Some fabric softeners are added to the rinse cycle of the washer and others are added to the dryer in sheet form. Follow label directions for use.

➤ **Various laundry products perform different jobs.** What are some of these products and their uses?

> **Remove clothes from the washing machine soon after the cycle is finished. Wet clothes left in a dark place will sour and smell bad enough to require rewashing.**

Select Cleaning Action

Different types of clothing require different water temperatures, water levels, and wash cycles. Be sure to choose the right settings for each load of laundry according to care label instructions.

Avoid overloading the washer. A washer is fully loaded when garments placed loosely in the empty washer tub almost reach the top.

Hand Washing

Some clothes require the gentle handling of hand washing. Here are a few tips:

- Use a sink or container large enough for the clothes to move freely.
- Choose a soap or detergent to suit the clothes.
- Put water into the sink, add the detergent and mix, then add the clothes.
- Soak clothes for 5 to 30 minutes, depending on the amount of soil and detergent directions.
- Drain the sink and add fresh water. Gently squeeze sudsy water through the garments. Use at least two clean rinses to remove both suds and soil.

DRYING CLOTHES

Most clothes can be either air-dried or dried in a dryer. Generally, articles that can be washed together can be dried together. However, some need to be dried in a particular way. Check all information on the care label.

Always shake out laundered clothes before tossing them into the dryer. This will help them dry faster. Avoid overloading the dryer. Overloading increases drying time and can cause uneven drying and wrinkles.

Select the dryer setting designed for the load you're drying. Avoid overdrying clothes. This can cause shrinkage. For best results, remove clothes from the dryer promptly. Clean the lint filter each time after using the dryer to improve air circulation, dry clothes faster, and avoid a fire hazard.

Air drying is an energy-saving alternative to machine drying. After washing, place clothes on a clothesline, rack, or on plastic hangers to dry. Lay loosely woven or knit garments on a flat surface to dry.

PRESSING AND IRONING

After washing and drying, some clothes are wrinkled and need to be pressed or ironed. **Pressing** is *the process of lifting and lowering the iron onto areas of the fabric.* **Ironing** involves *moving the iron back and forth over the fabric.* Knits and wool should be pressed to avoid stretching. Most woven fabrics can be ironed.

The correct iron temperature depends on the garment's fiber content. Check the care label before pressing or ironing. If the fabric is a blend, set the iron for the fiber requiring the lowest setting. If you don't know the fiber content, test a hidden seam or hem.

Always press or iron articles that need the lowest setting first. Move to higher settings later. Begin with small areas, such as collars, sleeves, and cuffs. Then move on to the body of the garment. Press dark and wool fabrics inside-out to keep them from becoming shiny.

DRY CLEANING

Some clothing-care labels tell you to dry clean garments. To **dry clean** means *to clean with chemicals rather than with water and detergent.* The cleaned garment is then steamed to remove wrinkles. Not all fabrics can be successfully dry cleaned. Check the care label.

Two types of dry cleaning services are available. Professional dry cleaners are more expensive, yet they can remove most spots and stains. Professional pressing is part of the service. Coin-operated machines cost less, but they don't always provide special treatment for spot or stain removal. You must do your own pressing.

> Remove clothes that wrinkle from the dryer before they are completely dry and hang on a hanger. This will help eliminate wrinkles and shrinkage of the garment.

> Iron with care. Some fabrics may melt when they are ironed. Read care labels on all clothing before laundering or ironing them.

New products are appearing on the market that enable you to do your own dry cleaning at home. Be sure to follow the label directions. Most clothes will still require treatment by a professional from time to time.

► Dry cleaning saves you time, but is very expensive. Be prepared to pay a high price for the service.

CLOTHING REPAIR

Clothes kept in good repair look better and last longer. Making simple repairs is easy. Here are some of the most common problems you will find.

Rips and Tears

Ripped seams are easily repaired. Use a color of thread that matches the fabric. By hand or with a sewing machine, make a new line of stitching. Begin and end the stitching just beyond the ripped section.

Tears on your clothing can be straight, diagonal, or three-cornered. Iron-on mending tape can help you repair them. Choose a color that matches the garment. Iron the tape to the inside of the garment, following package directions.

Tears can also be repaired with patches on the right side of the garment. Choose a fabric similar to the garment fabric. Use hand or machine stitching to attach the patch to the garment.

Buttons

There are two types of buttons, sew-through and shank. With sew-through buttons, the thread comes up through the button and shows on the top side. Shank buttons have a shank, or stem, underneath to hold the thread. The shank gives you room to work the button through the buttonhole. Because sew-through buttons don't have shanks, you should make a thread shank as you sew them on. See page 574 to learn how to make a thread shank.

Snaps, Hooks, and Eyes

An opening that doesn't have much strain, such as the top of a buttoned neckline, is often fastened with a snap. Use black snaps for dark fabrics and silver ones for light-colored fabrics.

Hooks and eyes are often used to fasten openings on which there's a strain. They're often found on the ends of collars, neck edges, and waistbands. Use black hooks and eyes for dark fabrics and silver ones for light-colored fabrics. On edges that overlap, such as a waistband, use a straight eye. On edges that meet, like a neck edge, use a round eye. The drawings on page 575 show how to sew on snaps, hooks, and eyes.

To press and iron safely:
- Keep your hands and face away from steam.
- Position the cord so you can't pull the iron off the ironing board.
- Keep the iron upright when not in use.
- Turn off and unplug the iron after using.

Making a DIFFERENCE

FAIR TRADE

Jarred had an idea and knocked on Mrs. Wilton's door. When his elderly neighbor opened it, Jarred smiled and said, "I have a good offer to make you, Mrs. Wilton."

"I'm always interested in a good offer, Jarred," Mrs. Wilton answered, smiling.

"Well, nobody in the neighborhood sews like you, and I have a few shirts in bad need of some buttons and minor repairs."

"I'm all ears," said Mrs. Wilton.

"Your backyard is full of leaves, and I'd rake it in exchange for a little of your expert sewing."

Mrs. Wilton considered it. "Tell you what. You rake my backyard *and* my front yard, and you've got a deal."

Jarred put his hand out. "Let's shake on it."

Taking Action

1. If your clothes needed repairs, could you get the repairs made by bartering one of your skills?
2. What are other ways you might consider having repairs made on your clothes?

HOW to...

Replace Buttons

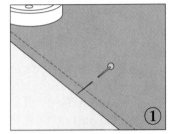

1. Place a pin where the missing button is to be located. Select a matching thread color.
2. Double the thread in the needle and knot both ends together. Bring the needle up from the wrong side to the right side of the garment.
3. Take a small stitch to secure the thread knot.
4. Remove the pin you used to locate the button.
5. Bring the needle through the button. Place a toothpick across the top of the button to allow for a thread shank.
6. Make several stitches through the fabric, the button, and over the toothpick.
7. Remove the toothpick. Bring the needle and thread between the button and the fabric. Wrap the thread around the threads under the button several times to make a thread shank.
8. Bring the needle back to the wrong side of the fabric and fasten the thread securely to the fabric. Clip the thread.
9. Your finished button.

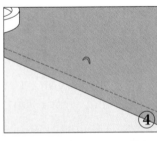

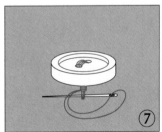

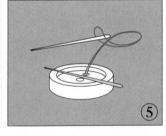

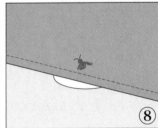

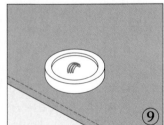

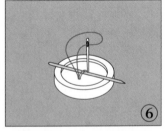

Sewing Snaps, HOOKS, AND EYES

Sewing on Snaps

- Start with the ball section of the snap. It is usually sewn to the underside of the overlap.

- Place the ball section of the snap about ⅛-inch (3 mm) from the edge of the overlap. Make several small stitches close together in each hole of the snap using a single thread in the needle. Sew through only one layer of fabric so that stitches don't show on the right side.

- Pin the closing together and mark the socket location, or flat part of the snap. Mark the position of the socket by placing a pin through the center hole of the ball section. Sew the socket section in place as you did the ball section.

- When going from hole to hole, slide the needle through one hole and under the snap to the next hole. Fasten the thread when finished.

Sewing Hooks and Eyes

- Place the hook on the underside of the overlap at least ⅛-inch (3 mm) from the edge. Using small stitches and a single thread in the needle, stitch around each loop or ring. Sew through only one layer of fabric so the stitches won't show on the right side.

- Bring the needle between the two thicknesses of fabric to the end of the hook. Take three to four stitches around the end of the hook so it is held down firmly.

- Overlap the edge and mark the position of the straight eye on the left-hand side with a pin. Stitch the eye in place around both loops using small stitches. Fasten the thread securely and clip.

- For edges that meet, sew the hook ⅛-inch (3 mm) from the edge. Stitch around each loop. Match the garment edges. Position the eye so the loop extends ⅛-inch (3 mm) beyond the edge. Stitch in place on the garment underside. When the hook and eye are attached, the edges should meet exactly. Secure the thread and clip it close to the fabric.

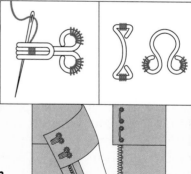

Chapter Summary

- Routine care and proper storage help to keep your clothes in good condition.
- Care labels provide important information about laundering, drying, and pressing clothes.
- Each laundry product is designed to perform a specific job.
- The correct iron temperature for pressing and ironing depends on the garment's fiber content.
- Dry cleaning involves the use of chemicals instead of water. It can be done by professionals or in coin-operated machines.
- Simple clothing repair done when needed prevents major problems later.

Reviewing the Chapter

1. What are five routine steps you can take to keep your clothes in good condition?
2. Suggest four ways to organize storage for clothes.
3. Identify five groups you'd use to sort laundry when preparing to wash clothes.
4. How would you pretreat clothes before laundering them?
5. Name three laundry products and explain what each is designed to do.
6. What important points would you keep in mind when you hand-wash clothes?
7. List six guidelines to remember when drying clothes.
8. Briefly describe four pointers to keep in mind when pressing or ironing clothes.

Family & Community

With Your Family
Talk with your family about how to make doing the family laundry an easier task. What can each person do to care for his or her clothes? Can responsibilities be shared differently? Why or why not?

In Your Community
Interview the owner or operator of a dry cleaning business. What are some common clothing-care mistakes people make that could be avoided? Find out more about the procedures used in dry cleaning clothes.

Review & Activities

Thinking Critically

1. **Analyze the situation.** How could you create storage room for clothes if closet and drawer space are very limited? Why is it important to be able to come up with creative solutions for clothing storage?

2. **Cause and effect.** If clothes came out of the wash and weren't clean, what might be the cause? How would you go about solving the problem?

Making Connections

1. **Science.** Try the following experiment to see how detergent works. Fill a glass with water and then pour 2 tablespoons (30 mL) of vegetable oil on top of the water. Stir the water and oil mixture. What are the results? Then, add 2 tablespoons (30mL) of laundry detergent to the oil and water mixture. What happens? What conclusions can you draw to explain the cleaning action of a detergent?

2. **Math.** Determine the cost of dry cleaning a pair of slacks for one year. Assume the slacks must be cleaned every two weeks. Use local dry cleaning prices.

Applying Your Learning

1. **Create additional space.** What are some of your biggest clothing storage problems? Brainstorm several solutions to one or more of your storage problems. What common household items could you use to help your storage situation? Follow through on one of your ideas.

2. **Remove stains.** Apply stains commonly found in family laundry to several fabric samples. Try removing the stains following the directions on a stain removal chart. Discuss your results.

3. **Sort it out.** Sort clothes or pictures of clothes that you'd typically find in your family laundry into appropriate wash loads. Explain your decisions.

What Would You Do?

A neighbor has given you and your family some clothes, which are in good condition. You like the clothes and could use them. Unfortunately, the care labels have been removed. How are you going to decide how to care for the clothes?

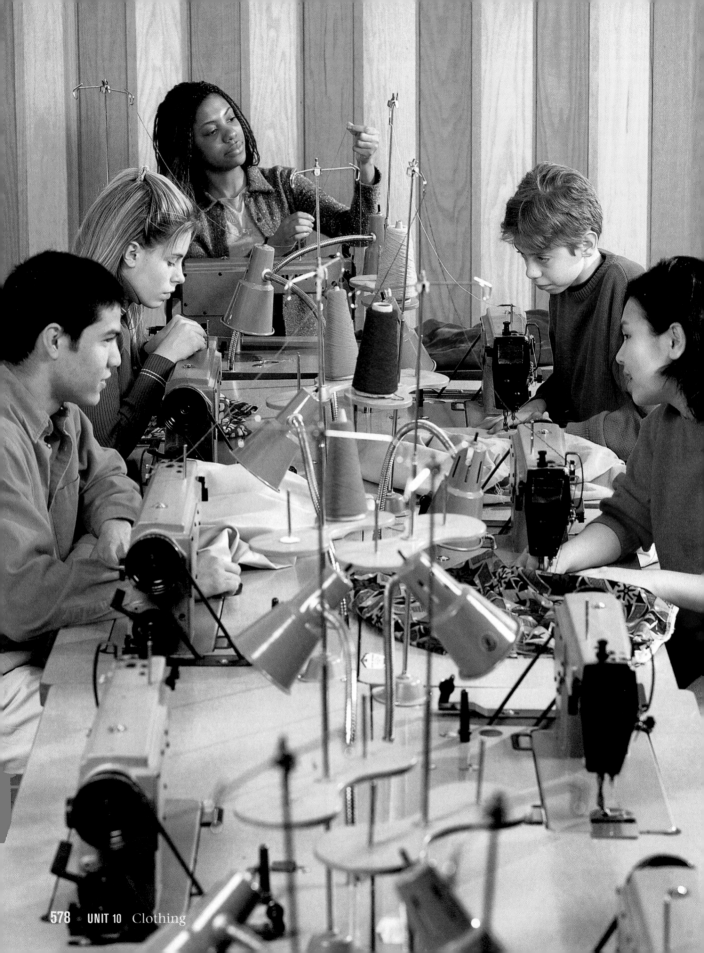

Sewing Equipment

YOU WILL LEARN . . .

➤ How small sewing equipment is used.
➤ How to operate a sewing machine.
➤ Why sergers are useful in sewing.

TERMS TO LEARN . . .

➤ backstitching
➤ serger
➤ tension
➤ trim

Imagine ...

... that you're a sewing machine at school. "Help! Help me. There's that kid who hurt me on Tuesday. He reminds me of the one who yanked on my feed dogs. Oh no, he's sitting down. He'd better not scratch my throat plate with those pins! I can't stand all this tension."

Think About

- How do you think your sewing machine "feels" when you sew?
- What does the way you handle a CD player or computer have in common with how you treat a sewing machine?
- If your sewing machine has a problem, does it mean you're careless? Why or why not?

LEARNING ABOUT SEWING EQUIPMENT

Everyone knows that sewing machines really don't have feelings. But what if they did? As you learn about sewing machines and other sewing equipment, think about the way the equipment is used and the best way to handle it. Knowing how to best care for your equipment helps maintain your investment.

SMALL SEWING EQUIPMENT

Having the right tools and using them the right way can make sewing faster, easier, and more fun. The small sewing equipment you'll read about is organized into groups according to their use.

Small scissors

Shears

Seam ripper

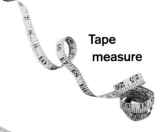

Tape measure

Measuring stick

Sewing gauge

Cutting and Measuring Equipment

All the pieces of cutting equipment used for sewing belong to the scissors family. Keep cutting equipment sharp by using it only for sewing. Using sewing scissors or shears to cut paper makes them dull. To measure the pattern, fabric, and garment pieces accurately as you sew, you need the proper measuring equipment. Here are the basics:

- **Small scissors.** Use small scissors to clip threads and **trim,** or *cut off,* fabric.
- **Shears.** Use shears for cutting fabric. Shears have long blades with one handle for the thumb and one handle for two or more fingers. Bent-handled shears improve your accuracy because the fabric is hardly lifted from the table as you cut.
- **Seam ripper.** The seam ripper has a hook-like point. It's handy for cutting and removing stitches.
- **Tape measure.** This is a narrow strip of durable plastic often marked with both inches and centimeters.
- **Measuring stick.** A measuring stick—yardstick or meterstick—is useful for measuring a pattern and fabric on a flat surface.
- **Sewing gauge.** This small ruler has a slide marker that can be set to gauge specific measurements, such as the width of a seam allowance or hem.

Marking Equipment

Marking equipment helps you transfer important construction markings from your pattern pieces to your fabric. It can be used to mark the position of details like pockets, buttonholes, and hems. Some of the most frequently used pieces of marking equipment are:

- **Tracing wheel.** This is used with a special waxed paper to transfer pattern markings to the wrong side of fabric.
- **Tailor's chalk.** Pencils, small squares, or small wheels of chalk or wax are used to mark fabric.
- **Fabric marker.** This special pen marks fabrics temporarily. Some fabric pen marks can be removed with water. Others fade in a short period of time. Test fabric markers on a scrap of fabric before using them.

Tracing wheel

Tailor's chalk

Fabric marker

Pressing Equipment

Pressing your project as you sew will give it a finished and professional look. Basic pressing equipment includes:

- **Iron and ironing board.** A steam iron and a well-padded ironing board enable you to press as you sew.
- **Press cloth.** Use a press cloth for dark fabrics. Place it between the fabric and iron to keep dark fabrics from developing a shine. You can buy a ready-made press cloth or use a clean, lightweight cloth or handkerchief.

Other Small Equipment

You'll use some additional equipment as you work on sewing projects.

SEWING MACHINES

A sewing machine is one of the most important and most expensive pieces of sewing equipment you'll use. Machines today range from basic models to computerized machines that perform machine embroidery and monogramming with the touch of a button. Basic models can handle most general sewing. Most machines today can do both straight and zigzag stitching and have built-in buttonholers.

SAFETY First

To use equipment safely:
- Keep shears, scissors, and seam rippers closed when not in use.
- Pass sharp objects handle first.
- Keep pins in a pincushion—not in your mouth or clothing.

Straight pins. These are used to anchor the pattern to the fabric and to hold layers of fabric together for sewing.

Pincushion. Use a pincushion to keep needles and pins handy while you work. Many pincushions come with an attached emery bag, often strawberry-shaped. Push rusty or sticky needles and pins into the bag a few times and it will clean them.

Thimble. A thimble can be used to push the needle through fabric while hand sewing. A thimble should fit snugly on the third finger of the hand that holds the needle.

Hand sewing needles. Needles are numbered from 1 (very thick) to 12 (very fine). A sharp point and medium length make "sharps" best for general hand sewing. Try a size 7 or 8.

Machine needles. Machine needles range from 60 (very fine for delicate fabrics) to 110 (very thick for coarse, heavy fabrics). Select the size best suited for your fabric. Use ballpoint needles for knit fabric. A needle that's dull, bent, or rough needs to be replaced.

For successful sewing, take time to learn about the sewing machine you'll use. Read the machine manual or have someone show you how to operate and care for the machine before you start to sew.

Threading the Machine

Before threading the machine, raise the presser foot and turn the handwheel toward you to raise the needle and take-up lever to the highest position. Follow the directions in the owner's manual for threading the machine.

Thread must also be wound onto a bobbin. The method will vary depending on the machine. Check your manual.

After threading the machine and putting the filled bobbin into the bobbin case, bring the bobbin thread up through the hole in the throat plate. Hold the end of the needle thread while turning the handwheel one full turn toward you. The needle thread will pull up a loop of bobbin thread. Pull up on this loop until the thread end is out of the throat plate.

Stitch Pattern Control ⑬

Tension Control ⑩

Thread Take-Up Lever ②

Presser Foot Lifter ⑨
(in back)

Thread Guide ⑯

Presser Foot ⑧

Feed Dogs ⑦

Throat Plate ③

Bobbin Area ④⑤

⑮ Spool Pins

⑥ Bobbin Winder

⑫ Stitch Width Control

① Handwheel

Buttonhole Knob

⑪ Stitch Length Control

⑭ Reverse Stitch Control

Parts of the Machine

All sewing machines function in a similar manner. Knowing the major parts helps you operate the machine easily and accurately. The parts shown and described here are found on most machines. Check your manual to see where they're located on your machine.

1. **Handwheel.** This large wheel on the right side of the machine controls the up-and-down movement of the needle and thread take-up lever.
2. **Thread take-up lever.** This lever feeds thread from the spool to the needle.
3. **Throat plate.** This is the metal plate under the machine needle. On most machines, the throat plate is also etched with seam allowance markings for accurate sewing.
4. **Bobbin.** A small, flat spool that holds the bottom thread.
5. **Bobbin case.** This holds the bobbin and is found beneath the throat plate.
6. **Bobbin winder spindle.** This spindle holds the bobbin while thread is wound from the thread spool to the bobbin. The location of this spindle varies with each machine.
7. **Feed dogs.** The feed dogs are a set of metal "teeth" that move the fabric during stitching.
8. **Presser foot.** This holds the fabric firmly in place against the feed dogs for sewing.

BUYING A SEWING MACHINE

When buying a sewing machine, check that...

- The machine starts and stops smoothly.
- The bobbin is easily wound and inserted.
- The foot pedal is comfortable to operate.
- The needle area is well-lighted.
- The machine makes attractive stitches.
- You understand the machine manual.

9. **Presser foot lifter.** A lever that raises and lowers the presser foot.
10. **Tension control.** A dial for adjusting the tightness or looseness of the needle thread.
11. **Stitch length control.** This is used to adjust the length of stitches from short to long.
12. **Stitch width control.** This control is used to adjust the width of stitches other than the straight stitch.
13. **Stitch pattern control.** The stitch pattern control can be adjusted to make different stitching patterns.
14. **Reverse stitch control.** Depending on the machine, this will be a button or a lever that allows you to stitch backward to secure the end of a seam.
15. **Spool pin.** This holds the spool of thread.
16. **Thread guides.** These guide the needle thread as it travels from the spool to the needle.
17. **Foot control.** The amount of pressure you apply with your foot to this control regulates the operation of the machine.

Machine Stitching

All machines straight stitch the same way. If you haven't sewn before or will be using a different machine, take time to practice stitching. Here are general directions:

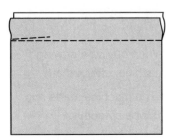

Reverse stitching or backstitching

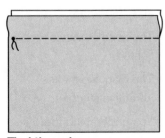

Tied threads

- **Raise the take-up lever and needle to the highest point.** Do the same when stitching is finished. This keeps the thread from pulling out of the needle or tangling in the bobbin.
- **Pull the needle thread and bobbin thread to the right side of the presser foot.** The threads should also be underneath the presser foot.
- **Place the fabric under the presser foot.** First lower the needle into the fabric at the beginning of the stitching line and then lower the presser foot. The bulk of the fabric should be to the left of the machine.
- **Start the machine slowly.** A smooth, steady speed allows better control than speed-ups and slow-downs.
- **Use the throat plate markings to guide your fabric through the machine.** This helps you keep an even seam width.
- **Slow the machine speed for the last few stitches.** This helps prevent you from stitching beyond the edge of the fabric.

- **Secure stitching at both ends of a seam.** There are several ways to do this. **Backstitching,** or *retracing your stitches* about ½-inch (1.3 cm), is done by using the reverse stitch control on the machine. Another way to secure stitching is to tie the threads at the end of the seam.

Adjusting Stitch Length and Tension

The correct stitch length and tension make a seam that's both attractive and strong. A medium-length stitch (2 to 2.5 mm or 10-12 stitches per inch) is used for most fabrics. But some fabrics and sewing steps require different stitch lengths. Check the machine stitching on a two-layer scrap of your fabric before beginning to sew. You can make changes in the stitch length by adjusting the stitch length control.

Tension refers to *the tightness or looseness of the thread.* The tension is balanced when the stitching looks the same on both sides. It's not in balance if thread loops form on either side of the fabric. Newer machines seldom require tension adjustments when regular sewing thread is used in the needle and the bobbin. If tension problems occur, check the machine and bobbin threading before adjusting the tension dial. Incorrect threading is often the cause. If the tension needs adjusting, your machine manual will tell you how to correct it.

Machine Care

To sew properly, the sewing machine needs to be cleaned regularly. Remove the throat plate and clean the teeth of the feed dogs with a small brush. Brush the bobbin case clean. Most machines also need occasional oiling. Check the machine manual for details.

If the machine jams because thread has become tangled in the bobbin area, the thread must be carefully removed. Turn off the machine and check the manual for further directions.

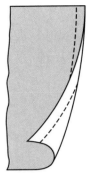

Balanced tension

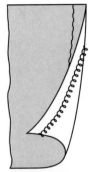

Upper tension too tight

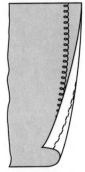

Lower tension too tight

➤ **Before changing your tension settings, check the machine threading first.**

SERGER SEWING

Have you ever wondered why the seams in ready-to-wear clothing look so smooth and neat? Thanks to new technology, people can now make garments at home that have the appearance of fine ready-to-wear clothing.

A **serger,** or *overlock sewing machine, is a machine that stitches, trims, and finishes a seam in one step.* Some garments, such as sweatshirts, can be sewn entirely on the serger. But many projects call for combining the use of a conventional sewing machine and a serger.

Sergers are different from conventional sewing machines in the following ways:

- Sergers sew much faster than conventional sewing machines.
- Sergers have cutters that trim the seam before it is stitched.
- Sergers use more thread. Most serger thread is on cones that hold 1,000 or more yards. Depending on the model, the serger uses two, three, four, or five cones of thread for stitching.

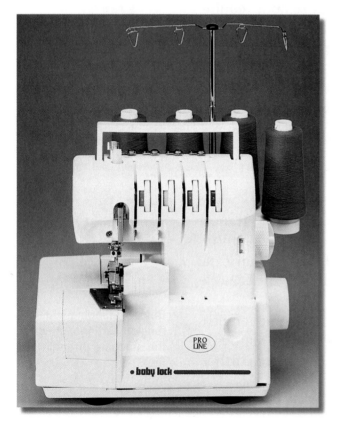

- Sergers may use one or two needles, depending on the model.
- Sergers have no bobbin. Two loopers take the place of bobbins.
- Lifting the presser foot isn't necessary when starting to sew unless fabric is thick. The serger feed dogs grip the fabric as you begin to sew.
- You can't sew over pins on a serger or the cutters will be damaged as they try to cut through a pin.

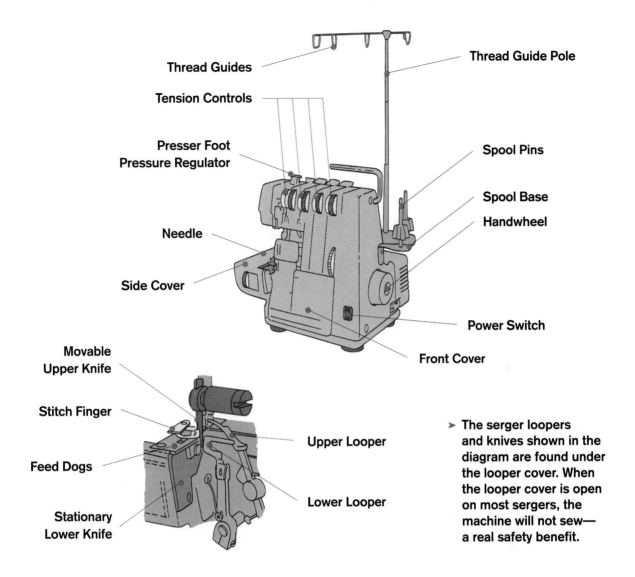

Thread Guides

Tension Controls

Presser Foot
Pressure Regulator

Needle

Side Cover

Thread Guide Pole

Spool Pins

Spool Base

Handwheel

Power Switch

Front Cover

Movable
Upper Knife

Stitch Finger

Feed Dogs

Stationary
Lower Knife

Upper Looper

Lower Looper

➤ The serger loopers
and knives shown in the
diagram are found under
the looper cover. When
the looper cover is open
on most sergers, the
machine will not sew—
a real safety benefit.

All brands of sergers sew basically the same way. As you feed the fabric into the machine, the feed dogs grip the fabric and pull it toward the cutters. The cutters trim the fabric edges before the fabric reaches the loopers and needles for stitching. Rather than backstitching, you simply run the fabric off the serger behind the needles. Securing the ends of stitching is not necessary for most applications.

Sewing with a serger has inspired many people to make their own clothing. Knit garments such as T-shirts and activewear can be made quickly and easily, and all garments can be given a professional finish with the serger.

Chapter Summary

- Small equipment for cutting, measuring, and marking is useful when working on sewing projects.
- Follow safety procedures when using sewing equipment to prevent accidents.
- Following the correct procedures for operating sewing machines and sergers ensures sewing success.
- Taking proper care of sewing machines and sergers keeps them in good working order.

Family & Community

With Your Family

If your family does not already have a sewing kit with small sewing equipment, talk with another family member and decide what items would be useful. Assemble a sewing kit.

In Your Community

Visit the notions departments of several stores that carry sewing supplies. Look for unusual articles of sewing equipment (or articles you are unfamiliar with). Write down the equipment names and purposes. Share your findings with the class.

Reviewing the Chapter

1. Identify at least three pieces of cutting equipment and explain how each is used.
2. Name two methods for marking fabric. Describe how each works.
3. When would it be helpful to use a press cloth?
4. Tell the difference between the best use for a sharp-pointed needle and a ball-point needle.
5. Explain the function of each of the following parts of a sewing machine: handwheel, bobbin, feed dog, presser foot, and tension control.
6. Identify at least five guidelines to follow when machine stitching.
7. What does tension refer to on a sewing machine? Describe the appearance of properly adjusted tension.
8. Briefly explain how a serger works.

Review & Activities

Thinking Critically

1. **Analyze decisions.** Assume you are going to purchase a sewing machine. What features do you consider important to have on the machine? Explain your choices.
2. **Compare and contrast.** What advantages does the serger have over a sewing machine and vice versa? If you could only purchase one of these machines, which would you choose and why?

Making Connections

1. **Math.** List the basic sewing equipment you would need for a beginning sewing project. Price the equipment and determine the total cost.
2. **Social Studies.** Research the way clothing was produced in the colonial period and in the following years. Summarize the highlights of your findings.

Applying Your Learning

1. **State your opinion.** Discuss your agreement or disagreement with the following statement: "Sewing is its own reward. It's a skill that can be used throughout life."
2. **Safety comes first.** Arrange a display of small sewing equipment. Point out safety features to keep in mind when using the equipment.
3. **Lab.** Try out some special sewing items, such as special fabric markers, disappearing basting thread, and liquid seam sealant. Evaluate their effectiveness. When would they be most helpful?

What Would You Do?

You're working in the sewing lab and see two students pretending they're dueling with scissors. The teacher is helping another student. A number of other students are around, but no one has said or done anything. What would you do?

Preparing to Sew

YOU WILL LEARN . . .

- ➤ How to select patterns.
- ➤ The importance of pattern information.
- ➤ What you should consider in preparing and selecting fabrics.
- ➤ The methods for laying out and marking a pattern.

TERMS TO LEARN . . .

- ➤ bias
- ➤ ease
- ➤ interfacing
- ➤ layouts
- ➤ notions
- ➤ seam allowances
- ➤ selvage
- ➤ views

Imagine ...

... that your retired uncle builds and paints birdhouses, and then sells them to a hardware store. "It makes me feel good to take some ordinary wood scraps and turn them into something useful," he explains. You're not interested in working with wood, but you do share his desire to create.

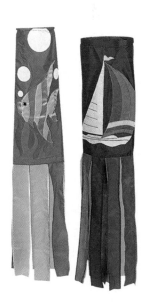

Think About

- Do you think people sew to save money or because they enjoy it?
- If you didn't sew clothing, what else might you try sewing?
- How might sewing help you with creative expression?

SELECTING A PATTERN

CHOOSING THE RIGHT PATTERN

If you're a true beginner, look for the easy-to-sew section of the pattern catalog. Patterns in this section have several things in common:

- They have fewer pattern pieces.
- They don't require much fitting.
- The designs are simple with few details.

➤ Pattern catalogs enable you to browse to find the perfect sewing project. Stores that sell fabric usually have several pattern catalogs.

The desire to be creative is a common one among people. As you think about the possibility of sewing, looking through a pattern catalog gives you an idea of the variety of sewing projects you might try to make. Catalogs are divided into different sections. You'll find easy-to-sew styles, sportswear, crafts, and other sections. The titles can help you make a selection that matches your interest and skill level.

Pattern catalogs also include numerical listings of all the pattern numbers and the page numbers on which they can be found. This makes it easy to look for a specific pattern number.

Pattern Envelopes

Both the front and the back of the pattern envelope contain important information that will help you select a project. See the next page for information on pattern envelopes.

Taking Measurements

Making a craft item such as a tote bag or pillow doesn't require taking personal measurements. If you're making a garment, however, you'll need to take several body measurements. Try to take measurements over a garment that fits well. Take off bulky sweaters, jackets, and belts before measuring.

When taking measurements, hold a tape measure so it fits snugly. It shouldn't be too tight or too loose. It's easier to work with a partner so that you can measure each other. Write your measurements down when you take them. See page 594 for information on taking measurements.

➤ You can't take accurate measurements by yourself. Get a friend to help you.

Special information, such as "Easy to Sew"

Garment description. An explanation of the garment with details that may not be obvious from the illustration.

Suggested fabrics. Your guide to selecting the fabric that will give you the best results.

Notions. The extra items, such as buttons, zippers, and trims, needed to make the garment.

Yardage chart. Lists the amount of fabric needed for each view, size, and fabric width.

Body measurements. Guidelines for helping you to determine your correct pattern size.

Colorful views, or garment styles, that can be made from the pattern.

Views. Shows design lines and details not easily seen on the envelope front.

➤ The front of a pattern shows the item you can make. The back of the pattern is your guide for selecting the proper fabric and notions.

TAKING MEASUREMENTS

For Males	For Females
Neck. Measure around the base of the neck and add ½-inch (1.3 cm) or buy pattern by the shirt size you regularly purchase.	**Back waist length.** Measure from the base of the neck to the waistline.
Chest. Measure around the fullest part of the chest.	**Bust.** Measure around the fullest part of the bust, under the arms.
Arm. With the arm bent up at the elbow, measure from the bone at the base of the neck, around the elbow, and up to the wrist bone.	**Arm.** Measure from the shoulder, over the bent elbow, down to the wrist.
Waist. Measure around the natural waistline over a shirt, but not over pants.	**Waist.** Tie a string around the waist to identify the narrowest point. Measure around the body at this point.
Hip/Seat. Measure around the fullest part of the hip/seat, usually about 8 inches (20.5 cm) below the waist.	**Hip.** Measure around the fullest part of the hips, 7-9 inches (18-23 cm) below the waist.
Outseam. Measure along the outside of the leg from the waist to the desired length of pants.	**Outseam.** Measure along the outside of the leg from the waist, over the hips, to the desired length of skirt or pants.
Inseam. Measure a pair of pants that fit well and are the correct length, measuring from the bottom of one leg to the crotch seam.	

Use these measuring methods to determine your pattern size. These could help you in purchasing clothing as well as sewing it.

Figure Types

Figure types are size categories based on height and body proportions. You need three pieces of information: your height, back waist length (females), and body proportion. Compare this information with the body measurement charts in the back of the pattern catalog to determine your figure type.

Pattern Size

After identifying your figure type, you need to find your pattern size. Compare your chest or bust, waist, and hip measurements with those listed on the measurement chart. Choose your pattern size for most garments by your chest or bust measurement. When making pants or a skirt, use your waist measurement for the pattern size. If your hips are large in relation to your waist, however, use the hip measurement for the best fit. When your measurements fall between two sizes, pick the smaller size unless the design is very close-fitting.

SELECTING FABRIC AND NOTIONS

Before you buy a piece of fabric, think about how appropriate the fabric is for your pattern and your sewing skills. If you're making a garment, think about how the fabric will look on you. What kind of care will the fabric need?

Buy fabric you like and will enjoy working with. Use your own good judgement to choose fabrics. If you're making an active sportswear garment, look at fabrics that are durable and hard-wearing. The fabric will also have to stand up to frequent washings. If you're making something for a special occasion, then you'll probably want dressier fabric.

➤ Selecting the proper fabric is important for success of the finished garment. It is also important to consider whether the fabric is washable or requires dry cleaning.

➤ Different fabrics require different interfacing weights. For example, heavy interfacing would not work well for a silky fabric.

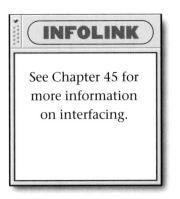

INFOLINK

See Chapter 45 for more information on interfacing.

Interfacing

Interfacing is *a special fabric that gives support and body to a garment or project.* It's placed between the facing and the outer fabric so that it's not visible. Interfacing adds body and support to hats, belts, or bags. You also find it used around necklines to keep them from stretching.

You can buy sew-in or fusible interfacing. *Sew-in interfacing* is stitched to the garment. *Fusible interfacing* is pressed on with a hot iron. Choose an interfacing that has similar weight, body, and care requirements to your fabric.

Notions

Notions are the *small items, such as thread, zippers, buttons, trim, seam binding, hooks and eyes, and snaps needed to complete a garment.* The back of the pattern envelope lists the notions you need.

Thread of 100 percent polyester or cotton-covered polyester is a good choice for most projects. Select thread that's just slightly darker than the fabric. If you have a print, match the thread with the main color in the print.

Zippers come in a variety of colors, lengths, and styles. Check the pattern envelope for the zipper length and type suggested. Match the color of the zipper to the fabric as closely as possible. If the fabric has several colors, match the zipper to the background color.

➤ Choosing thread for your project involves color, weight, and quality concerns. Take time to select the proper threads.

USING THE PATTERN

You'll find the guide sheet and pattern pieces inside the pattern envelope. The guide sheet contains:

- Sketches of different styles or views that can be made from the pattern.
- A list and diagram of pattern pieces.
- Cutting **layouts,** or *diagrams,* that show how to lay pattern pieces on the fabric for different sizes, fabric widths, and types of fabric.
- Step-by-step instructions for sewing the garment or project.

Each pattern piece has a number of pattern symbols or markings. These will serve as your guides for laying out and sewing your project. The most common symbols you'll see include:

1. **Cutting line.** The heavy line you follow on the outside of the pattern to cut out the fabric.
2. **Grainline.** A straight line with arrows on each end to be placed in the direction of the lengthwise grain, crosswise grain, or bias.
3. **Place on fold.** A bracketed grainline that indicates the pattern edge is to be placed exactly on the fold of the fabric.
4. **Darts.** The broken lines show the stitching line.
5. **Placement line.** A solid line to show where to locate pockets, trims, and other features.

Pattern Symbols

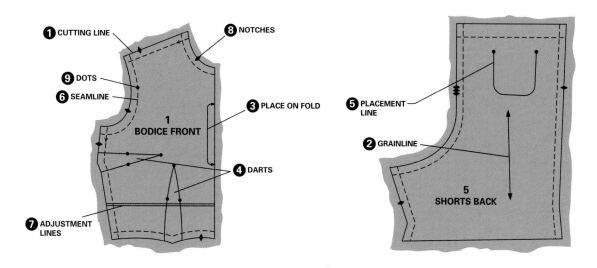

➤ Pattern pieces are generally larger than your exact body measurements. Always remeasure before cutting to avoid costly mistakes.

6. **Seamline or stitching line.** A broken line, usually ⅝-inch (1.5 cm) inside the cutting line that shows where to stitch the seams.
7. **Adjustment line.** Two parallel lines that indicate where to cut or fold a pattern for lengthening or shortening.
8. **Notches.** Diamond-shaped symbols along the cutting line that show where to join the pattern pieces together.
9. **Dots, squares, and triangles.** Symbols that help you match and join project sections together.

FITTING THE PATTERN

When you're making a garment, you'll want to check how well the pattern will fit you. You can do this by comparing your measurements with those of the pattern. Follow these guidelines:

• Smooth out the pattern with your hands, or if necessary, press the pattern pieces with a warm, dry iron.

- Measure the pattern between stitching lines at the same places where the body measurements were taken and write them down.
- Don't include **seam allowances**—*the fabric between the cutting line and the stitching line*—or darts when measuring the pattern pieces.

In most cases, you can expect the pattern pieces to be larger than your exact body measurements. Don't panic! Your pattern should be larger to account for wearing and design ease. **Ease** is *the extra room needed for movement and comfort.* Of course, some garments are very loose with plenty of ease. But if the garment is close-fitting and the pattern measurements are much larger (or smaller) than your body measurements, you need to make some adjustment in the pattern.

PREPARING FABRIC

All woven fabric is made up of two sets of yarn, one going lengthwise and the other crosswise. Lengthwise grain, running the length of the fabric, has little or no stretch. The **selvage** is *the finished lengthwise edge of the fabric.* It will not ravel. The crosswise yarns, running horizontally from selvage to selvage, have more stretch than the lengthwise grain.

The true bias has the most stretch. True **bias** is *the diagonal edge formed when the fabric is folded with the crosswise grain parallel to the selvage, or lengthwise grain.*

A fabric's crosswise and lengthwise grains must be square (at right angles to each other) when you cut out your pattern, or the finished garment may not hang properly.

Straightening Fabric Ends

It's difficult to check whether the fabric grain is straight if the crosswise edges are uneven.

To straighten the fabric ends, clip into the selvage and pull one thread (yarn) with one hand while pushing the fabric back with the other hand. Cut along this pulled-thread line. If the thread breaks before you reach the other selvage, pick up the end of the broken thread and continue pulling and cutting as necessary.

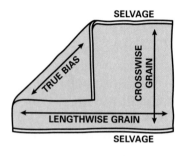

➤ How you position your pattern pieces depends on the grain of the fabric. The pattern will show you how to lay the pattern pieces on the fabric.

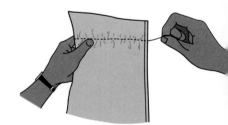

➤ Before cutting woven fabrics, make sure they are on-grain. A garment that is made with off-grain fabric will not hang properly.

Alter Your Pattern

For successful pattern alterations, make adjustments for length and width on both front and back pattern pieces. Use a measuring stick to extend the grainline, making sure the grainline is straight. Be sure to redraw any seamlines, design details, or darts changed by the alteration.

Here are some common adjustments:

- **Increasing pattern width.** A width adjustment of 2 inches (5 cm) or less can be made along the garment side seams. Tape tissue paper along both front and back pattern pieces at the seam allowance. Divide the total adjustment by the number of seam allowances. For example, to increase the waistline by 1 inch (2.5 cm) on a garment with two side seams, you'll add ¼-inch (6.3 mm) to the side seam of both the front and back pattern pieces. Each side seam will then increase by ½-inch (1.3 cm), which adds up to the 1 inch (2.5 cm) total needed. Measure from the cutting line and mark the amount needed on the tissue paper. Redraw the cutting lines and stitching lines carefully.

- **Decreasing pattern width.** To decrease pattern width, divide the total adjustment needed by the number of seam allowances. Measure the amount needed and redraw cutting lines and stitching lines to blend in with areas that don't need to be decreased.

Increase waistline

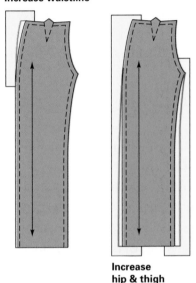

Increase hip & thigh

Decrease waistline

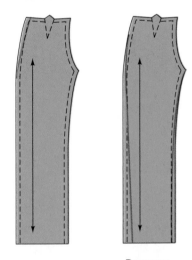

Decrease hip & thigh

- Lengthening a pattern. Cut the pattern apart on the adjustment lines. Tape tissue paper to one pattern piece. Redraw the grainline through the tissue using the edge of a measuring stick as a guide. Measure from the adjustment line and mark the tissue for the extra length needed. Tape the second pattern piece at this point, matching the grainlines. Redraw cutting and stitching lines.

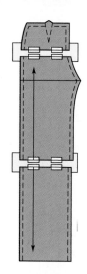

- Shortening a pattern. Measure the amount to be shortened upwards from the adjustment line on the pattern. Draw a line at this point parallel to the adjustment line. Fold along the adjustment line and bring the fold up to the second line. Match grainline markings. Tape the fold in place.

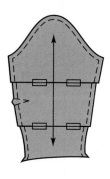

Preshrinking Fabric

Fabrics need to be preshrunk before you make your project for two reasons. Preshrinking makes sure that your project won't shrink after you make it. Also, preshrinking "relaxes" the fabric so you can check the grain more accurately. Washable fabrics should be preshrunk in the same manner that you plan to launder the finished garment. (Be sure to ask for a care label when you make your purchase.) For fabrics that ravel easily, zigzag stitch or serge the cut edges before washing the material. All woven interfacings, zippers, and trims should also be preshrunk.

PATTERN LAYOUT

The pattern guide sheet lists the pattern pieces needed for each view. Before you lay out the pattern, do the following:

- Cut apart the pattern pieces you need. Leave some extra paper outside of the cutting lines on all pieces.
- Check off the pattern pieces needed as you find them. Put the extra ones back into the envelope.
- Press the pattern pieces with a warm, dry iron if they're very wrinkled.
- Write your name on the pattern pieces so you don't lose them when you're in the clothing lab.

Positioning Pattern Pieces

It's important to place pattern pieces on the fabric correctly. Once fabric has been cut, it's difficult to correct layout mistakes. Follow these steps:

1. **Circle the layout you're using on the pattern guide sheet.** This shows how to place the pattern pieces for the view, fabric width, and size you're making.
2. **Check the layout instructions carefully**. Note the following markings: the right and wrong sides of the fabric; the right and wrong sides of the pattern; and the pattern pieces to be cut a second time. Are there any pieces to be cut from a single layer of fabric?
3. **Fold the fabric as shown in the layout diagram.** Generally, fabric is folded in half on the lengthwise grain with right sides together.
4. **Position the large pattern pieces to be placed on the fold first.** Then position the remaining pattern pieces so their grainline symbols are straight on the fabric grain. Pin securely, inserting the pins perpendicular to the cutting line, but not on the cutting line.

Cutting Out the Pattern

Use a sharp shears to cut out the fabric. Follow the outside cutting lines carefully. Don't cut on the fold line. Hold the pattern and fabric flat with one hand as you cut with

➤ Pre-washing washable fabrics before you cut the pattern out, prevents the final garment from shrinking. Be sure to follow the fabric care instructions listed on the bolt or care label.

the other to prevent the fabric from moving under the pattern. Move around the table as you work instead of moving the fabric.

Cut the notches outward, not inward. Cutting inward can weaken the seam. You could also accidentally cut into the garment. If two or three notches are together, cut them across the top as one long notch.

Keep pattern pieces pinned to the fabric for marking and identification. If you're using interfacing, cut out the interfacing when you finish cutting the fabric.

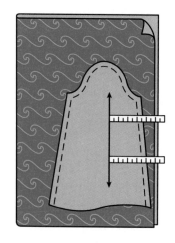

➤ A pattern's layout depends on the width of the fabric selected. Follow the instructions carefully. Extra fabric is often needed for matching the fabric designs.

Marking the Fabric

The lines and symbols on your pattern pieces serve as a guide for sewing accurately. Transfer these markings to the *wrong* side of your fabric before the pattern is unpinned. They must be visible as you sew, but should not show on the outside of the finished project.

Markings can be transferred to fabric in several ways. Fabric markers and a tracing wheel with tracing paper are popular methods.

- **Fabric markers.** Special liquid fabric markers can be used to make temporary markings on fabric. Test markers on a fabric scrap to be sure the markings can be removed.
- **Tracing paper and tracing wheel.** Choose a color of tracing paper that can be easily seen, but is close to the color of your fabric. Slide the tracing paper under the pattern so the colored side is against the wrong side of the fabric. If you need to mark two layers of fabric, use two sheets of tracing paper. Roll the tracing wheel along the marking lines. Using a ruler will help keep the lines straight. Mark dots with an X.
- **Chalk and pins.** Put a pin through the pattern and fabric at the place to be marked. Make a chalk mark on the wrong side of both fabric layers at the pin marking.

➤ Accurately transferring the pattern markings to your fabric leads to professional looking finished results.

Chapter Summary

- Use pattern guidelines to select a pattern that matches your ability level.
- Fabric and notions selected should be appropriate for the pattern and your sewing skills.
- Use the pattern guide sheet and pattern pieces as guides when sewing.
- Fit adjustments should be made before the pattern is cut out.
- Preshrink and straighten the grain of fabrics before cutting out fabric.
- Follow pattern markings carefully as you construct your sewing project.

Family & Community

With Your Family

Work with another family member to make a sewn craft item for your family. Consider a door-draft stopper, a decorative pillow, or other home accessory.

In Your Community

Imagine that one of your neighbors has always enjoyed sewing, but arthritis has made it difficult to do so in recent years. She's mentioned that some of her friends have similar problems. You'd like to be able to help. What might you do?

Reviewing the Chapter

1. List five important pieces of information on a pattern envelope back.
2. What are three major guidelines to follow when taking body measurements for a pattern?
3. How do you identify your correct pattern size?
4. Suggest guidelines you would keep in mind when selecting fabric for a project?
5. What are notions? List six notions you might use in constructing a sewing project.
6. Name four important pieces of information found on a pattern guide sheet.
7. Explain why it's important to preshrink fabric before you lay out a pattern.
8. Briefly describe how to check the grain of fabric.
9. List four steps to follow when laying out a pattern.
10. Describe six points to remember when cutting out a pattern.

Thinking Critically

1. **Compare and contrast.** Describe the types of garments on which accurate measurements are important for appearance and fit. On what types of garments are very accurate measurements somewhat less important?

2. **Predict consequences.** Why is it helpful to understand fabric construction and fabric grain when shopping for fabric? What could be some consequences of not being knowledgeable about fabric grain?

3. **Identify evidence.** Suppose one of your classmates made a mistake in laying out and cutting a pattern on the fabric. What would you look for to see whether the project could be saved? What mistakes would be difficult to correct?

Making Connections

1. **Math.** Select a pattern and estimate the total cost of constructing the view you selected. Include the pattern, fabric, and notions in your estimate.

2. **Language Arts.** Write a paragraph explaining to first-time sewers the important information found on a pattern envelope.

Applying Your Learning

1. **Compare choices.** Obtain two patterns, each from different companies. How are the patterns similar and different? Locate information such as body measurements, fabric suggestions, notions needed, and yardage needed for several sizes. Is the information easier to find on one pattern brand than another? How?

2. **Make a selection.** Collect five small pieces of different types of fabrics. Mount each fabric type on a separate sheet of paper. On each paper under the fabric, explain whether or not the fabric would be a good choice for someone who is just learning to sew.

3. **Identify the grain.** Locate several samples of fabric, some on-grain and some off-grain. See how many people can correctly identify the fabrics on- and off-grain. Discuss how off-grain fabrics can be straightened. If possible, demonstrate straightening the grain of fabric.

What Would You Do?

Suppose you laid out a pattern and cut it out. As you were beginning to put your project together, you realized you made a mistake and didn't lay one of the major pieces on the fold. What would you do?

Basic Sewing Techniques

YOU WILL LEARN . . .

➤ Various clothing construction techniques.
➤ Guidelines to follow when constructing sewing projects.

TERMS TO LEARN . . .

➤ basting
➤ clipping
➤ directional stitching
➤ grading
➤ notching
➤ staystitching
➤ understitching

Imagine ...

… waiting in line at the fabric store or movie theater. Some people stand patiently while others look at their watches and the progress of the line with frustration. A few switch lines, hoping to save a minute or two. Does this sound like anyone you know?

Think About

• Would an impatient person enjoy sewing? Why or why not?
• What type of project should he or she choose?
• Do you think shortcuts, just like changing lines, are possible in sewing? Why or why not?

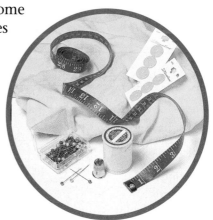

GETTING STARTED

Now that you've become familiar with the equipment and tools needed to sew, you can begin to develop your sewing skills. You will find that sewing skills are useful throughout your life. You can use them not only for making clothes, but also for repairing and altering garments. They also enable you to personalize your clothes and items in your home. The techniques explained in this chapter will help you develop these skills. All it will take is a little practice and patience.

Basting

If you altered your pattern correctly before cutting it out, you'll probably have few adjustments to make as you sew. To be certain about fit, you may need to baste parts of your garment together. **Basting** means *holding two or more pieces of fabric together temporarily until they are permanently stitched.*

There are several types of basting. Thread basting uses long stitches, about ¼-inch (6 mm) long by hand or by machine with the stitch length set at 4 or longer. For pin basting, the pins substitute for stitching. You may want to experiment with basting tape or disappearing basting thread, which dissolves when you wash or iron it.

When basting, make sure the stitches or pins are next to, but not directly on, the seamline. This makes the basting easy to remove after the permanent seam is sewn.

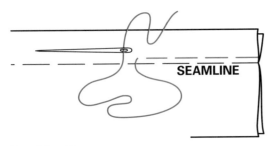

Hand basting

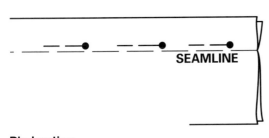

Pin basting

MACHINE STITCHING

Machine stitching is used for the major seams of your sewing project and for directional stitching and staystitching. You'll usually use a stitch length setting of 2.5 for most fabrics.

Directional Stitching

All the stitching on a garment should be sewn with the grain of the fabric. *Stitching in the direction of the grain* is called **directional stitching.** If you sew with the grain, you're less likely to stretch the fabric.

How do you determine the direction for stitching?

- Move your finger along the raw edge of the fabric. The direction that smooths the yarns against the fabric is going with the grain.
- Pattern tissues have arrows pointing to grain direction.
- As a general rule, stitch from the wide to the narrow part of the garment. For example, sew from the hem to the waist of a skirt.

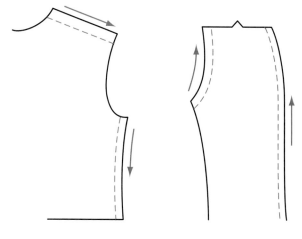

Staystitching

Before you begin to put a garment together, it should be staystitched. **Staystitching** is *a row of stitching on one layer of fabric that prevents the edges from stretching* as you handle the fabric. Staystitch after your fabric is marked, but before pinning or basting is done.

- Staystitch in the direction of the grain.
- Use the same thread tension and stitch length you'll use for the project seams.
- Staystitch ½-inch (1.3 cm) from the raw edge. This is ⅛-inch (3 mm) inside the seamline. Staystitching shouldn't show on the outside.
- Staystitch edges that are curved, on the bias, or cut off-grain, such as shoulder seams, necklines, and armholes.

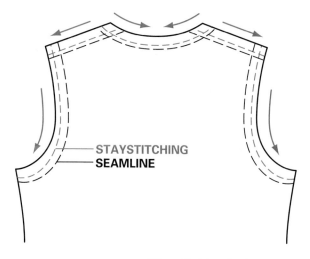

STAYSTITCHING
SEAMLINE

➤ Staystitching is done on curved areas to prevent the fabric from stretching.

SEWING TECHNIQUES

As you work on sewing projects, you'll use several different sewing techniques. Here are some useful techniques.

Seams

Seams hold a garment together. A seam is made by sewing two pieces of fabric together. In general, seams are ⅝-inch (1.5 cm) wide. The fabric between the seamline and the cut edge is the seam allowance.

Before you begin to sew, make a sample seam on a scrap of your fabric. Check the tension, stitch length, and general appearance. To make a plain seam, follow these steps:

1. Place right sides of the fabric together. Match notches, cut edges, and both ends of the fabric. Place pins at right angles to the seamline at the ends and notches. Pin the rest of the seam, placing pins 2 to 3 inches (5 to 7.5 cm) apart with the pin heads outward.
2. Place the fabric under the presser foot with the cut edges of the seam allowance lined up with the proper seam guide on the throat plate. Turn the handwheel to lower the needle into the fabric ½-inch (1.3 cm) from the top. Lower the presser foot.
3. Backstitch to secure the top end of the seam. Backstitch by retracing your stitches about ½-inch (1.3 cm). Use the reverse button or lever on your sewing machine.
4. Using a medium speed and an even pace, stitch to the other end of the seam.
5. Backstitch to secure the bottom end of the seam.
6. Seams are usually pressed open flat.

Seam Finishes

Seam finishes are often used to prevent raveling on the cut edges of seams and facings. The seam finish to use depends on the type of fabric and the amount of raveling. If you're unsure which finish to use, try different finishes on fabric scraps.

- **Zigzag finish.** For fabrics that ravel, zigzagging is a practical seam finish. Use a medium-width machine zigzag stitch and sew along the edge of each seam allowance.
- **Clean finish.** A clean finish is a turned and stitched finish used on lightweight and medium-weight fabrics. Machine stitch ¼-inch (6 mm) from the cut edge. Turn the cut edge toward the inside along the stitching line. Press. Machine stitch close to the folded edge.
- **Serged finish.** This may be used on any fabric. Serge along the cut edge of the seam, just skimming the edge as you sew. A serged finish is especially helpful on heavy or bulky fabric and fabric that ravels easily. See the next page for more information on how to serge seams successfully.

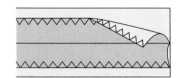

Zigzag seam finish

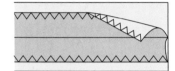

Clean finish

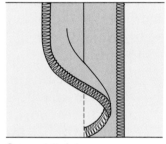

Serged finish

Interfacing

Interfacing is applied before the facing is attached to the garment. See the illustration that follows for two ways to apply interfacing.

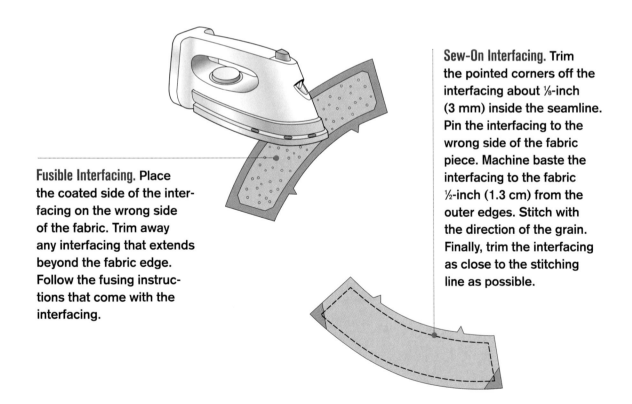

Fusible Interfacing. Place the coated side of the interfacing on the wrong side of the fabric. Trim away any interfacing that extends beyond the fabric edge. Follow the fusing instructions that come with the interfacing.

Sew-On Interfacing. Trim the pointed corners off the interfacing about ⅛-inch (3 mm) inside the seamline. Pin the interfacing to the wrong side of the fabric piece. Machine baste the interfacing to the fabric ½-inch (1.3 cm) from the outer edges. Stitch with the direction of the grain. Finally, trim the interfacing as close to the stitching line as possible.

Serge Seams Successfully

Serged seams work well on many garments. They're especially good on knits because serged seams stretch with the garment. You can also use serged seams with loosely woven fabrics for loose-fitting garments.

- Sew a test seam first. The seamline is where the needle enters the fabric—not where the knives cut. If you begin with a ⅝-inch (1.5 cm) seam allowance, and your knives cut off ⅜-inch (1 cm), a ¼-inch (6 mm) seam allowance remains.

- If your serger doesn't have a guide mark for sewing a ⅝-inch (1.5 cm) seam, simply measure ⅝-inch (1.5 cm) to the right of the needle and mark the spot on the machine with a permanent marker or piece of tape.

- Generally, pins aren't needed for serger sewing. The serger feeds fabric evenly through the machine. If you do use pins, remove them before they hit the knives. If a pin hits the knives, the blades can be seriously damaged. In addition, pins that break and fly away from the machine could cause injury.

- Press serged seams to one side, front or back, depending on the garment you are making.

Facings

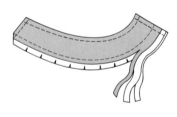
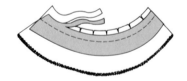

Facings are often used to finish a raw edge, such as necklines, front openings, armholes, or collars. There are several different types of facings. A shaped facing is used most often. It's cut the same shape as the edge onto which it is sewn.

Before sewing a facing to a garment, you need to understand several techniques. These techniques are:

- **Grading.** After facings are joined to a garment, the seams may be thick and bulky. **Grading** or *trimming the seam allowances in layers* is done to reduce the bulk.
- **Notching or clipping.** Outward-curved edges, as on collars, and inward-curved edges, as on necklines, need special treatment to lie flat. Outward curves need **notching,** which means *clipping V-shaped notches from the seam allowance.* Inward curves need **clipping,** or *making small, straight cuts in the seam allowance.*

- **Understitching.** This row of stitching gives facings a smooth, flat edge. **Understitching,** or *stitching the facing to the seam allowances,* also keeps seams and facings from rolling to the outside of the garment.

Sewing a Facing

After learning about grading, notching, and understitching, it's easier to sew on a facing. Follow these steps to attach a facing:

Step 1. Staystitch curved facing edges that are to be attached to the garment. Sew facing pieces together as directed in the pattern. Trim the seams to ¼-inch (6 mm) and press open.

Step 2. Finish the unnotched outer edges of the facing to prevent raveling. Use one of the finishing methods discussed earlier. Press.

Step 3. Place the *right* side of the facing against the *right* side of the garment. Match notches and seams, and pin together.

Step 4. Stitch the facing to the garment at ½-inch (1.3 cm), sewing as evenly as possible.

Step 5. Grade and clip the seams to reduce bulk.

Step 6. Press the facing and seam allowance away from the garment.

Step 7. Understitch the facing. Turn the facing to the inside and press.

Step 8. Hand sew the facing to the inside of the garment at the seam allowances only to avoid pulling along the stitching line.

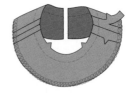
Step 1

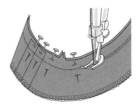
Step 4

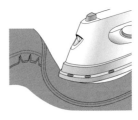
Step 6

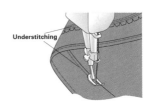
Understitching

Step 7

Gathering

Gathers are soft folds of fabric. They're formed by pulling up basting stitches to make a larger piece of fabric fit onto a smaller space. Fullness on shirts, skirts, and sometimes window curtains is often created by gathers. To make gathers:

Step 1. Sew two evenly spaced rows of machine basting on the right side of the fabric, with a stitch length of at least 4. Leave a 2-inch (5 cm) tail of thread at the beginning and the end of each row. Don't backstitch. Stitch the first row on the seamline. Stitch the second row about ¼-inch (6 mm) from the seamline inside the seam allowance.

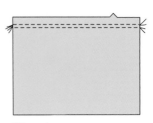
Step 1

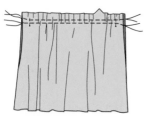

Step 2

Steps 3–4

Step 5

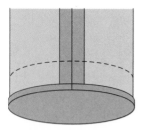

Finish casing edge.

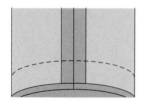

Opening for elastic or drawstring.

Step 2. If a large amount of fabric is to be gathered, divide the amount to be gathered into equal parts. Stitch and gather each part separately.

Step 3. Pin the edge to be gathered to the corresponding straight edge (such as a ruffle to a curtain edge) with the right sides together. Match all markings, notches, and seams.

Step 4. Tie a knot in each pair of bobbin thread tails. Gently pull up these bobbin thread tails at each end. Slide the fabric along with your fingers until it fits the shorter section. At both ends, wrap the excess bobbin thread around the pins in figure eights. Adjust the gathers evenly. Pin about every ½-inch (1.3 cm).

Step 5. When stitching a gathered seam, sew with the gathered edge on top. In this way, stitching is more accurate and the gathers will not be caught in the stitching. For safe sewing, remove the pins as you sew.

Casings

A casing is a closed tunnel or space of fabric that can hold an elastic or a drawstring in a waistband. Casings are also used as curtain rod pockets for simple curtains or valances.

A casing is made like a hem. You generally fold over the edge of the waistband or the top of the curtain and sew it in place. The width of the casing will vary depending on the size opening needed. For example, waistband casings are usually 1-inch (2.5 cm) wide. To sew a self-casing:

- Finish the raw edge of fabric by turning it under ¼-inch (6 mm) and press. Otherwise, zigzag or serge the raw edge.
- Turn the casing to the inside on the foldline with wrong sides together. Pin in place. Press the outer edge of the casing.
- Stitch close to the inner pinned edge of the casing. If you're inserting elastic or a drawstring, you need to leave a small opening.

Elastic Waistband

The width of the elastic needs to be about 1-inch (2.5 cm) narrower than the finished casing so you can pull it through the casing. If the casing is too wide, the elastic will twist inside the casing when the garment is worn.

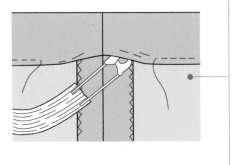

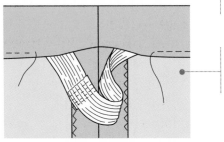

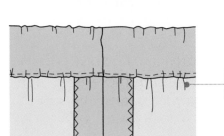

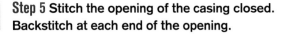

Step 1. Leave a 1½-inch (3.8 cm) opening when stitching the inner edge of the casing to insert elastic. Backstitch at each end of the seam.

Step 2. Cut a piece of elastic to fit snugly around your waist. Remember, it must be able to slide over your hips. Add 2 inches (5 cm) to overlap.

Step 3. Put a safety pin in one end of the elastic. Insert the pin and elastic into the opening in the casing. Pull the pin and elastic through the casing, using the pin to guide the elastic. Hold onto the loose end of the elastic.

Step 4. Overlap the elastic ends 1 inch (2.5 cm). Machine stitch the overlap securely in a square pattern.

Step 5 Stitch the opening of the casing closed. Backstitch at each end of the opening.

Hems

The bottom edges of pants, skirts, sleeves, and curtains are finished with hems. The type of hem you'll use depends on the type of fabric and the design of the project.

Marking the Hem

To mark the length of the hemline, put on shoes of the heel height you expect to wear with the finished garment. Decide on the best length for the garment. Have another person measure the correct length up from the floor using a measuring stick. Place pins or chalk marks at the same distance all the way around the garment. Check to be sure the markings form an even line.

Using the marked line as a guide, turn the hem to the wrong side of the garment. Insert pins at right angles along the fold line. The depth of the hem varies depending on

Marking with chalk   Marking with pins

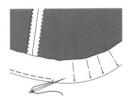

Pin and baste the hem along the fold.

Mark and trim the hem depth to make it even.

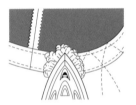

Shrink hem fullness with steam in fabrics that shrink.

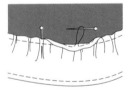

For fabrics that do not shrink with steam, machine baste close to cut edge. Pull up bobbin thread to ease in fullness.

the fullness of the garment. Pants usually have a hem of 1½ to 2 inches (3.8 to 5 cm). Skirt hems vary from 1 to 3 inches (2.5 to 7.5 cm), depending on the fullness.

Measure the hem depth needed plus ¼-inch (6 mm) for finishing. Cut off the extra fabric from the edge of the hem. Machine stitch ½-inch (1.3 cm) from the cut edge. Stitch only through the hem, not the outside of the garment.

Finishing the Hem

When a garment has extra fullness, it has to be eased in to fit flat against the garment. Otherwise, it will be bulky and lumpy. The illustrations on this page show how to ease in fullness.

There are several ways to finish raw edges of hems, such as zigzagging, clean finishing, and serging. Choose a method that best suits your fabric.

Next, attach the hem to the garment. Two methods include slipstitching—a method of hand stitching—and machine stitching.

- **Slipstitching.** To slipstitch a hem, use a single strand of thread in the needle. Make sure the stitches don't show on the outside of the garment. Keep the stitches somewhat loose so the fabric doesn't pull. Start by attaching the thread to a seam. Pick up only one or two threads on the outer layer of the garment or fabric. Space the stitches about ½-inch (1.3 cm) apart.
- **Machine stitching.** Blindstitching or topstitching can also be used to attach a hem to a garment. If your machine has a built-in blindstitch, follow the machine manual. For topstitching, fold the hem to the width you want and press. Stitch close to the upper edge of the hem.

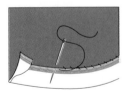

Hem edge finished by serging the fabric edge.

Slipstitch the hem edge to the garment.

HOW to...

Make Pop Can Wrap-Arounds

To make four wrap-arounds, you will need:

- ⅜-yd. (0.35 m) of 45-inch (115 cm) wide cotton-blend fabric
- 11-by-16-inch (28-by-40.5-cm) piece of ½-inch (1.3 cm) thick foam rubber
- 14-inch (35.5 cm) strip of hook-and-loop fastener tape

Step 1: Cut fabric into four pieces, each 12½ by 10 inches (31.8 by 25.5 cm). Cut foam rubber into four strips, each 10½ by 4 inches (26.8 by 10 cm). Cut the hook-and-loop tape into four 3½-inch (9 cm) pieces.

Step 2: Press one long edge of fabric under ½-inch (1.3 cm).

Step 3: Lay one foam piece lengthwise across each length of fabric. Center the foam, both horizontally and vertically, on the fabric. The short ends of the fabric should extend 1 inch (2.5 cm) beyond the short ends of the foam. To encase the foam in the fabric, bring the bottom of the fabric up toward the center of the foam and the top of the fabric (with the folded edge) down toward the center of the foam. Overlap the folded edge over the raw edge of the fabric at the center of the foam. Pin the overlapped layers of fabric to the foam to hold the layers in place.

Step 4: Set your machine's stitch length on 4, or the longest stitch length. Topstitch next to the folded edge on the overlap. Remove the

pins as you come to them. Stitch again ¼-inch (6 mm) from the folded edge of this seam.

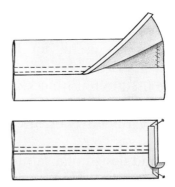

Step 5: With the seam side up, fold one end of the fabric over ½-inch (1.3 cm) and press. Tuck the corners in and pin the folded end in place. Cover the raw edges with the loop section of the tape and stitch it in place through all layers, removing pins as you sew. Begin stitching in the middle of one long edge of the loop section, and continue around. Backstitch to secure the thread ends.

Step 6: Turn the wrap-around over. Fold the other end over ½-inch (1.3 cm) and press. Tuck the corners in, pin, and cover with the hook section of the tape. (The hook-and-loop sections should be on opposite sides of the wrap-around.) Stitch the hook section of the tape in place through all layers.

Chapter Summary

- Learning basic sewing techniques is helpful for constructing projects and for repairs and alterations.
- Accurate stitching is important in any sewing project.
- Appropriate seam finishes prevent the cut edges of fabric from raveling.
- Serged seams are useful for knits and loosely woven fabrics.
- Facings are used to finish necklines, front openings, armholes, and collars.
- Fullness on garments is often created by gathering.
- The fabric and design of a garment determine the type of hem used.

Reviewing the Chapter

1. Identify two types of basting. Briefly describe each.
2. What are two ways you can determine the correct stitching direction for sewing a seam?
3. Briefly describe how to stitch a seam.
4. List three seam finishes. Briefly explain when it's best to use each.
5. Why is it important to grade a seam when attaching interfacing to a garment?
6. Explain how to make the two rows of stitching used in gathering.
7. What is a casing? Where are casings used?
8. Identify three ways to finish the raw edges of a hem.

Family & Community

With Your Family

If you'd like to learn some new sewing techniques, ask someone in your family who is more experienced if he or she can help you.

In Your Community

Organize a clothing repair workshop along with some classmates to benefit a local shelter or food pantry. As a class, decide what types of repairs you'll make, such as repairing seams, replacing buttons, or hemming garments.

- Set a date for your workshop and determine the fee for each type of repair.
- Prepare flyers to put out in the community.
- Evaluate the success of your repair workshop.

Thinking Critically

1. **Draw conclusions.** Why might some of your classmates be more satisfied when working on their sewing projects than others? How could their attitudes affect other construction projects?
2. **Analyze the situation.** If you saw a neckline seam that was very bulky and unattractive, what could have caused the problem? Explain how this could have been avoided.
3. **Draw conclusions.** Assume you read that hanging a skirt at the waistline for a day before hemming it was advisable. Speculate why this might be a good idea.

Making Connections

1. **Art.** Collect drawings or photographs that show gathering used in a variety of places on clothing or projects for the home. Arrange an attractive display that illustrates how gathering creates interest in each example. Top your display with an appealing title.
2. **Speech.** Present a brief demonstration for the class on how to apply interfacing. Prepare oversized visual aids with paper to show each of the various steps before you actually sew them.

Applying Your Learning

1. **Test basting methods.** Experiment with different methods of basting on samples of fabric. When would you use each of these basting methods?
2. **Finish the edge.** Collect samples of different types of fabric. Decide which seam finish would be appropriate for each type of fabric. Try the finishes on the fabric samples.
3. **Make a casing.** If your project does not include an elastic casing, make a sample casing to fit your wrist out of some scrap fabric. Practice putting in the elastic and securing it to fit your wrist.

What Would You Do?

As you're completing a new garment, you find that there's not enough hem allowance for the length you need. What are some ideas you might try to make a satisfactory hem without shortening the garment?

Career Network

FASHION AND APPAREL

RETAIL MANAGER

Large retail store needs manager for children's clothing department. Will supervise employees and manage daily activities.
- Good customer service skills needed.
- Associate's degree required.
- Formal training provided.

FASHION BUYER

Women's clothing store seeks individual who will choose suppliers, negotiate prices, and monitor quality and service. Must be well informed and able to anticipate customer demand.
- Frequent overseas travel.
- Ability to work under pressure.
- Bachelor's degree preferred.

FASHION DESIGNER

Apparel manufacturer seeks entry-level fashion designer for children's clothing and accessories.
- Two-year degree necessary.
- Knowledge of textiles and fabrics required
- Training provided.

PATTERNMAKER

Garment manufacturer seeks skilled patternmaker to convert original designs into patterns, and to prepare patterns of different sizes.
- Artistic ability needed.
- Strong computer skills essential.
- Must have eye for detail and ability to work as part of a team.

MANAGEMENT CONSULTANT

Growing fashion industry consulting firm has opening for consultant with strong problem-solving ability. Will develop plans to expand operations in large client companies.
- Master's degree plus experience required.
- Excellent communication skills necessary.

SEWING MACHINE OPERATOR

Clothing manufacturer seeks individuals to operate computerized sewing machines. Work involves sewing parts together, attaching buttons, and performing other tasks to produce clothing.
- Training provided.
- Good hand-eye coordination needed.
- Ability to work under pressure.

More Career Options

Entry Level
- Laundry Worker
- Cutter
- Presser
- Clothing Salesperson
- Stock Clerk

Technical Level
- Dyer
- Textile Engineer
- Weaving Machine Operator

Professional Level
- Model
- Stylist
- Fashion Coordinator
- Wardrobe Consultant
- Jeweler

CLOTHIER/TAILOR

Store specializing in wedding clothes seeks experienced clothier/tailor to make alterations.
• Must have eye for detail and ability to use design elements.
• Must be tactful and patient when dealing with clients.
• Must be able to work extra hours when needed to meet deadlines.

PERSONAL SHOPPER

Upscale department store seeks knowledgeable personal shopper to help customers find suitable clothing and accessories.
• Experience in fashion merchandising.
• Ability to anticipate fashion trends.
• Good communication and interpersonal skills.

FABRIC DESIGNER

Textile manufacturer has opening for creative fabric designer who will create designs on computer and recommend suitable textures, weaves, and colors.
• Eye for detail and color essential.
• Ability to present ideas and accept criticism.
• Bachelor's degree and fashion merchandising experience preferred.

DRY CLEANER

Individual needed to work in busy dry cleaning business. Responsibilities include removing stains, applying pretreatments, using cleaning machines, and pressing and shaping garments.
• Training provided.
• High school diploma preferred.

Linking School to Career

1. **Your Career Plan:** Imagine you are the Human Resources Director and a classmate is applying for a job with your company. Write down the questions that you will ask. Conduct an interview with your classmate. Would you hire your classmate for the job? Now you give it a try and be the one applying. Did you get the job? Together make a list of dos and don'ts for a job interview.

2. **Researching Careers:** Some jobs in fashion and apparel are threatened by stiff competition from overseas. Investigate a career that interests you and find out whether the demand for people in that career is likely to grow, decline, or stay the same. Why is it important to investigate future trends for careers that interest you?

3. **Reading:** Look up the definitions of the following terms that are found in the want ad listings:
• Negotiate
• Anticipate
• Tactful
• Hand-eye coordination
• Merchandising

Unit 11

Housing and Interiors

Chapter
46

Where You Live

YOU WILL LEARN . . .

- ➤ The basic needs that housing fulfills.
- ➤ Factors that influence housing choices.
- ➤ Various kinds of housing and their advantages and disadvantages.
- ➤ The pros and cons of renting and owning housing.

TERMS TO LEARN . . .

- ➤ condominiums
- ➤ cooperative
- ➤ duplex
- ➤ landlords
- ➤ lease
- ➤ mortgage
- ➤ multiple-family housing
- ➤ multiplex
- ➤ single-family housing
- ➤ townhomes
- ➤ utilities

Imagine ...

... that you're five years old again. Your favorite thing to draw is a home. There's always a door and windows, some flowers, and a big sun in the sky.

Think About

- Why do children like to draw homes?
- At your age now, how would your drawing be different?
- What will your home in the future be like?

HOUSING TO FULFILL HUMAN NEEDS

What does a one-story brick bungalow in Milwaukee have in common with a sprawling ranch house near Dallas? With an apartment in the nation's capital or a cabin in rural Georgia? Each living unit is someone's home. Whether large or small, each structure fulfills its residents' basic needs.

All people have basic needs in common:

- **Physical needs.** Physical needs are air, sunlight, sleep, food, and other things the body needs to survive. Housing helps people meet physical needs by protecting them from the weather and by providing a place to eat, sleep, and be safe.

- **Emotional needs.** Housing meets people's emotional needs by allowing them to relax and pursue their own interests in privacy and comfort. Many people decorate their homes to reflect their personal taste.

- **Social needs.** The need for love and belonging to a group is a social need. Housing serves as a gathering place for family and friends. A home promotes family strength by giving family members a place to live, work, play, and relax together.

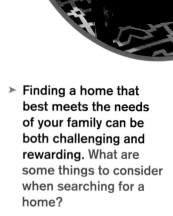

➤ Finding a home that best meets the needs of your family can be both challenging and rewarding. What are some things to consider when searching for a home?

When housing offers opportunities to meet emotional and social needs, it's more than just a structure— it's a home!

INFLUENCES ON HOUSING DECISIONS

Although people share basic human needs, they also have individual needs and wants. When families and individuals choose a place to live, they first need to consider specific needs and wants. The next step is to find a way to balance those needs and wants with available resources.

> People's housing needs vary. A person with physical limitations may require special adaptations.

Considering Needs and Wants

Needs and wants differ from family to family. What one family considers necessary might be considered a drawback to another family. The following are some questions that families should consider when choosing housing:

- **Family size.** How much room does the family need? Ari lives with his foster parents and five other children. His family's need for space is quite different from that of Annie's family, which includes herself, her brother, and her father.

- **Family life cycle.** What type of housing suits the family's life cycle stage? As explained in Chapter 15, every family goes through a life cycle. Changes during the life cycle can affect housing needs and wants. Desiree and Darren just became parents. Soon they'll look for a larger place to live with an outdoor play area nearby. Meanwhile, Darren's grandfather is also planning ahead. Now that he lives alone, he'd prefer a smaller place that requires little upkeep.

- **Special needs of family members.** Do any family members have special needs? Someone with limited mobility, for example, may require a single-level home. A person who uses a wheelchair or walker requires a home with doors and hallways wide enough to easily pass through.

> Because of increased technology, searching for a new home can be done on the Internet.

- **Location.** Is it important for any family member to be close to a job or certain transportation? Would the family prefer a quiet location or a busy neighborhood with easy access to stores and public transportation?
- **Environment.** What kind of environment best suits the family's needs? Some families seek to avoid the noise and air pollution associated with cities. A family concerned about the environment might look for a community that conserves or recycles resources.
- **Technology.** Some families have a greater need than others for modern technology in the home. Is the home wired for high-speed telephone or cable access?
- **Lifestyle.** What interests and activities are part of the family's lifestyle?

Meet Special Family Needs

Some families have members who require special housing considerations. Whether it be a parent in a wheelchair or a grandparent with limited mobility, adapting living space can improve independence. Here are some suggestions:

- Kitchens. Kitchens can be made more convenient by offering lower counters to accommodate wheelchairs, open shelves rather than closed cabinets, and special faucets with long spouts and handles. For visually impaired persons, Braille knobs, appliance control panels, and instruction books can be ordered.
- Bathrooms. To make bathrooms safe and convenient, install grab bars in the tub and around the toilet, add a hand-held shower, and put nonslip strips on the shower or tub floor.
- Floors. Floors with hard, smooth finishes make it easier for people who use wheelchairs and walkers. Avoid throw rugs—they can cause falls.
- Stairs. Install railings on both sides of stairs and hallways. For people in wheelchairs, use ramps rather than stairs, if possible.
- Lighting. Adequate lighting is especially important for those with poor vision. Check the number, brightness, and placement of lights in the home. Be sure a light can be turned on near the entrance of each room.

What simple changes could be made to your home to accommodate someone with a disability, even a temporary disability, such as a broken leg?

Considering Family Resources

Once a family has considered the factors discussed above, they'll have a good idea of the location and type of housing they want. If the family can't find what they're looking for, they may have to rethink their housing needs and wants.

The housing you choose must be affordable. Financial advisers recommend spending no more than 28 percent of household income on housing expenses. When calculating the cost of housing, take all expenses into account. In addition to monthly payments for the housing unit itself, consider other possible costs, such as insurance, taxes, repairs, and utilities. **Utilities** are *basic services, such as electricity, gas or oil, water, and sewer service.*

➤ Additional living costs must be considered when determining how much a family can afford to spend on a home. What do these include?

Most people must make some compromises in order to find housing that fits their budget. Lindsay's family hoped to find a home where she and her younger sister could have their own bedrooms. Because her mother worked at home as a hairdresser, they needed space for her salon, too. The best value they could find met all the family's needs, except for separate bedrooms for the girls.

Human resources, such as construction and decorating skills, time, energy, and creativity can stretch housing dollars. For instance, Ari's foster parents bought an old house that needed repairs. Without their skills and willingness to make improvements themselves, they would have had to settle for a much smaller house.

TYPES OF HOUSING

The two most basic categories of housing are single-family housing and multiple-family housing. **Single-family housing** is *built to house one family.* **Multiple-family housing** contains *several single-family housing units in one structure.*

Learning more about the kinds of single-family and multiple-family housing available, and understanding the advantages and disadvantages of each, can help you make good housing decisions in the future.

Single-Family Housing

Single-family homes are freestanding—they don't share any walls with another housing unit. They may be small or large, one story or several stories high.

Single-family houses offer more privacy than other types of housing. They're also usually more expensive, because they require more land and materials.

One kind of single-family home is a manufactured home (sometimes called a "mobile home"). Manufactured homes are built in a factory and are installed at a specific site. Some communities restrict where manufactured homes can be placed. Most manufactured homes are less expensive than a traditional single-family house. They may come complete with carpeting, window coverings, appliances, and furniture.

➤ **This neighborhood consists of single family dwellings. What are** some other types of single-family dwellings?

Multiple-Family Housing

There are many kinds of multiple-family dwellings, including the following:

- A **duplex** is *one building that contains two separate units.* The units may be side by side, sharing one wall, or they may be on separate floors.
- A **multiplex** is similar to a duplex, but *three or more units share one building.*
- **Townhomes** are *houses built in rows and attached to one another at the side walls.*
- The term "apartment building" covers any structure that has rental units for more than two families. Apartment buildings range from a large older home divided into three or four apartments to a high-rise with hundreds of units. A number of separate buildings may be grouped together to form an apartment complex.

➤ Sharing common walls and outdoor spaces makes multiple-family housing less expensive to build.

Multiple-family dwellings meet the needs of many people. This type of housing is often more affordable and more readily available than single-family houses. Cost, however, varies with location, size, and features. Individual units may be small or large. Residents may or may not share the use of a laundry, swimming pool, or other special features.

Multiple-family dwellings require much less land per person than single-family houses require. It's no surprise that multiple-family housing is especially common in large cities where land is scarce and single-family housing is expensive.

Multiple-family dwellings also have their disadvantages. They tend to be noisier and less private than single-family homes. Storage space may be limited, and there may be little or no yard area. Pets may not be allowed.

➤ Name some of the advantages and disadvantages of living in a townhome.

WAYS TO OBTAIN HOUSING

Some individuals and families own the housing unit in which they live. Others rent their home either directly or indirectly from its owner. Renting and buying both have advantages and disadvantages.

Renting a Home

Renting means paying money to live in a housing unit that is owned by someone else. *Owners of rental housing* are sometimes called **landlords.** Rental units come in a wide range of prices and may be furnished or unfurnished.

All the kinds of housing units described in this chapter may be rented. In addition, you might rent a room in a house or a dormitory. A room just for sleeping, with no private kitchen or bath facilities, is a relatively inexpensive form of housing.

When you rent a housing unit, you may have to fill out an application and sign a **lease,** *a written rental agreement.* The lease states that you agree to pay rent for a certain number of months. It specifies the monthly fee and any rules you must follow. Always read a lease carefully before you sign it. If you don't understand part of the lease, ask a qualified third person to explain it to you. Many landlords require a security deposit equal to one month's rent or more. The deposit is returned when you move out if the unit hasn't been damaged. The landlord may keep a portion of the deposit if you don't leave the apartment or house clean and in good condition.

➤ Signing a lease commits you to a long-term financial obligation. Make sure everything in the lease is clearly explained.

Many people enjoy the advantages of renting. They include:

- **Convenience.** The landlord rather than the tenant usually does tasks such as painting and household repairs.
- **Flexibility.** Renters don't have to sell their home when it's time to move. Selling a home can be a long and costly process.
- **Financial advantages.** Both renting and owning have month-to-month costs. However, tenants don't face unexpected costs for repairs.

Owning a Home

Many people choose to buy a home because they value a feeling of permanence. Owning a home also offers freedom. Homeowners can redecorate or remodel their home to meet their personal needs and tastes. A home is also a major investment and can provide a sense of financial security.

Purchasing a place to live isn't a decision to be made lightly. Buying a home is the costliest purchase most families will ever make.

➤ Applying for a mortgage loan is a long process. Your family should look for the best interest rate available.

In order to buy a home, most people take out *a long-term loan,* called a **mortgage.** The mortgage is typically for 15 to 30 years. The interest paid on the mortgage can be deducted on the homeowner's income tax return. This is an incentive for many people to buy instead of rent a home.

The part of the purchase price that is paid in cash is called a *down payment.* The down payment can be quite large, often at least 10 percent of the cost. Other costs must also be considered. A homeowner usually must pay property taxes and insurance, as well as for utilities and repairs.

Many people want to invest in a home but don't want the responsibilities of yard work and outside maintenance. Two special kinds of housing, which combine some advantages of home ownership and apartment living, offer a solution.

➤ Condominiums offer ownership without the responsibility of yard work and outside maintenance. A monthly fee, paid by each owner of a condominium, covers the expense of outside chores.

Condominiums are *individually owned units in a multiple-family dwelling.* The owner of each unit pays a fee to help cover the cost of maintaining hallways, landscaping, parking lots, and other common areas.

A less common form of ownership is a **cooperative,** or co-op. In a co-op, *residents of a multiple-family dwelling form an organization that owns the building.* Instead of buying or renting an individual unit, organization members buy shares in the organization and contribute to its monthly costs. In return, each member receives use of one of the living units.

Sharing a Home

Sharing a home is an option chosen by many people. Families or individuals combine their finances to better meet their housing needs.

Classmates may share an apartment to save money. Adult children sometimes return to live with a parent for a time. An elderly mother or father may move in with their adult child's family for care and companionship.

Sharing a home only works if people are thoughtful of one another. If possible, every member of the household should have some degree of privacy, a place to call his or her own.

TRY IT OUT

Your Ideal Home

What You'll Need
- Pictures of housing
- Current salary information for a career of your choice
- Paper, glue, pen or pencil

What to Do
1. Collect pictures of five homes along with their prices. Glue each to a separate sheet of paper. Write the price on the back of each.
2. Identify a job that interests you and use current salary information to find out what the job might pay annually.
3. Combine your house pictures with those of other students. Choose a picture of a home that appeals to you. Assuming that you'll spend two times your annual income, can you afford the home you chose? If not, choose again until you find one you can afford.

To Discuss
- How does choice of career affect the amount you can afford to spend on housing? What role do values play in housing choices?
- Why might families with the same amount of income spend different amounts on housing? What resources can be used to lower the costs of buying and maintaining a home?

CHOOSING A PLACE TO LIVE

People often change housing as their needs and resources change. Most people live in several different types of housing during their lifetime.

The decision to move should be made carefully. Moving can be expensive. You may need to hire movers or rent a truck. Having the phone hooked up or changing electric service, for instance, involves additional fees. What other moving-related expenses can you think of?

When it does make sense to move, the more information you have to make a housing decision, the more satisfied you're likely to be with your choice.

Review & Activities

Chapter Summary

- All people share the same basic needs.
- Not every family has the same housing needs and wants.
- Compromises are usually necessary when choosing housing to fit an individual or family's budget.
- Human resources can be used to stretch housing dollars or to meet special needs.
- Single-family homes usually are more expensive but offer more privacy than other types of housing.
- There are different types of multiple-family dwellings, each with its own advantages and disadvantages.

Family & Community

With Your Family
Talk with your family about what a home means to them. What's the most important feature to them? What is the least important feature?

In Your Community
Habitat for Humanity International helps to renovate and build homes for people who would otherwise not be able to afford a home. Find out more information about this organization and how people in a community can help.

- Renters need to read carefully and understand all parts of a rental agreement before signing it.
- Choosing to buy a place to live is a major decision. It's the costliest purchase most families will ever make.
- Many individuals and families satisfy their housing needs by combining finances and sharing a home.
- You're likely to live in several different types of housing during your lifetime.

Reviewing the Chapter

1. Briefly describe and give examples of three basic needs everyone has in common.
2. Explain how changes during a family's life cycle can affect their housing needs and wants.
3. Give an example showing how a family member's special needs might affect the family's housing choices.
4. Name four human resources. Describe a situation where human resources can be used to stretch housing dollars.
5. List and describe the two basic categories of housing. Which type tends to be more expensive? Why?
6. Identify four types of multiple-family dwellings. Why are multiple-family dwellings common in most large cities?
7. What is the difference between a landlord and a tenant?
8. Name three advantages of renting and three advantages of owning a home.
9. Give three situations in which people may choose to share a home.

Review & Activities

Thinking Critically

1. **Analyze decisions.** Think about the different influences on housing decisions. In what ways have those influences affected your family's housing decisions?

2. **Assess outcomes.** What human resources might you develop or strengthen to help stretch your present or future housing dollars? Explain your answer.

3. **Predict consequences.** Describe possible consequences that might occur when people with different housekeeping standards, privacy standards, or social needs decide to share housing.

Making Connections

1. **Language Arts.** Write a paragraph about the type of housing you think you'll be living in five, ten, and fifteen years from now. Explain your reasoning.

2. **Math.** Assume you are renting an apartment for $425 a month and have to pay a two-month refundable security deposit. How much would you pay for your apartment the first year?

Applying Your Learning

1. **Take a survey.** Use the real estate section of the newspaper to see what types of housing are available in your community. What type of housing seems to be the most available? Least available?

2. **Share ideas.** Brainstorm a list of situations when sharing housing might be a good option.

3. **Think about it.** Imagine you're in a wheelchair. What difficulties would you encounter trying to get around in your own home? What accommodations could you make?

What Would You Do?

On several occasions you've seen younger neighborhood children doing minor damage to neighborhood property. You know the children and their families, and they've always been good neighbors. What would you do about this?

Decorating Living Space

YOU WILL LEARN . . .

- ➤ How to create pleasing room designs.
- ➤ Elements that make up a room's background.
- ➤ Strategies for selecting and arranging furniture and accessories.
- ➤ Three types of lighting and the unique purpose of each.
- ➤ Ways to make sharing space easier.

TERMS TO LEARN . . .

- ➤ accent lighting
- ➤ functional furniture
- ➤ general lighting
- ➤ task lighting
- ➤ traffic patterns

Imagine ...

… that your family has moved to an apartment where you'll have a small room of your own. The landlord might give it a fresh coat of paint, but that won't help the ugly carpet. You're eager to make the room reflect your own taste.

Think About

- If you had $75 to spend, where would you start? Why?
- Where could you find decorating ideas?
- Would you be willing to spend some of your own money on your room? Why or why not?

DESIGNING LIVING SPACE

Some people just seem to have a natural flair for decorating a room. But anyone can learn to apply the basic elements and principles of design to create attractive living spaces.

Whether you're planning merely to brighten a room by adding a few new posters, or to redecorate entirely, think the project through before you begin. You're much more likely to be pleased with the results. Here are some suggestions:

- **Identify your needs and preferences.** Ask yourself these questions: What's my major goal? For what activities will the space be used? What type of storage is needed? What kind of look do I want to achieve?
- **Evaluate your current space.** What parts of the present design work well? What needs improvement? What specifically would you like to keep or change?
- **Consider your resources.** There's no point in planning expensive changes if they're beyond your budget. Remember that skills are resources, too. Changing a room's look can mean adding a few new touches to what you already have.

As you plan, consider the elements and principles of design to combine backgrounds, furniture, and accessories into a successful design that expresses *you*.

INFOLINK

See Chapter 40 for more information on the elements and principles of design.

➤ When designing a room, allowing for ample space is important. It allows people to move easily from one area to another.

Backgrounds

When you design a living area, first think about the space you have to work with. That space is defined by walls, windows, and flooring. Well-chosen backgrounds help display your furniture and other possessions to their best advantage.

Walls

Walls define areas, provide privacy, and help absorb noise. The number of ways you can decorate walls, however, is limited only by your imagination.

The two most popular ways to decorate walls are painting and wallpapering. If you paint, you can choose from many colors. You might even paint a design on all or part of a wall. Wallpaper can add interesting patterns and textures.

Windows

Window treatments (also called window coverings) can provide both privacy and decoration. Window treatment choices include curtains, drapes, shutters, blinds, and shades. Some people like to combine treatments. For example, you might want to use shutters and curtains on the same window.

➤ Color affects people's feelings. Choice of color can create the mood you want. Blue, for example, creates a cool, relaxed feeling.

➤ Window coverings change the look of a room. Before selecting window coverings, decide on the amount of privacy you want.

Design in Housing

The Elements of Design

The elements of design are five basic building blocks of any design: space, line, shape, texture, and color. As you read about these elements, think about how each is used to add comfort and beauty to the room shown on the next page.

Space refers to the three-dimensional area to be designed, such as the room itself, as well as the area around or between objects within that space. Space can make a room seem quite different depending on how it's used. For example, a room containing many pieces of furniture may give some people a cozy feeling. Others may find the same room uncomfortably crowded.

Line refers to the outline of an object or to obvious lines within it. Lines can cause your eyes to move up and down or across an object. For example, tall bookcases create the illusion of height, while the long, horizontal lines of a sofa draw the eye across the room.

Shape, or the form and structure of solid objects, is created when lines are combined. The shapes of objects can make them seem heavy or light. A large, heavy object like a sofa gives a feeling of stability to a room. Spindly chairs in the same space produce the opposite effect.

Texture describes the way an object's surfaces look and feel. In turn, texture often influences the way people feel in a room. Plush rugs and furniture covered with soft fabric provide a sense of comfort and luxury, while nubby, rough materials convey a casual, country feeling.

Color is often called the most important of all decorating tools. Color influences how people feel, so it can be used to create a certain mood. Because warm colors appear closer than cool colors, red-painted walls seem to draw closer together, creating a sense of intimacy.

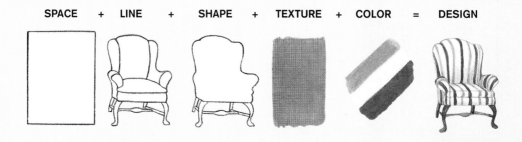

SPACE + LINE + SHAPE + TEXTURE + COLOR = DESIGN

The Principles of Design

All good designs follow certain principles that have evolved over time. These principles are balance, emphasis, harmony, proportion, rhythm, and scale. By applying these principles to the elements of design, you can achieve appealing decorating results that fit your personality.

Balance gives a feeling of equal weight among all parts of a design. Balance can be formal or informal. In formal balance, the objects on each side of an imaginary centerline are the same. In informal balance, the objects on each side of the center are different in size, form, texture, or color.

Emphasis is the point of greatest interest. This room's point of emphasis is the fireplace wall.

Harmony is the feeling that all parts of a design belong together. That doesn't mean everything has to match. Variety is interesting if objects grouped together have something in common, such as the repetition of the color red in the walls, rug, chairs, and pillows.

Proportion is the way one part of a design relates in size or shape to another or to the whole. The ancient Greeks discovered that certain uneven proportions are more pleasing than even ones, and rectangles are more desirable than squares.

Rhythm is a feeling of movement, leading the eye from one point to another. Repeating one or more elements of design does this. For example, there is rhythm in the white-painted woodwork of the bookshelves and fireplace.

Scale refers to the overall size of an object or its size compared to other objects. Without arms, for example, the chair in this room looks smaller, in keeping with the room's smaller scale.

DECORATING WALLS

Pictures and other items hung on the walls give a room a warm, personal look. When planning wall decorations, keep these tips in mind.

- Hang decorations at eye level.

- Place single wall decorations over a piece of furniture that is in proportion to the decoration.

- Use an uneven number of items if you are creating a wall arrangement. Uneven numbers are more pleasing to the eye.

- When arranging a wall grouping, trace each item on paper and cut out the shapes. Practice arranging these paper "wall decorations" (using masking tape on the back) before fastening the hangers or nails to the wall.

Floors

Flooring materials, such as concrete, wood, ceramic tile, slate, and brick are considered a permanent part of the floor. Floor coverings, which aren't considered permanent, may be installed over permanent flooring. They can add comfort, warmth, and beauty to a room. Vinyl, for example, is easy to clean. It's warmer and quieter to walk on than ceramic tile and other hard materials, but vinyl is more easily damaged. Carpets and rugs provide extra warmth and comfort, muffle noise, and add color.

Furniture

Furniture provides a place for all kinds of activities. Most furniture is **functional furniture,** or *meets specific needs.* Chests, for example, are used to store things. Tables provide space for eating or perhaps doing homework. Of course, functional furniture is usually decorative as well.

Furniture Styles

Because people's tastes differ, manufacturers make many styles of furniture. These styles can be divided into two basic types: traditional and contemporary.

Traditional styles are based on designs used for hundreds of years. Traditional furniture can be formal or informal and fancy or plain.

Contemporary furniture is simple and reflects today's lifestyles. It has straight or smoothly curved lines with little or no decoration. Plastic, glass, and metal are used for contemporary furniture, but wood and fabric are often used too.

When choosing furniture for a room, look for styles that have a similar feeling, such as different wood furniture pieces with similar simple lines. Even if they're from different time periods, they'll still look good together.

Choosing Furniture

Before selecting furniture, determine what you need and what you have. If your budget is limited, put your creativity to work. Garage sales, flea markets, and secondhand shops often have used furniture bargains. With a coat of paint or a new cushion, these pieces might become just what you have in mind.

Arranging Furniture

The smart way to arrange furniture is to use paper (or a special computer program) before you use your muscles. Take time to think about your arrangement plan. Ask others for their ideas. Check to see if the **traffic patterns,** or *the paths people use to get from one area or room to another,* are uncluttered and fairly direct. Avoid blocking your traffic pattern with furniture.

Accessories

Lamps, plants, posters, books, baskets, pictures, and other accessories are the easiest and least expensive way to change a room. They can make the difference between an interesting room and one that is only ho-hum. When selecting accessories, keep in mind the elements and principles of design.

When you consider accessories, don't limit yourself to the conventional. You can also accessorize a room by displaying your collection of hats, sports memorabilia, jewelry, or other items that express your personality.

 When shopping for furniture, look for sturdy, well-made pieces that will last.

Lighting

Lighting is part of interior design, and lighting needs should be considered during the planning stage. Each of the three main types of lighting has a unique purpose.

- **General lighting,** such as an overhead ceiling light, *provides enough light so that you can move around the room safely and comfortably.* In most cases, general lighting isn't a good light for reading or studying.
- **Task lighting** *focuses light where it's needed.* You use task lighting to prevent eyestrain when reading, working on hobbies, and playing games. Task lighting should be free of distracting glare and shadows. If you use a table or floor lamp for reading, the bottom of the shade should be slightly below eye level when you are seated. If the lighting is above your eye level, the lamp should be about 10 inches (4 cm) behind your shoulder.

HOW to...

Try Out Furniture Arrangements

It's possible to try out different arrangements without having to drag around the furniture itself. Professional designers use computer-aided design (CAD) programs, which give lifelike views of how a finished room will look. A commercial floor-plan kit is simpler to use. Such a kit contains precut plastic furniture shapes that cling to a flat plastic grid for marking your room's measurements. You can experiment with different arrangements simply by moving the plastic shapes.

Try making your own "kit." All you need is graph paper, a ruler, and a measuring tape.

1. Measure the size of the room. Use your measurements to draw the outline of the room on graph paper. Make each square on the graph paper represent 12 inches (30.5 cm).

2. Mark the size and placement of windows, doors, and other features.

3. On another sheet of graph paper, draw each piece of furniture to the same scale as you drew the room outline, using simple shapes. Cut out the furniture shapes.

4. Use your paper furniture and room outline to try different furniture arrangements.

➤ Small changes, such as adding bright pillows or rearranging furniture, can improve a room. What differences do you notice in this updated room?

BEFORE

AFTER

- **Accent lighting** is *an intense beam of light aimed at a painting, sculpture, or other object to create a dramatic effect.* Accent lighting can be installed in the ceiling or can be freestanding lighting.

SHARING SPACE

Sharing space is part of life. Whether you're at school, in stores and restaurants, or at work, you must share space and facilities with other people. In a family, everyone shares areas such as the kitchen and living room. Bathrooms are usually shared, too.

Many teens share a bedroom with one or more siblings. If you share a room, you've probably discovered that differences in age, interests, friends, and study habits can create occasional conflicts.

That's where furniture arrangement might offer a solution. Is there a way you can arrange your furniture to help make sharing easier? In a shared bedroom, you might try separating the sleeping and activity areas of the room. Another possibility is to divide the room so you each have a private area.

Whenever people share the same space, it also helps to agree on a few ground rules. Rules will keep conflicts to a minimum and help you enjoy each other more.

Respect and consideration for everyone sharing the space are the keys to effective rules. You might, for example, agree not to use each other's books or clothes without permission. Once you agree on a list of rules, make a commitment to stick to the rules you made.

Think of sharing space as a plus, not a minus. Learning how to share space can teach you a lot about yourself and others. The cooperation and communication skills you develop will help you now and in the future.

➤ How does this room arrangement make sharing space easier?

Review & Activities

Chapter Summary

- Use the elements and principles of design to create living space that you and your family enjoy.
- Before beginning any decorating project, consider individual and family needs and preferences, current space, and available resources.
- Walls, windows, and flooring serve as backgrounds that help to display furniture and other objects to their best advantage.
- Color affects people's emotions and can be used to create certain moods.

- Most furniture is functional and meets specific needs. Before selecting furniture, think of pieces you need, the functions they will serve, and what you already have.
- Before moving furniture, take time to plan your arrangement on paper or on the computer. Traffic patterns should be uncluttered and fairly direct.
- Three types of interior lighting are general lighting, task lighting, and accent lighting.
- Respect and consideration for everyone can help make sharing space easier for family members.

Family & Community

With Your Family

Talk with your family about the furnishings in your home. Would any pieces of furniture be more useful if they were refinished or repaired? How could this be done? Do you have the necessary skills? If not, how could you learn them?

In Your Community

What educational opportunities are available in your community for learning to make decorative and functional home accessories? What type of instruction is offered? How much does the instruction cost?

Reviewing the Chapter

1. What are three purposes of walls? Name two of the most popular ways to decorate walls.
2. List five types of window treatments. Give an example of treatments that are combined.
3. Briefly list and describe the five elements of design. Which one is often considered the most important? Why?
4. Explain the six principles of design and ways they can be used in various rooms of a home.
5. Should only one furniture style be used in a room? Explain.
6. Why is it important to consider the traffic pattern when arranging furniture in a room?
7. Name the purposes of the three main types of home lighting.
8. How can furniture arrangement help reduce conflicts among people who share space?

Thinking Critically

1. **Predict consequences.** What consequences might result if the traffic patterns between rooms in a family's small apartment were blocked with furniture? What steps might the family take to help make the patterns more direct?

2. **Compare and contrast.** Visualize some of the colors in nature. Compare and contrast colors you see in the spring with colors you see during the winter. In what ways are they similar? How are they different? How do the colors make you feel?

3. **Draw conclusions.** Think about college roommates who share a small dormitory room. What do you think they may learn from sharing space that they will be able to use in the future?

Making Connections

1. **Social Studies.** How has home lighting changed from the colonial period to modern times? How have these changes improved the quality of life?

2. **Math.** Estimate what the total cost would be for you to buy new furniture for your bedroom. Check a furniture store or newspaper ads for pricing. How could you save money when buying furniture?

Applying Your Learning

1. **Plan an arrangement.** Using graph paper and paper furniture cut to scale, rearrange the furniture in your bedroom to make the best use of space. Show your plan to others to see what suggestions they can offer.

2. **Create an accessory.** Draw sketches or write descriptions of at least three ways to use items as decorative accessories instead of storing them out of sight. If possible, try out one of your ideas.

3. **Make a selection.** Find a picture of a lamp that would give you good lighting for a study desk. Explain why your choice is a good one.

What Would You Do?

Assume you share a room with a brother or sister. What are some things you'd have to agree upon so that problems or conflicts would be kept to a minimum?

A Clean, Safe Home

YOU WILL LEARN . . .

➤ How to develop a maintenance plan for your home.
➤ Ways to organize storage.
➤ Hints for selecting appropriate cleaning products and equipment.
➤ Strategies for keeping your home environment healthful and safe.

TERMS TO LEARN . . .

➤ hazard
➤ home maintenance

Imagine ...

... that your grandma with failing eyesight is coming to live with your family. Grandma fell and broke her wrist last year. You have mixed feelings about the plan— Grandma has always been fun to be around, but you know daily life is going to change.

Think About

• What would have to be done to make your home safe for an elderly person?
• What if the person were almost blind?
• Could these changes benefit your family today— even without a relative coming to stay?

MAKING A PLAN

Maintaining a home so that it benefits everyone who lives there takes thought and planning. So does making changes to accommodate a new resident like a grandparent. One way to agree on household organization is to develop a home maintenance plan. **Home maintenance** includes *eliminating clutter, cleaning, making minor repairs or changes, and keeping household equipment in good working order.* A good home maintenance plan can catch small problems before they develop into large and costly ones.

The most successful home maintenance plans are those that family members work together to develop. Your family can begin by listing maintenance tasks for each room of your home. Together, decide how often each task should be done—daily, weekly, monthly, or occasionally. Consider how much time each job will take and if it needs to be done in a certain order. Then decide who'll be responsible for each job. Even young children can be given simple tasks. Many families rotate job assignments.

➤ When families join forces, home maintenance is done more efficiently.

Daily Tasks

Although the amount of clutter that's acceptable can be open to family discussion, household tasks that protect health and safety should never be compromised. The following should be carried out daily to protect health and safety:
- Wash dishes with hot water and soap.
- Dispose of garbage.
- Wipe up food spills as they occur.
- Keep traffic patterns, stairs, and doorways free of clutter.

Many families also carry out these tasks daily:
- Clean kitchen sink and counters.
- Sweep or vacuum the kitchen floor.
- Put away clothes and other belongings.

TRY IT OUT

Create a Cleaning Schedule

ACTIVITY

What You'll Need
- Paper
- Pen or pencil

What to Do
1. With a partner, pretend that the two of you are to share an apartment. Together, make a list of all the cleaning and maintenance chores that should be done.
2. Create a schedule that distributes the work fairly. Don't agree to any responsibility that you wouldn't actually be willing to assume.
3. Share your schedule with the class, and discuss how you reached the agreement.

To Discuss
- Which tasks were easiest to agree upon? Which were most difficult? What roles do values and standards play in making cleaning decisions?
- Did you agree on how often the tasks should be done? If not, how did you decide? What factors did you consider in dividing the tasks?

Making beds is another daily job in many households. "One rule my stepdad made was making your bed everyday," says Keith. "I hated it at first, but now my room seems really messy if the bed's not made."

Regular Tasks

Each family decides how often vacuuming, dusting, cleaning bathrooms, washing floors, doing laundry, and other cleaning tasks must be done. Many families undertake a general overall cleaning once a week. Others may do this more or less often.

➤ Families need to agree on an acceptable standard of tidiness and abide by the rules that are set.

Occasional Tasks

Your list of maintenance tasks will also include some to be taken care of occasionally or seasonally. Occasional tasks include cleaning the refrigerator, washing walls and windows, cleaning blinds and curtains, washing blankets, and cleaning closets.

Cleaning drawers is another worthwhile task. Tara sorted through a seldom-used drawer one day, and later teased her mother because she found diaper coupons that had expired ten years earlier! The cleaned space became the perfect spot for greeting cards and stationery.

If you have instruction books that come with furnishings and equipment, check them to find out what special care is required. Add these jobs to your list. Many families also need to add outdoor jobs, such as raking leaves and cutting grass, to their home maintenance task list.

➤ Cleaning and organizing your home regularly are important for your family's comfort, health, and safety. How can families benefit by doing household chores together?

Storage

The best way to control clutter is to pick up and put away things as you use them. When possible, every room should have space for storing items. Organized storage that's easy to use is especially important in kitchens, bathrooms, and children's rooms.

How you organize your storage will depend on what you have to store and the kind and size of storage space you have. There are two general guidelines:
• Store items near the area they're used.
• Store frequently used items where they can be reached easily.

Cleaning Products and Equipment

Part of getting organized for cleaning means selecting products and equipment to do various household cleaning jobs. Products that clean more than one type of surface often are a good buy. Jobs such as cleaning an oven, however, may require a specific product.

As you shop, compare labels on various brands. You may find a product very similar to a name brand for less cost.

Many basic cleaning products are both inexpensive and "environmentally friendly." Baking soda, for instance, is an effective, gentle cleansing powder for sinks, refrigerators, and microwave ovens. It can also be used to remove odors. Adding a little white vinegar to baking soda boosts its cleaning power even more.

Using the proper equipment also makes cleaning easier. A broom, mop, bucket, vacuum cleaner, as well as brushes, sponges, and dusting cloths are basic cleaning tools. No matter what ads say, you'll need to wipe or even vigorously scrub to loosen dirt and grime.

MAINTAINING A HEALTHY ENVIRONMENT

Keeping your home neat and organized helps to make it a desirable place to live. But keeping your home free of dirt and bacteria that can lead to illness is even more important. By removing dust and dirt, disposing of garbage, and controlling pests, you help to make your home a healthy place to live.

Dust and Dirt

Dust and dirt can be removed by sweeping, dusting, vacuuming, washing, and mopping. Sweeping with a broom removes dirt from hard floors. You can also use brooms for seasonal jobs, such as cleaning window screens and dusting cobwebs from walls and ceilings.

Wipe windowsills and baseboards. Then dust all furnishings except upholstered pieces. Don't forget areas such as chair legs and lampshades. Wood furniture needs occasional polishing to keep it in good condition.

A vacuum cleaner can remove dust and dirt from carpeting, hard floors, upholstered furniture, and draperies. It uses suction to draw soil into the machine, where it's trapped inside a bag or container. For proper operation, vacuum bags and containers must be changed or cleaned frequently.

To use cleaning products safely:

- Follow the directions on cleaning products exactly. Never mix products. The results could be poisonous, explosive, or fatal.
- Keep cleaning products in their original containers. That way you'll always know what they are and how they should be used.
- Never store cleaning products near food.
- Store cleaning products in a locked cabinet, out of the reach of small children.
- Some cleaners give off powerful fumes. Use a fan and open windows to bring in fresh air.

Washable hard floors need regular washing to remove stubborn dirt. Use a mop, water, and a cleaner that is safe for the type of floors you have.

Cleaning is usually most efficient if certain tasks are performed in a particular order. For example, as you dust, work from the top to the bottom. Working from top to bottom ensures that dust doesn't end up on already dusted areas. Some people prefer first cleaning the outside edges of a room. Then they clean the center, and finish with the floor. This sequence helps make sure no areas are skipped.

> ➤ Dirt and harmful bacteria can lead to illness. Therefore, it is important to keep your home clean.

Garbage

An overflowing garbage can and dirty dishes in the sink can make an otherwise clean house look unkempt. Because standing garbage may contain thousands of germs and can give off a bad odor, dispose of garbage daily.

Pests

> ➤ Many products are available for pest control. Select the product that best meets the needs of your family. Read label directions and warnings carefully.

Roaches, ants, flies, and mice are all types of household pests that carry germs that can cause illness. With regular home maintenance, you can usually keep pests under control. If you use pest control products, read and follow directions carefully. Always store the products out of the reach of children. If a pest problem becomes severe, call a professional.

KEEPING YOUR HOME SAFE

Proper home maintenance can't guarantee your family's safety. However, it can prevent unnecessary risks. For example, keeping toys and sports equipment off the floor can prevent falls. Following directions for using electrical equipment can keep it from becoming a **hazard,** or *source of danger.* Storing flammable products correctly will prevent fires. Secure and properly labeled storage of cleaning products and other poisons will prevent accidental poisoning.

Making a DIFFERENCE

CLEAN UP

When Van went to visit his granddad, he noticed the apartment was musty and needed cleaning. "Grandpa, when was the last time you scrubbed this place?"

Van's granddad shook his head. "Look, you know it's not easy for me to move around a lot, and frankly, I can't afford help right now."

Van had always been close to his granddad. They used to fish together in a nearby river, and spent lots of time together. Van also didn't like cleaning up his own room very much. But he realized his granddad needed help. "Okay, grandpa, get out the cleaning supplies, and I'll have a go at it. But don't get used to this."

They both laughed.

Taking Action

1. Have you ever helped a friend or relative take care of a living space in some way?
2. How could Van make cleaning his granddad's apartment more fun for both of them?

Falls

Most falls or other injuries in the home are preventable. You can avoid such falls by taking the following precautions:

- If you use throw rugs, make sure they have a nonskid backing.
- Use a sturdy ladder or stepstool instead of a chair to reach items.
- Keep traffic patterns, stairs, and doorways free of clutter.
- Use adequate lighting, especially on stairs. Use nightlights.
- Stairways should have railings. Use them.
- Use a rubber mat in the bathtub.

Misuse of electrical cords may cause a fire in a home. What can you do to prevent electrical hazards? What electrical hazard do you see in this photo?

Electrical Hazards

Electricity is so much a part of everyday life that it's easy to forget it can be very dangerous or even fatal. To avoid electrical hazards:

- Don't plug too many cords into one outlet.
- Never use electrical appliances near water, or touch them with wet hands.
- Don't run electrical cords underneath rugs or carpeting.
- Cover outlets that small children can reach.
- Repair or replace damaged cords and appliances.

Fires

When Tiffany received a candle as a birthday gift, her parents insisted that she burn it only in the living room. Why do you think it wasn't allowed in her bedroom?

It's not surprising that matches, candles, cigarettes, grease, and electrical appliances cause most fires. Garbage cans, mattresses, and upholstered furniture are common places for a fire to start.

Every home should have fire extinguishers. Keep a chemical extinguisher near, but not above, the kitchen range for grease and electrical fires. Be sure you know how to use it. Keep matches out of children's reach. Store flammable products away from all heat sources.

Smoke detectors can provide early warning in case of fire and smoke. Make sure your home has smoke detectors near bedroom areas and on each floor. Check all detectors once a month to see that they function properly and replace batteries regularly.

Saving your home isn't as important as saving your life. It's a good idea to schedule fire drills, so that everyone in the family knows the quickest way to exit your home in case of fire. You and your family need to know how to escape from every room.

Plan ahead for emergencies! You'll be prepared if one arises.

Poisons

Poisons can be found in nearly every room of your home. Prescription drugs, some cleaning products, and other materials can be harmful. Small children are the most common victims of accidental poisoning. Therefore, always store poisonous products out of children's reach in a locked cabinet.

Sometimes children mistake a poison for something else. Never store poisons in another container, such as a soda bottle. Also, never encourage children to take medicine by telling them medicine is candy. They may go back for more. A little poisoning prevention can save a life.

➤ Poisonous products must be stored out of a child's reach. A cabinet with a lock is ideal.

MAKING REPAIRS

If a toilet overflows or a fuse blows, would you know what to do if you were the only person at home? Do you know where to find the water shut-off valve?

What about minor structure repairs? Could you open a stuck door or fix a leaky faucet? Learning to handle minor repairs can save your family money now and prepare you to handle these tasks in your own future home.

When repairs have to be made or small emergencies arise in your home, take advantage of the opportunity to watch the person who handles the problem. In many communities, low-cost classes that teach repair skills are available.

KEEPING A POSITIVE ATTITUDE

Home maintenance tasks can be easier, and even enjoyable, if you approach them with a positive attitude. Consider these other suggestions:
• Play your favorite music as you work.
• Think of vigorous chores as part of your exercise program.
• Work with someone else and visit as you work.
• Use household tasks as a way to reduce stress.

Chapter Summary

- A home maintenance plan can help stop small problems from developing into large and expensive ones.
- Household tasks that protect health and safety should be carried out on a daily basis.
- When organizing storage space, store items near areas where they are used. Store frequently used items where they can be easily reached.
- Consider the effect on the environment when selecting cleaning products.
- You can make cleaning more efficient by performing certain tasks in a particular order, such as by dusting from top to bottom.
- Falls, electrical hazards, fires, and poisons are frequent causes of injuries and deaths in today's households.

Family & Community

With Your Family

Talk with your family about doing a safety check in your home. Make a checklist of possible safety hazards and use the list to evaluate your home. (You might begin by using the suggestions in this chapter.) Develop a plan to correct the problems you discover.

In Your Community

Do you know of any people in your community who have difficulty maintaining their homes due to physical limitations or due to age? What community help is available for them? What assistance can teens offer?

- Learning to make minor repairs and deal with small emergencies can save you money now and provide skills for handling these tasks in your own future home.
- A positive attitude helps make home maintenance tasks easier and even enjoyable.

Reviewing the Chapter

1. What is home maintenance? What can family members do to help make a home maintenance plan successful?
2. What four tasks should be carried out daily to protect health and safety?
3. Name five maintenance tasks that need to be done occasionally or seasonally.
4. Describe two general guidelines for organizing storage space.
5. How can comparing the chemicals listed on various brands of cleaning products help you save money when shopping?
6. List five ways to remove dust and dirt. Why is it more efficient to dust from the top to the bottom, instead of the other way around?
7. Why is it important to dispose of garbage every day?
8. Give five precautions for avoiding falls.
9. Why should poisonous products always be stored in their original containers?
10. Briefly describe three ideas for making household tasks easier and more enjoyable.

Thinking Critically

1. **Draw conclusions.** How would you rate your family's fire safety awareness and preparation? Do you have fire extinguishers? Do you know where the extinguishers are stored? Do you know how to use them? Do you have an escape plan and a place to meet outdoors?

2. **Predict consequences.** What consequences might result if someone poured poisonous cleaning products or pesticides down the drain? How should the products be discarded instead? What steps has your community taken to deal with the disposal of poisonous or hazardous household products?

3. **Make generalizations.** Which household tasks do you enjoy doing? Which do you not enjoy? How might you make certain tasks easier or more pleasant?

Making Connections

1. **Health.** Read the information on the labels of cleaning supply products. What types of precautions are listed? How clear are the instructions? What other information would be helpful?

2. **Language Arts.** Compose a 30-second commercial for public service radio stressing the importance of home safety.

Applying Your Learning

1. **Check storage.** Brainstorm suggestions for improving drawer and closet storage space in bedroom areas. Select several ideas that would be easy to do. Try one or more of them.

2. **Plan maintenance tasks.** Identify three cleaning or maintenance tasks you dislike doing. Come up with a plan for making each easier to do.

3. **Gather opinions.** At what age should children become involved in home maintenance and cleaning? What tasks would be appropriate for a three-year-old? An eight-year old?

What Would You Do?

Your family has asked you to take on some additional home chores. You think: "This couldn't come at a worse time. I have a couple of reports to do for school, and I'm worried about my grades. But I know my folks are depending on me to help out." What would you do in this situation?

Career Network

INTERIOR DESIGNER

Established consulting firm seeks experienced interior designer to develop plans for commercial business offices.
- Four-year degree required.
- Knowledge of Americans with Disabilities Act accessibility requirements needed.

ARCHITECT

Small firm has opening for architect to develop design concepts and manage production of construction plans.
- Bachelor's degree, strong design skills, and AutoCAD experience required.
- Minimum 3 years experience desired.

FLORAL DESIGNER

Large floral shop has full-time opening for floral designer.
- Exceptional creativity desired.
- Must work well with people.
- At least 3 years experience required.

REAL ESTATE AGENT

Join our dynamic team selling commercial and residential property.
- State license and high school diploma required.
- Training provided for entry-level agent.

LANDSCAPE ARCHITECT

Metropolitan park district seeks certified landscape architect to assist with the design, development, and improvement of city park facilities.
- Manage new and renovation projects through all phases.
- Bachelor's degree required.

SPACE PLANNER

Interior design firm seeks space planner to work with clients in the hotel and restaurant industry.
- Applicants must have completed courses in interior design and computer-aided drafting.
- Ability to sketch freehand as well as on computer.
- Good interpersonal skills.

More Career Options

Entry Level
- Furniture Salesperson
- Carpet Installer
- Construction Worker
- Apprentice Upholsterer

Technical Level
- Home Appliance Repairer
- Home Inspector
- Plumber
- Electrician
- Home Inspector

Professional Level
- Landscape Gardener
- General Contractor
- Furniture Designer
- Mortgage Loan Officer

COLOR SPECIALIST

Wallcovering manufacturer seeks color specialist to work with design team to select and recommend colors for various product lines.
- Must be creative and imaginative.
- Bachelor' degree required; courses in interior design, color theory, and art desirable.

ELECTRICIAN'S APPRENTICE

Electrical contracting firm specializing in residential work offers 4-year apprenticeship program. Apprentice will learn all aspects of the trade while helping licensed electricians install electrical systems.
- Must have good dexterity.
- Good color vision essential.
- High school diploma or equivalent.

URBAN AND REGIONAL PLANNER

Department of Health Services seeks regional planner to oversee the development of waterfront property in growing areas of the state.
- Master's degree desired.
- Knowledge of environmental issues necessary.
- Excellent communication skills and ability to collaborate with other agencies required.

KITCHEN PLANNER

Kitchen design firm seeks planner who will work with clients to organize kitchen space and select fixtures and appliances.
- Knowledge of building codes essential.
- Understanding of electrical and ventilation systems.
- Ability to work within client's budget.

Linking School to Career

1. **Your Career Plan:** Spotting trends is how people start businesses. These people are called entrepreneurs; they see a need and figure out a way to meet the need. Think about the community where you live. What business do you think is needed? If you were to start the business, how many people would you hire? What would their job duties be? What would your job duties be?

2. **Researching Careers:** Many entrepreneurs have opened small businesses to cater to the needs of homeowners. If you could start a business of your own in the housing and interiors field, what would it be? How would you determine the kind of business that is most likely to succeed? What kind of research would you need to do before starting your business?

3. **Reading:** Look up the definitions of the following terms that are found in the want ad listings:
- Creativity
- Certified
- Collaborate
- Apprenticeship
- Building codes

FCCLA (Family, Career and Community Leaders of America) is a dynamic and effective national vocational student organization for family and consumer sciences students. With thousands of young women and men involved at the middle level and high school level, FCCLA seeks to challenge and enrich the lives of students with diverse backgrounds and interests.

Benefits of Joining FCCLA

As part of its mission, FCCLA promotes personal growth and leadership development through family and consumer sciences courses. It will help you focus on your multiple roles of family member, wage earner, and community leader through challenging and fun activities. In addition, involvement in FCCLA helps you develop the following life skills:

- Character development.
- Creative and critical thinking.
- Interpersonal communication.
- Practical knowledge.
- Career preparation.

Activities, Service and Recognition

As a member in FCCLA, you will learn and develop practical, real-world skills and talents—keys to success whether you enter the workforce after high school or go on to college. With the guidance of your teacher/adviser, FCCLA can help you grow through:

- Exciting, well-planned activities that integrate vocational and academic learning. Individual and team projects introduce and strengthen critical thinking and decision-making skills.
- Emphasis on family and community service that builds bridges between school, family, and community.
- Recognition of student achievement as individual and team members. FCCLA members have an opportunity to shine through "high-challenge, low-threat" competitions.

For more information contact:
Family, Career and Community
Leaders of America
1910 Association Drive
Reston, VA 20191-1584
Phone: (703) 476-4900
FAX: (703) 869-2713
www.fcclainc.org

Glossary

(Numbers indicate chapters where term can be found.)

A

abbreviation: A short form of a word. (35)

abstinence: A conscious decision to avoid harmful behaviors. (26)

accent lighting: An intense beam of light aimed at a painting, sculpture, or other object to create a dramatic effect. (47)

accessories: Small items of clothing that complete an outfit. (40)

acne: A skin problem that develops when glands below the pores become blocked. (24)

acquaintances: People you know but who are not personal friends. (12)

acquired immunodeficiency syndrome-AIDS: A life-threatening disease that interferes with the body's natural ability to fight infection. (26)

addiction: A physical or psychological dependence on a substance. (15, 26)

additives: Substances added to food for a specific purpose. (29)

adolescence: The stage of growth between childhood and adulthood. (2)

aerobic exercise: Vigorous activity that causes your heart to beat faster for a sustained amount of time. (25)

age span: The number of years between children. (14)

à la carte: On a menu, describes items that are priced separately. (32)

al dente: Tender but firm to the bite. (38)

alcoholics: People who are addicted to alcohol. (15)

alcoholism: Physical and mental dependence on alcohol. (15)

alternatives: The different options you have for dealing with a situation. (4)

amino acids: The chemical compounds that make up protein. (28)

anorexia: An eating disorder characterized by self-starvation. (25)

appetizer: The optional first course of a meal. (32)

aptitude: A natural tendency that makes it easier for you to perform certain types of tasks. (5)

assertive: Able to stand up for yourself and your beliefs in firm, but positive ways. (9)

B

backstitching: A reverse stitch used to secure the ends of a seam. (43)

bacteria: One-celled living organisms so small they can be seen only with a microscope. (34)

baking: Cooking food uncovered in an oven with dry heat. (37)

basal metabolic rate: The rate at which your body uses energy when you are inactive. (25)

basic skills: Tools for learning, such as reading, writing, listening, and mathematics. (6)

basting: Holding fabric in place temporarily with pins or long stitches. (45)

bias: The diagonal edge formed when fabric is folded with the crosswise grain parallel to the selvage. (44)

binge eating disorder: A condition characterized by compulsive overeating. (25)

body language: The way in which you use gestures and body movement to communicate. (9)

boiling: Heating liquid at a high temperature so that bubbles rise and break on the surface of the liquid. (37)

braising: Browning food in a small amount of fat, then simmering in very little added liquid. (37)

bran: The outside covering of the grain kernel. (38)

broiling: A method of cooking in which food is cooked directly over or under the source of heat. (37)

budget: A plan for spending and saving the money you have available. (20)

bulimia: An eating disorder in which people eat large quantities in a short period of time and then purge. (25)

C

calories: Units for measuring energy. (28)

carbohydrates: Sugars and starches; the body's main source of energy. (28)

career: A series of occupations over a lifetime. (5)

career cluster: A large grouping of occupations that have certain things in common. (5)

character: A combination of traits that show strong ethical principles and maturity. (3)

check register: A small booklet in which you keep a record of your checking account. (20)

cholesterol: A fat-like substance that is part of every cell in the body. (28)

citizen: A member of a community, such as a city, town, state, or country. (3)

citizenship: The way you handle your responsibilities as a citizen. (3)

clipping: Making small, straight cuts in the seam allowance. (45)

clique: A group of people who exclude others from their circle. (12)

clothing inventory: An organized list of the clothing you have. (40)

communication: The process of sending messages to, and receiving messages from, others. (9)

community: A group of people with common interests who live in a certain area. (8)

comparison shopping: Taking the time to shop around and compare products, prices, and services. (22)

compromise: Coming to an agreement in which each person gives up something in order to get what they both want. (10)

condominiums: Individually owned units in a multiple-family dwelling. (46)

conflict: A disagreement or struggle between two or more people or groups who have opposing points of view. (10)

conflict resolution: The process of settling a conflict by cooperating and problem solving. (10)

conscience: An inner sense of right or wrong. (16)

conservation: Protecting natural resources against waste and harm. (23)

consumer: A person who purchases goods and services produced by others. (22)

convenience foods: Prepared or partially prepared foods. (36)

cookware: Pots, pans, and other containers for use on top of the range, in the conventional oven, or in the microwave oven. (33)

cooperative: A form of ownership in which residents of a multiple-family dwelling form an organization that owns the building. (46)

courses: Parts of a meal. (32)

cover letter: A letter that accompanies a résumé and that informs an employer that you are applying for a position within the company. (7)

credit: An arrangement by which you purchase things now and are allowed to pay for them later. (20)

credit rating: A record that shows your ability and willingness to pay your debts. (15)

creditors: People or companies to whom you owe money. (15)

crime: An illegal act committed against someone or something. (27)

crisis: An extreme change that is often negative. (15)

cross-contamination: Situation in which harmful bacteria are transferred from one food to another. (34)

crush: A strong attraction to someone that is one-sided. (13)

decibel: A unit that measures the loudness of sound. (24)

decision-making: The act of making a choice or coming to a solution. (4)

deep-fat frying: Cooking method in which food is completely covered in fat. (37)

deficiency: A shortage. (28)

dependable: Able to be counted on. (12)

deposit: Money paid into an account. (20)

depressants: Drugs that reduce blood pressure, and slow down heart and breathing rates. (26)

dermatologist: A doctor who specializes in skin problems. (24)

desktop publishing: Using computers and special software to create professional-looking documents. (21)

developmental tasks: The skills and abilities that children master during each stage of their development. (16)

Dietary Guidelines for Americans: Six simple suggestions for making healthful food choices. (29)

directional stitching: Stitching in the direction of the grain of the fabric. (45)

discipline: Training given by parents and caregivers that helps children become responsible and cooperative. (18)

dovetail: To fit tasks together to make the best use of time. (36)

dry clean: To clean with chemicals rather than with detergent and water. (42)

duplex: One building that contains two separate housing units. (46)

D

dandruff: Scales and flakes on the scalp. (24)

E

ease: The extra room in a garment, needed for movement and comfort. (44)

elements of design: Line, color, texture, shape, and pattern. (40)

e-mail: Electronic mail. (9)

empathy: The ability to understand what someone else is experiencing. (8)

endorse: To sign over your rights to a check by writing your name on the back. (20)

endosperm: The largest part of the grain kernel. (38)

entrée: The main course of a meal. (32)

enriched: Used to describe foods that have had nutrients added back in after processing. (38)

environment: Everything around you, including people, places, and events. (2)

equivalents: Amounts that are equal to each other. (35)

escalate: To increase in intensity. (10)

ethical principles: Standards for right and wrong behavior. (3)

etiquette: Accepted rules of behavior. (32)

expenses: The goods and services on which you spend your money. (20)

F

fads: Fashions that last only a short time. (40)

family life cycle: The stages that families go through during their lifetime together. (14)

fashions: Styles that are currently popular. (40)

fetus: An unborn child. (16)

fiber: Plant material that does not break down when you digest food. (28)

fibers: Hairlike substances twisted together to make yarns and fabric. (41)

financial: Relating to money. (15)

first aid classes: Classes that provide instruction in basic emergency care. (17)

flatware: Eating utensils. (32)

flextime: A work schedule that allows workers to adjust their start and stop times to meet the needs of their families. (7)

foodborne illness: Illness caused by eating spoiled food or food contaminated with harmful bacteria. (34)

Food Guide Pyramid: A simple method of meal planning based on food groups. (29)

food product dating: The process of using a date to indicate product freshness. (31)

freezer burn: A white discoloration on a food that lowers quality and nutrition. (39)

fringe benefits: Employment benefits such as vacation time, sick leave, healthcare insurance, and retirement programs. (5)

frying: Cooking with fat. (37)

functional furniture: Furniture that meets specific needs. (47)

G

general lighting: Lighting that provides enough light so that you can move around the room safely and comfortably. (47)

generic name: The common name for a group of similar fibers. (41)

germ: The sprouting section of the grain kernel. (38)

goal: Something you plan to be, do, or have, and for which you are willing to work. (1)

grading: Cutting seams in layers to reduce bulk. (45)

graffiti: Unwanted drawings and writing on walls and other property. (8)

graze: To eat several mini-meals throughout the day. (36)

grooming: The personal care routine you follow to keep yourself clean and attractive. (24)

H

hallucinogens: Street drugs that distort thoughts, moods, and senses. (26)

hazard: A source of danger. (48)

health: The total state of your physical, mental, emotional, and social well-being. (24)

heredity: The qualities and traits passed from parents to children through genes. (2)

home maintenance: Eliminating clutter, cleaning, making minor repairs, and keeping appliances and equipment in good working order. (48)

homogenized: Processed milk that has had the fats broken up and blended into the liquid. (31)

hormones: Chemical substances in your body. (2)

human resources: Resources that have to do with people. (1)

I

illusion: An image that fools the eye. (40)

immersible: Able to be put into water safely. (33)

immunizations: Protection against common childhood diseases. (18)

impulse buying: Making unplanned purchases on the spur of the moment. (22)

income: The amount of money that you have coming in. (20)

infatuation: A feeling brought about by an intense attraction to another person. (13)

inhalants: Substances with dangerous fumes that are sniffed to produce a mind-altering high. (26)

initiative: The ability to start activities on your own. (16)

interest: *On savings:* the money a financial institution pays you at regular intervals for the use of your money; *on a loan:* the amount of money you pay the lenders for using their money. (20)

interfacing: Special fabric that gives hidden support and body to a garment. (44)

ironing: The process of moving the iron back and forth over fabric to remove wrinkles. (42)

irradiated foods: Foods that have been passed through a field of radiant energy to destroy bacteria, mold, and insects. (30)

L

landlords: Owners of rental housing. (46)

layouts: Diagrams included on the pattern guide sheet that show how to place the pattern pieces on the fabric. (44)

leader: A person who has influence over a group. (4)

leadership: The ability to lead. (4)

leavening agent: Substance that causes baked products to rise. (38)

lease: A written rental agreement. (46)

legumes: Plants whose seeds grow in pods, such as beans, peas, and lentils. (31)

long-term goals: Goals that are far-reaching and take time to achieve. (1)

M

manipulation: A dishonest way to control or influence someone. (11)

manufactured fibers: Fibers produced through chemical processes. (41)

marbling: Tiny veins of fat throughout the meat muscle. (39)

marijuana: A drug made from the hemp plant that can be eaten or smoked. (26)

marketplace: Anywhere goods and services are bought and sold. (22)

material resources: Resources such as money, time, and tools, that you use to accomplish something. (1)

meal pattern: Way of grouping daily food choices into meals and snacks. (36)

mediation: A process in which a neutral third party is used to help reach a solution that's agreeable to both sides. (10)

menstruation: A monthly discharge of blood from the uterus. (2)

mentors: Successful workers who share their expert knowledge and demonstrate correct work behaviors. (5)

microprocessors: Tiny, single-purpose computers. (21)

modem: A device that connects a computer to a phone line. (21)

mortgage: A long-term loan used to buy a home. (46)

multi-family housing: A structure that contains several housing units. (46)

multiplex: A building similar to a duplex, but containing three or more units. (46)

multipurpose clothes: Clothes suitable for a variety of situations. (40)

muscular endurance: The ability of your muscles to work continuously over a long time. (25)

myth: An untrue statement that some people believe. (29)

N

natural environment: The living and the nonliving elements around you. (23)

natural fibers: Fibers made from plant or animal products. (41)

natural resources: Resources that occur in nature. (23)

needs: Things that are essential to one's health or well-being. (4)

negotiation: The process of discussing problems face-to-face in order to reach a solution. (10)

nonrenewable resources: Natural resources that can't replace themselves and that are therefore limited in supply. (23)

nonverbal communication: Communication without words. (9)

notching: Clipping v-shaped notches from the seam allowance. (45)

notions: The smaller items, such as thread, zippers, and buttons, needed to construct a garment. (44)

nutrient density: The amount of nutrients in a food relative to the number of calories. (28)

nutrients: The substances found in food that keep your body in good working order. (28)

nurturing: Providing love, affection, attention, and encouragement. (18)

O

obesity: A condition in which a person is seriously overweight. (29)

occupations: Groups of similar jobs. (5)

organic food: Food that is produced without manufactured chemicals. (29)

P

pan frying: Method used to cook tender cuts of meat, fish and eggs with a small amount of fat. (37)

parenting: The process of caring for children and helping them grow and develop. (18)

pasteurized: Heated and cooled to destroy harmful bacteria. (31)

peer mediator: A young person who acts as a neutral third party between two students who are locked in conflict. (10)

peer pressure: The pressure you feel to do what others your age are doing. (11)

peers: People of similar age. (11)

personality: The combination of the feelings, character traits, attitudes, and habits that you display to others. (2)

place setting: The arrangement of tableware and flatware for each person. (32)

plaque: A sticky film of harmful bacteria that forms on the teeth. (24)

poison control centers: Special hospital units that advise and treat poison victims. (17)

potential: The possibility of becoming more than you are right now. (1)

precycling: A way of conserving resources before you use them. (23)

prejudice: An unfair or biased opinion. (8)

pressing: The process of lifting and lowering the iron onto an area of fabric. (42)

pretreatment: Giving special treatment to a garment before laundering it. (42)

principles of design: Proportion, emphasis, harmony, scale, balance, and rhythm. (40)

priorities: Goals, tasks, or activities that are more important than all others. (19)

proteins: Nutrients used to build, maintain, and repair body tissues. (28)

puberty: The time when boys and girls start to develop the physical characteristics of adult men and women. (2)

R

rapport: Harmony or understanding between people. (9)

recipe: A set of directions used in cooking. (35)

redress: The right to have a wrong corrected quickly and fairly. (22)

refusal skills: Communication skills you can use to say *no* effectively. (11)

renewable resources: Natural resources that can renew or replace themselves over time. (23)

resource: Anything you use to accomplish something. (1)

resourceful: Able to solve problems and succeed in life. (1)

respect: Showing regard for the worth of someone or something. (8)

responsibility: Reliability; showing that you are accountable for your actions. (3)

résumé: A document that provides a brief history of your work experience and education. (7)

roasting: Cooking food uncovered in an oven with dry heat. (37)

S

salmonella: Bacteria that can cause foodborne illness. (39)

sanitize: To clean to eliminate harmful bacteria. (34)

sautéing: Method used to cook thinly sliced foods in a very small amount of fat. (37)

scorch: Burn. (39)

seam allowances: The fabric between the cutting line and the stitching line. (44)

sedentary: Inactive. (25)

self-concept: The mental picture you have of yourself, and the way you believe others see you. (2)

self-confidence: Confidence in yourself and in your abilities. (1)

self-esteem: The confidence and worth you have in yourself. (2)

selvage: The finished lengthwise edge of the fabric. (44)

serger: An overlock sewing machine that stitches, finishes, and trims a seam in one step. (43)

sexually transmitted diseases (STDs): Diseases passed from one person to another through sexual contact. (26)

short-term goals: Goals that can be accomplished in the near future. (1)

sibling rivalry: Competition between siblings for the love and attention of parents. (14)

siblings: Brothers and sisters. (14)

silhouette: The outline of a garment. (40)

simmering: Heating a liquid to a temperature just below the boiling point until bubbles barely break on the surface of the liquid. (37)

single-family housing: A structure built to house one family. (46)

spouse: A husband or wife. (15)

staples: Food that you are likely to use often, such as flour, salt, pepper, eggs, milk, and bread. (31)

staystitching: A row of stitching on one layer of fabric that prevents fabric edges from stretching as you sew. (45)

steaming: Cooking food over boiling water rather than in it. (37)

stereotype: A belief that an entire group of people shares a fixed, common pattern. (8)

stimulants: Drugs that increase heart rates, speed up the central nervous system, increase breathing rates, and raise blood pressure. (26)

stir-frying: Cooking method in which small pieces of food are stirred and cooked very quickly at high heat in very little fat. (37)

stress: The pressure people feel as the result of their ability or inability to meet the expectations of others and themselves. (7)

systems: Orderly ways of doing things. (6)

T

tableware: Dishes, glasses, and flatware. (32)

tact: Knowing what to do or say in order to show sensitivity to another's feelings. (8)

task lighting: Lighting that focuses light where it is needed. (47)

technology: The way in which science and inventions are put to practical use in everyday life. (21)

teleconferencing: System that enables people in different locations to see and hear each other at the same time. (21)

tension: Tightness or looseness of the thread on a sewing machine. (43)

thinking skills: The mental skills you use to learn and solve problems. (6)

toddlers: Children from one to two years of age. (16)

tolerance: Accepting and respecting other people's customs and beliefs. (10)

townhomes: Houses that are built in rows and attached to one another at the side walls. (46)

trade name: The manufacturers' name for a specific fiber or fabric. (41)

traditions: Customs that are followed again and again. (14)

traffic patterns: The paths people use to get from one area or room to another. (47)

trim: To cut off extra fabric. (43)

U

understitching: Stitching the seam allowance to the facing to prevent the seam from rolling to the outside. (45)

unit price: The price per ounce, pound, or other unit of measure. (31)

universal product code: A combination of a bar code and numbers that identifies a product and usually assigns a price. (21)

universal values: Values that are generally accepted and shared worldwide. (3)

utensils: Small kitchen tools. (33)

utilities: Basic services such as electricity, gas or oil, water, and sewer service. (46)

V

values: The beliefs and ideas that help guide the way you live. (3)

vandalize: To cause damage to public or private property. (8)

vegetarian: Someone who avoids meat and fish, and who lives on vegetables, fruits, grains, nuts, and sometimes eggs and dairy products. (29)

verbal communication: Communication with spoken words. (9)

views: Garment styles that can be made from a particular pattern. (44)

W

wants: Things that you desire but that are not essential. (4)

warranty: A written guarantee that a product will work properly for a specified length of time unless misused or mishandled by the consumer. (22)

wellness: A way of living based on healthful attitudes and actions. (24)

work: Doing something productive with your time. (5)

work simplification: Determining the easiest and quickest way to do a job well. (19)

Y

yield: The amount of food or the number of servings a recipe makes. (35)

Glosario

A

abbreviation/abreviatura: Palabra reducida a varias de sus letras. (35)

abstinence/abstinencia: La decisión de evitar conductas peligrosas. (26)

accent lighting/luz direccional: Una luz intensa que se hace brillar sobre una pintura, escultura u otro objeto para destacarlo y producir un efecto dramático. (47)

accessories/accesorios: Pequeños artículos que complementan un traje. (40)

acne/acné: Un problema del cutis causado por el bloqueo de las glándulas que están debajo de los poros. (24)

acquaintances/conocidos: Personas que uno conoce pero con quién no tiene amistad. (12)

acquired immunodeficiency syndrome (AIDS)/Síndrome de inmunodeficiencia adquirida (SIDA): Una enfermedad mortal que interfiere con la capacidad del cuerpo de combatir la infección. (26)

addiction/adicción: La dependencia física o psicológica de una sustancia. (15, 26)

additives/aditivos: Sustancias que se añaden a los alimentos por ciertas razones. (30)

adolescence/adolescencia: La etapa de crecimiento entre la niñez y la adultez. (2)

aerobic exercise/ejercicio aeróbico: Actividad enérgica que hace latir el corazón rápidamente por un período continuo de tiempo. (25)

age span/diferencia de edad: El número de años entre hijos. (14)

a la carte/a la carta: En un menú, describe los platos que tienen precios individuales. (32)

alcoholics/alcohólicos: Personas adictas al alcohol. (15)

alcoholism/alcoholismo: La dependencia física y mental del alcohol. (15)

al dente/al dente: Tierno pero firme. (38)

alternatives/alternativas: Las distintas opciones que uno tiene para resolver una situación. (4)

amino acids/aminoácidos: Los compuestos químicos que forman las proteínas. (28)

anorexia/anorexia: Un trastorno alimenticio que hace que el enfermo deje de comer. (25)

appetizer/aperitivo: El primer plato de una comida, que es opcional. (32)

aptitude/aptitud: Una tendencia natural que le permite a una persona hacer ciertas tareas con facilidad. (5)

assertive/firme: Que puede sostener las ideas y creencias personales de manera constante y positiva. (9)

B

backstitching/pespuntear: Un punto hacia atrás que se usa para rematar las terminaciones de una costura. (43)

bacteria/bacteria: Organismos de una sola célula, tan pequeños que solamente se pueden ver con un microscopio. (34)

baking/hornear: Cocinar en seco un alimento descubierto en el horno. (37)

basal metabolic rate/tasa metabólica básica: El ritmo al cual el cuerpo utiliza energía cuando uno está inactivo. (25)

basic skills/conocimientos básicos: Las habilidades necesarias para aprender, como saber leer, escribir, escuchar y matemáticas. (6)

basting/hilvanar: Asegurar una tela a su sitio temporalmente con alfileres o puntadas largas. (45)

bias/bies: El doblez diagonal que se forma cuando se dobla una tela con los hilos de trama paralelos al orillo. (44)

binge eating disorder/trastorno de ingestión excesiva: Una condición caracterizada por comer desmedidamente por compulsión. (25)

body language/lenguaje corporal: La manera en que uno usa los gestos y movimientos del cuerpo para comunicarse. (9)

boiling/hervir: Calentar un líquido a una temperatura alta hasta que las burbujas suban a la superficie y se rompan. (37)

braising/estofar: Dorar un alimento en una cantidad pequeña de grasa y después cocinarlo con muy poco líquido. (37)

bran/salvado: La cáscara que cubre el grano o semilla de los cereales. (38)

broiling/asar a la parrilla: Cocinar un alimento directamente arriba o debajo del calor. (37)

budget/presupuesto: Un plan para gastar y ahorrar el dinero que uno tiene disponible. (20)

bulimia/bulimia: Un trastorno alimenticio que hace que el enfermo ingiera grandes cantidades de comida en un corto período de tiempo y después se purga. (25)

C

calories/calorías: Unidades para medir la energía. (28)

carbohydrates/carbohidratos: Azúcares y féculas; la fuente principal de energía del cuerpo. (28)

career/carrera: Una serie de ocupaciones durante toda la vida. (5)

career cluster/concentración de carreras: Un grupo grande de carreras que tienen ciertas cosas en común. (5)

character/carácter: Una combinación de rasgos que muestran fuertes principios éticos y madurez. (3)

check register/libreta de operaciones: Un cuaderno pequeño en que se mantiene un registro de una cuenta de cheques. (20)

cholesterol/colesterol: Una sustancia grasosa que forma parte de todas las células. (28)

citizen/ciudadano: Un miembro de una comunidad, tal como una ciudad, pueblo, estado o país. (3)

citizenship/ciudadanía: La manera en que uno cumple sus responsabilidades de ciudadano. (3)

clipping/hacer cortecitos: Hacer una serie de cortes rectos y pequeños en la orilla de la tela junto a una costura. (45)

clique/camarilla: Un grupo de personas que no permiten que otros entren en su círculo. (12)

clothing inventory/inventario de ropa: Una lista organizada de la ropa que uno tiene. (40)

communication/comunicación: El proceso de mandar mensajes y recibirlos de otras personas. (9)

community/comunidad: Un grupo de personas con intereses en común que viven en la misma zona. (8)

comparison shopping/compras comparadas: Tomarse el tiempo para comparar productos, precios y servicios. (22)

compromise/transigir: Llegar a un acuerdo en que cada persona cede algo para que las dos obtengan lo que quieren. (10)

condominiums/condominios: Unidades individuales que se pueden comprar en un edificio de múltiples viviendas. (46)

conflict/conflicto: Un desacuerdo o lucha entre dos o más personas o grupos con distintos puntos de vista. (10)

conflict resolution/resolución de conflictos: El proceso de solucionar un conflicto por medio de la cooperación y las habilidades para resolver problemas. (10)

conscience/conciencia: El sentido interno del bien y el mal. (16)

conservation/conservación: La protección de recursos naturales contra el daño y malgasto. (23)

consumer/consumidor: Una persona que compra bienes y servicios producidos por otros. (22)

convenience foods/comidas de preparación rápida: Comidas que están preparadas o parcialmente preparadas con antelación. (36)

cookware/batería de cocina: Cazuelas, sartenes y otras vasijas que se usan para cocinar alimentos sobre una hornilla, en el horno corriente o en el horno de microondas. (33)

cooperative/cooperativa: Un tipo de propiedad en que los residentes de un edificio de múltiples viviendas forman una organización que se hace dueña del edificio. (46)

courses/platos: Partes de una comida. (32)

cover letter/carta de introducción: Una carta que acompaña un curriculum vitae para informar a un empleador que una persona está solicitando un puesto en su compañía. (7)

credit/crédito: Un arreglo mediante el cual uno puede comprar mercancía ahora y pagar por ella más adelante. (20)

creditors/acreedores: Personas o compañías a quienes se les debe dinero. (15)

credit rating/calificación crediticia: Un historial que muestra la capacidad y voluntad de una persona para pagar sus deudas. (15)

crime/crimen: Un acto ilegal cometido contra alguien o algo. (27)

crisis/crisis: Un cambio total que a menudo es negativo. (15)

cross-contamination/contaminación: Situación en que bacterias dañinas se trasladan de un alimento a otro. (34)

crush/enamoramiento: Una atracción fuerte hacia alguien que no es correspondida. (13)

D

dandruff/caspa: Escamas que se forman en el cuero cabelludo. (24)

decibel/decibel: Una unidad para medir el volumen del sonido. (24)

decision-making/tomar una decisión: El acto de elegir o llegar a una solución. (4)

deep-fat frying/freír en grasa abundante: Técnica de cocina en que el alimento se cubre totalmente de grasa. (37)

deficiency/deficiencia: La falta de alguna cosa. (28)

dependable/confiable: Que se puede contar con él. (12)

deposit/depósito: Dinero que se pone en una cuenta. (20)

depressants/depresores: Drogas que bajan la presión arterial y reducen el ritmo del corazón y de la respiración. (26)

dermatologist/dermatólogo: Un médico que se especializa en problemas de la piel. (24)

desktop publishing/edición electrónica: Usar computadoras y software especial para crear documentos con toda apariencia profesional. (21)

developmental tasks/tareas de desarrollo: Las destrezas y habilidades que los niños aprenden en cada etapa de su desarrollo. (15)

Dietary Guidelines for Americans/ Recomendaciones dietéticas para los estadounidenses: Nueve sugerencias sencillas para elegir alimentos saludables. (29)

directional stitching/coser con el hilo: Coser en la dirección del hilo de la tela. (45)

discipline/disciplina: Enseñanza que los padres y cuidadores dan a los niños para que sean responsables y cooperadores. (18)

dovetail/organizarse: Realizar varias tareas en conjunto para hacer mejor uso del tiempo. (36)

dry clean/limpiar en seco: Limpiar con sustancias químicas en vez de agua y detergente. (42)

duplex/dúplex: Un edificio que tiene dos viviendas separadas. (46)

E

ease/holgura: La anchura extra que tiene una prenda de vestir, necesaria para el movimiento y la comodidad. (44)

elements of design/elementos del diseño: Línea, color, textura, contorno y motivo. (40)

e-mail/correo electrónico: Correspondencia por Internet. (9)

empathy/empatía: La habilidad de comprender lo que otra persona siente. (8)

endorse/endosar: Entregar los derechos propios a un cheque al firmarlo por el dorso (la parte de atrás). (20)

endosperm/endospermo: La parte más grande del grano. (38)

enriched/enriquecidos: Se usa para describir aquellos alimentos a los que se les han devuelto los nutrientes que perdieron al ser procesados. (38)

entrée/plato fuerte: El plato principal de una comida. (32)

environment/medio ambiente: Todo lo que rodea a una persona, incluyendo gente, lugares y sucesos. (2)

equivalents/equivalentes: Cantidades iguales. (35)

escalate/intensificarse: Acrecentarse o excitarse. (10)

ethical principles/principios éticos: Criterios para la buena y mala conducta. (3)

etiquette/etiqueta: Las reglas para la conducta y trato. (32)

expenses/gastos: Los bienes y servicios en que uno gasta su dinero. (20)

F

fads/modas pasajeras: Modas que duran muy poco tiempo. (40)

family life cycle/ciclo de vida familiar: Las etapas por las que pasan juntos los miembros de una familia. (14)

fashions/modas: Los estilos que son populares en una temporada. (40)

fetus/feto: Un niño que no ha nacido. (16)

fiber/fibra: Material vegetal que no se descompone al digerirse las comidas. (28)

fibers/fibras: Hebras que se tuercen juntas para formar el estambre y la tela. (41)

financial/económico: Que tiene que ver con el dinero. (15)

first aid classes/clases de primeros auxilios: Clases que proporcionan instrucción en el manejo de emergencias médicas. (17)

flatware/cubiertos: Utensilios para comer. (32)

flextime/horario flexible: Horario que permite a los trabajadores cambiar las horas en que comienzan y terminan de trabajar para poder atender a sus familias. (7)

foodborne illness/enfermedad portada por los alimentos: Enfermedad causada por comer alimentos que se han echado a perder o que están contaminados por bacterias dañinas. (34)

Food Guide Pyramid/Pirámide de los Alimentos: Un método sencillo de planificar las comidas, basado en los grupos alimenticios. (29)

food product dating/fechar alimentos: El proceso de ponerles fechas a los alimentos para indicar hasta cuando están frescos. (39)

freezer burn/quemadura por congelación: Manchas blancas en un alimento que significan que ha perdido nutrientes y buena calidad. (39)

fringe benefits/extras: Complementos al sueldo como días de vacación, días por enfermedad, seguro de salud y programas de jubilación. (5)

frying/freír: Cocinar con grasa. (37)

functional furniture/muebles funcionales: Muebles que satisfacen ciertas necesidades. (47)

G

general lighting/iluminación general: Alumbrado que da luz suficiente para poderse mover por una habitación con seguridad y comodidad. (47)

generic name/nombre genérico: El nombre común de un grupo de fibras semejantes. (41)

germ/germen: La parte del grano de donde brota la planta. (38)

goal/meta: Algo que una persona quiere ser, hacer u obtener y por el cual está dispuesta a trabajar. (1)

grading/escalonar: Cortar las costuras en capas para reducir el grosor. (45)

graffiti/graffiti: Escritura y dibujos indeseados en paredes y otros tipos de propiedad. (8)

graze/pastar: Comer varias comidas pequeñas durante el día. (36)

grooming/arreglo personal: La rutina para el cuidado personal que uno sigue para lucir limpio y atractivo. (24)

H

hallucinogens/alucinógenos: Drogas callejeras que distorsionan el pensar, el ánimo y los sentidos. (26)

hazard/peligro: Algo arriesgado o inseguro. (48)

health/salud: El bienestar físico, mental, emocional y social de una persona en su totalidad. (24)

heredity/herencia: Las cualidades y rasgos que los padres transmiten a los hijos por medio de los genes. (2)

home maintenance/mantenimiento del hogar: Eliminar el desorden, limpiar, hacer arreglos pequeños y ocuparse de que los electrodomésticos y otros aparatos funcionen bien. (48)

homogenized/homogeneizada: Procesada de manera que las grasas de la leche se descomponen y se mezclan con el líquido. (31)

hormones/hormonas: Sustancias químicas en el cuerpo. (2)

human resources/recursos humanos: Recursos que poseen las personas. (1)

I

illusion/ilusión: Una imagen engañosa. (40)

immersible/sumergible: Que se puede meter debajo del agua sin peligro. (33)

immunizations/inmunizaciones: Protección contra las enfermedades comunes de la niñez. (18)

impulse buying/hacer compras impulsivas: Comprar algo repentinamente que uno no tenía intención de comprar. (22)

income/ingresos: La cantidad de dinero que uno tiene de entrada. (20)

infatuation/encaprichamiento: Una atracción intensa que uno siente por otra persona. (13)

inhalants/inhalantes: Sustancias que despiden gases peligrosos que al olerse producen una intoxicación que altera la realidad. (26)

initiative/iniciativa: La habilidad de comenzar actividades por sí mismo. (16)

interest/interés: *En cuentas de ahorro,* el dinero que una institución financiera le paga a uno a intervalos regulares por el uso de su dinero; *en préstamos,* la cantidad de dinero que uno paga a unas personas o instituciones por el uso de sus dinero. (20)

interfacing/entretela: Una tela especial escondida dentro de una prenda de vestir para darle forma y cuerpo. (44)

ironing/planchar: El proceso de mover la plancha sobre la tela para quitar las arrugas. (42)

irradiated foods/alimentos irradiados: Comidas que han sido pasadas por un campo de energía radiante que destruye las bacterias, hongos e insectos. (30)

L

landlords/dueños: Los propietarios de viviendas que se alquilan. (46)

layouts/distribución: Diagramas que muestran cómo colocar las piezas de un patrón sobre la tela. (44)

leader/líder: Una persona que tiene influencia sobre un grupo. (4)

leadership/liderazgo: La habilidad para guiar y motivar. (4)

lease/contrato de arrendamiento: Un acuerdo escrito que detalla las condiciones de alquiler. (46)

leavening agent/levadura: Sustancia que hace que se expandan los panes y otros productos hechos al horno. (38)

legumes/legumbres: Plantas cuyas semillas crecen en vainas, como los frijoles, guisantes y lentejas. (31)

long-term goals/metas a largo plazo: Metas de gran alcance que toman tiempo en lograr. (1)

M

manipulation/manipulación: Una manera deshonesta de controlar o influenciar a otra persona. (11)

manufactured fibers/fibras artificiales: Fibras producidas mediante procesos químicos. (41)

marbling/vetas de grasa: Pequeñas franjas de grasa mezcladas por todo el músculo (la carne). (39)

marijuana/marihuana: Una droga hecha del cáñamo, que se puede comer o fumar. (26)

marketplace/mercado: Cualquier sitio donde se venden y compran bienes y servicios. (22)

material resources/recursos materiales: Recursos que uno usa para realizar algo, como el dinero, tiempo y herramientas. (1)

meal pattern/patrón alimenticio: Una manera de agrupar los alimentos diarios en comidas y refrigerios. (36)

mediation/mediación: El proceso en el que un tercero sin interés en un asunto ayuda a llegar a una solución que es satisfactoria a ambas partes. (10)

menstruation/menstruación: El flujo mensual de sangre del útero. (2)

mentors/mentores: Personas expertas en su trabajo que comparten sus conocimientos y muestran cómo comportarse en el trabajo. (5)

microprocessors/microprocesadores: Pequeñas computadoras para un solo uso. (21)

modem/módem: Un aparato que conecta una computadora con una línea telefónica. (21)

mortgage/hipoteca: Un préstamo a largo plazo que se usa para comprar una casa. (46)

multifamily housing/viviendas para múltiples familias: Una estructura que contiene varias residencias. (46)

multiplex/múltiplex: Un edificio parecido a un dúplex, con tres o más residencias. (46)

multipurpose clothes/ropa de muchos usos: Ropa que se puede usar en distintas ocasiones. (40)

muscular endurance/resistencia muscular: La habilidad de los músculos para trabajar continuamente por un largo período de tiempo. (25)

myth/mito: Un cuento falso que alguna gente cree. (29)

N

natural environment/ambiente natural: Los elementos vivos y sin vida que rodean a una persona. (23)

natural fibers/fibras naturales: Fibras hechas de plantas o productos animales. (41)

natural resources/recursos naturales: Recursos que vienen de la naturaleza. (23)

needs/necesidades: Cosas esenciales para la salud o bienestar de una persona. (4)

negotiation/negociación: El proceso de hablar sobre problemas cara a cara para llegar a una solución. (10)

nonrenewable resources/recursos no renovables: Recursos naturales que no se pueden reemplazar y, por lo tanto, existen en cantidades limitadas. (23)

nonverbal communication/comunicación no verbal: Comunicación sin palabras. (9)

notching/cortar: Hacer cortes en forma de V en la orilla de la tela. (45)

notions/artículos de mercería: Los artículos pequeños (como hilo, zíperes y botones) que se usan para hacer una prenda. (44)

nutrient density/densidad nutritiva: La cantidad de nutrientes de un alimento en relación con la cantidad de calorías. (28)

nutrients/nutrientes: Las sustancias que tiene la comida que ayudan al cuerpo a mantenerse sano. (28)

nurturing/cuidar: Dar cariño, atender y alentar. (18)

O

obesity/obesidad: Una afección en que una persona está muy por encima del peso normal. (29)

occupations/ocupaciones: Grupos de trabajos semejantes. (5)

organic food/alimentos orgánicos: Alimentos producidos sin sustancias químicas artificiales. (29)

P

pan frying/freír con poca grasa: Técnica de cocina en que cortes tiernos de carne, pescado o huevos se cocinan en un sartén con poca grasa. (37)

parenting/criar: El proceso de cuidar y ayudar a los niños a crecer y desarrollarse. (18)

pasteurized/pasteurizado: Calentado y enfriado para matar las bacterias dañinas. (31)

peer mediator/intermediario contemporáneo: Un joven tercero sin interés en el asunto que ayuda a otros dos estudiantes envueltos en un conflicto. (10)

peer pressure/presión de contemporáneos: La presión que siente un joven para hacer lo mismo que las demás personas de su edad. (11)

peers/contemporáneos: Personas de la misma edad. (11)

personality/personalidad: La combinación de sentimientos, cualidades, actitudes y hábitos que uno muestra a los demás. (2)

place setting/servicio de mesa: El conjunto de vajilla y cubiertos necesarios para cada persona. (32)

plaque/placa dental: Una capa pegajosa de bacterias dañinas que se forma sobre los dientes. (24)

poison control center/centro de control del envenenamiento: Unidad especializada de un hospital que aconseja y atiende a víctimas del envenenamiento. (17)

potential/potencial: La posibilidad de ser más de lo que uno es. (1)

precycling/preciclar: Un modo de conservar recursos antes de usarlos. (23)

prejudice/prejuicio: Una opinión injusta o parcial. (8)

pressing/planchar: El proceso de subir y bajar la plancha sobre una parte de la tela. (42)

pretreatment/tratamiento de antemano: Hacer un tratamiento especial a una prenda de vestir antes de lavarla. (42)

principles of design/principios del diseño: Proporción, énfasis, armonía, escala, balance y ritmo. (40)

priorities/prioridades: Las metas, tareas y actividades más importantes. (19)

proteins/proteínas: Nutrientes necesarios para fabricar, mantener y reparar los tejidos del cuerpo. (28)

puberty/pubertad: La etapa en que los niños y niñas comienzan a desarrollar las características físicas de hombres y mujeres. (2)

R

rapport/buen entendimiento: Armonía y comprensión entre personas. (9)

recipe/receta: Instrucciones para cocinar un plato. (35)

redress/compensación: el derecho a que se corrija una injusticia de manera rápida y justa. (22)

refusal skills/habilidades de rechazo: Técnicas de comunicación para decir que *no* de manera efectiva. (11)

renewable resources/recursos renovables: Recursos naturales que se pueden reemplazar solos con el transcurso del tiempo. (23)

resource/recurso: Cualquier cosa que se utiliza para lograr algo. (1)

resourceful/hábil: Que puede resolver problemas y tener éxito en la vida. (1)

respect/respetar: Mostrar consideración hacia alguien o algo. (8)

responsibility/formalidad: Ser confiable y tomar responsabilidad por sus propios actos. (3)

résumé/currículum vitae: Un documento que proporciona un resumen de la experiencia laboral y educación de una persona. (7)

roasting/asar: Cocinar al horno alimentos destapados y en seco. (37)

S

salmonella/salmonella: Bacteria que puede causar una enfermedad portada por los alimentos. (39)

sanitize/desinfectar: Limpiar para eliminar las bacterias dañinas. (34)

sautéing/sofreír: Técnica en que alimentos cortados en pedazos finos se cocinan en muy poca grasa. (37)

scorch/quemar: Quemar la superficie. (39)

seam allowances/orilla de la tela: La tela entre la línea de cortar y la de coser. (44)

sedentary/sedentario: Inactivo. (25)

self-concept/autoconcepto: La imagen que una persona tiene de sí misma y la manera que piensa que los demás la ven. (2)

self-confidence/confianza en sí mismo: Tener confianza en uno mismo y en las habilidades propias. (1)

self-esteem/autoestima: El valor e importancia que uno se da a sí mismo. (2)

selvage/orillo: El borde terminado del largo de la tela. (44)

serger/remalladora: Una máquina de coser de alta velocidad que cose, corta y remata una costura en un solo paso. (43)

sexually transmitted diseases (STDs) /enfermedades transmitidas sexualmente: Enfermedades que se pasan de una persona a otra por medio del contacto sexual. (26)

short-term goals/metas a corto plazo: Metas que se pueden realizar en el futuro próximo. (1)

sibling rivalry/rivalidad entre hermanos: Competencia entre hermanos por el amor y atención de los padres. (14)

siblings/hermanos: Hermanos y hermanas. (14)

silhouette/silueta: El contorno de una prenda de vestir. (40)

simmering/hervir a fuego lento: Calentar un líquido lo más posible, permitiendo que las burbujas apenas se rompan en la superficie. (37)

single-family housing/vivienda unifamiliar: Una estructura construida como residencia para una sola familia. (46)

spouse/cónyuge: El esposo o la esposa. (15)

staples/alimentos básicos: Alimentos que se usan con frecuencia, como la harina, sal, pimienta, huevos, leche y pan. (31)

staystitching/puntadas de fijar: Una línea de puntadas que se hacen a un pedazo de tela para que no se estiren los bordes de la tela al coserse. (45)

steaming/cocinar al vapor: Cocinar alimentos arriba del agua hirviendo en vez de dentro de ella. (37)

stereotype/estereotipo: La creencia que todos los miembros de un grupo siguen el mismo patrón. (8)

stimulants/estimulantes: Drogas que aumentan el ritmo del corazón, del sistema nervioso central y de la respiración y suben la presión arterial. (26)

stir-frying/sofreír revolviendo: Técnica de cocina en que pequeños trozos de alimentos se revuelven mientras se cocinan rápidamente sobre fuego alto con poca grasa. (37)

stress/estrés: La presión que uno siente como consecuencia de poder o no poder realizar las expectativas de los demás o de uno mismo. (7)

systems/sistemas: Métodos ordenados de hacer las cosas. (6)

T

tableware/vajilla y cubiertos: Platos, vasos y utensilios de comer. (32)

tact/tacto: Saber hablar o actuar con delicadeza para mostrar consideración por los sentimientos de otra persona. (8)

task lighting/iluminación sobre la labor: Alumbrar de manera que brille la luz donde haga falta. (47)

technology/tecnología: El modo en que la ciencia y los inventos se usan de manera práctica en la vida diaria. (21)

teleconferencing/teleconferencia: Sistema que permite que personas en distintos lugares se vean y se oigan. (21)

tension/tensión: Lo estirado o flojo que está el hilo en una máquina de coser. (43)

thinking skills/uso de razón: Las habilidades mentales que se usan para aprender y para resolver problemas. (6)

toddlers/niños pequeños: Niños entre uno y dos años de edad. (16)

tolerance/tolerancia: Aceptar y respetar las costumbres y creencias de otras personas. (10)

townhomes/casas unifamiliares en hilera: Casas construidas en filas con las paredes de los lados pegadas. (46)

trade name/nombre comercial: El nombre que el fabricante le da a una fibra o tela. (41)

traditions/tradiciones: Costumbres que se siguen repetidamente. (14)

traffic patterns/patrones de movimiento: Las sendas que se usan para ir de un área o cuarto a otro. (47)

trim/recortar: Cortar la tela extra. (43)

U

understitching/costura por debajo: Coser la orilla de la tela al refuerzo para impedir que la costura se ruede hacia afuera. (45)

unit price/precio por unidad: El precio por onza, libra u otra unidad de medir. (31)

universal product code/código universal de productos: Una combinación de barras y números que identifica un producto y generalmente le fija el precio. (21)

universal values/valores universales: Valores que son aceptados y compartidos alrededor del mundo. (3)

utensils/utensilios: Artículos pequeños para la cocina. (33)

utilities/servicios públicos: Servicios básicos como la electricidad, gas, petróleo para la calefacción, agua o alcantarillado. (46)

V

values/valores: Las creencias o ideas que determinan la manera en que uno vive. (3)

vandalize/destruir: Destrozar o estropear propiedad pública o privada. (8)

vegetarian/vegetariano: Alguien que no come carne o pescado y se alimenta de vegetales, frutas, granos, nueces y, a veces, huevos y productos lácteos. (29)

verbal communication/comunicación verbal: Comunicarse a través de palabras habladas. (9)

views/modelos: Variaciones de una prenda que se pueden hacer de un mismo patrón de costura. (44)

W

wants/deseos: Cosas que uno quiere pero que no son necesarias. (4)

warranty/garantía: Seguridad dada por escrito que un producto funcionará bien por un período específico de tiempo, a menos que el consumidor no lo use correctamente. (22)

wellness/bienestar: Un modo de vida basado en conducta y actitudes sanas. (24)

work/trabajar: Hacer algo productivo con el tiempo que uno tiene. (5)

work simplification/simplificar el trabajo: Hallar la manera más fácil y rápida de hacer bien un trabajo. (19)

Y

yield/número de porciones: La cantidad de comida o el número de raciones que rinde una receta. (35)

Index

O

Oatmeal Muffins, 514
Obesity, 408
The Occupational Information Quarterly (OIQ), 84
The Occupational Outlook Handbook (OOH), 84
Occupations, 77
Oil, getting out of clothes, 570
Optimism, 96
Organic foods, 420
Outdoors, safety in, 252–53
Over-the-counter (OTC) drugs, 371–72

P

Packaged foods, buying, 431, 433
Pan frying, 502, 503
Pare, 477
Parents
    deciding to be, 258
    getting along with, 205–6
    responsibilities of, 259–63
    resources for, 263
    teen, 259
Paring knives, 453
Passive responses, 161
Pasta, 511
    cooking, 511–12
Pasteurized, 432
Pastry blenders, 453
Patience, 52
Pattern, 541
    fitting, 598–99, 600–601
    selecting, 592–95
    using, 597–98

Pattern envelopes, 592
Pattern layout, 602–3
Pattern size, 595
PCP, 371
Peelers, 454
Peer friendships, 176
Peer mediator, 151–52
Peer pressure, 157–65, 310
    definition of, 158
    negative, 160
    positive, 158
Peers, definition of, 158
Pent-up anger, 149
Permanent press, 561
Perseverance, 52
Personal computers, 303
Personal connections in investigating careers, 83
Personal goals, 27–29
Personality, 41–42
    differences as cause of conflict, 145
Personal responsibility, 53
    taking, 53
Perspiration, 344, 421
Pests, 656
Phosphorus, 398
Physical activity, 359
Physical changes, 36
Physical development, 235, 236
Physical growth and development, 237
Physical health, 340–46
Physical needs, 626
Piece-dyeing, 560
Pie pans, 455
Pile weave, 558
Pincushion, 582
Placement line, 597
Place on fold, 597
Place setting, 439, 444
Plain weave, 558
Plaque, 346

Plastic scrapers, 453
Plate service, 438
Playgrounds, 253
Playing with children, 251
Poison control centers, 252
Poisoning, preventing, 467
Poisons, 659
    safety with, 252
Polyester, 556
Pop can wrap-arounds, 617
Positive attitude, keeping, 659
Positive influence, 159
Positive peer pressure, 158
Potassium, 398
Potential
    identifying your, 23–24
    impact of resources on, 24–25
Poultry
    buying, 523
    cooking, 524
Power issues as cause of conflict, 145
Praise, 262
Precycling, 330
Pregnancy
    avoiding early, 373
    teen, 373
Prejudice, 122–23
    overcoming, 122–23
Prenatal stage, 234
Preschool, 234, 237
Preschoolers
    caring for, 247
    meals and snacks for, 249
Prescription drugs, 371–72
Preservatives, effect of, on foods, 419
Preshrinking fabric, 601
Press cloth, 581
Pressing, 571, 610
Pressing equipment, 581
Pretreatment, 568
Primary colors, 544

Credits

Design:
Squarecrow Creative Group, Washington, IL

Allsport (UK) Limited/ Getty Images 352
Allsport/Getty Images, Jamie Squire 382
American Honda Corp., 326
America's Dairy Farmers and Milk Processors, 528
AP/Wide World Photos, 421T
Articulate Graphics/Joel & Sharon Harris, 290
Roger Bean, 490T
Bernina of America, Inc., 583
Bruce Coleman, Inc.
D. & J. McClure, 250T
S. Nielson, 321
Stephen Kline, 234
Burlington Industries, Inc., 561
Ken Clubb, 464
Corbis
Paul Barton, 629T
Ed Bock, 179
George Disario, 64
Craig Hammell, 231
John Henley, 336
Ted Horowitz, 18
Michael Keller, 622
Charles Krebs, 428
Rob Lewine, 21
Gabe Palmer/Mugshots, 120
Jose L. Pelaez, Inc., 268, 534
Chuck Savage, 168

Cover Photography:
Getty Images

Ariel Skelley, 236
Tom Stewart, 52
Joe Towers, 305
Chris Trotman, 43
Jon S. Yeager, 72
Bob Daemmrich, 37
Design Office, 136, 288B, 544, 545, 546
DesignNet, 197
Digital Stock, 203T, 210
Cheryl Fenton, 35, 59, 84, 103, 143, 171, 187, 213, 233, 237, 245, 271, 283, 297, 327, 353, 365, 377, 391, 394, 403, 405, 408T, 409, 411T, 418B, 423, 425, 429, 432, 451, 452, 456T, 456TR, 456BR, 461, 471, 476B, 485, 486, 487T, 488, 497, 498L, 498R, 501TL, 501TR, 501BL, 501MB, 501BR, 502T, 502M, 502B, 505, 506, 509, 512B, 516, 518, 521, 553, 565, 579, 591, 625, 639, 651
Curt Fischer, 417, 567
FoodPix, Jackson Vereen, 388, 448
David R. Frazier Photolibrary, Trent Steffler, 175
Tim Fuller, 194, 440B
Ann Garvin, 76, 456M, 456BL, 476TL,

Photo Editing:
Design Office, San Francisco, CA

476TM, 476TR, 476ML, 476M, 476MR, 477BL, 477TL, 477TR, 477ML, 477MR, 477MB, 477RB, 522, 527, 580, 581, 582, 596T, 596B
Getty Images
Jim Cummins, 22, 30
EyeWire, 289, 311
Zigy Kaluzny, 239
Chuck Keeler, 241
Michael Krasowitz, 28, 51, 97, 110, 124, 152, 163, 177, 218, 248, 278, 324, 358, 382, 400, 439, 491, 466, 573, 657
David Leahy, 296
Lester Lefkowitz, 85
Bill Losh, 232
Ghislain & Marie David de Lossy, 308
Dick Lunia, 196, 203L, 380
Mike Malyszko, 368
Alan R. Moller, 383
Stephen Simpson, 116, 340
David Stewart, 350
Arthur Tilley, 3, 23, 38, 260B, 401
David Young-Wolff, 144, 357
Lane Gregory, 542, 543, 548, 549
Linda K. Henson, 240, 263

Esbin-Anderson Photography, 279
Jeff Greenberg, 55
Jenny Hager, 127
Willie Hill, Jr., 258
Fritz Hoffmann, 198
Szen Martson, 376
Network Productions, 202B
Skjold Photography, 126B
Lee Snider, 631B
Jenny Thomas, 24, 53, 88, 89, 118, 119, 123, 153, 200B, 202T, 212, 219, 322, 323, 378, 379, 420, 466, 467, 539
USDA, 410
Dana White, 50, 67, 80, 83, 284, 285
Woodfin Camp & Assoc.
  Nathan Benn, 299
  Robert Frerck, 40
  Catherine Karnow, 630
  A. Ramey, 301T
Duane Zehr, 478TM, 478TR, 478ML, 478M, 478M, 478MR, 478

Special thanks to the following for their assistance on this project: Fashion Institute of Technology, State University of New York, College of Staten Island, New York.